# Strings
## OF CONNECTEDNESS

ESSAYS IN HONOUR OF IAN KEEN

# Strings
## OF CONNECTEDNESS

ESSAYS IN HONOUR OF IAN KEEN

EDITED BY P.G. TONER

PRESS

Published by ANU Press
The Australian National University
Acton ACT 2601, Australia
Email: anupress@anu.edu.au
This title is also available online at http://press.anu.edu.au

---

National Library of Australia Cataloguing-in-Publication entry

Title:      Strings of connectedness : essays in honour of Ian Keen / edited by Peter Toner.

ISBN:       9781925022629 (paperback) 9781925022636 (ebook)

Subjects:   Aboriginal Australians--Australia.
            Research--Northern Territory--Arnhem Land.
            Aboriginal Australians--Religious life.
            Language and culture--Australia.

Other Creators/Contributors:
            Toner, Peter, editor.

Dewey Number:   305.89915

---

All rights reserved. No part of this publication may be reproduced, stored in a retrieval system or transmitted in any form or by any means, electronic, mechanical, photocopying or otherwise, without the prior permission of the publisher.

Cover design and layout by ANU Press.

Cover image: Ian taking notes while observing a ceremony overseen by Djäwa, senior informant and Gupapuyngu elder, Milingimbi, 1974. Photo: Brad Harris.

This edition © 2015 ANU Press

Cultural warning: Aboriginal and Torres Strait Islander readers are warned that this work contains images of deceased persons.

# Contents

List of Figures . . . . . . . . . . . . . . . . . . . . . . . . . . . . . . . . . . . . . . . . . vii
List of Tables . . . . . . . . . . . . . . . . . . . . . . . . . . . . . . . . . . . . . . . . . . ix
Acknowledgements . . . . . . . . . . . . . . . . . . . . . . . . . . . . . . . . . . . . xi
Contributors . . . . . . . . . . . . . . . . . . . . . . . . . . . . . . . . . . . . . . . . . xiii
Foreword . . . . . . . . . . . . . . . . . . . . . . . . . . . . . . . . . . . . . . . . . . . xix
NICOLAS PETERSON

1. Introduction: Strings of Connectedness in Ian Keen's Scholarship . . . . . . . 1
   PETER TONER

2. Judicial Understandings of Aboriginality and Language Use in
   Criminal Cases . . . . . . . . . . . . . . . . . . . . . . . . . . . . . . . . . . . . . . 27
   DIANA EADES

3. Change and Succession in Australian Aboriginal Claims to Land . . . . . . . 53
   DAVID TRIGGER

4. From Skills to Stories: Land Rights, Life Histories and the Terms
   of Engagement . . . . . . . . . . . . . . . . . . . . . . . . . . . . . . . . . . . . . . 75
   ROBERT LEVITUS

5. Conceptual Dynamism and Ambiguity in Marrangu Djinang
   Cosmology, North-Central Arnhem Land . . . . . . . . . . . . . . . . . . . . . 101
   CRAIG ELLIOTT

6. Steppe Riders in the East Kimberley Contact Zone: Zoroastrianism,
   Apocalyptic Judeo-Christianity and Evangelical Missionaries in
   Australia's Colonised Periphery . . . . . . . . . . . . . . . . . . . . . . . . . . 119
   HEATHER MCDONALD

7. The Failures of Translation across Incommensurable Knowledge
   Systems: A Case Study of Arabic Grammar Instruction . . . . . . . . . . . . 143
   ALLON J. UHLMANN

8. Bakhtin's Theory of the Utterance and Dha_lwangu *Manikay* . . . . . . . . . . *161*
   PETER TONER

9. Development of Collecting at the Milingimbi Mission . . . . . . . . . . . . . . . . 187
   LOUISE HAMBY WITH DR GUMBULA

10. Rupture and Readjustment of Tradition: Personal Autonomy in the Feminised Warlpiri Diaspora in Australia . . . . . . . . . . . . . . . . . . . . . . . . 215
    PAUL BURKE

11. The Language of 'Spiritual Power': From *Mana* to *Märr* on the Crocodile Islands . . . . . . . . . . . . . . . . . . . . . . . . . . . . . . . . . . . . . . . . . 235
    BENTLEY JAMES

12. Reconstructing Aboriginal Economy and Society: The New South Wales South Coast at the Threshold of Colonisation . . . . . . . . . . . . . . . . 263
    JOHN M. WHITE

13. Long-Distance Diffusion of Affinal Kinship Terms as Evidence of Late Holocene Change in Marriage Systems in Aboriginal Australia . . . . 287
    PATRICK MCCONVELL

Afterword . . . . . . . . . . . . . . . . . . . . . . . . . . . . . . . . . . . . . . . . . . . . . . . . . . . 317
AD BORSBOOM

Appendix: Ian Keen's Publications, 1977–2015 . . . . . . . . . . . . . . . . . . . . . . 323

Index . . . . . . . . . . . . . . . . . . . . . . . . . . . . . . . . . . . . . . . . . . . . . . . . . . . . . . 331

# List of Figures

Figure 1.1 Ian's attempt to represent the proposed restructuring of the University . . . . . . . . . . . . . . . . . . . . . . . . . . . . . . . . . . . . . . . .xxiii

Figure 3.1 Traditional succession, Gulf Country. . . . . . . . . . . . . . . . . . . . . . . 56

Figure 3.2 Roth sketch map (arrows and numbers show historical movement eastwards). . . . . . . . . . . . . . . . . . . . . . . . . . . . . . . . . . . . 60

Figure 4.1 Kakadu National Park and surrounds . . . . . . . . . . . . . . . . . . . . . 78

Figure 4.2 Kabirriki on the cover of *Kakadu*. . . . . . . . . . . . . . . . . . . . . . . . . 89

Figure 4.3 Kabirriki on the cover of *Archaeology of the Dreamtime*. . . . . . . . . . . 90

Figure 4.4 Dedication page from George Chaloupka, *Journey in Time* . . . . . . . 91

Figure 5.1 Location Map—North-central Arnhem Land, Australia. . . . . . . . . . . 103

Figure 5.2 *Merri* and *Mewal* in Marrangu Djinang art and ceremony. . . . . . . . . 111

Figure 8.1 The Dhalwangu *yuṯa* A melody. . . . . . . . . . . . . . . . . . . . . . . . . . 183

Figure 9.1 Djäwa and Wulili from Goulburn Island, c. 1926–39. . . . . . . . . . . . 189

Figure 9.2 Beach at Top Camp, Milingimbi, 2013. . . . . . . . . . . . . . . . . . . . . . 190

Figure 9.3 Rev. James Watson distributing food to children assisted by Rosie from Goulburn Island, wife of Andrew Birrinydjawuy Garawirrtja, Milingimbi, 1924. . . . . . . . . . . . . . . . . . . . . . . . . . . . . 192

Figure 9.4 *Murayana* by Djäwa Daygurrgurr. . . . . . . . . . . . . . . . . . . . . . . . . 194

Figure 9.5 Djäwa Daygurrgurr and Edgar Wells at Milingimbi, c. 1955. . . . . . . . 197

Figure 9.6 Arnhem Land dancers performing for Queen Elizabeth II and the Duke of Edinburgh at Toowoomba, 1954. . . . . . . . . . . . . . . 201

Figure 9.7 George Milaybuma, Matthew Baltha, Ian Keen and Dr Gumbula at Djiliwirri, 2005. . . . . . . . . . . . . . . . . . . . . . . . . . . . 203

Figure 9.8 Gupapuyngu family and researchers including Ian Keen,
    Aaron Corn and Louise Hamby at Djilwirri, 2005. . . . . . . . . . . . . . . . . . . 204

Figure 9.9 Dr Gumbula in a storeroom at The Peabody Museum
    of Archaeology and Ethnology, Harvard University, 2010. . . . . . . . . . . . . 205

Figure 9.10 Court case for Ngalandir; Djäwa, Edgar Wells and
    Jacky Badaltja seated at table at Milingimbi, 1955.. . . . . . . . . . . . . . . . . 206

Figure 9.11 *Burala Rite* by Djäwa Daygurrgurr, 1972, collected by
    Ed Ruhe at Milingimbi. . . . . . . . . . . . . . . . . . . . . . . . . . . . . . . . . . . . . 208

Figure 13.1 Spread of *ramparr/lamparr(a)*. . . . . . . . . . . . . . . . . . . . . . . . . . . . . . . 291

Figure 13.2 Recent eastward diffusion in the eastern Northern Territory. . . . . . 292

Figure 13.3 *TyamVny* in non-Pama-Nyungan. . . . . . . . . . . . . . . . . . . . . . . . . . . 305

# List of Tables

Table 3.1 Waanyi families by pre-succession estates and post-succession areas. . . . . . . . . . . . . . . . . . . . . . . . . . . . . . . . . . . 64

Table 5.1 Groupings of Marrangu Djinang *manikay* song subjects. . . . . . . . . . 109

Table 7.1 A schematic approximation of some differences between the two systems. . . . . . . . . . . . . . . . . . . . . . . . . . . . . . . . . . . . . . . . . . 157

Table 11.1 Body part initial verbal idioms in Gupapuyngu.. . . . . . . . . . . . . . . . 250

Table 11.2 *Märr* initial verbal idioms. . . . . . . . . . . . . . . . . . . . . . . . . . . . . . . 251

Table 11.3 *Märr* initial verbal idioms in two different Yolngu languages. . . . . . . 252

Table 12.1 Key features of Yuin economy and society in the Eurobodalla in the late eighteenth century. . . . . . . . . . . . . . . . . . . . . . . . . . . . . 280

Table 13.1 Grandparental loanwords from Marrngu in Nyulnyulan. . . . . . . . . . 299

Table 13.2 Diffusion and change of meaning of affinal terms from north to west to southeast Kimberley. . . . . . . . . . . . . . . . . . . . . . . . . . . . 301

# Acknowledgements

A book of this kind cannot be produced without a great deal of help from many quarters. My first thanks go to Ian and Libby Keen—Ian for his unfailing support throughout my career and for his cooperation with this volume, and Libby for initiating the whole project and inviting me to steer the ship. Nicolas Peterson, Christine Huber and Liz Walters of the Humanities and Creative Arts Editorial Board, and Emily Tinker and Teresa Prowse of ANU Press, provided valuable logistical support and advice, and my colleague here in Fredericton, Douglas Vipond, provided expert copyediting. Of course, my sincere thanks go to all of the authors, who stuck with the project despite required revisions, some delays, and numerous requests from me, both large and small.

On a personal note, my thanks and love to Peta Fussell and our children, Charlotte, Jack, and Harry, for their support throughout, and for tolerating my presence in front of a computer when a million other activities beckoned.

As this book was about to go to press, I received word of the passing of Dr Gumbula, co-author with Louise Hamby of Chapter 9, 'Development of Collecting at the Milingimbi Mission'. Dr Gumbula had devoted well over a decade of his life to research on the documentation, collection, digitisation and repatriation of Yolngu cultural heritage materials, both tangible and intangible, and was widely regarded as a leading cultural authority on these matters. His death is a loss for Yolngu people throughout northeast Arnhem Land, but he has left behind a strong foundation and legacy for others to follow. R.I.P.

# Contributors

**Ad Borsboom** is Emeritus Professor of Pacific Studies at the Radboud University Nijmegen, The Netherlands. Since 1972 he has conducted fieldwork in Arnhem Land investigating religion and social change, identity and land rights. His writings include *De Clan van de Wilde Honing* (popular-science book on Arnhem Land Aborigines) and Thomson at Gaartji (in *Donald Thomson, the Man and Scholar*), and he is, together with Ton Otto, editor of *Cultural Dynamics of Religious Change in Oceania*.

**Paul Burke** is currently a Visiting Fellow in the School of Archaeology and Anthropology at The Australian National University. During 2009–13 he undertook research among the Warlpiri diaspora all over Australia via an Australian Research Council Postdoctoral Fellowship. His previous work on anthropologists in native title claims, *Law's Anthropology*, was published in 2011.

**Diana Eades**, Adjunct Professor at the University of New England, is a sociolinguist who specialises in language in the legal process, especially in the use of English by, to, and about Aboriginal Australians. Recent books include *Aboriginal Ways of Using English* (Aboriginal Studies Press, 2013), *Sociolinguistics and the Legal Process* (Multilingual Matters, 2010), and *Courtroom Talk and Neocolonial Control* (Mouton de Gruyter, 2008). Her 1983 PhD in linguistic anthropology at the University of Queensland was supervised by Bruce Rigsby and Ian Keen.

**Craig Elliott** holds a Bachelor of Arts degree (Anthropology) from Macquarie University and a Master of Arts degree (Anthropology) from The Australian National University. He has conducted anthropological field research with Aboriginal people since 1989 and has worked in Central Australia since 1991 as a consultant anthropologist and Senior Anthropologist with the Central

Land Council (CLC). Between 1990 and 2014 he tutored in anthropology at The Australian National University, University of Canberra and New York University (Sydney campus). He has conducted research and peer review in land claim proceedings under the *Aboriginal Land Rights Act (NT) 1976* since 1993, and in native title claim proceedings under the *Native Title Act 1993* since 1994, authoring numerous reports for the CLC and giving expert evidence before the Federal Court and the Aboriginal Land Commissioner.

**Dr Gumbula (1954–2015)** was a Daygurrgurr Gupapuyngu elder who was awarded the degree of Doctor of Music (*honoris causa*) from the University of Sydney. From 2003–05 he was a Research Fellow in Australian Indigenous Studies at the University of Melbourne, where he worked on identifying and documenting items to help form a Gupapuyngu 'legacy collection'. In 2007 he became the University of Sydney's first Australian Research Council Indigenous Research Fellow, and in 2010 he was awarded an Australian Research Council Discovery Indigenous grant to pursue research on issues pertaining to digitisation, repatriation, and access to collections. His book *Mali'Buku-Runanmaram: Images from Milingimbi and Surrounds, 1926–1948* (Darlington Press and the University of Sydney Archives) was published in 2012. His final research project at The Australian National University, funded by the Australian Research Council, was entitled 'Clouded and mobile delivery platforms for early collections of Yolngu cultural heritage in Arnhem Land'.

**Louise Hamby** is a Research Fellow in the School of Archaeology and Anthropology at The Australian National University in Canberra. She is a leading researcher in Indigenous fibre arts, the material culture of Arnhem Land, Indigenous collection-based research, and in the digital repatriation and re-documentation of museum collections and archival material. She has been awarded a number of Australian Research Council grants investigating Indigenous museum collections in Australia and overseas and has been an honorary associate of Museum Victoria since 2003. Her experience undertaking fieldwork in Yolngu communities started in 1992. Through her research she has developed a number of collaborative curatorial projects working with Indigenous Australians supported by VISIONS grants: *Art on a String, Twined Together: Kunmadj Njalehnjaleken* and *Women With Clever Hands: Gapuwiyak Miyalkurrwurr Gong Djambatjmala*. She is currently the chief investigator of an ARC Linkage grant, *The Legacy of 50 Years Collecting at Milingimbi Mission*.

**Bentley James** has lived and worked in northeast Arnhem Land for over 20 years. His linguistic and anthropological research, which started in the Central Desert in the late 1980s and then with continued with Yolngu people, led to the first *Yan-nhangu Dictionary* (2003) and the *Atlas and Illustrated Dictionary of the Crocodile Islands* (2014). His long-term engagement has yielded a family of interrelated projects on the islands. He founded ranger and heritage programs, language nests and local language resources to protect linguistic, cultural and biological diversity and support bilingual education. Affiliated with the Australian Centre for Indigenous Knowledges and Education at Charles Darwin University, he continues to promote the intergenerational transmission of local languages, conservation, and traditional ecological knowledge for meaningful livelihoods on country, and he continues to lecture internationally in ethnography, linguistics and education.

**Robert Levitus** has researched the social history, politics and environment of the Alligator Rivers region of the Northern Territory, especially Kakadu National Park, since 1981. He has done applied research into traditional land attachments in the east Kimberley and southwest Queensland, and into Australian Aboriginal policy issues. In recent years he has been attached to the Department of Archaeology and Natural History at The Australian National University, where he has worked on an ARC Linkage project researching human ecology and environmental change on the South Alligator River wetlands.

**Patrick McConvell** is currently an Australian Research Council DORA (Discovery Outstanding Research Award) Fellow at The Australian National University, working on the project AustKin, on Australian kinship and social categories. Among recent publications of this project are *Kinship Systems: Change and Reconstruction* (University of Utah Press, 2013) and the forthcoming book *Southern Anthropology – a History of Fison and Howitt's* Kamilaroi and Kurnai, with Helen Gardner (Palgrave MacMillan, 2015). McConvell was trained in anthropology and linguistics at the University of London (SOAS) and came to Australia in 1973. He has worked on several languages of northern Australia and carried out anthropological work on many land and native title claims, as well as teaching anthropology at Northern Territory University (now Charles Darwin University) and Griffith University, and holding the position of Research Fellow, Language and Society at the Australian Institute of Aboriginal and Torres Strait Islander Studies before moving to ANU in 2008. His publications range over linguistics, sociolinguistics, anthropological linguistics and linguistic prehistory.

**Heather McDonald** studied anthropology at the University of Queensland and The Australian National University, gaining her PhD in 1998. Her book, *Blood, Bones and Spirit: Aboriginal Christianity in an East Kimberley Town* (Melbourne University Press, 2001), won the Stanner Award in 2002. She was a Research Fellow at the Australian Institute of Aboriginal and Torres Strait Islander Studies in Canberra. This was followed by research positions at Charles Darwin University and the University of Sydney. She is currently living in East Kimberley, assisting Aboriginal people with the recording of family histories.

**Nicolas Peterson** is Professor of Anthropology in the School of Archaeology and Anthropology at The Australian National University. His main areas of research have been with Aboriginal Australians in northeast Arnhem Land and the Tanami Desert. His research interests include economic anthropology, social change, applied anthropology, land and marine tenure, fourth-world people and the state, and the anthropology of photography.

**Peter Toner** is a social anthropologist and ethnomusicologist who has conducted more than two years of field research in Yolngu communities in Arnhem Land, principally in Gapuwiyak, NT. His PhD research at The Australian National University (1995–2001) was conducted under the supervision of Ian Keen. In addition to his research on music and sociality among the Yolngu, he conducts research on folk music and Irish cultural identity in Atlantic Canada. He is currently an Associate Professor in the Department of Anthropology at St Thomas University in Fredericton, New Brunswick, Canada.

**David Trigger** is Professor of Anthropology at the University of Queensland. His research interests encompass the different meanings attributed to land and nature across diverse sectors of society. His research on Australian society includes projects focused on a comparison of pro-development, environmentalist and Aboriginal perspectives on land and nature. In Australian Aboriginal Studies, he has carried out more than 35 years of anthropological study on Indigenous systems of land tenure, including applied research on resource development negotiations and native title. He is the author of more than 60 major applied research reports and has acted as an expert witness in multiple native title claims and associated criminal matters involving Aboriginal customary law. He is the author of *Whitefella Comin': Aboriginal Responses to Colonialism in Northern Australia* (Cambridge University Press, 1992) and a wide range of scholarly articles.

**Allon Uhlmann** conducted his PhD research in anthropology under Ian Keen's supervision at The Australian National University. He has conducted ethnographic fieldwork in urban Australia and the Middle East, investigating such diverse issues as kinship, sexuality, cognition and education. He has also published on social theory and methodology. He has held academic positions in Australia and overseas, and for the last two years has been conducting independent research in the private and public sectors. He is currently a visitor at the School of Archaeology and Anthropology at The Australian National University, and lives in Canberra with his wife and two daughters.

**John White** completed his PhD in 2010 at The Australian National University as part of an Australian Research Council Linkage project on Indigenous participation in the Australian colonial economy. His ethnographic and archival research focuses on the character of the changes brought about by European colonisation and the expansion of the settler economy on the New South Wales south coast. For the past four years he has worked as a senior researcher for several parliamentary inquiries into aspects of Indigenous affairs and social policy.

# Foreword

Nicolas Peterson
The Australian National University

Shortly after Derek Freeman took up the position of head of the Department of Anthropology in the Research School of Pacific Studies in 1972, following the departure of Bill Epstein, he approached me as a recently appointed research fellow to say it was about time I was supervising a graduate student. He asked me to draft an advertisement for a person to work on the kind of project that I thought was important. Instead of one advertisement I provided him with two drafts on 18 March 1973, two because the two areas I felt needed urgent attention were affected by the gender of the researcher:

> Applications are invited for a post-graduate research scholarship from persons interested in carrying out research on aspects of men's religious life in Aboriginal Australia. It is envisaged that the successful applicant will work in north Australia, in an area where some substantial work has already been completed on social organisation devoting much of his attention to the analysis of the symbolism in the large but neglected song vocabulary. Preference will be given to applicants whose interest in ritual and symbolism extends beyond a purely structural approach.

> Applications are invited for a post-graduate research scholarship from persons interested in carrying out research on aspects of women's life in Aboriginal Australia. Women's life remains the most neglected aspect of Aboriginal studies with only one recent major publication in this field. Preferences will be given to applicants with either an interest in child socialisation and development or women's ritual life.

At the very same time, the latest list of applicants for PhD scholarships arrived, Ian Keen among them. He indicated that he wanted to work in Oceania or Indonesia, but Derek suggested that I get in direct contact with him to see if he would be interested in working in Arnhem Land. One problem was Ian's age. At that time the University was reluctant to give a scholarship to anybody over 30 and Ian was approaching 35. Nevertheless, Derek thought Ian was deserving of special attention and suggested that we press ahead with encouraging him. Things were humming in the anthropology field in 1973, with Roger Keesing and Anthony Forge both being offered chairs of anthropology, the one in the Research School and the other in the School of General Studies, later to be called the Faculties. Derek's enormous energy was also making a lot of things happen with visitors and conferences: Ken Burridge was visiting, Aram Yengoyan was passing through, ethology was having its profile raised, and there were plans for new research fellowships in a range of areas.

I had a chance to be in England in late 1973 and caught up with Ian at a pub near the LSE where we had a long talk and I spruiked the virtues of ANU and research in Arnhem Land at Milingimbi, where nobody had worked since Lloyd Warner in 1927–29 and Ronald and Catherine Berndt shortly after the war.

Ian had excellent references from Bob Layton, Peter Ucko and Mary Douglas. Mary Douglas commented that he was a very committed student 'achieving five times as much reading and writing as expected in a very heavy programme of course work', and Bob Layton sang his praises as a fieldworker on the basis of a summer project in the French Jura. With these references, and Derek at the full height of his influence, nobody raised the age issue at the Faculty Board.

Persuading the missionaries at Milingimbi to accept Ian and family was another hurdle that required assuring them there would be none of the challenges that the missionaries at Elcho had recently experienced with a graduate student. I envisaged the family living in a large caravan with a tent annex. However, on 1 May 1974 Ian received a memo from Derek: 'You would be good enough to draw up a plan together with specifications and notional costing of the habitat in which you and your family would, if possible, like to live at Milingimbi'.

And so Ian began his preparations for fieldwork by drawing up a very professional-looking specification for a modest 'Timber Frame House 18 feet by 15 feet' to house himself, Libby, John and Imogen, which he costed at $1,515.62. Shortly afterwards we received a message that there was a contractor's camp facility available for $950 made up of a tin shed that slept six men and another tin shed that served as a day and meal room with an electric stove, a large table, two benches and a sink, as well as an outside shower and a pit latrine. Because fieldwork funds were scarce, the AIAS agreed to pay for the buildings.

Foreword

On 3 July Ian presented his pre-fieldwork seminar, 'Forthcoming research in northeast Arnhem Land ceremony and song', which, thankfully, Derek was unable to attend. At the end of August Ian and family left for Milingimbi, missing the booked plane from Darwin to Milingimbi and instead taking a charter for $80, which even with inflation seems remarkably cheap for a two-hour flight. They were met by Matthew, one of the sons of the senior man at the mission, Djäwa, who was to become Ian's firm friend and teacher. Ian was lucky he was not going to Yirrkala where there were six anthropologists, including Howard and Frances Morphy, Jan Reid, and a film crew of four, with the result that Nancy Williams was turned back.

To improve his language skills Ian worked with the all-Aboriginal house-building crew for three days a week for two months, which stood him in excellent stead. He was also the beneficiary of a tobacco shortage, which allowed him to get a lot of work done as neither of his chief instructors, Binyinyiwuy or Djäwa, wanted money; but after a while somebody commented to him 'I think your work will be very slow. Everyone knows you haven't got much money'. Ian was hampered by his necessary parsimony: unlike Howard and Frances, who were spending the equivalent of an award wage a month (around $400), Ian only had $830 for 12 months, which was made even worse as only two months into the field he was talking about staying for two years. However, a visit to Howard, Frances and Nancy at Yirrkala in March 1975 led him to realise that he would have to obtain greater funds, as Aboriginal life was becoming increasingly commoditised.

Fieldwork was very busy with Djäwa reprimanding him for not attending a small mortuary ceremony, which Ian explained he didn't know about. Djäwa declared this a 'mistake'. Indeed there was a great deal of ceremonial activity going on, but even so six months into his fieldwork Ian commented: 'The complete bafflement a ceremony induces is depressing, but with patience some of the fog may lift ... I can't really say anything about the thesis yet. The problem is not really interpretation and analysis but finding out the "facts".'

As we all know now, the fieldwork was a huge success, and the six months put into learning Gupapuyngu was richly worthwhile. He brought back with him over 100 hours of recordings of mortuary song cycles, many transcribed and translated.

In 1974 I applied for and got a lectureship in the newly formed anthropology section of the Department of Prehistory and Anthropology under Anthony Forge, so we considered Ian transferring to this department. It did not make much sense, however, as we were very much the poor relation relative to the department in the Research School of Pacific Studies: lower status, smaller, and with fewer resources of all kinds. At this point, Jim Fox, who had newly arrived in RSPacS, became involved in Ian's project. This was an important lesson for me as I realised that we would remain the Cinderella location for graduate students for some time. I approached newly arrived Roger Keesing about the issue and he agreed that since there were no anthropologists on staff working in the Aboriginal field he would leave Australian Aboriginal anthropology to us. This was generous of him and it has played an important role in the growth and profile of our school ever since. Indeed, Di Bell was the first student to come under that agreement after briefly flirting with the idea of going to RSPacS—I think our underdog status appealed to her at the time.

Just before Ian left the field he spent one month working with George Chaloupka for the newly established Northern Land Council, mapping in the Oenpelli region in response to the Ranger Uranium Environmental Inquiry (Fox Inquiry). This was to be the beginning of a major body of land claim research in the region, totalling eight months in connection with the Alligator Rivers land claim, in which he helped lift the quality of land claim reports enormously. Later he extended his claim research down to Central Australia at McLaren Creek Station. The Fox Inquiry brought Ian, Basil Sansom and myself together to present evidence to the inquiry including our jointly written paper on succession (Peterson, Keen, and Sansom 1977). Who said nothing significant comes out of applied anthropology?

From ANU Ian ended up at the University of Queensland and a friendly competition started between us for graduate students, but by 1987 he was back at ANU, this time in the Department of Prehistory and Anthropology as a senior lecturer. Shortly after arriving his still-to-be-surpassed edited collection of papers on Aboriginal cultures in settled Australia, *Being Black* (1988), appeared. When Anthony retired from the department in 1991, Ian and Libby were on study leave in Oxford, where Ian completed his outstanding ethnography on Yolngu religion, *Knowledge and Secrecy in an Aboriginal Religion* (1994), which at one stage he had light-heartedly thought he might call 'On the sunny side of the creek: the Djang'kawu in eastern Arnhem Land'. Imogen, who had stayed behind at the Art School, helped us make and bind a splendid scrapbook for Anthony, celebrating events in the history of his reign as a retirement gift from the department.

Throughout the 1990s, Ian carried a heavy teaching load and provided inspired supervision for a raft of graduate students. At the same time he found time to prepare a major native title report for the Gippsland region and to work on his hugely informative comparative study of seven regions of Aboriginal Australia, *Aboriginal Economy and Society: Australia at the Threshold of Colonisation* (2004). In November 2002, Ian decided it was time to retire—it wasn't really necessary to ask him why. As an ex-art school student he summed it up brilliantly in a diagram he drew of yet another bout of university restructuring in order to create a more 'unified structure' (Figure 1.1). Since his retirement there have been further elaborations! Retirement has not meant Ian's withdrawal from research but involvement as a chief investigator in two ARC grants, one on Aboriginal involvement in the colonial economy, resulting in two edited volumes, and the other a grant that is playing a substantial part in the revival of interest in kinship studies.

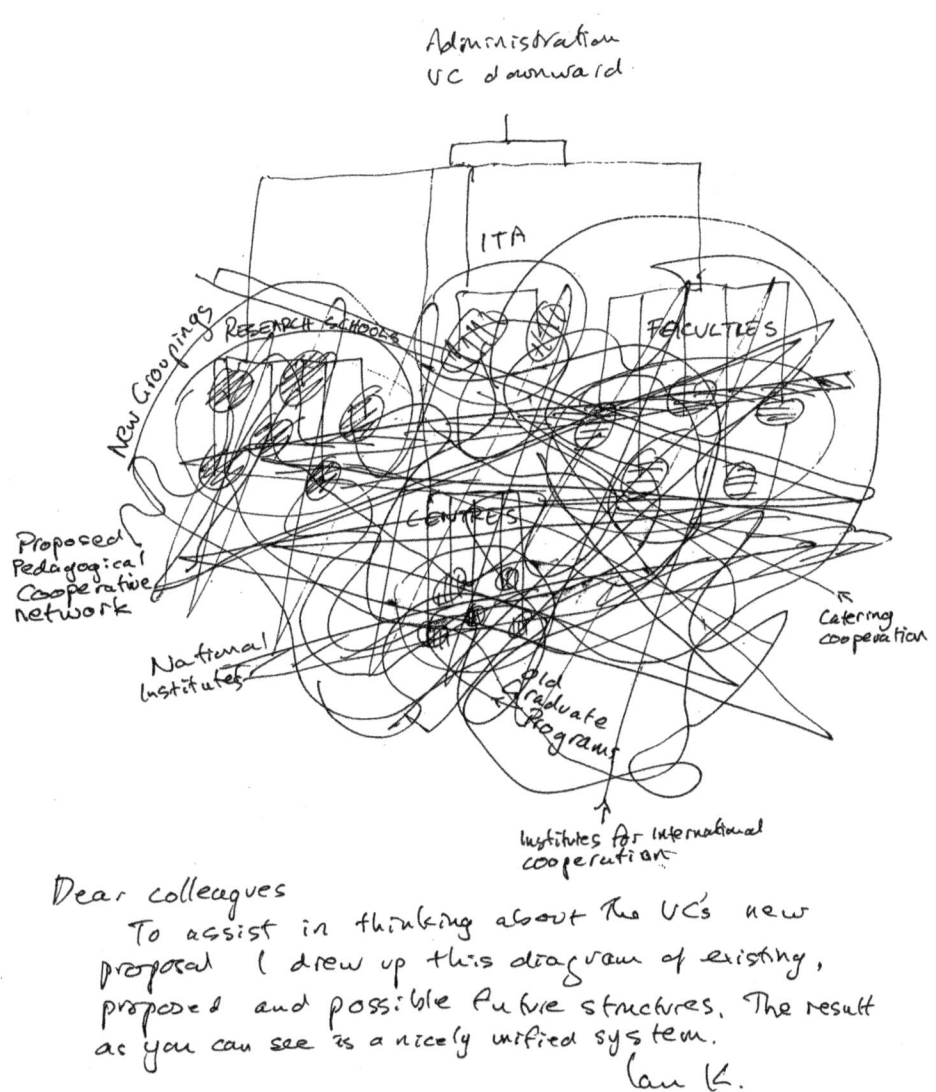

Figure 1.1 Ian's attempt to represent the proposed restructuring of the University.
Source: Ian Keen.

Not all that long after retirement, Libby and Ian moved into the bush at Harold's Cross. Since then Rosalind and I, and many colleagues and friends, have had wonderful Sunday lunches in the utter tranquillity of the haven they have built out there. The scholarly craftsmanship and attention to detail that he has lavished on his field research and the many publications that have come out of it, are now partially directed towards maintaining life in the bush, but Ian is still an active member of the emeritus faculty, publishing, presenting seminars and participating in the academic life.

## References

Keen, I. 1988. *Being Black: Aboriginal Cultures in 'Settled' Australia*. Canberra: Aboriginal Studies Press.

Keen, I. 1994. *Knowledge and Secrecy in an Aboriginal Religion*. Oxford: Clarendon Press.

Keen, I. 2004. *Aboriginal Economy and Society: Australia at the Threshold of Colonisation*. Melbourne: Oxford University Press.

Peterson, N., I. Keen and B. Sansom. 1977. Succession to land: primary and secondary rights to Aboriginal estates. In *Official Hansard Report of the Joint Select Committee on Aboriginal Land Rights in the Northern Territory*. Canberra: Government Printer. pp. 1002–14.

# 1

# Introduction: Strings of Connectedness in Ian Keen's Scholarship

Peter Toner
St Thomas University

On a brisk early winter day in late 1994, I was on my way from my home in Fredericton, New Brunswick, to Halifax, Nova Scotia, about a five-hour drive away, to meet Ian Keen. I had just been accepted into the PhD program at The Australian National University, and Ian was to be my supervisor. As luck would have it, he was visiting his late brother's family in Halifax, and I decided to take the opportunity to make an overnight trip to meet him as I prepared for what was to become the most important decade, professionally, in my life. I had spent much of that northern hemisphere autumn reading and re-reading *Knowledge and Secrecy in an Aboriginal Religion*, which had just been published and which I had ordered through my local bookstore. This was a powerfully liminal period for me, personally and professionally. I had completed my honours degree earlier in the year, and was to leave for Australia the following February. Those crisp autumn days were spent immersing myself in the Arnhem Land ethnographic literature and daydreaming about fieldwork. *Knowledge and Secrecy* loomed large in that period—for me, it represented an imaginary future. For Ian, as I came to learn, it represented the midpoint of a very distinguished career.

Ian welcomed me into his sister-in-law's home and we spoke for a couple of hours about scholarship on the Yolngu in general and my own upcoming PhD research in particular. Outwardly, Ian was not at all as I had imagined him from reading his work. Small of stature, soft-spoken, with a grey beard and bright, glinting eyes, he had a scholarly and jovial demeanour that suggested to me a career spent pondering rather abstract and complex religious and social systems. He was very kind and encouraging, especially given that, I now realise, I actually knew very little about the Yolngu and must have seemed every inch the fresh-faced 22-year-old that I was. I left our meeting with a sense of elation at the prospect of starting a new chapter of my life.

It is appropriate that I first met Ian in the Maritimes, as my home region of Canada is known. After nearly a decade in Australia, spent living either in Canberra or in Arnhem Land, I returned home to take up my current position, coming full circle. In my ongoing research and writing, his ideas remain profoundly influential in how I have come to understand Yolngu music and society, even as I contemplate those issues from the other side of the world. In a less obvious way, the lessons that I learned from Ian also influence my 'other' research on music and cultural identity in Atlantic Canada, which include research sites a short walk away from the house in Halifax where we first met. And, of course, all of my work on this volume of essays in Ian's honour has been done in the same city where I first encountered Ian's work, daydreaming, on those crisp autumn days more than 20 years ago.

---

Editing the present volume of essays has provided me with the opportunity to re-examine all of Ian's scholarly work in a new light. Rather than making use of selected ideas for particular purposes of my own, as I had done previously, I have been able to take a more holistic and synthetic perspective on more than 40 years' worth of writing. Several themes have emerged for me during this process. One is the quite remarkable breadth of Ian's interests and expertise over this period. His earliest work focused predominantly on matters pertaining to kinship, social organisation, and religious practice (and the interconnections between these), topics that have retained their importance in much of his more recent writing. His research on Aboriginal land rights elsewhere in the Northern Territory augmented the insights based on his Milingimbi fieldwork, evident in increased attention in his publications to matters of property and connections to country. His edited volume *Being Black* (1988a) was a landmark publication on Aboriginal cultures in 'settled' Australian society. During my closest association with Ian, from the mid-1990s until the early 2000s, he was publishing very stimulating, challenging, and theoretically engaged work re-evaluating the principles of Yolngu sociality. He then moved into a very productive period involving the comparative study of Aboriginal economy and society, and most recently has returned to a series of sophisticated studies of Aboriginal kinship.

Along the way, he has also published on songs, symbolism, dreams, art, and even classical music. This impressive range of scholarly interests is a clear demonstration of a stimulated and stimulating mind at work.

Another theme that has emerged in my re-examination of Ian's work is a willingness to critically appraise the scholarly work of his colleagues and contemporaries, and to develop and defend ideas that are unconventional or controversial. This critical engagement with the work of others is the lifeblood of our academic institutions, as it requires us all to re-evaluate our positions and sharpen our scholarly tools in the spirit of debate and discussion. My first taste of this came during my attendance at many anthropology seminars at ANU, where Ian could always be relied on for an astute observation or probing question in his appreciation of the work of his colleagues. Given his quiet good nature and gentle humour, these interventions were always understood to be cases of constructive criticism in the best sense of the term. His published reviews of the work of his colleagues could be reasonably critical (1986, 1993), but always demonstrated a considered and serious engagement with the work under consideration. In his own work he followed a strain of Australianist anthropology developed by Les Hiatt in challenging established orthodoxies and proposing alternative interpretations that were rigorously researched and strongly argued, but also intellectually risky (1994, 1995, 1997, 2000). As Ian's student during this period, I was inspired and encouraged to resist standard interpretations of Yolngu social life and to explore alternate ways of understanding and framing my own ethnographic data. Ian's comparative work (2003, 2004, 2006) and his return (2013a) to the study of kinship (although he never really left it) are the latest iterations of an independent attitude toward his scholarly work, finding value in topics and approaches that have fallen out of favour.

A third theme running through Ian's work is his impressive erudition. This is perhaps best illustrated in his writing on kinship, that old chestnut of Australian Aboriginal studies that has generated an enormous amount of ethnographic data and a bewildering variety of interpretations, some firmly grounded in that data, and some speculative. This is a segment of the scholarly literature that is not only complex, but requires a mastery of theories going back to the very earliest days of Australian anthropology. Ian's writing on kinship (both among the Yolngu and more broadly across Australia) moves confidently across this sometimes perplexing terrain, generating insights that are then used to shed light on his own research. The same holds true for his writing on Aboriginal religion, or his use of theory on metaphor to re-examine Yolngu sociality, or his quite extensive research on Howitt's anthropological work in Gippsland, or his very ambitious comparative study of seven different Aboriginal societies as they existed at 'the threshold of colonisation' (Keen 2004): in each case, Ian demonstrates a great depth of understanding based on his close reading of a wide range of the scholarly literature.

Ian has been a very productive scholar: 7 books, 14 encyclopedia entries, more than 25 articles in academic journals, and more than 30 book chapters over a 38-year span—and the number is still rising, with more than 20 of those publications appearing in the last 10 years alone. This is a rich oeuvre which rewards regular re-examination.

---

Ian's path to his prominent position in Australian anthropology has not been a conventional one. Born on 21 November 1938 in the semi-rural community of Finchley, on the northern outskirts of London, Ian was the younger of John and Susanah Keen's two sons. John Keen ran a grocery store before joining the signal corps of the Royal Air Force during the war, and the family lived in London during the Blitz. After the war, Susanah taught at a school and John was a commercial traveller, later doing a theological course, becoming ordained into the Anglican Church, and directing a parish in Suffolk. Ian left high school before taking his advanced-level exams, opting instead to attend art school where he studied stained glass and lithography. Drawn to the practical, craft aspect of stained glass art, Ian worked as a stained glass artist in Norwich for a couple of years, doing mostly restoration work, but eventually realised that he did not want a career in the field.

By the mid-1960s Ian was in London, doing a variety of jobs at different times: barman, petrol pump attendant, working for a sculptor, and teaching art part-time, including at the Ruskin School of Drawing at Oxford University. By the late 1960s he had decided to do a university course, but he first had to take night classes in history and English in order to complete his advanced-level exams. In 1970 he began his studies at University College London, where he became interested in anthropology and took courses from Mary Douglas, among others. Completing his honours degree in three years, he considered various options for postgraduate study, including universities in the U.S., and enrolled at the London School of Economics. A more generous offer from The Australian National University, however, brought him and his family to Canberra in early 1974. By September of that year, they were in Milingimbi in northeast Arnhem Land.

Ian's fieldwork among the Yolngu consisted of two main periods: a 14-month stint based at Milingimbi; and a further 10 months based at Nanggalala on the mainland. After a slow start, he was taken on by the local Liyagawumirr men and spent much of his time working on their ritual life, which led to significant amount of time spent on Howard Island, as the Liyagawumirr had connections to the Wobulkarra traditional owners there. He worked a great deal with Bäriya, Banhdharrawuy, Buwa'nandu, and Durrng, as well as with Gupapuyngu men, including Djäwa. Living conditions were challenging for the young family, as they inhabited a rather rudimentary former contractor's camp consisting of a tin shed with no glass on the windows. This situation improved on his second trip based at Nanggalala, where they had a small caravan. On this trip, Ian was primarily attached to the Liyagalawumirr elder Paddy Dhathangu and attended numerous ceremonies in his company, including a Djungguwan, a Gunapipi, and a Mandayala. Near the end of this second field trip he was invited back to Milingimbi to attend a Ngärra ceremony being organised by Bäriya, the analysis of which featured prominently in both his PhD dissertation and *Knowledge and Secrecy*. This lengthy and intensive exposure to Yolngu religious life provided the basis for his doctoral dissertation, as well as a score of publications to the present day.

---

Bugs was snoring—loudly—on the floor beside me. Ming was asleep on my lap, drooling copiously. The former was Ian and Libby's elderly dog, the latter their cat, and I was house-sitting for them in their cosy house in O'Connor with my future wife, Peta. Ian and Libby were very generous with opening their house to us on numerous occasions, allowing us to escape the rather close confines of our residential college. Their house always seemed to me to be a quiet place of contemplation, located on a leafy lot with a beautiful native garden and two laying bantam hens out the back. I invariably brought with me my own research materials in the hope of an especially productive weekend of thesis-writing, but a bottle of wine left for us on the dining room table and the possibility of pet time usually meant that my time there was a combination of work and play.

I clearly recall spending a couple of long afternoons there, midway through my writing-up phase, working away on an analysis of some of my song texts. A developing argument on the centrality of place names and other place references in Dhalwangu songs required a time-consuming, word-for-word analysis of an entire five-hour performance, a task that seems retrospectively to have been facilitated greatly by the lack of distractions offered by our occasional O'Connor getaways.

Ian and Libby not only opened their home for house-sitting when they were away, but they also were gracious hosts. I first visited with them the day after I arrived in Canberra from Canada, still jet-lagged, for lunch outside in the garden. I first met Ad Borsboom, Nigel Lendon, and other Arnhem Land scholars at dinners at their house. This hospitality later extended to a townhouse they owned on the south coast at Moruya Head, which they again allowed us to use from time to time. I proposed to my wife there.

---

> You can say in private that yours is the true story, for your father told it to you, and those other people have it all mixed up, but there is a convention to leave these differences unsaid. This convention, and the ambiguity of Yolngu song language, allows Yolngu groups to perform together, each retaining its own identity and holding to its own truths. (Keen 1977: 49)

In 1977, before his PhD dissertation was completed, some of the principal themes running through much of Ian Keen's work were already apparent. His article 'Ambiguity in Yolngu Religious Language' (1977) was published in the inaugural issue of the journal *Canberra Anthropology* (now *The Asia Pacific Journal of Anthropology*). In it he examined the role of deliberate ambiguity in Yolngu song texts in the constitution of an 'economy of knowledge'[1] (1977: 33). In contrasting the songs of the Yolngu Madayin ceremony with those of the Gunapipi ceremony, Keen was able to demonstrate that the former were structured in terms of different levels of access to knowledge, from the public and exoteric to the restricted and esoteric, with the inherent polysemy of the song texts functioning as the key ingredient in this differential interpretability based on relative age and gender (ibid.: 43). Interpretations of the Gunapipi song texts, by contrast, were radically different from one another because they were not based in everyday language, allowing different groups to participate together because the differences are not commented upon publicly (ibid.: 46). Both forms of song are based in ambiguity, but the Madayin songs allow for the development of a true 'economy of knowledge' because they allow for such a wide range of levels of access to meaning, which relates in turn to the structure of group identities (ibid.: 49).

These formulations about the economy of Yolngu religious knowledge and its relationship to Yolngu social structures became a recurring theme in Keen's scholarly work over the next two decades, and is one of his most valuable contributions to Australian Aboriginal studies. His doctoral dissertation, 'One Ceremony, One Song' (Keen 1978), explored these themes in depth, drawing upon a substantial amount of ethnographic data acquired during his very successful fieldwork in Milingimbi and surrounding communities. His analysis of kinship and marriage uncovered important patterns regarding bestowal and marriage from the standpoint of the individual, but also indicated the role of

---

1   An 'economy of knowledge' refers to a system of control over knowledge, especially in a form whereby older Yolngu men retained control over valuable resources (namely wives) by controlling access to religious knowledge (Keen 1978).

sociocentric 'clan' structures in maintaining and reinforcing the system. His diagram depicting 'Marriages over three generations between clans in the Woollen River area' (Keen 1978: 130) shows a dense web of interconnections between 35 groups that quite literally boggles the mind; it is a testament to his analytical powers that he is able to reduce this complexity to a coherent set of principles that underlie it. Similarly, his chapter on the Ngärra ceremony is a definitive account, documenting an iteration of the ceremony over an incredible 33 days with a level of detail that enabled a compelling analysis (ibid.: 257–74). His conclusions brought together into an integrated framework his interpretation of kinship, marriage, group structure, and religious knowledge and practice, demonstrating that the organisation of Yolngu religion enables age-related polygyny, a complex bundle of themes further explored in his oft-cited article 'How Some Murngin Men Marry Ten Wives' (Keen 1982).

Themes arising out of Keen's doctoral work continued to be important in his writing during the 15 years following the end of his fieldwork, most notably his important contributions to the anthropological study of Aboriginal kinship (Keen 1985, 1986, 1988b) and of Aboriginal religion (Keen 1987, 1988c, 1990, 1991, 1993). These writings cemented his status as an important figure in Australian anthropology, one whose works became widely read and who attracted a cohort of students working on a wide variety of topics.

---

Although Ian Keen is primarily recognised as a scholar of Yolngu society, he has extensive experience in conducting research on other Aboriginal societies, including a combined total of more than a year and a half of field research for the purpose of land claims. This work is perhaps less widely known, in some circles anyway, but indicates a clear commitment to the field of applied anthropology over his entire career. This research has also been influential in the reinterpretation of his Yolngu research, as well as the development of new areas of interest.

Between his two field trips in and around Milingimbi, Keen acted as a consultant on the Alligator Rivers (Stage I) land claim, carrying out an intensive six-week period of field research in western Arnhem Land with George Chaloupka, and later continued this work for Alligator Rivers Stage II; these land claims on behalf of the Northern Land Council included a total of seven months of fieldwork in that area of Arnhem Land. These consultancies, Keen's first, are notable because of the tension between the claimants' sense of their own sociality and the 'orthodox' model of social organisation set out under the Northern Territory Land Rights Act, a theme that Keen returned to regularly in his later academic writing. Land claims research across the Northern Territory in this period revealed that claimant groups used a variety of rationales for determining group membership, rights, responsibilities, and succession—real life, as it turns out, did not provide a neat fit for the Radcliffe-Brownian model of Aboriginal social organisation—and the work of anthropologists documenting and interpreting ethnographic data proved to be crucial not only at the coalface of the new land rights era, but also for developing new interpretations of Aboriginal sociality in more 'academic' contexts. Ian Keen was among a small group of dedicated scholars working at this crucial juncture.

Alligator Rivers Stages I and II were the first components of a string of consultancies that spanned Keen's academic career. They were followed by the Milingimbi closure of seas hearings (1981), the Timber Creek land claim (1984), the McLaren Creek land claim (1986–88), a Northern Land Council consultancy concerning mining royalties on the Gove Peninsula (1987), the Coronation Hill inquiry (1991), and the Kŭnai Native Title claim in Gippsland (1996–2005), among others. These consultancies have made important contributions to the field of native title anthropology in Australia, and so are valuable in their own right. It is important to note, however, their significance for the development of Keen's interpretations of Aboriginal sociality over the past two decades. Keen has noted that his 'brief but intensive' fieldwork in Yirrkala, Gapuwiyak, and Galiwin'ku in 1987, on behalf of the Northern Land Council, was pivotal in his rethinking of the 'clan' concept in the Yolngu ethnographic literature (Keen 2000a: 39), which led to a very challenging and thought-provoking counter-interpretation developed in his writing (Keen 1994, 1995, 2000a, 2000b). The suitability of concepts like 'clan corporation', and 'patrilineal descent group' for describing Aboriginal sociality and relations to country was also an important consideration in his interpretation of the ethnographic data resulting from the McLaren Creek land claim (Keen 1997), demonstrating the importance of challenging prevailing anthropological orthodoxies across Aboriginal Australia.

---

It is this period of research and writing about the reinterpretation of Yolngu sociality that I think of as the 'middle period' of Ian Keen's career, marked by the publication of *Knowledge and Secrecy* (1994), his important article 'Metaphor and the Metalanguage' (1995), and a set of other publications restating, defending, and extending his basic position (1997, 2000a, 2000b). This is, no doubt, a very personal way of framing an important career, as this 'middle period' relates to the beginning of my own association with Ian and his work until the point when I left Canberra and returned to Canada. For me, Ian's 'early period' represents everything prior to *Knowledge and Secrecy*, and his 'late period' everything from *Aboriginal Economy and Society* (2004) until the present. Ian's other colleagues and students, no doubt, mark the milestones of Ian's career somewhat differently; and yet, it is objectively true that this period marks a concentration of writing about Yolngu sociality unlike anything else in his career.

In *Knowledge and Secrecy,* Keen brings the interrelated themes of heterogeneity, indeterminacy, and power—themes first developed in his PhD dissertation and returned to with some regularity—together in their best-developed synthesis. He challenged the notion that 'Yolngu' social organisation could be thought of as a unified or homogeneous system. The 'same story' was only contingently the same for different groups or individuals; religious 'truths' were only relatively so; sociality seemed to be based on open and flexible networks defined by discourse and action rather than segmentary and clearly defined groups like 'clans'; the definition and ascription of rights over country was not agreed upon but contested; people could interpret their religious beliefs in ways which allowed for cooperation in ritual, but preserved their distinctive differences. As Keen writes:

> The form given to groups, the character of country, a group's complement of ceremonies, and local styles were heterogeneous. People sometimes profoundly disagreed over group structure, leadership, identity of country, and the meaning of a ceremony or *maḏayin* element. Perspectives on ancestral events and the interpretation of ceremonies were relative to a network centred on a group or subgroup, the locus of the greatest degree of orthodoxy, and to the individual. More profoundly perhaps, ambiguity and indeterminacy lay at heart of the construction of ancestral worlds, so that typologies of beings were found wanting. (Keen 1994: 167)

Although other scholars of Yolngu society and ritual had noted and interpreted similar points of detail, *Knowledge and Secrecy* represents the most systematic attempt to re-interpret the 'orthodox' view of Aboriginal social organisation in the light of contemporary social theory. He extended his reinterpretation of Yolngu sociality in his article 'Metaphor and the Metalanguage' (1995), focusing on the analytical slippage between the metaphorical bases of the anthropological metalanguage, on the one hand, and those of Yolngu discourse and action, on the other. The metalanguage of anthropological description, particularly notions of segmentation, corporateness, and boundaries inherent in the 'clan' concept, are based on a set of tropes that are incompatible with Yolngu tropes pertaining to *mala* and *bäpurru*, pertaining to the body, ancestral journeys and traces, and other domains of Yolngu life.

Keen's position on these matters generated what I consider to be academic debate in its ideal form. The 'orthodox' position on Aboriginal sociality, once hegemonic in its scope and influence, had been under increasing scrutiny for decades, and anthropologists working with the Yolngu had been modifying their views based on a wealth of ethnographic data. Keen developed a wide-ranging and systematic critique of the vestiges of anthropological orthodoxy as a necessary step in developing a coherent analysis of his own ethnographic data, extending important insights for work across the region. His colleagues in Aboriginal research engaged with his challenge in the light of their own work and renewed their commitment to or extended their own positions as a result (Morphy 1997, Morton 1997, Sutton 1999, Williams 1999), but also countered Keen's analysis with their own critiques that had to be addressed (Keen 2000a, 2000b). Keen has written of this extended debate that 'while the critique has aroused some interest, it has not been received with unalloyed enthusiasm' (Keen 2000a: 33). I would posit that unalloyed enthusiasm, if it had occurred, would have represented a failure of academic debate in its ideal form. Valuable ideas are forged in the heat of robust, and even contentious, debate, and some of the most valuable ideas are those that are most hotly contested. In my own research and writing, Keen's challenge has proven to be very productive, and has helped me to develop my own coherent interpretations of my own data.

---

In December 2014, my family and I made a return trip to Ian and Libby's farm at Harold's Cross, near Braidwood, NSW. On one previous visit there, in 2007, our children had a great time playing with Ian and Libby's grandchildren, who are close to the same age, and they renewed their acquaintance with the property again in 2010. The road from Queanbeyan to Captain's Flat, and then through the Tallaganda State Forest to their farm, was familiar from these previous visits, and we spent an enjoyable and relaxing day and night in their company in the midst of a rather whirlwind trip from Canada. As was customary, after lunch we all took a long stroll around the property, through wooded areas, across paddocks, and along a stream that runs behind their house. This was a purely social visit, but I couldn't help but notice that the study contained many signs of Ian's ongoing scholarly interests, with a variety of books and notes relating to several different projects. I imagined the books that could be written in this bucolic setting.

---

When one commences an academic career, an initial period of familiarising oneself with a body of literature is followed by a process of backtracking, filling in all of the missing details that came before. My own period of time under Ian's tutelage began with an intensive engagement with *Knowledge and Secrecy* and his research on the Yolngu that led up to it. My fieldwork in Gapuwiyak coincided with Ian's fieldwork in Gippsland on the Kŭnai Native Title claim, but it was only later that I read and appreciated his work on Aboriginal societies in 'settled' Australia. While at The Australian National University I was a 'Yolngu-ologist' (to borrow an apt phrase from Francesca Merlan), but I came to realise that Ian's work could not be reduced to 'Yolngu-ology'.

*Being Black: Aboriginal Cultures in 'Settled' Australia* (1988a) was, at the time of its publication, an important contribution to our understanding of contemporary Aboriginal societies in those parts of Australia that are less remote and were more intensively colonised than Arnhem Land, the Western and Central Deserts, the Kimberley, and Cape York Peninsula, regions that have produced a larger share of the ethnographic literature. It remains a widely read book on this topic and played a part in generating important research by a new generation of scholars. Inspired in part by the work of his former PhD student Diana Eades (whom Keen had accompanied on a short trip to her field location in southern Queensland), as well as the work of Gaynor MacDonald and Marcia Langton, *Being Black* brought together contributions by a range of scholars who had worked with the Aboriginal peoples of Victoria, the northern and southern coasts and the central and western regions of New South Wales, Adelaide, southeast Queensland, southwest Western Australia, and the urban fringe of Darwin. In his editorial introduction, Keen provided a framework for the volume as a whole, reviewing the literature on themes pertaining to cultural continuity, identity, heterogeneity, language, kinship and household, economics, politics, belief, and history.

At the time that *Being Black* was published, Keen had not conducted any of his own research into 'settled' Aboriginal society, although his consulting work had certainly exposed him to a range of Aboriginal social formations. That changed with his extensive field and archival research in Gippsland in the mid-1990s on behalf of the Mirimbiak Aboriginal Corporation. His findings during this research were in keeping with the conclusions of many of the authors of the chapters of *Being Black*, especially that there are important continuities in Koori culture with their precolonial past. These include spiritual beliefs, language, and kinship networks, the latter demonstrated by Keen's own genealogical research supplemented by earlier scholars like Norman Tindale (Keen 1999a). His concern with the impact of anthropological models on the interpretation of ethnographic data, so important to his Yolngu research, also became a feature of his consideration of cultural continuity in native title claims in the southeast and southwest of Australia (Keen 1999b). The success of the Kŭnai people in gaining the recognition of native title over their traditional country is an indication that Keen's research on Aboriginal society in 'settled' Australia has made an impact.

Keen's research in Gippsland, involving as it did the detailed examination of documentary records created during the colonial period in this region, seems to have led naturally to an interest in the depiction of Aboriginal societies in the historical record and the reconstruction of what those societies must have looked like when the British first arrived in Australia. The earliest anthropological research on the Aboriginal societies of Gippsland was conducted by A.W. Howitt, who made use of the theoretical frameworks of Lewis Henry Morgan and indeed corresponded with him (Keen 2000c). Keen was clear that his interest in Howitt's work stemmed from the possibility of reinterpreting that research in the light of contemporary concerns, namely native title research (ibid.: 95). His next major research project incorporating materials from this region, however, was not a second native title claim, but rather a bold project comparing seven different Aboriginal societies as they existed just prior to colonisation. *Aboriginal Economy and Society: Australia at the Threshold of Colonisation* (Keen 2004), the culmination of this period of research, made use of the earliest ethnographic materials on these societies, representing a wide geographical and ecological spread.

*Aboriginal Economy and Society* (as well as a later article in *Current Anthropology* using the same analytical framework (Keen 2006)) is an ambitious comparative work seeking to fill a gap in the literature by providing a focused and comprehensive analytical framework for understanding the commonalities and differences among Aboriginal societies relative to their time of first intensive colonisation (roughly from the 1830s to the 1930s, depending on the region). Not only do these societies differ in terms of time frame of historical contact, but also in terms of their environmental conditions and constraints, taking in temperate, desert, and tropical regions. Keen surveys a wide range of ecological aspects and 'institutional fields', but the volume is unified by a focus on the economy because that aspect of Aboriginal life can be usefully integrated into most others. Each chapter's topical focus proceeds through an examination of each of the seven case studies, together with comparative analysis. While collections bringing together a range of papers on a shared topic are common enough, explicitly comparative works like *Aboriginal Economy and Society* are relatively rare in the literature. I believe that taking on a project of this nature demonstrates an important aspect of Keen's approach to scholarship—that is, his willingness to develop serious analyses of topics that may be considered controversial or simply unfashionable. In doing so, he does all of us a great service, as he enriches our shared academic discourse and stimulates the critical engagement of his colleagues.

Keen's next major research project, on Indigenous participation in the Australian frontier economy, pursues similar themes in a slightly different way. On a multidisciplinary and collaborative project funded by an Australian

Research Council Linkage grant, Keen worked with economic historian Christopher Lloyd, historian Fiona Skyring, archaeologist and curator Michael Pickering, and anthropologists Anthony Redmond and John White, resulting in not one but two edited collections (Keen 2010a; Fijn, Keen, Lloyd, and Pickering 2012). These volumes demonstrate the extension of Keen's developing interest in the Aboriginal economy, specifically in the context of Australian colonisation and settlement. In his introduction to the first volume, Keen surveys the existing literature on the Aboriginal economy under two headings: those studies concerned with the 'internal' economic mechanisms operative within Aboriginal domains, and those dealing with 'external' engagements with the mainstream market economy and the state (Keen 2010: 4). The individual chapters of that volume engage with both of these perspectives and, as was the case in *Aboriginal Economy and Society*, they include contributions on Aboriginal societies across the entire continent. The second volume extends the scope and range of topics, focusing primarily on the 'hybrid economy model' and its utility in understanding Indigenous economic participation (Keen and Lloyd 2012: 2).

---

In surveying the work of a scholar with very broad and diverse academic interests, like Ian Keen, it is of course no surprise to find certain themes emerging with some regularity, developed and redeveloped in various guises and as a result of new data and re-analysis. One such theme in Keen's work that jumps out at me is property, on which he published over the course of more than two decades. A companion theme linked to property in Keen's writing, however, concerns the incommensurability of Western European and Aboriginal tropes in the description and analysis of social life. The latter, as I mentioned above, was the central thrust of his re-evaluation of Yolngu sociality, most carefully developed in the article 'Metaphor and the Metalanguage' (1995). Concerns about the different metaphorical bases for Western European analytical frameworks, as compared to Aboriginal discourses and practices, appear earlier in Keen's scholarly work, and are maintained in some of his very recent publications.

Even in his PhD dissertation (1978), notions of 'property' and 'ownership' among the Yolngu emerged in his interpretation of his ethnographic data. The ownership of land and religious property forms the basis for his definition of the 'clan' and of the 'land-owning group' (one or more lineages affiliated to one country) (Keen 1978: 21). It was in the chapter 'Yolngu Religious Property' (1988c), though, that he clearly began 'to enquire into whether the concept of property is appropriate for thinking about the relation of the Yolngu to ritual and land' (Keen 1988c: 272). He notes that European concepts of property are characterised by 'the notion of possession, the right to use and enjoy, the right to exclude others from use and enjoyment, and the right to dispose of an object' (ibid.), but that these may not be applicable to Aboriginal rights in land and ritual, despite some commonalities that have led to anthropologists using such concepts in their analyses (ibid.: 273). The Yolngu gift economy does not include much in the way of private property, rights in land are distributed in a variety of ways, and land and ritual objects are inalienable (ibid.: 275–7). Importantly for Keen's broader analytical concerns, Yolngu have no general terms for 'property' or 'ownership' (ibid.: 278); the suffix '-*waṯangu*' ('holder of') is applied to land and sacra (i.e. '*wänga-waṯangu*' = 'land-holders'), but there is some slippage between the Yolngu notion of 'holding' and the Western European notion of 'owning' (ibid.: 280–1). Keen concludes that the concept of property is appropriate for understanding certain elements of Yolngu social and ritual life, but there are crucial differences as well that should not be overlooked (ibid.: 290–1). As he develops later in relation to Yolngu sociality (although he does not use the term in his 1988 chapter), anthropological thinking about property includes elements of an anthropological analytical metalanguage that can create anomalies when applied cross-culturally.

Keen's critique of the property concept continued and was extended in two subsequent chapters, both obviously informed by the broader 'metalinguistic' concerns developed in his 1995 article. In a chapter on Yolngu relations to country (Keen 2011), Keen explicitly examines the ways in which the language of 'rights' has dominated discussions of Aboriginal property and land tenure, both in anthropological work and in legislative frameworks. Western legal theory, Keen points out, viewed property in terms of a 'disaggregated "bundle of rights"' (ibid.: 104) to use a resource, although there was a high degree of contestation in legal circles (ibid.: 105–7). Although some dissenting voices appeared in anthropology, overall 'rights' and 'property' have been used uncritically in our discipline. As Keen writes:

> The problem with the dominance of the language of 'rights' and 'property' … is that it obscures Indigenous concepts and discourse … Unfortunately, the majority of ethnographies simply translate ways of possessing things in terms of 'property' and of 'rights' (ibid.: 110).

After reviewing other anthropologists' work on Yolngu relations to land, Keen calls for a focus on the ways in which the relations typically described in terms of 'rights' are constituted in Yolngu discourse (ibid.: 115).

His third chapter on the topic of property extends the analysis to an examination of how 'property' was interpreted on the colonial frontier. Keen also returns to an analytical framework based on a comparative analysis of historical sources in different regions of Australia at the time of contact, including a variety of colonial officials and amateur and professional anthropologists.

The language of 'property' and 'rights' is evident in writings in all regions, together with associated notions of 'families' tribes' or 'clans' that are the owners (Keen 2010b: 48, 52, 54). As a result, writes Keen, 'Aboriginal society—at least in its dimension of "property"—is depicted through the nineteenth and early twentieth centuries as a primitive form of English society' (ibid.: 55). Contemporary anthropological writing has indicated that, in fact, Aboriginal discourse and practice differs substantially from these early interpretations, and there seems to be 'no equivalent to the overarching concept of property' (ibid.: 56). Nevertheless, as with our use of 'clan' or 'corporation' in writing of 'ownership rights' and 'property', anthropologists may (wittingly or not) incorporate incommensurable Western tropes instead of exploring Indigenous discourses.

---

A rolling stone gathers no moss, even in academic circles. More than 40 years after he commenced his fieldwork in Milingimbi, Keen is a contributor to a collaborative, multidisciplinary project that relates to but extends some of his long-standing research interests. His involvement with the AustKin project and databases of kinship and social category terms has led to his latest book-length publication, *Kinship Systems: Change and Reconstruction* (McConvell, Keen, and Hendery 2013). Like his other projects of the past decade or more, AustKin demonstrates a concern with comparative and historical analyses, and so can be seen as a natural extension of *Aboriginal Economy and Society* in a new direction. It also brings Keen's scholarly work full circle, as he returns to the study of kinship that was such an integral element of his PhD research.

He is also developing research and writing interests on language and sociality, a topic of long-standing interest for him. Having used Searle's speech act theory in his doctoral dissertation, the important links between language and sociality are apparent in *Knowledge and Secrecy*, and were developed in subsequent publications (Keen 1995, 2011). However, it is only now, post-retirement, that he has been able to develop this interest to its fullest extent, with two recent publications (Keen 2013b, 2015), and more on the way.

---

Ian developed the metaphor of 'strings of connectedness' in his examination of the anthropological metalanguage and its relation to Yolngu society. Arguing against the idea that the complexity of Yolngu sociality could be represented by anthropological metaphors of segmentary structures, taxonomic hierarchies, enclosed sets, or enclosure within boundaries, he proposed that Yolngu social identities extend outward from foci and may be represented by 'open and extendible "strings" of connectedness' (Keen 1995: 502). Upon reflection, it seems to me that Ian's metaphor is an apt one to describe his own diverse scholarly interests, as well as his influence on students and colleagues. Ian is not a scholar who is easily pigeonholed, or who is content to work within a safe and 'enclosed' set of research and writing projects, or who restricts supervision to only those students working closely on his own topics of interest. Rather, his scholarly interests extend outward from a wide range of foci: kinship, religion, language, relations to country, and economy, among others. These topical foci are joined together by conceptual and theoretical strings of connectedness: ambiguity, change, agency, sociality, metaphor, and comparison. Likewise, during his career as a supervisor he extended strings of connectedness from his own foci to those of his students. The result is a diverse but coherent network of scholarship that both enlightens and challenges, and that is open to reviving old interests or developing new ones.

The present volume contains contributions from a number of Ian's former students and one of his current colleagues, representing the full span of Ian's distinguished career and the diversity of his scholarly interests. Rather than impose an arbitrary thematic order on the volume, I have opted to present the chapters in a rough chronological order, based on the beginning of each author's association with Ian; the exception here is Patrick McConvell who, although a long-standing colleague of Ian's, is presented here last because his chapter represents their collaboration at the present time. So the volume represents a version of Ian's own research interests as they developed through his career, but refracted through the projects of those upon whom he had (and continues to have) such an important influence.

Diana Eades, Ian's first PhD student at the University of Queensland, opens the proceedings with yet another contribution to her very important work on Aboriginality and language use in Australian criminal courts. Citing the central thrust of *Being Black* (Keen 1988a)—that there are distinctively Aboriginal ways of life in 'settled' southern Australia—Eades examines issues of intercultural communication during courtroom questioning and interviews with police, lawyers, and other judicial officers. Important advances in the sentencing of Aboriginal people in criminal cases have been made over the past 25 years with the recognition of mitigating factors such as alcohol abuse, economic disadvantage, and educational limitations. Eades notes, however, that this focus on problems associated with Aboriginal social life in the realm of sentencing has affected other parts of the legal process, leading to a 'deficit' view of Aboriginal identity that is problematic when considering issues of communication. As she writes in her chapter, 'It is not people's problems which are at issue, but their socialisation and sociolinguistic experiences and abilities, as well as differences in ways of using language'. Eades argues cogently for attention to the erasure of Aboriginal identity in these contexts, demonstrating that the fundamental insights contained in *Being Black* are still relevant today.

Ian's connection to the University of Queensland continues in Chapter 3, with David Trigger's contribution on change and succession in Aboriginal land claims. As noted above, this topic pertains to Ian's earliest consulting work during the Alligator Rivers claim, in which succession was an important feature. Trigger uses this as a stepping-off point for an analysis of two cases of succession to country that featured in native title claims in the Gulf Country of Queensland: the Ganggalida people who inhabit country near Burketown, and the Waanyi people who live further to the west. Both groups were claimants in native title cases that included not only their own traditional country, but also succession areas that had once belonged to other groups. Both were cases of legitimate succession based on customary law, rationalised by language similarities, subsection or 'skin' names, Dreaming sites and tracks, and actual occupation and use, and in both cases succession occurred despite widespread social and economic changes. Trigger's research demonstrates, as he points out, the need for strong ethnography in order to understand traditional processes of succession, as well as an understanding of the legal framework within which such claims to country are made.

In Chapter 4, Robert Levitus also takes the reader back to Ian's Alligator Rivers work in his account of the life and work of Nipper Kabirriki. Levitus carefully charts the shifting political economy and policy frameworks that transformed the Kakadu region from a backwater of marginal employment to a cauldron of political contestation and engagement. He develops the argument that the coincidence of three factors—the discovery of uranium deposits and the subsequent Ranger Uranium Environmental Inquiry, the passing into legislation of the Northern Territory Land Rights Act, and the establishment of Kakadu National Park—led to a situation in which a new set of cultural capacities focused on 'stories' supplanted the earlier focus on 'skills' among Aboriginal people in the region. A case study examining Kabirriki and how he negotiated this shifting political landscape personalises the land rights era, and situates Ian Keen as one of the earliest of a series of interlocutors interested in his 'stories' pertaining to traditional land ownership and use.

Ian's important contributions to the understanding of ambiguity in Arnhem Land religion, which is fundamental to an understanding of cosmology, sociality, and political life, are extended by Craig Elliott in Chapter 5 in his study of the Marrangu Djinang spirit beings *Merri* and *Mewal*. Referencing Ian's studies of Yolngu social life and cosmology, Elliott describes the social and ritual connectedness of the Marrangu Djinang to other groups, both their immediate neighbours (to whom they are connected by residence and marriage), as well as those connected across a wide region based on their shared Wild Honey Dreaming. In mythology, *Mewal*, a part-bee, part-human spirit being, collected honey in Marrangu Djinang country and is symbolic of procreative power; her association with the origins of group identity, however, is tempered by her connection to the 'symbolically malign' monsoonal jungles, an attribute shared with *Merri*, as both spirit beings are believed to roam the jungle at night and are associated with antisocial and corrupted attributes. This essential ambiguity inherent in Marrangu Djinang cosmology is personified by *Mewal* and *Merri*, occupying as they do separate but overlapping cosmological domains. Elliott's analysis examines geographical, historical, and demographic factors to account for this ambiguity, and concludes by arguing that Marrangu Djinang belief is not unified or fully integrated, but is, rather, characterised by a conceptual dynamism that was such an important feature of Ian Keen's analyses of the same kinds of phenomena.

In addition to an extended study of Yolngu beliefs in the context of a range of traditional ceremonies, *Knowledge and Secrecy* contains an analysis of Yolngu Christianity as a form of universalistic religious belief and practice comparable to Gunapipi. In the context of widespread social change, both Gunapipi and Christianity allowed broader cooperation between groups, and between men and women; in addition, Ian argued that Yolngu Christianity also represented an attempt to develop 'a common moral order' (Keen 1994: 287) with white society, as well as to reassert a measure of autonomy, although Christianity in the Yolngu context did not displace traditional religious practice. In Chapter 6, Heather McDonald explores a very different dynamic at play in Aboriginal Christianity in the East Kimberley. She begins with a Foucauldian 'archaeology' of Zoroastrian cosmology and the ways in which it was adopted by Judaism and early Christianity, and subsequently revived after the Protestant Reformation and ultimately imported into the 'contact zone' of the East Kimberley. In early Iranian traditions, good/evil and heaven/hell dichotomies were strongly developed in religious beliefs, based on oppositional relations between settled agriculturalists and nomadic herders, and notions of the apocalypse to rid the world of evil-doers became prominent. Such apocalyptic ideas gradually spread into Jewish and then early Christian thought, diminished during the Middle Ages, but then returned with the Protestant Reformation and its literalist reading of scripture, and eventually travelled with missionaries to the East Kimberley, where McDonald conducted her fieldwork. Beliefs in the coming apocalypse were widespread among Halls Creek Aboriginal people, but the cosmological dualisms derived from Zoroastrian ideas became blurred when applied to Aboriginal spiritual beliefs and practices and kin-based morality. Although this represents a very different situation than the syncretism described by Keen, McDonald's insights are nevertheless reminiscent of Ian Keen's emphasis on indeterminacies in post-contact religious beliefs.

This indeterminacy in the bringing together of once-separate systems of thought is a theme Ian pursued in his article 'Metaphor and the Metalanguage' (1995), demonstrating that the use of Western analytical concepts (based on a recognisable set of Western metaphors) generates anomalies when applied to the social practices of the Yolngu (based on a quite different set of metaphors). This incommensurability of knowledge systems is a theme developed by Allon Uhlmann in Chapter 7, in which he examines two competing approaches to Arabic grammatical instruction in Israeli universities. Arab and Jewish students in these courses have been schooled in two quite different approaches to Arabic, the Arabic tradition and the European Orientalist tradition, which are ontologically distinct and draw upon different kinds of tropes. Also, again reminiscent of Ian's work, the two systems are locked into a set of unequal power relations with the indigenous system subordinate, and with Arab students coming to feel a sense of failure when faced with an institutionalised but incommensurable system of instruction. Uhlmann analyses a range of different 'failures of translation' on the part of the European Orientalist tradition, which then generate anomalies experienced by the Arab students and create a false sense of equivalence between the Arabic language and the European Orientalist translation of it. Although analysing ethnographic materials quite different from Ian's, Uhlmann develops similar themes and draws similar conclusions that underscore the productivity of Ian's ideas and the influence that he had on his students, Aboriginalist and non-Aboriginalist alike.

In Chapter 8, I also pick up on the themes of indeterminacy and heterogeneity that have been so important in Ian's interpretations of Yolngu ritual, as well as his recent resurgence of interest in language and sociality, in my analysis of Dhalwangu song texts using the framework of Bakhtin's theory of the utterance. For Bakhtin, the utterance is the unit of living speech communication (as opposed to the sentence, the unit of language as an abstract system), and is characterised by fundamentally dialogical features. In my analysis I take song textual phrases performed by Dhalwangu singers to be utterances in a Bakhtinian sense, and *manikay* as a genre of public song to be a speech genre (another Bakhtinian term). A poetic analysis of Dhalwangu song using Bakhtin's ideas not only generates insights into *manikay* as a living and dynamic tradition, but also lends support to Ian Keen's long-standing interest in the indeterminacies and ambiguities of Yolngu ritual and social life.

Milingimbi as a place was enormously influential on the development of Ian Keen's thought, being the location of his earliest intensive and long-term field research. In Chapter 9, Louise Hamby and Dr Gumbula focus their attention on Milingimbi as a centre of material culture collecting over the last century. Chronicling the long history of the collection of material culture at Milingimbi since the mission was established in the early 1920s, Hamby and Gumbula note the importance of both mission staff and visiting academics in the development of numerous collections dispersed throughout the globe. These collections provide a tangible history of Milingimbi, and shed light on the central place of material culture in the engagement between Yolngu and Europeans. This chapter also conveys a strong sense of the importance of these collections for contemporary Yolngu, not as relics collecting dust on shelves in faraway places, but rather as living components of Yolngu cultural heritage that have an ongoing importance in Yolngu social life. This is especially significant given that Gumbula was the son of Djäwa, one of Ian's main research collaborators during his Milingimbi research.

In Chapter 10, Paul Burke provides a compelling and ethnographically grounded analysis of the women of the Warlpiri diaspora and their diverse strategies for asserting personal autonomy by severing ties to kin and country and moving away to towns and cities far removed from Warlpiri settlements. The analysis necessarily engages critically with the work of Diane Bell, who posited a return to traditionalism for Aboriginal women's empowerment, and argues instead that Warlpiri women pursue diverse and heterogeneous strategies, which in turn help us to re-examine and redefine concepts of personal autonomy and of active and constructive agency. Burke's case studies include women escaping promised marriages, women who had become leaders in Christian religious communities in Darwin, those who had established semi-traditional women's spaces in Alice Springs or foster homes for Warlpiri children to attend school in Adelaide, and women artists who established an ongoing relationship with a non-Aboriginal art wholesaler in Adelaide. Burke acknowledges that his project has no straightforward relationship with Ian Keen's own scholarly work, but is instead characterised by the more general (but no less important) scholarly influences of being empirically grounded, open to critical and theoretical engagement, and committed to a clear style of writing. That these characteristics are so much in evidence in this chapter attests to Ian's abilities as a mentor and his willingness to allow his students to pursue their own interests, rather than impose his own perspective.

Chapter 11 takes the reader again to the Crocodile Islands, the site of Ian's PhD fieldwork, and again back to issues pertaining to language and meaning. This time, Bentley James considers challenges in the translation and interpretation of the concept of *märr*, in the light of not only the ethnographic literature on the Yolngu, but also in relation to anthropological writings pertaining to the concept of *mana* in the Pacific. Both concepts pertain to notions of spiritual power, and both are inadequately translated when the tropes of the anthropological metalanguage are allowed to obscure the specific contextual features of their originary cultures. After critically surveying the relevant literature, James embarks on an ethnolinguistic reinterpretation of *märr*, focusing on its polysemy, complexity, and ambiguity, and the lessons to be learned by its use in everyday language. The power of *märr* is also omnipresent in the Yolngu experience of the lived environment as it is believed to reside in the land, and can be harnessed through ritual means. James's chapter neatly encapsulates a range of interpretive themes that have been present in Ian Keen's work over the past four decades: the links between language and culture, the nature of Yolngu religious beliefs and practices, and the challenges of cross-cultural translation. Careful attention to these issues can have the beneficial result of demanding self-reflexive questions about the rituals, institutions, and ontology of the anthropological project, a goal Ian himself would no doubt support.

John White, in Chapter 12, provides a systematic profiling of the Yuin people of the Eurobodalla region of southeast New South Wales, adopting the analytical approach Ian developed in *Aboriginal Economy and Society* (Keen 2004). Indeed, White was Ian's student during the study period for this book, and he demonstrates convincingly that the categories of ecology, institutional fields, and economy provide a very productive basis for the extension of this comparative study of Aboriginal societies at the threshold of colonisation, opening the way for further studies of this type. White also draws a specific comparison with the Kŭnai people of Gippsland, one of Ian's case studies, as both Kŭnai and Yuin occupied similar ecological zones which gave rise to similar relations between economy and society. The productivity of Ian's framework when applied to other societies validates his approach and underscores the importance of *Aboriginal Economy and Society* as a work of lasting importance.

The book closes with a contribution by Ian's long-standing colleague and current research collaborator, Pat McConvell, and his study of the diffusion of kin terms in northern Australia. This chapter arises out of their collaboration on the AustKin project which, broadly speaking, seeks to use kinship terminology to generate a comparative framework for understanding Aboriginal social organisation across Australia. The project is an excellent fit for Ian's interests in kinship, the comparative and historical study of Aboriginal societies, and the relationship between language and culture. McConvell's chapter examines affinal terms as noteworthy examples of long-distance loanwords, focusing on two particular kinship terms that diffused broadly across the Kimberley and into the Northern Territory. In its intricate detail and thorough analysis, McConvell not only provides a comprehensive account of two particular cases of linguistic diffusion, but also establishes a clear case for the importance of an historical examination of the links between language, kinship, and other elements of social organisation like avoidance relations. Indeed, as McConvell notes, the diachronic study of Aboriginal kinship systems is augmented considerably by the focus on linguistic materials. Ian's early and ongoing interests in kinship, his later development of comparative historical frameworks, and his abiding interest in language and society, combine in a way that makes the research goals of the AustKin project a natural and productive fit.

---

In late November 2011, Ian and I were standing in front of Salvador Dali's massive *Santiago El Grande*, which hangs in Fredericton's Beaverbrook Art Gallery. Ian had been in Montreal for the American Anthropological Association meetings, and then in Nova Scotia to visit his family there, and managed a visit to Fredericton on his way back to Australia. It was the first time Ian had visited us in Canada, and so it was a special occasion for us. It was also special because we were joined for dinner the previous evening by the anthropologist Alan Mason, who had been my undergraduate mentor and who had supervised my honours thesis on the topic of Yolngu religion. I felt that a circle had been closed, with the teacher who had first introduced me to the Yolngu, the teacher who had guided me through my own study of the Yolngu, and I all sharing a meal.

*Santiago El Grande* is a monumental work that inspires contemplation: physically huge, brilliantly conceived, masterfully executed, and full of symbolism. As we stood there, I was reminded that Ian began his professional life not as an anthropologist, but as an artist. As an anthropologist, though, he has created an *oeuvre* of lasting significance that deserves careful contemplation as well. Ian has pursued a broad variety of different scholarly interests, which nevertheless are linked by a set of overlapping and consistent themes. And, as with a great work of art, careful contemplation is abundantly repaid with additional new insights and inspirations. The chapters collected here represent just one set of examples, of which there will, no doubt, be more to come.

## References

Fijn, N., I. Keen, C. Lloyd, and M. Pickering (eds). 2012. *Indigenous Participation in Australian Economies II: Historical Engagements and Current Enterprises*. Canberra: ANU E Press.

Keen, I. 1977. Ambiguity in Yolngu religious language. *Canberra Anthropology* 1: 33–50.

Keen, I. 1978. One Ceremony, One Song: An Economy of Religious Knowledge among the Yolngu of North-East Arnhem Land. PhD Thesis, The Australian National University, Canberra.

Keen, I. 1982. How some Murngin men marry ten wives: the marital implications of matrilateral cross-cousin structures. *Man* 17(4): 620–42.

Keen, I. 1985. Definitions of kin. *Journal of Anthropological Research* 41: 62–90.

Keen, I. 1986. New perspectives on Yolngu affinity. *Oceania* 56(3): 218–30.

Keen, I. 1987. Stanner on Aboriginal religion. *Canberra Anthropology* 9(2): 26–50.

Keen, I. 1988a. *Being Black: Aboriginal Cultures in 'Settled' Australia*. Canberra: Aboriginal Studies Press.

Keen, I. 1988b. Twenty-five years of Aboriginal kinship studies. In R.M. Berndt and R. Tonkinson (eds), *Social Anthropology and Australian Aboriginal Studies: A Contemporary Overview*, pp. 79–123. Canberra: Australian Institute of Aboriginal Studies.

Keen, I. 1988c. Yolngu religious property. In T. Ingold, D. Riches and J. Woodburn (eds), *Property, Power and Ideology in Hunting and Gathering Societies*, pp. 272–91. London: Berg.

Keen, I. 1990. Ecological community and species attributes in Yolngu religious symbolism. In R. Willis (ed.), *Signifying Animals: Human Meaning in the Natural World*. London and Boston: Unwin Hyman.

Keen, I. 1991. Images of reproduction in the Yolngu Madayin ceremony. *The Australian Journal of Anthropology* 1(2–3): 192–207.

Keen, I. 1993. Ubiquitous ubiety of dubious uniformity. *The Australian Journal of Anthropology* 4(2): 96–110.

Keen, I. 1994. *Knowledge and Secrecy in an Aboriginal Religion*. Oxford: Clarendon Press.

Keen, I. 1995. Metaphor and the metalanguage: 'groups' in northeast Arnhem Land. *American Ethnologist* 22(3): 502–27.

Keen, I. 1997. The western desert vs the rest: rethinking the contrast. In F. Merlan, J. Morton and A. Rumsey (eds), *Scholar and Sceptic: Australian Aboriginal Studies in Honour of L.R. Hiatt*, pp. 65–93. Canberra: Aboriginal Studies Press.

Keen, I. 1999a. Norman Tindale and me: anthropology, genealogy, authenticity. In J.D. Finlayson, B. Rigsby and H.J. Bek (eds), *Connections in Native Title: Genealogies, Kinship and Groups*, pp. 13–57. Canberra: Centre for Aboriginal Economic Policy Research.

Keen, I. 1999b. Cultural continuity and native title claims. *Land, Rights, Laws: Issues of Native Title* (Issues Paper no. 28). Canberra: Native Title Research Unit, Australian Institute of Aboriginal and Torres Strait Islander Studies.

Keen, I. 2000a. The debate over Yolngu clans. *Anthropological Forum* 10(1): 31–41.

Keen, I. 2000b. A bundle of sticks: the debate over Yolngu clans. *Journal of the Royal Anthropological Institute* 6: 419–36.

Keen, I. 2000c. The anthropologist as geologist: Howitt in colonial Gippsland. *The Australian Journal of Anthropology* 11(1): 78–97.

Keen, I. 2003. Aboriginal economy and society at the threshold of colonisation: a comparative study. *Before Farming* 2003(3): 1–24.

Keen, I. 2004. *Aboriginal Economy and Society: Australia at the Threshold of Colonisation*. Melbourne: Oxford University Press.

Keen, I. 2006. Constraints on the development of enduring inequalities in Late Holocene Australia. *Current Anthropology* 47(1): 7–38.

Keen, I. (ed.). 2010a. *Indigenous Participation in Australian Economies: Historical and Anthropological Perspectives*. Canberra: ANU E Press.

Keen, I. 2010b. The interpretation of Aboriginal 'property' on the Australian colonial frontier. In I. Keen (ed.), *Indigenous Participation in Australian Economies: Historical and Anthropological Perspectives*, pp. 41–61. Canberra: ANU E Press.

Keen, I. 2011. The language of property: analyses of Yolngu relations to country. In Y. Musharbash and M. Barber (eds), *Ethnography and the Production of Anthropological Knowledge: Essays in Honour of Nicolas Peterson*, pp. 101–19. Canberra: ANU E Press.

Keen, I. 2013a. The legacy of Radcliffe-Brown's typology of Australian Aboriginal kinship systems. *Structure and Dynamics* 6(1): 1–31.

Keen, I. 2013b. The language of possession: three case studies. *Language in Society* 42(2): 187–214.

Keen, I. 2015. Language in the constitution of kinship. *Anthropological Linguistics* 56(1): 1–53.

Keen, I. and C. Lloyd. 2012. Introduction. In N. Fijn, I. Keen, C. Lloyd, and M. Pickering (eds), *Indigenous Participation in Australian Economies II: Historical Engagements and Current Enterprises*, pp. 1–15. Canberra: ANU E Press.

McConvell, P., I. Keen, and R. Hendery. 2013. *Kinship Systems: Change and Reconstruction*. Salt Lake City: University of Utah Press.

Morphy, H. 1997. Death, exchange, and the reproduction of Yolngu society. In F. Merlan, J. Morton, and A. Rumsey (eds), *Scholar and Sceptic: Australian Aboriginal Studies in Honour of L.R. Hiatt*, pp. 123–50. Canberra: Aboriginal Studies Press.

Morton, J. 1997. Arrernte (Aranda) land tenure: an evaluation of the Strehlow model. *Strehlow Research Centre, Occasional Papers 1*, pp. 107–25. Alice Springs: Strehlow Research Centre.

Sutton, P. 1999. The system as it was straining to become: fluidity, stability, and Aboriginal country groups. In J.D. Finlayson, B. Rigsby and H.J. Bek (eds), *Connections in Native Title: Genealogies, Kinship and Groups*, pp. 13–57. Canberra: Centre for Aboriginal Economic Policy Research.

Williams, N. 1999. The relationship of genealogical reckoning and group formation: Yolngu examples. In J.D. Finlayson, B. Rigsby and H.J. Bek (eds), *Connections in Native Title: Genealogies, Kinship and Groups*, pp. 125–39. Canberra: Centre for Aboriginal Economic Policy Research.

# 2 Judicial Understandings of Aboriginality and Language Use in Criminal Cases[1]

Diana Eades
University of New England

## Introduction

Ian Keen is highly respected for his seminal research on complex relationships between social group, kinship, religion, economy, knowledge and territory, particularly in remote Australia. Much of this work has been applied in land rights and native title claims, in which contests over the social identities of claimants are often central. As highlighted in the Yorta Yorta native title claim in Victoria, judicial officers have considerable power to accept or reject who people say they are, with far-reaching implications. But Ian's contributions to the study and understanding of Aboriginal identity have extended much further than his research in remote Australia and its connections to land. His early interest in diverse aspects of identity led to his 1988 edited book *Being Black: Aboriginal Cultures in 'Settled' Australia*, which was a groundbreaking work in the understanding of Aboriginal identity, interactions, and culture in non-remote Australia. As he wrote in the introduction, there had been a tendency

---

[1] I am grateful to Ian Keen whose patient, supportive and insightful supervision of my PhD in the early 1980s played a important role in launching my ongoing investigations into Aboriginal ways of using English. In expanding my understanding of some of the issues canvassed in this chapter, I owe gratitude to participants in the 2012 Uluru Criminal Lawyers conference, especially Judge Dean Mildren, retired judge John Nicholson, and then Senior Public Defender Dina Yehia (now District Court Judge). Thanks also to Jeff Siegel and Peter Toner and two anonymous reviewers for helpful comments on the draft. All remaining errors are my responsibility. I do not intend to imply that any of these people agree with my analysis.

by many—scholars and others—to regard Aboriginal people who did not live in remote Australia from a deficit perspective. They were seen as people who had 'lost their culture', and were somehow less Aboriginal (if indeed they were Aboriginal at all) than those whose remote location had resulted in less disruption to their lives. Keen's book was the first to bring together and extend ethnographic studies which recognised and exemplified contemporary Aboriginal identities and cultures in 'settled' Australia.

While Keen's use of Rowley's (1971) term 'settled' Australia worked well in 1988, more than two decades later this term seems less appropriate, given the possible present-day connotations of 'at rest' or no longer contested. This chapter deals with identity issues of Aboriginal people who do not live in remote Australia and who speak varieties of English as their main language, often their only language. Where necessary, I will refer to Aboriginal people in 'southern Australia', while recognising that this label is less than ideal. To Keen's (1988: 3) observation of such people forming 'part of a distinct, though heterogenous and loosely bounded ethnic category', we can add the twenty-first century understanding that ethnic identities are typically hybrid, dynamic and multiple.

This chapter discusses how judicial decision-makers understand Aboriginal identity, specifically in the criminal justice system. As in land claim and native title processes, the criminal justice process centres on fundamental questions about whose story can be believed, or which parts of which stories can be believed, and in these questions Aboriginal identity and culture can be important considerations. Length limitations will prevent me from considering further parallels between these different legal processes. And a longer work would situate this discussion of Aboriginality in southern Australia in the current contests and misunderstandings among Australians from a wide range of backgrounds, which is frequently seen in public discourse, (such as then Opposition Leader Tony Abbott's November 2012 comment that Western Australia's first Aboriginal member of parliament, Ken Wyatt, is 'not a man of culture' (Aikman 2012)).

Aboriginality has been a prominent focus of the criminal justice system in the past 25 years, particularly in terms of one of the most fundamental human rights, namely that 'all people are equal before the law' (Article 7, Universal Declaration of Human Rights). This right entails being 'entitled without any discrimination to the equal protection of the law' (International Covenant on Civil and Political Rights 1966). Judicial officers (judges and magistrates) take an oath to administer the law 'without fear or favour, affection or ill-will'. Guidance for Australian judicial officers about their day-to-day practice in court is clear about equal treatment being different from the same treatment, as seen in the opening section of the NSW *Equality before the Law Bench Book* (Judicial Commission of NSW 2009: 1103):

Equality before the law is sometimes misunderstood. It does not necessarily mean 'same treatment'. As McHugh J succinctly explained: 'discrimination can arise just as readily from an act which treats as equals those who are different as it can from an act which treats differently persons whose circumstances are not materially different'.[2]

The principle explained by Justice McHugh is pertinent all over Australia on a daily basis in the ways that the criminal justice system deals with Aboriginal people. This chapter considers one factor which can be central to the participation of many Aboriginal people in the criminal justice process, namely ways in which judicial officers understand Aboriginal identities, practice and culture.

The discussion will start with a 1987 case that highlights an approach to Aboriginal identity which centres on biological and phenotypical assessment, and which exemplifies important real-world consequences of the denial of Aboriginality which Keen (1988) set out to counter. I then briefly sketch some important developments in judicial understandings. I outline the main judicial context in which Aboriginality has been considered, namely in sentencing convicted offenders. Sentencing contexts are not the main focus of this chapter, however, which instead turns to matters concerning communication between witnesses (including defendants) and officers within the legal process, including police officers, lawyers, magistrates and judges. The discussion of selected cases between 1993 and 2006, together with consideration of related judiciary-led developments underline my argument (e.g. 1992, 1993, 1996a, 2008, 2013) for the need for the legal system to recognise Aboriginal ways of using English. In this discussion we will see evidence of the difficult task that judicial officers can be faced with in deciding whether and how Aboriginal identity is relevant in individual cases.

The chapter will argue that judicial officers need to distinguish between sentencing contexts on one hand, and contexts of communication in legal settings on the other, in their consideration of Aboriginality. The role of alcohol in lives characterised by often extreme disadvantage, including illiteracy and other 'grave social difficulties' (see 'Grave Social Difficulties') is often central to the judicial consideration of Aboriginality in sentencing. But there is no inherent connection between these negative (and distressing) living conditions experienced by many Aboriginal people and their language variety—in southern Australia, their Aboriginal use of English. Yet in cases in which communication with Aboriginal English speakers is central (for example, with prosecution witnesses in a murder case, see 'A Problem-Centred Approach to Aboriginal Ways of Using English'), a focus on problems experienced by Aboriginal people can sometimes connect to a deficit view of Aboriginal identity and social

---

2  In *Waters v Public Transport Corporation* (1991: 402). See also Queensland Supreme Court (2005: 14).

practice, while at the same time preventing the court from engaging in effective intercultural communication. Thus, this chapter highlights how an ongoing deficit approach to Aboriginal identity in southern Australia, addressed by Keen and others in his 1988 book, can still, at times, play a role in the criminal justice system, with disturbing social consequences.

The discussion in this chapter will draw primarily on judgments, that is written decisions of one or more judges in a case, which outline the facts, discuss the evidence and refer to legislation and case law on which the judicial decision is based (Family Court of Australia). In discussing judgments, this chapter will use the legal convention of referring to judges with the form 'Last Name J' and to judges who are President of the Appeal Court as 'Last Name P'. It is not my intention to comment on legal reasoning or to analyse the complexity of individual cases, nor do I have the expertise required.

## '... Of Only Partly Aboriginal Extraction'

The year before Keen's (1988) book on Aboriginal identity and culture in 'settled' Australia was published, an appeal judgment in a Queensland case (*R v Condren* 1987) highlighted the conception of Aboriginality through the discourse of race, as well as the language ideology that language acquisition and use is dependent on biology.

Kelvin Condren, who had grown up in Townsville, was found guilty of the brutal murder of a woman in Mount Isa in 1983, on the basis of a signed confession allegedly given in answers to questions he was asked in a police interview. One of the grounds for Condren's 1987 appeal was related to linguistic evidence which supported his claim that the police transcript of their interview with him had not been typed verbatim, as they had claimed. (Thus, this case revolved around Condren's allegation that his 'confession' had been fabricated.) This linguistic evidence compared the grammatical structures and ways of communicating (or pragmatic patterns) in answers in the so-called confession to those in other interviews Condren had had in legal contexts, and to general research about Aboriginal English patterns (see Eades 1993, 2013: Chapter 8). Although the linguistic evidence was heard in full in the appeal hearing, it was ruled as legally inadmissible.

Several reasons were given for the inadmissibility ruling (see Eades 1997), including the judges' refusal to accept that there could be a specialised field of knowledge that could analyse the English spoken by Aboriginal people. The reason pertinent to the discussion in this chapter can be characterised as the judges' finding that Condren was not 'Aboriginal enough' (my term, see also Flynn 2005) for evidence about Aboriginal use of English to be relevant, if indeed they had accepted that there could have been such a kind of expertise.

This finding drew on the discourse of skin colour and fractions of racial descent, which had predominated for decades in colonial and neocolonial discourse. While no longer used in government censuses after the 1967 referendum (Rowse 2012: 9), and also discredited in the social sciences by 1987, these crude biological and phenotypical assessments of Aboriginal people in the 1987 *Condren* judgment mirrored much public discourse at that time. Ambrose J (*R v Condren* 1987: 276) drew a general distinction between 'full-blooded tribal Aboriginals' and 'part-blooded urban Aboriginals'. Referring specifically to Condren, he mentioned the 'absence of any clear evidence as to the genealogy of the appellant and … the fact that neither of his parents were full-blooded Aboriginals' (p. 297). Ambrose J also observed Condren's mother giving evidence at the appeal and commented in his judgment: 'Upon my assessment of that lady's appearance and manner, I certainly formed the impression that she was of only partly Aboriginal extraction and indeed that part was not predominant' (p. 275).[3]

Condren's appeal judgment illustrates a taken-for-granted perspective that biological characteristics, such as skin colour and fraction of racial descent, can account for language acquisition, exposing acceptance of a general approach which has been disparagingly labelled 'the pathology of ethnicity'. It highlighted the way in which (possibly most) members of the judiciary at that time were both removed from and ignorant of Aboriginal social life and culture.[4]

## Contexts of Developing Judicial Understandings

Within just a few years of Condren's appeal, the Royal Commission into Aboriginal Deaths in Custody exposed and explored the complex relationships between the criminal justice system and Aboriginal people, in its investigation into their extraordinary over-representation in the country's police cells and prisons. The Royal Commission found that 'the most significant contributing factor' to this over-representation was 'the disadvantaged and unequal position in which people find themselves in the society—socially, economically, and culturally' (Johnston 1991: 15). The extensive report on the ways in which this

---

3   It appears that many, if not most, of the decisions which consider whether a person is 'Aboriginal enough' are from southern Australian cases. In contrast, Condren had lived in and near the north Queensland cities of Townsville and Mount Isa most of his life (on 'the rolling side of the frontier', in Langton's (1981: 17) terms) and also in an Aboriginal community in Central Australia.
4   In 1990, the Queensland appeal court found that Condren had been wrongfully convicted, and his seven years in prison came to an end.

'disadvantaged and unequal position' brings Aboriginal people 'into conflict with the criminal justice system' marked a watershed in terms of making the legal system realise that Aboriginal people and societies could no longer be ignored. The Royal Commission's extensive investigations and findings have impacted the criminal justice system, and the judiciary specifically, in numerous and diverse ways.[5] Of its 339 recommendations, one specifically addressed judicial awareness, dealing with the need for judicial officers (among others) to have training about 'contemporary Aboriginal society, customs and traditions', as well as participating 'in discussion with members of the Aboriginal community in an informal way in order to improve cross-cultural understanding' (Johnston 1991: 53).

In response, several state courts have established court committees or programs to promote understanding of Aboriginal people and cultures, such as the NSW Judicial Commission's Ngara Yura Program (since 1992). In addition to conventional judicial training approaches, such as workshops, conferences and publications, this program runs a popular series of community visits. Judicial officers make a field trip to a selected Aboriginal community, where they have the opportunity to talk to local people, 'to enhance their understanding and appreciation of the history and culture' and 'to exchange information and ideas on issues of mutual concern, including cultural and language differences' (Judicial Commission of New South Wales n.d.).

At the national level, professional development programs for judicial officers are central to the work of the National Judicial College of Australia, established in 2002. With programs developed and delivered by committees of judges or magistrates, and drawing on other expertise as required, the college deals with a vast range of topics impacting judicial work. Many of these programs incorporate issues about understanding Aboriginal communities and witnesses (for example, in programs on Judging in Remote Localities (2008), Solution Focussed Judging (2011) and Witness Assessment (2012, 2014)).

Other significant developments in the context of judicial understandings about Aboriginal people and cultures relate to the people being appointed to judicial positions. There is a very small but growing number of Aboriginal magistrates, including Pat O'Shane (NSW, 1986–2013), Jacqui Payne (Queensland, since 1999) and Rose Falla (Victoria, appointed 2013). There has only been one Aboriginal judge, the late Bob Bellear, who was a NSW District Court judge from 1996–2004. However, there are now judges at the highest levels who had earlier

---

5  However, this over-representation has not been reduced. Statistics for 2013 show that Indigenous people (of whom the majority are Aboriginal) are imprisoned at 13 times the rate of the general population (age-adjusted figures), while Indigenous young people are in juvenile detention at about 24 times the rate of the general population (SCRGSP 2014).

worked as young lawyers in the newly established Aboriginal Legal Services in the 1970s. Over decades, these Aboriginal organisations, which have provided unparalleled service to Aboriginal people, have also trained many lawyers in understanding Aboriginal social and cultural life, and many of these lawyers have gone on to work as judicial officers. One such example is the current Chief Justice of the High Court of Australia, Robert French (Skyring 2011: 13). Other contemporary judges have had other close involvements with Aboriginal people and issues over many decades since their student days or early work as lawyers. For example, the Chief Justice of the NSW Supreme Court from 1988–2011, Jim Spigelman, was one of the 34 university students who made the 1965 Freedom Ride to expose and protest about segregation and racism against Aboriginal people in NSW country towns (Curthoys 2002).

## 'Grave Social Difficulties'

The judiciary's expanded awareness of the need to understand Aboriginal social life has been particularly focused, in the criminal justice system, on decisions about sentencing. This is perhaps their most significant and difficult job in most cases where an offender is convicted. In making the decision about sentencing, judicial officers usually have discretion in exercising their responsibility to balance the main punishment aims of retribution, deterrence and rehabilitation.[6] The sentencing decision involves not only balancing these punishment aims, but also taking into account a wide range of relevant 'material facts' concerning the nature of the offence, the nature of the offender, and the effect of the offence and the penalty (Findlay, Odgers and Yeo 2005: Chapter 8). One of the cases which established that an offender's Aboriginality may often be a relevant consideration was the 1982 *Neal* High Court case. Brennan J held that material facts to be taken into account in sentencing include 'those facts which exist only by reason of the offender's membership of an ethnic or other group' (*Neal v R* 1982: 326).

Ten years later, with the benefit of the final report and recommendations of the Royal Commission into Aboriginal Deaths in Custody, as well as judgments in a number of cases, including *Neal*, Wood J set out 12 specific principles in *R v Fernando* (p. 61). The principles from this 1992 NSW Supreme Court trial have become one of the most important and detailed precedents in the sentencing of Aboriginal people throughout the country. At the centre of these sentencing principles is recognition of 'the problems of alcohol abuse and violence which to a very significant degree go hand in hand with Aboriginal

---

[6] However, judicial officers are sometimes provided with little sentencing discretion, namely in jurisdictions where governments have legislated mandatory sentences for some offences.

communities' and that the 'cure [of these problems] requires more subtle remedies than the criminal law can provide by way of imprisonment' (p. 61). A key element includes the need for

> the realistic recognition by the court of the endemic presence of alcohol within Aboriginal communities, and the grave social difficulties faced by those communities where poor self-image, absence of education and work opportunity and other demoralising factors have placed heavy stresses on them, reinforcing their resort to alcohol and compounding its worst effects. (*R v Fernando* 1992: 62–3)

But concerns are being expressed about the ways in which the *Fernando* principles are being 'narrow[ed]' in application (Flynn 2005), or 'retreat[ed] from' (Edney 2006; see also Anthony 2010: 3; Nicholson 2012 and Yehia 2012). Edney argues that in a number of NSW appeal court judgments the application of these principles has been restricted because of judicial officers 'fundamentally misapprehending the nature of [Aboriginal] identity in a post-colonial society' (p. 17). Examples of this 'misapprehended' approach to Aboriginal identity are cited from judgments which find that the *Fernando* principles are not relevant because of such factors as the defendant having an urban background (*R v Newman, R v Simpson* 2004), or having a 'part-aboriginal' grandfather (*R v Ceissman* 2001) or having 'had many dealings with the police, and not [being] intimidated by the idea of being questioned by them' (*R v Helmhout* 2001: 259). The Aboriginal identity of many people who have been described in these ways has been thus legally 'erased' or 'extinguished', in Edney's (2006) terms.[7] Yet, such factors as fractional descent, place of residence and experience with the police manifestly do not enable many Aboriginal people to escape the 'grave social difficulties' enunciated by Wood. An important 2013 High Court case about the sentencing of a New South Wales Aboriginal man (*Bugmy v R* 2013), found that 'Aboriginal Australians who live in an urban environment do not lose their Aboriginal identity and they, too, may be subject to the grave social difficulties discussed in *Fernando*' (§41).[8]

The fact that the *Fernando* principles are focused on Aboriginal alcohol abuse and violence, and linked to 'poor self-image, absence of education and work opportunity and other demoralising factors' in Aboriginal communities, was doubtless central to Fernando's case. And these negative social issues, and others such as foetal alcohol syndrome, are also relevant to many other

---

7   This approach to Aboriginal identity and resulting legal erasure highlights the need for scholarly writing in the social sciences (such as Keen 1988) to be accessed in law school training, and more widely made available for judicial officers and other legal professionals.

8   In this case, the High Court rejected the decision of the NSW Court of Criminal Appeal (CCA) that the social disadvantage referred to in the *Fernando* principles diminishes over time, especially during a person's period of incarceration. While the decision in this case is important for the issue of Aboriginal sentencing, further comment is beyond the scope of this chapter (but see Judicial Commission of New South Wales 2013, Williams 2013).

Aboriginal offenders, and to central considerations in their sentencing. But, as Nicholson (2012: 4) points out, an offender's Aboriginality can also be relevant to sentencing in positive ways (for example, in cases where an offender has been making a positive contribution to the community in their role as an elder).

## Communication with Aboriginal Witnesses

The *Fernando* principles highlight the relevance of having 'a deprived background' or being 'otherwise disadvantaged', which must often be taken into account when a judicial officer sentences an Aboriginal offender. But the life experiences focused on in these principles are seen to revolve around 'abuse of alcohol' and 'resort to violence'. While these experiences may be common to many Aboriginal people who have not learned general Australian English, they are not necessarily relevant to the way that a person speaks English, which depends on the much richer fabric of socialisation, both primary and secondary (and further), and patterns of social networking, interaction, and residence. This chapter now turns away from issues involved in the sentencing of Aboriginal offenders, to those involved in communication with Aboriginal witnesses (including defendants) and to hearing their stories in the criminal justice process. In my view Aboriginality is often relevant to the judicial officers' responsibility of ensuring that the proceedings are conducted fairly. But, it seems that this relevance of Aboriginal identity—specifically in terms of communication in interviews with police or lawyers, or during courtroom questioning—is often ignored. We will see examples of this in decisions about admissibility of evidence and directions to the jury. We turn first to two judgments in which issues concerning Aboriginal ways of using English were relevant to appeals against guilty verdicts, as with the Condren appeal discussed above. The first case discussed here deals with miscommunication between an accused person and her lawyer, and the second with communication in a police interview. Initiatives by judicial officers and state justice departments concerning trial communication with Aboriginal speakers of English are also considered. We then examine judicial decisions in two cases where Aboriginal use of English was raised in relation to courtroom communication.

Elsewhere (e.g. Eades 1992, 1994, 2008, 2013) I have written about features of Aboriginal use of English—often referred to as Aboriginal English—which are particularly relevant to communication in the legal process.[9] These features can be structural (including grammatical patterns, word choice and meaning), and/or pragmatic, that is features of language usage (including patterns of discourse

---

9   For discussion of the advantages and disadvantages of the terms 'Aboriginal English' and 'Aboriginal ways of speaking/using English' see Eades (2013: Chapter 1).

and conversation). Several pragmatic features impact on Aboriginal participation in legal interviews, even when structurally the variety of English may be close to general Australian English. For example, in many western Anglo societies, silence (or a pause of more than about one second) in an interview is generally taken to mean that a speaker has nothing to say, or could be trying to invent an answer. In contrast, in much Aboriginal interaction (whether the language spoken is a variety of English or a traditional Aboriginal language) silence is used as a positive and productive part of communication. The implications of this difference in language use are extensive for the participation of Aboriginal people in legal interviews, as is the widespread use of the phenomenon known as 'gratuitous concurrence'. This term refers to the act of saying 'yes' to a question, regardless of whether the speaker agrees with the proposition being questioned, or even understands it. The strong Aboriginal tendency to use gratuitous concurrence in interviews has been documented since the mid-1800s, and makes many Aboriginal people suggestible, or highly suggestible, in police interviews and courtroom questioning, an issue we will return to below. The use of Aboriginal patterns of communication (or pragmatic language features) is not inherently connected to 'social difficulties' centred around abuse of alcohol and violence. Thus criteria such as those derived from sentencing principles will not necessarily be relevant to questions about an Aboriginal person's English usage or patterns of communication.

## Pre-Trial Communication Issues for Defendants

A 1993 Queensland Appeal Court case provides a positive example of how and why Aboriginal patterns of communication can be relevant. Just six years after this court used racial and biological constructions of Aboriginal identity to reject expert sociolinguistic evidence (in *Condren* 1987, discussed above), the same court raised no objections to the admissibility of expert sociolinguistic evidence, this time in relation to issues involved in communication between an Aboriginal woman from southeast Queensland and her lawyers (in *R v Kina* 1993). Kina had appealed her murder conviction on the basis that her lawyers did not find out her story and thus the jury had found her guilty in the absence of any opportunity for her to present her defence. The sociolinguistic report, which was admitted into evidence without contest, referred in part to some of the characteristics of Aboriginal ways of using English mentioned above (see Eades 1996a, 2003). The court was unanimous in finding there had been a miscarriage of justice. The judgment by Fitzgerald P and Davies J accepted Kina's Aboriginality without qualification, and noted that none of her lawyers had 'received any training or instructions concerning how to communicate or deal with Aborigines' (*R v Kina* 1993: 21). In finding that Kina's trial had involved a miscarriage of justice, this judgment cited 'cultural, psychological and personal factors' which 'presented exceptional difficulties of communication between her legal representatives and the appellant'. These factors 'bore upon the adequacy of the advice and legal representation which the appellant received and effectively denied her satisfactory representation or the capacity to make informed decisions on the basis of proper advice' (pp. 35–6). (The judgment by McPherson J did not mention Kina's Aboriginality.)

Another judgment in the same court, two years later, involved more detailed consideration of southeast Queensland Aboriginal identity—this time for a teenager from Cherbourg community—in relation to issues concerning his communication with arresting police officers (*R v Aubrey* 1995). Sixteen-year-old Aubrey was appealing his conviction for manslaughter following the death of a man whom he had punched outside a hotel. One of the grounds of the appeal was that the confession contained in answers in the police interview should not have been admissible. This was because the interviewing officers had not followed a Queensland police directive requiring the presence of a lawyer/legal officer when interviewing 'persons under disability' (which included 'many Aborigines', see below). The appeal was unsuccessful, and the judgments of both the two majority judges and the dissenting judge considered the issue of the appellant's Aboriginality.

In his dissenting judgment, Fitzgerald P referred to 'cultural problems associated with the reliability of confessional statements made by aborigines who are interrogated by white persons in positions of authority'. He held that the police commissioner's regulations, both about interviewing young people and interviewing Aboriginal people, had been ignored in Aubrey's case, and the resulting admissions that Aubrey made to police should not have been received into evidence. For Fitzgerald, the Aboriginality of this appellant from the largest Aboriginal community in Queensland was not at issue. Not only did he recognise that Aubrey was Aboriginal (as did the other two judges), but for Fitzgerald, this Aboriginality needed to be taken account of in considering the non-application of the police directive (a view in which he diverged from the decision of the other two judges). Further, Fitzgerald described as 'too narrow' the view of the trial judge that the regulations concerning police interviews of Aboriginal people were 'particularly directed to tribal people withdrawn from the European way of living', thus rejecting a consideration of Aboriginality in terms of the appellant living in a non-remote area and non-traditionally oriented lifestyle. Fitzgerald P found that 'by reason of his aboriginality and life experience, the appellant was "at a disadvantage in respect of the investigation, in comparison with members of the general Australia community"'. Here Fitzgerald P cited Kearney J's finding (in *R v Butler* 1991) that the Anunga guidelines—on which the Queensland police guidelines were based—were designed to overcome 'a particular vulnerability of Aboriginals to police interrogation, and in the exercise of the right to silence'. (While Fitzgerald P did not refer specifically to gratuitous concurrence, this phenomenon is clearly one of the issues addressed in the Anunga guidelines for police interviews with Aboriginal people (see Douglas 1998).)

While the two majority judges in this appeal did not question that Aubrey was Aboriginal, they questioned whether he was an Aboriginal person under disability in terms of the police regulations. Unlike the trial judge and some of the judges in the sentencing cases referred to above, they did not draw on the fact that the appellant lived in a non-remote area and non-traditionally oriented lifestyle. Nor did they use the discourse of racial fractions or skin colour, as the judges had in Condren's appeal. Indeed the police commissioner's directive specifically eschewed such a consideration:

> Whilst many Aborigines and Torres Strait Islanders would fall into the category of persons under disability, pigmentation of the skin or genealogical background should not be used as a basis for this assessment. Whilst all of the factors outlined above [including age and developmental disability] should be considered, particular attention should be given to the suspect person's educational standards, knowledge of the English language, or any gross cultural differences. (as cited by Fitzgerald P in *R v Aubrey* 1995)

In taking account of the directive, Davies J found that Aubrey had 'no difficulty in speaking and understanding English'. This finding was made on the basis of reading transcripts of Aubrey's evidence in the trial court, and on the decision of the trial judge that his 'command of the English language in the record of [police] interview was good, and he gave some quite long descriptive answers to questions'. It is quite likely that, as with many other people in Cherbourg, Aubrey's variety of Aboriginal English was close to general Australian English in terms of grammar and vocabulary, and thus he might be considered by many to have a 'good command of the English language'. However, this would be difficult to assess from reading answers to questions on a courtroom transcript. And it is also quite likely that he used pragmatic features such as those outlined above, and presented in the Queensland lawyers' handbook *Aboriginal English and the Law* (Eades 1992), which was referred to in Fitzgerald P's dissenting judgment.

It is relevant to point out that Fitzgerald P also took account of social conditions in Cherbourg, saying that the appellant's 'all-too-common life experience had left him poorly educated, unemployed, angry, aggressive and sometimes violent, especially when intoxicated'. While this is consistent with some of the factors in the *Fernando* principles, it was not invoked in relation to sentencing in this case, but as part (but not all) of the context for the appellant's engagement with police, which impacted on the extent of his 'disability' in the police interview.

The differing approaches in Aubrey's case highlight the complexity for judicial officers in understanding and assessing both the likelihood that a person may be using English in an Aboriginal way, and the fact that this may need to be considered, regardless of whether this person is living with the 'grave social difficulties' at the heart of the *Fernando* decision about Aboriginality and sentencing. And this same complexity is also faced by police officers in their decision about their interviews with Aboriginal suspects.

It is interesting to compare this development in the three Queensland Appeal Court judgments, from the 1987 *Condren* judgment on the one hand, to the 1993 *Kina* judgment and the dissenting 1995 *Aubrey* judgment on the other hand. It might perhaps be suggested that the reports of the Royal Commission into Aboriginal Deaths in Custody and the Queensland lawyers' handbook (Eades 1992) could have contributed to change in judicial thinking about Aboriginal identity, although a causal connection would be impossible to establish. However, the contrasting ways of conceptualising Aboriginality in these cases probably had more to do with the individual judicial officers than with any widespread development in judicial thinking about Aboriginality over that time, thus highlighting the significance of judicial discretion. Justice Fitzgerald, who was the President of the Appeal Court of Queensland during the 1993 and 1995 appeals, had been the barrister defending Condren in his 1987 appeal (in which he called sociolinguistic evidence about Aboriginal English).

## Trial Communication: Leading Questions and Jury Directions

When we turn to communication with Aboriginal witnesses in court, we see a number of initiatives both from judicial officers and from state justice departments. Since the three Queensland appeal cases discussed above, several states have drawn from research on Aboriginal ways of communicating in English in their publications intended to provide guidance for judicial officers and court staff (e.g. CJC 1996; Fryer-Smith 2008; Judicial Commission of New South Wales 2009; Queensland Department of Justice 2000; Queensland Supreme Court 2005). The Queensland lawyers' handbook (Eades 1992) has been extensively relied on. Within the judiciary, Justice Dean Mildren, who has been a Northern Territory Supreme Court judge since 1991, brings his extensive experience and his attention to sociolinguistic research to his judgments (e.g. *R v Kenny Charlie* 1995), publications (e.g. Mildren 1997, 1999) and keynote addresses at conferences (e.g. Mildren 2012). Mildren has taken a strong lead in dealing with communication issues for Aboriginal people in court in two important areas. Firstly, while leading questions are typically considered central to the testing of witnesses in cross-examination, Mildren points out that the trial judge has the power 'to disallow questions, or forms of questions, which are unfair'

(Mildren 1997: 14; also CJC 1996: 52).[10] Recognising the role of gratuitous concurrence in rendering some Aboriginal people too suggestible for the fair use of leading questions in cross-examination, Mildren disallows leading questions in such situations (Mildren 1999: 147).

Secondly, for many years Mildren has been giving directions to juries about Aboriginal ways of using English. In 1995, the Criminal Justice Commission in Queensland asked Mildren and me to prepare a pro forma set of directions to be given to juries in Queensland cases involving witnesses who are speakers of Aboriginal English (published in CJC 1996: pp. A9–11; see also Mildren 1997, 1999).[11] These directions have also been published in Queensland Supreme Court's 2005 *Equal Treatment Benchbook* (Appendix B in Chapter 9) and discussed in the NSW and WA equivalents (Judicial Commission of New South Wales 2009 and Fryer-Smith 2008). These specific directions, sometimes referred to as 'Mildren directions' or 'Mildren-style directions', are 'designed to assist a jury assessing the evidence of Aboriginal witnesses and/or an Aboriginal accused's record of interview. This is achieved by drawing the jury's attention to the possibility that sociolinguistic features of an Aboriginal witness's evidence may lead to misunderstandings (Fryer-Smith 2008: 7.4.1). Mildren (1997: 14) points out that the directions 'would obviously have to be moulded to the circumstances of the case'. And an important feature of the pro forma directions is the explicit warning of variation in the ways that Aboriginal people use English, as well as the frequent use of modifying expressions such as 'many Aboriginal people', 'often', and 'may'. That is, the directions should be impossible to apply in a categorical manner, and jurors are explicitly reminded that it is their 'function to decide which evidence [they] accept, and which evidence [they] reject' (CJC 1996: A9). While Justice Mildren has been using jury directions in the Northern Territory Supreme Court for at least 15 years, they are also used in some Western Australian cases (see Fryer-Smith 2008: 7.9–7.10), but they are reportedly not used in Queensland (Lauchs 2010: 17).

While it might perhaps be expected that Mildren's experience in the Northern Territory could result in a remote-area focus in his understandings of Aboriginality, this is not the case. Speaking at a national conference of criminal lawyers in 2012, he said 'even [Aboriginal] people who live in the major cities and towns are often influenced by their social or cultural background—even if they speak English quite well, and even if English is their first language' (2012: 6).

---

10 Leading questions are typically considered central to the testing of witnesses in cross-examination. While they most commonly have the syntactic form of yes/no questions, they are not defined in grammatical terms, but in legal terms: as questions which suggest a particular answer, or assume the existence of a fact which is in dispute.
11 A version of the directions was modified by Helen Harper for speakers of Torres Strait Creole.

But, how do judicial officers (and police officers) decide when to use Mildren directions? How do they decide if information about Aboriginal ways of using English is relevant to the case at hand? Similarly, when is it relevant for a court to take note of expert evidence about differences between Aboriginal English and standard Australian English? It would presumably not be relevant if the Aboriginal witnesses in a case were Marcia Langton and Warren Mundine. But when is it relevant for others from southern Australia? What factors should lawyers and judges consider when addressing this question?[12]

In discussions and workshops with judicial officers and legal professionals, I respond to such questions in terms of the bicultural/bidialectal ability to switch between Aboriginal ways of communicating in English in some situations, and mainstream Anglo ways in other situations. Bicultural and/or bidialectal ability is demonstrated in public life by Aboriginal political leaders, legal professionals, judicial officers, educators, public servants, filmmakers, musicians and more. But how can judicial officers and police officers know whether someone has considerable, or sufficient, bicultural and/or bidialectal ability? While this is clearly not always straightforward, to frame an answer to this question in terms of whether or not a person is a 'tribal [person] withdrawn from the European way of living' (as in the judge's decision in Aubrey's trial, see above) is clearly inadequate. It would also be inadequate to answer this question in terms of fractional descent, or the extent of a person's experience with police officers, following some of the sentencing decisions mentioned above. And it would not be relevant to consider the relevance of the witness's Aboriginality in terms of whether or not he had suffered from violence and alcohol abuse (which are central issues in the *Fernando* sentencing principles, as explained in 'Grave Social Difficulties', above). In the lawyers' handbook published more than two decades ago, I addressed this issue in terms of the socialisation of the person in question, and the evidence suggested by their successful participation in education, employment and leisure with non-Aboriginal people (Eades 1992: 12). Anthropologists might debate the basis for Aboriginal people's identity, and sociolinguists might debate contexts for the strategic essentialist use of 'Aboriginal English' versus 'Aboriginal ways of speaking English' (see Eades 2013). But in courts in southern Australia where Aboriginal people regularly give evidence, much more fundamental applications of our research are required, as the following examples will illustrate.

---

12   Parallel questions are relevant in situations in police interviews and courtroom hearings for Aboriginal—and any other—witnesses who speak English as a second language: how do judicial officers (and police officers) decide if the L2 speaker needs an interpreter? (see Cooke 2009).

## Leading Questions and Jury Directions: Questions of Specific Relevance

The question of the relevance of sociolinguistic research about Aboriginal ways of using English was the subject of considerable deliberation in the 2004 *Stack* appeal in the Supreme Court of Western Australia. The specific focus of this deliberation comprised the two areas discussed above in which Justice Mildren has provided judicial leadership in relation to Aboriginal people's communication issues in court. In *Stack,* the Aboriginal applicant appealed his conviction, on manslaughter and unlawful wounding charges, because of the trial judge's Mildren-style directions to the jury (both at the commencement and the end of the trial) and his decision to stop leading questions being asked in the cross-examination of one of the prosecution witnesses, an 18-year-old Perth Aboriginal man. Thus, the communication issues were not raised in relation to the defendant, but to one of the witnesses giving evidence in his prosecution. The appeal was successful (with a two-to-one majority) on the grounds that leading questions in cross-examination should not have been stopped, and that it was 'not possible to be satisfied that no substantial miscarriage of justice resulted from the trial judge's ruling' on leading questions. That is, the conviction was overturned because of the appeal court's decision that the defendant's lawyer had been prevented from a thorough cross-examination of one of the prosecution witnesses.

In relation to the relevance of the Mildren directions about sociolinguistic features such as gratuitous concurrence, the judges considered several biographical factors, namely the witness's area of residence, his education and the fact that he spoke no Aboriginal languages. For example, Steytler J said (*Stack v Western Australia* 2004: 553) that the witness

> was an Aboriginal man who lived with his father in a Perth suburb and that he studied art and photography at TAFE in Kwinana [a Perth suburb] ... Subsequent evidence established that he attended Kwinana Senior High School up to halfway through year 10, that he did well at school and that he did not speak any Aboriginal languages. There is nothing in any of this evidence which would indicate that any generalised phenomenon, such as that of gratuitous concurrence, or any other failure to give appropriately responsive answers, was applicable to him.

The dissenting judge (Murray J) drew on similar biographical details of the witness, also highlighting the fact that the witness 'spoke no Aboriginal languages' (p. 535). While the factors of area of residence, education to midway through Year 10, followed by a TAFE course, and not speaking an Aboriginal language may often correlate with considerable ability to use English in a mainstream Australian way, this correlation is not a necessary one. That speaking 'no Aboriginal languages' was a criterion for all three appeal judges highlights the way that judicial officers (like many lawyers) still tend to look to clear markers of traditionally oriented practice to evaluate the relevance of a person's Aboriginality. However, sociolinguistic research on Aboriginal ways of using English, which are at the heart of the Mildren directions, do not appeal to use of an Aboriginal language to help provide guidance on a person's likely bicultural communication ability.[13]

Murray J also observed that 'there was no evidence that [the witness] lived a lifestyle different from any young person within the socioeconomic group of which his family and relatives appeared to be members' (p. 535). However, it should be noted that this apparent similarity of lifestyle with non-Aboriginal people could well mask subtle distinctively Aboriginal features of communicative practice, which still characterise Aboriginal family interactions in southern towns and cities, including Perth (see Malcolm et al. 2002).

In their careful consideration of the relevance of Aboriginal ways of using English to the witness in question, the appeal judges discussed not just the witness's biographical information, but they also gave evaluations of the witness's actual communication while giving evidence during the trial. Murray J commented that from his reading of the transcript of trial evidence, the witness 'appears to speak ordinary English and to display no signs of difficulty in expressing himself'. However, focusing on whether an Aboriginal speaker of English appears to have problems in expressing themselves, could well miss the subtle communication differences that arise from Aboriginal use of gratuitous concurrence, or silence, or different ways of giving specific information (see Eades 1992). Using English in an Aboriginal way may not sound like difficulty in communication, and indeed it may not comprise difficulty in communication. But it can contribute to miscommunication, where interlocutors are unaware of differences in the use and interpretation of English. While all three judges indicated general acceptance of the idea of gratuitous concurrence, two of them cited passages from the cross-examination which seemed to show the witness in question was able to disagree, sometimes 'vigorously', with propositions put to him.

But there was a difference between the two majority judges (Steytler J and Templeman J) and the third, dissenting judge (Murray J) which pointed to Murray J's recognition that reading a transcript of interaction is not the same as listening to it (see Eades 1996b, 2008). Murray J found that the trial judge's decision to stop leading questions and to give jury directions was made on the basis of information not accessible to the appeal court, which had 'not had the benefit of seeing and hearing [the witness] give evidence' (p. 535). Thus, his

---

13 Further, it is unlikely that many judicial officers in criminal jurisdictions would be aware of the complex relationships between self-reports about whether a person speaks an Aboriginal language, and actual linguistic and sociolinguistic practice (see McConvell and Thieberger 2001: 22–3).

acceptance of the trial judge's decision concerning Aboriginal ways of using English was based on the fact that the trial judge's 'view of the way in which the witness was handling the process of questioning and giving evidence depended, not only upon the nature of his responses but upon the demeanour of the witness while giving evidence'.

The *Stack* case provides evidence of four judges addressing communication issues for Aboriginal speakers of English, and navigating the tricky question which we could express in terms of deciding the relevance of these issues for a particular witness, who may or may not have been socialised with these norms of language use, and who may or may not have bicultural communication abilities.

## A Problem-Centred Approach to Aboriginal Ways of Using English

In contrast, these communication issues appear to have been dismissed with little consideration, and seemingly little understanding, in a NSW trial less than two years later. *R v Hart* 2006 was the Supreme Court trial of a (non-Aboriginal) man for the murder of one of three local Aboriginal children in the small town of Bowraville.[14] The prosecution was intending to call 50 Aboriginal witnesses from that town or with links to that community, where Aboriginal people make up 13 per cent of the population, and where Aboriginal ways of interacting, including ways of using English, are strong.

The investigating police officer had commissioned me to write a sociolinguistic report on communication issues which might have caused difficulties for the Aboriginal witnesses in communicating with police over the early years of the investigation, and which might also make it difficult for them to tell the court what they had seen and what they knew that was relevant to this case, and for their evidence to be understood. In this report I wrote about several ways in which Aboriginal use of English differs from mainstream Anglo use, such as gratuitous concurrence and the use and interpretation of silence, discussed above. This report included a recommendation about directions to the jury similar to those prepared for the Queensland CJC (1996) report, also discussed above.

Before the jury came into court, there was a brief courtroom discussion between lawyers and judge about the substance of the sociolinguistic report. The defence barrister said that he 'did not dispute the general thrust of Dr Eades' observations', saying that 'many people from the background of a large number of witnesses in this case do have the sorts of communication

---

14  This case is an important one for Aboriginal people's participation in the criminal justice system for many reasons, as exposed by a parliamentary inquiry (NSWPLC 2014); see also Knox (2010) and ABC (2011).

eccentricities, to put it neutrally, as suggested by Dr Eades'. The fact that a lawyer can refer to sociolinguistic features described in an expert report in terms of 'communication eccentricities', and can attribute 'neutrality' to such a derogatory reference to linguistic features, shows just how little recognition and understanding there is among some members of the legal profession about cultural and dialectal differences in ways of using English. Further, this lawyer's erasure of Aboriginal identity with the euphemistic reference to 'people from the background of a large number of witnesses in this case' was consistent with the wider complaints from the Bowraville Aboriginal community that they were ignored by the criminal justice process (NSWPLC 2014; ABC 2011).

Having expressed lack of disagreement with the content of the sociolinguistic report, the defence barrister then argued against the use of such jury directions as recommended in my report, saying that it 'will introduce into an evaluation of [the Aboriginal] witnesses, an assessment of them, a whole range of assumptions which may or may not be appropriate'. This is despite the qualifications and caveats made explicit in the recommended directions, discussed above.

Interestingly, the prosecution (Crown) barrister had the opportunity to argue in favour of the relevance of the sociolinguistic report when he formally tendered (submitted) it to the court, but he did not do so, and he did not disagree with the defence argument about it.[15] Nor did he take up the report's recommendation about directions to the jury.

This short general discussion between defence counsel, prosecuting counsel and judge, before the jury came into court, resulted in agreement not to present anything specific to the jury about Aboriginal use of English. However, seemingly prompted by this discussion, the judge (Hulme J) made the following general comment to the jury:

> I understand that some of the witnesses are going to be Aboriginal and some people, particularly where their first language is not English, have some problems in terms of understanding or expressing themselves. Whether that is going to occur in this case, I have not got the foggiest idea. When it does, I will deal with it as I think appropriate, but you, in considering what you think of a witness, also bear in mind their apparent level of education or any other attributes. (from official trial transcript *R v Hart* 2006)

Unlike the *Stack* appeal, in this case there was no discussion about the applicability of sociolinguistic differences to any particular witness. Thus, there was no assessment of Aboriginality. While the judge's stance is not overtly

---

15  An experienced lawyer has pointed out that the issue is complicated by legal complexities regarding the admissibility of expert evidence about language use and understanding. An examination of these complexities, while beyond the scope of this chapter, would in my view be valuable in providing further impetus for the recognition of the role of jury directions in many cases involving Aboriginal witnesses.

demeaning or deficit-based, his comments are arguably more disturbing than the defence counsel's comment, revealing several problems which appear to prevent the understanding of Aboriginal identity, culture and social practice and its relevance to cases such as this.

Ignoring the two-way nature of communication, the judge's comment implies that the possibility of jurors misunderstanding Aboriginal witnesses occurs only to the extent that Aboriginal people might have *problems* of communication. It gives no indication of the much more common cause of intercultural miscommunication between Aboriginal and non-Aboriginal people, namely where there is no recognition of different ways of using English, for example that silence is used and interpreted differently, and that there are differences in the use of 'yes' answers to questions. Thus, this comment to the jury effectively invites jurors to base their evaluation of witnesses on ignorance, stereotypes, or even misunderstanding of Aboriginal communication, as it was made in the absence of any specific information about this topic. This is somewhat ironic, given the defence barrister's concerns about jurors bringing into their evaluation of Aboriginal witnesses 'a whole range of assumptions which may or may not be appropriate'. These comments by the judge to the jury also reveal apparent ignorance of the nature of the cultural and dialectal differences discussed in the expert report. It also revealed ignorance of the fact that Aboriginal people in Bowraville specifically, as throughout the state of NSW generally, are not second-language speakers of English.

## Conclusion

Perhaps the judge's focus in the *Hart* case on Aboriginal *problems* in communication should not be surprising when we consider that so much judicial energy has focused on Aboriginal sentencing, in which individual histories of troubled Aboriginal people figure so prominently. Further, the leading judicial authority on the relevance of Aboriginality to sentencing in southern Australia—the 1992 *Fernando* judgment—highlights problems common to the experience of many Aboriginal people which can add significant weight to mitigating factors concerning the nature of the offender and the effect of the penalty (for example, reasons to weigh in the consideration of a prison term). Foremost among these mitigating factors are the 'grave social difficulties' including endemic alcohol problems referred to above.

But this chapter has argued that understanding Aboriginality is relevant not only to sentencing, but that it is also crucial to the way that Aboriginal witnesses are heard and how their stories are evaluated. In considering the relevance of Aboriginality to issues of communication, sentencing is not the goal, but rather a fair hearing of witnesses' stories, in interviews with lawyers and police officers, and in courtroom questioning. Thus, it is not people's individual problems stemming from alcohol abuse and violence which are at issue, but their linguistic socialisation and sociolinguistic experiences and abilities, as well as differences in ways of using language. It is true that many Aboriginal people who have suffered greatly in the colonisation and decolonisation process (and who thus would presumably meet the *Fernando* test) have, as a result, had limited opportunities to develop bicultural communication abilities. Thus, for example, many have not been successful participants in mainstream education and employment, two of the major social contexts where socialisation in the norms and practices of mainstream use of English occur. But there is not necessarily a neat overlap here between factors relevant to the application of the *Fernando* principles and those which call for the use of Mildren directions for the jury for example. Further, issues of alcohol abuse and violence, which often figure prominently in Aboriginal sentencing cases, are irrelevant to the sociolinguistic issues involved in Aboriginal ways of using English, and connected questions of intercultural communication. For example, there are many teetotaller speakers of Aboriginal English in rural and urban regions of southern Australia (as in other regions), and in order for them to communicate in court and in other legal contexts, it is issues of socialisation and language variety usage which need to be considered.

Thus, in cases where communication rather than sentencing is at issue, knowledge of the *Fernando* principles can provide a framework—whether consciously or unconsciously—for thinking about Aboriginality in terms of problems. Such an approach runs the risk of erasing Aboriginal identity, ignoring the two-way process of communication, and obscuring cultural and dialectal differences in ways of speaking English. The central premise of Ian Keen's (1988) book—that there are distinctive Aboriginal ways of life (or social practice) in southern Australia—remains just as relevant more than a quarter of a century after the initial publication of the book. Focusing on social practices involved in the Aboriginal use of English, we now have a clearer picture of how and why this is crucial in the criminal justice system. As we have seen in the discussion of *Hart*, effective intercultural communication and fair interpretation of the character and credibility of witnesses and their evidence requires abandoning a deficit view of Aboriginal identity and social practice, and developing understandings of culturally different ways of using the same language.

# Cases Cited

*Bugmy v R.* 2013. Unreported, High Court of Australia 37, 2 October.

*Neal v R.* 1982. Commonwealth Law Reports 149, 305–26 (High Court).

*R v Anunga*. 1976. *Australian Law Reports* 11, 412–7 (Northern Territory Supreme Court).

*R v Aubrey*. 1995. Unreported, Queensland Court of Appeal, 28 April.

*R v Butler*. 1991. *Federal Law Reports* 102, 341–9 (Northern Territory Supreme Court).

*R v Ceissman*. 2001. Unreported, New South Wales Court of Criminal Appeal 73.

*R v Condren*. 1987. *Australian Criminal Reports* 28, 261–99 (Queensland Court of Criminal Appeal).

*R v Fernando*. 1992. *Australian Criminal Reports* 76, 58–65 (New South Wales Supreme Court).

*R v Hart*. 2006. Unreported, New South Wales Supreme Court 1501, 7 July.

*R v Helmhout*. 2001. *Australian Criminal Reports* 125, 257–67 (New South Wales Court of Criminal Appeal).

*R v Kenny Charlie*. 1995. Unreported, Northern Territory Supreme Court. 28 September.

*R v Kina*. 1993. Unreported, Queensland Court of Appeal, 29 November.

*R v Newman, R v Simpson*. 2004. *Australian Criminal Reports* 145, 361–89 (New South Wales Court of Criminal Appeal).

*Stack v Western Australia*. 2004. *Western Australian Reports* 29, 526–65 (Western Australian Court of Criminal Appeal).

*Waters v Public Transport Corporation*. 1991. Commonwealth Law Reports 173, 349–416.

# References

ABC (Australian Broadcasting Commission). 2011. Bowraville: Unfinished Business. *Four Corners* [television documentary], 4 April 2011.

Aikman, A. 2012. Voices of authenticity. *The Australian,* 15 November, p. 13.

Anthony, T. 2010. Sentencing indigenous offenders. *Indigenous Justice Clearinghouse* Brief 7.

CJC (Criminal Justice Commission). 1996. *Aboriginal Witnesses in Queensland's Criminal Courts*. Brisbane: Criminal Justice Commission.

Cooke, M. 2009. Anglo/Aboriginal communication in the criminal justice process: a collective responsibility. *Journal of Judicial Administration* 19: 26–35.

Curthoys, A. 2002. *Freedom Ride: A Freedom Rider Remembers.* Sydney: Allen and Unwin.

Douglas, H. 1998. The cultural specificity of evidence: the current scope and relevance of the *Anunga* guidelines. *UNSW Law Journal* 21(1): 27–54.

Eades, D. 1992. *Aboriginal English and the Law: Communicating with Aboriginal English Speaking Clients: A Handbook for Legal Practitioners.* Brisbane: Queensland Law Society.

Eades, D. 1993. The case for Condren: Aboriginal English, pragmatics and the law. *Journal of Pragmatics* 20(2): 141–62.

Eades, D. 1994. A case of communicative clash: Aboriginal English and the legal system. In J. Gibbons (ed.), *Language and the Law,* pp. 234–64. London: Longman.

Eades, D. 1996a. Legal recognition of cultural differences in communication: the case of Robyn Kina. *Language and Communication* 16(3): 215–27.

Eades, D. 1996b. Verbatim courtroom transcripts and discourse analysis. In H. Kniffka (ed.), *Recent Developments in Forensic Linguistics,* pp. 241–54. Frankfurt: Peter Lang.

Eades, D. 1997. The acceptance of linguistic evidence about indigenous Australians. *Australian Aboriginal Studies* 1997 (1): 15–27.

Eades, D. 2003. 'I don't think the lawyers were communicating with me': misunderstanding cultural differences in communicative style. *Emory Law Journal* 52: 1109–34.

Eades, D. 2008. Telling and retelling your story in court: questions, assumptions, and intercultural implications. *Current Issues in Criminal Justice* 20(2): 209–30.

Eades, D. 2013. *Aboriginal Ways of Using English.* Canberra: Aboriginal Studies Press.

Edney, R. 2006. The retreat from *Fernando* and the erasure of Indigenous identity in sentencing. *Indigenous Law Bulletin* 6(17): 8–11.

Family Court of Australia. n.d. Finding out about judgments. Accessed online 19 March 2013: www.familycourt.gov.au/wps/wcm/connect/FCOA/home/judgments/about_judgments/.

Findlay, M., S. Odgers and S. Yeo. 2005. *Australian Criminal Justice*. Third edition. (First edition 1994). Oxford: Oxford University Press.

Flynn, M. 2005. Not 'Aboriginal enough' for particular consideration when sentencing? *Indigenous Law Bulletin* 6(9): 15–8.

Fryer-Smith, S. 2008. *Aboriginal Cultural Awareness Benchbook for Western Australian Courts*. Second edition. Perth: Australian Institute of Judicial Administration.

Johnston, E. 1991. Royal Commission into Aboriginal Deaths in Custody National Report: Overview and Recommendations. Canberra: Australian Government Publishing Service.

Judicial Commission of New South Wales. 2009. *Equality before the Law Benchbook*. Sydney: Judicial Commission of New South Wales.

Judicial Commission of New South Wales. 2013. Relevance of deprived background of an Aboriginal offender: *Bugmy v The Queen* [2013] HCA 37; *Munda v Western Australia* [2013] HCA 38. Special Bulletin 4, October 2013.

Judicial Commission of New South Wales. n.d. Ngara Yura Program. Accessed online 4 March 2013: www.judcom.nsw.gov.au/Ngara-Yura.

Keen, I. 1988. *Being Black: Aboriginal Cultures in Settled Australia*. Canberra: Aboriginal Studies Press.

Knox, M. 2010. The mission. *The Monthly* October: 40–7.

Langton, M. 1981. Urbanizing Aborigines: the social scientists' great deception. *Social Alternatives* 2(2): 16–22.

Lauchs, M. 2010. Rights versus reality: the difficulty of providing 'access to English' in Queensland courts. Report published by Faculty of Law, Queensland University of Technology, Brisbane.

Malcolm, I.G., P. Königsberg, G. Collard, A. Hill, E. Grote, F. Sharifian, A. Kickett and E. Sahanna. 2002. *Umob Deadly: Recognized and Unrecognized Literacy Skills of Aboriginal Youth*. Mt Lawley, WA: Edith Cowan University.

McConvell, P. and N. Thieberger. 2001. State of Indigenous Languages in Australia—2001. Australia State of the Environment Second Technical Paper Series (Natural and Cultural Heritage). Canberra: Department of the Environment and Heritage.

Mildren, D. 1997. Redressing the imbalance against Aboriginals in the criminal justice system. *Criminal Law Journal* 21(1): 7–22.

Mildren, D. 1999. Redressing the imbalance: Aboriginal people in the criminal justice system. *Forensic Linguistics* 6(1): 137–60.

Mildren, D. 2012. Indigenous Australians and the criminal justice system. Paper presented to the Uluru Criminal Lawyers Conference, August.

NSWPLC (New South Wales Parliament Legislative Council Standing Committee on Law and Justice). 2014. *The Family Response to the Murders in Bowraville* (Report 55). Sydney: New South Wales Parliament Legislative Council.

Nicholson, J. 2012. Sentencing Aboriginal offenders: A judge's perspective. Paper presented to the Uluru Criminal Lawyers Conference, August.

Queensland Department of Justice. 2000. *Aboriginal English in the Courts: A Handbook*. Brisbane: Department of Justice.

Queensland Supreme Court. 2005. *Equal Treatment Benchbook*. Brisbane: Supreme Court of Queensland Library.

Rowley, C.D. 1971. *Outcasts in White Australia*. Canberra: Australian National University Press.

Rowse, T. 2012. *Rethinking Social Justice: From 'Peoples' to 'Populations'*. Canberra: Aboriginal Studies Press.

SCRGSP (Steering Committee for the Review of Government Service Provision). 2014. *Overcoming Indigenous Disadvantage: Key Indicators 2014*. Canberra: Productivity Commission.

Skyring, F. 2011. *Justice: A History of the Aboriginal Legal Service of Western Australia*. Perth: UWA Publishing.

Williams, M.S. 2013. High Court to give 'full weight' to Indigenous disadvantage. *The Conversation*. Accessed online 22 January 2014 at: theconversation.com/high-court-to-give-full-weight-to-indigenous-disadvantage-18880.

Yehia, D. 2012. Admissibility of admissions: Aboriginal and Torres Strait Islander suspects. Paper presented to the Uluru Criminal Lawyers Conference, August.

# 3 Change and Succession in Australian Aboriginal Claims to Land

David Trigger
University of Queensland

Since the advent of land rights legislation, and then native title laws, Aboriginal people in Australia have grappled with presenting tradition-based claims in light of cultural change to their lifestyles and customary relations with land and waters. While arguments are reasonably made that the legislative requirement to prove continuing customary law places unwarranted burdens on claimants (Strelein 2006; Pearson 2009: 100–32), it is also important to note that commitment to the idea of continuing cultural traditions retains its significance across Indigenous Australia. If Aboriginal associations with land have been 'pushed in a culturalist direction' by essentialist assertions about Indigenous 'consubstantiality' with place (Merlan 2007: 129–36), this has surely arisen from core beliefs among Aboriginal people themselves at least as much as from romanticism across the wider Australian public. The emergence of 'the economic Aborigine' is rightfully recognised as key to contemporary Indigenous life (Langton 2013: 59–80), but a major challenge for the courts and those sectors of Australian society embroiled in the language of land and native title claims is to understand how Indigenous cultural traditions underpinning assertions of rights both continue and change over time.

Ian Keen (1999: 5–6) pointed out that in the context of Australian native title claims 'the demonstration of continuities with the past requires a kind of winnowing process, blowing away the chaff of culture-change to leave the kernels of persisting Indigenous forms'. This is a peculiar feature of native title whereby embraced aspects of Australian society are positioned as negative in relation to asserting inherited rights to land. Keen is doubtless correct in that 'it is not enough to demonstrate a general cultural distinctiveness' in negotiating such claims (p. 5). Relations to land must be regarded as constituting 'some kind of system' that is 'grounded' in the past, though 'the form of the group holding title and the content of that title have changed' (p. 6).

Keen's discussion was focused particularly on the southeast and southwest of Australia 'where the degree of change in the lives of Aboriginal people has been greatest' (Keen 1999: 1), and indeed, it is in those settings that a 'cultural lack, loss and deficit' perspective has particularly continued to influence 'the native title sector' (Macdonald and Bauman 2011: 1). In part, this derives from very considerable physical dislocation (in some cases over several generations) from what is now presented as ancestral country, parts of Queensland constituting indicative cases (Trigger 1983; Babidge 2011).

However, the challenge of great historical and demographic change in relations with land and waters is also far from an easy matter in regions where Indigenous populations are regarded as 'more traditional'. Writing of the north, clearly with his Arnhem Land research in mind, Keen (1994a: 29) pointed out that changes in Aboriginal 'relations with country' are commonly 'about succession, and occur among those who claim to have taken over responsibility' for land in which others once had traditional rights. An early and highly influential report in the context of then emerging land rights legislation in the Northern Territory (Peterson, Keen and Sansom 1977) confirmed that there were traditional mechanisms for managing changing rights at a local scale. In the context of small local groups, the authors listed various kinds of 'secondary rights' which could be mobilised and translated into primary rights; hence, secondary rights could derive from place of spiritual conception, place of birth, place of death/burial of an important relative, kinship ties of various kinds, totemic and ceremonial links, and being the child of a female clan member. This type of rule-governed succession involved a clan, family group or individual succeeding to traditional ownership of a nearby estate which became vacant in the course of demographic and/or historical change.

The intervention by Peterson, Keen and Sansom (1977) in anthropological and legal debates about Indigenous rights to land, and then the resulting recognition of succession as encompassed within traditional customary law, was, as Layton (1985: 157) has pointed out, 'an important decision, because it acknowledged Aboriginal land tenure to be a living system'. The significance of the issue was, according to Layton, not missed among other Australians concerned about Indigenous land claims at the time. The majority leader of the Northern Territory Assembly reportedly went so far as to assert that recognising Aboriginal succession 'could have disastrous consequences for law and order in the Northern Territory'. Layton (1985: 151) surmises that succession raised for such Australians an anxiety that it would become impossible to distinguish between genuine and opportunist claims. In any case, with the passing of the Federal Native Title Act some 16 years later, the critical issue has arisen across many cases of whether succession to country has occurred legitimately in terms of customary law.

## The Ganggalida Case

Rather than movement and changing rights among small local groups, the issue in native title in the Gulf Country of northern Australia appears more about what Sutton (2003: 6) discusses for larger collectivities as 'group succession': 'Whole language groups or similar sized regional groups may be involved. For this reason I refer to such processes as instances of conjoint succession' (Sutton 2003: 6).

An indicative case from my research involved Ganggalida people as one of the four named language or tribal groups claiming rights in seas and adjacent mainland coastal areas in the southern Gulf of Carpentaria.[1] As summarised by Behrendt (2004), a solicitor engaged by the applicants, the relevant judge's decision accepted the claimants' evidence and my anthropological opinion that a section of the mainland coast in the vicinity of Burketown had been subject to a process of succession by the Ganggalida people,[2] this area having been occupied by a different group of Mingginda people at the time of European colonisation. While it was argued by the Commonwealth government that such succession could not exist as a matter of Australian law, that position was rejected by Justice Cooper who held:

> The new legal order at the time of sovereignty recognised both existing rights and interests in relation to lands and also 'the efficiency of rules of transmission of rights and interests under traditional laws and traditional customs which existed at sovereignty.': Yorta Yorta at [44]. If the rights and interests in respect of the Mingginda peoples' countries was acquired under traditional laws and customs which provided for such a succession and those laws and customs existed at sovereignty, then the interests of the Gangalidda peoples in respect of those lands and waters will be recognised and protected under the NTA. (*Lardil Peoples,* paragraph 131; cited in Behrendt 2004)

---

1   *Lardil Peoples v State of Queensland* (the 'Wellesley Sea Claim') [2004] FCA 298 (hereafter *Lardil Peoples*). I have carried out academic and applied anthropological research in this region since 1978 when I first began work as a site recorder.
2   I use here my spelling of the name of this language and 'tribal' group. The alternative 'Gangalidda' is the spelling used in the legal documents for the case.

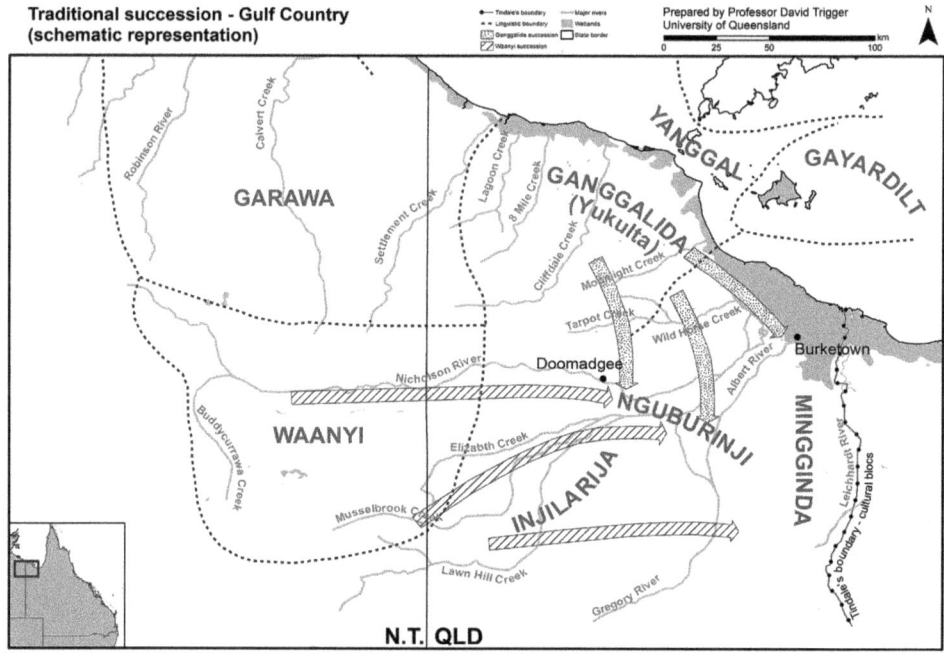

Figure 3.1 Traditional succession, Gulf Country.
Source: David Trigger.

The anthropological research, which benefited from my lengthy academic and applied work in the region, examined available early sources. These supported the view that the area west from the Leichhardt River (Figure 3.1) was once 'Minkin' (or Mingginda) territory (Evans 1990; Palmer 1883: 227; Curr 1886: 314; Turnbull 1896: 13; Old 1899). Causes of the demise of Mingginda people doubtless included violent encounters with Europeans and also disease. We can note Sharp's comment (1939: 454, footnote 41) that the 'Minkin' tribe was at the time of his research 'apparently extinct, probably having suffered severely from the yellow fever which decimated Burketown in the 1860s'. Tindale (1974: 181) draws on some of these sources to reach similar conclusions. Dymock (1977) reports on an interview he conducted with a senior Ganggalida woman, in 1972, in which she recounted an oral tradition telling of early encounters between 'Minkin' people and intruders on the Albert River. Linguist Sandra Keen (1983: 193) comments that 'Burketown was [in the past] Mingin country not Yukulta [Ganggalida] country'.

Recorded accounts from the most senior Ganggalida people with whom I had conducted academic inquiries from 1978 indicated that a language known as Mingginda (or Minggin/Minkin) was once spoken around the Burketown area (Figure 3.1). Ganggalida people had thus 'taken over' Mingginda country as its original occupants did not survive the impacts of European colonisation. By the time of my writing an expert report for the native title claim in 1998, there remained a few older living people who still acknowledged Mingginda people as having once occupied the area, with most Ganggalida persons considering it as having always been part of their country. Interviews with eight women conducted in 1998 all confirmed the view among Ganggalida people that the Albert River area had always belonged to their families. Given the history of demographic change and the well-documented 'strategic amnesia' evident in Aboriginal law and custom (Sansom 2001; Trigger 2011: 150), I concluded that especially the convictions among younger people on this issue were indicative that the process of succession had been completed (see *Lardil Peoples,* paragraphs 128–9).

In the coastal area surrounding Burketown that was at issue in the Wellesley native title claim, Ganggalida claimants referred to their forebears' presence since the early 1900s and to their traditional knowledge and use of the country. Ganggalida people had lived at camps on the fringes of the town and exploited bush resources along the Albert and Nicholson Rivers down to the sea (Figure 3.1). There were memories of fishing as children, of Ganggalida people travelling from the coast up and down the rivers, and discussions of several significant Dreaming places on the open saltpan country not far from the sea. A woman indicatively commented that she was 'born and bred in Burketown'. Another pointed out that her father's maternal grandmother's personal name was taken from the Aboriginal language name of a site in the Albert River area (*Lardil Peoples,* paragraphs 128–9).

This data obtained during native title investigations in the late 1990s mirrored that from my early academic research when I had recorded nine then deceased Ganggalida forebears said to have succeeded to ownership of the Albert River area on the basis of birth and spiritual conception ties to Dreamings and sites there. An illustrative quotation from a senior man, whose father's pre-succession estate was located to the west of Burketown, discussed a named lagoon in what was once Mingginda country as his son's spiritual conception place:

> I was fishin' down here [near the Albert River] and big whirly-wind come … straight across, and pull up here end of the waterhole. And that's a sign … come along the river then … all the way. His mother said: 'Oh well this is [their son's] country'. And then they all give [their son] this country then, this lagoon, they just said: 'Oh well, this is little boy country here'. (1978. Field Audio Tape 10, DT General Field Book 1)

Twenty years later during the 1998 research, the man whose conception site was so noted, sang a song said to refer to Rainbow Snake Dreaming in the vicinity of the Albert River mouth, once part of Mingginda territory. There was discussion of a 'whirly water' (water spout) Dreaming story which belongs to the mouth of the Albert River with an individual asserting his grandmother told him this was a place where the Rainbow Snake entered the sea and created whirlpools. Two special places were designated as 'belonging to the Rain Dreaming', and as having 'a big story', as the following woman in her 40s described:

> My mum has the story of the rain. If you break anything then it will pour and pour with rain and smoke comes and you can't see anything. There is a lot of [traditional] law [at this site]. Lightning hits the water and trees hard, it can kill you … There are a lot of rules … We were not allowed to go there when we were kids. Tribal men would go fishing and take young boys and the women and children would stay home, waiting for the fish and crabs, to prepare. It was the rules of the Dreamtime stories, maybe sacred places, only young boys were allowed out there [i.e. males only]. [A particular named man] used to go out there.

This information was consistent with what this woman's mother had explained to me in the late 1970s and early 1980s (DT Field Book 5, Trip 2).[3]

A potentially persuasive piece of further relevant evidence on the issue of succession and change was an elicited linguistic analysis of recorded place names. In the context of the native title claim litigation Nicolas Evans examined the Aboriginal language names for locations I had recorded in the early 1980s. His hypothesis was that in a case of succession we should expect to find a mixture of language sources—some place names from the language of the original group, some from the succeeding group, and some where there might possibly be two alternative names. On the basis of available knowledge of linguistic features of both Ganggalida and Mingginda languages, Evans found that of the 50 or so place names recorded by me in the Albert River / lower Nicholson River / Gin Arm Creek area (Figure 3.1), there were clear Ganggalida (Yukulta) etymologies for 17, possible or partial Ganggalida etymologies for another eight, and clear or partial Mingginda etymologies for five place names (plus another six ending in what looked to be a Mingginda locative suffix). To quote Evans's conclusion:

> Within the limits of our knowledge of the languages concerned … the toponymic evidence conforms to a succession scenario in which Yukulta [Ganggalida] speakers have succeeded to Minkin speakers as the primary landholders. (N. Evans, personal communication to D. Trigger, 5 August 1998)

This, then, is a case evident from the requirements of native title processes, where the descendants of deceased Ganggalida forebears now trace ties to the Burketown and surrounding area through their genealogical connections to those who were born there and assimilated customary knowledge of the country into Ganggalida traditions. Several living individuals at the time of the claim research were known to have spiritual conception sites in the area and also had their own birth affiliations there. Of significance at the time of the claim was

---

3   See *Lardil Peoples*, paragraph 133, for a noting of such spiritual beliefs.

that few if any living Aboriginal people disputed the fact that for many years the Burketown, Albert River, lower Nicholson River area had been Ganggalida country. This conviction was evident even among the few who nevertheless knew they had a likely Mingginda forebear in their own ancestry.[4]

The case material enabled my conclusions that Ganggalida occupation and ownership of Mingginda coastal areas is a case of completed succession (*Lardil Peoples,* paragraphs 128–9). The process occurred from the early 1900s and may be considered consistent with a regional body of custom and tradition. Ganggalida and Mingginda peoples shared closely related languages (Evans 1995: 9), as commented upon by senior informants in my research. To quote one man: the two groups 'nearly talk the same language' except 'one was a bit heavy, one a bit light'. Tindale (1974: 181, Map of Aboriginal Tribes) suggests that the Mingginda group, like Ganggalida and other language groups west of the Leichhardt River (see Figure 3.1), also shared features of traditional law associated with male initiation. Circumcision was not practised east of the Leichhardt River and nor were subsection terms used in the traditional forms of social organisation. The Leichhardt River can thus be regarded as a traditional regional societal boundary of considerable importance and both Ganggalida and Mingginda belonged to the cultural bloc extending to its west.

## The Waanyi Case

The second Gulf Country case that is productive for our understanding of succession to rights in land and waters is Waanyi. Waanyi people historically moved eastwards into Nguburindi territory and southwards into parts of Injilarija country (Figure 3.1), both areas believed by claimants to be culturally familiar, and since European arrival taken over according to Waanyi traditional law and custom with the demise of these two groups. My research, from 1978 through several decades to then encompass work for native title claim proceedings, documented the nature of Waanyi movements and the assimilation of the cultural significance of land and waters into Waanyi traditions. The focus of the research was on the facilitation of this process of succession via understandings of the country in terms of its 'skin' or subsection/semimoiety attributes, its totemic Dreamings, its flora and fauna species, and the general spiritual and material topography of the land. These aspects of tradition-based relationships with land and waters coexisted with Waanyi knowledge of the cattle industry, its dams,

---

4   However, this is not to conclude there was complete agreement of this kind in relation to other inland parts of Mingginda country.

fences, yards and camps that have been significant in the cultural landscapes of both Aboriginal people and others for more than 100 years. The anthropological research assembled considerable cultural data of relevance to these issues.[5]

Some movement eastwards from the tableland and ranges that traditionally bounded Waanyi people from their eastern and southern neighbours would likely have occurred before the impact of European incursions began. Intermarriage, ritual obligations, and trade of resources amongst known networks would have seen Waanyi and other local groups interacting for a range of purposes. Indeed, there is evidence that the easterly movements occurred along customary routes that were already in use for ceremonial and trade purposes. Roth (1901), then occupying the office of Queensland Government Protector of Aborigines, produced a sketch map (Figure 3.2) showing a number of trade and travel routes from the Northern Territory border (near the eastern boundary of Waanyi country at the time of European arrival) into Queensland and the territories of other language groups.

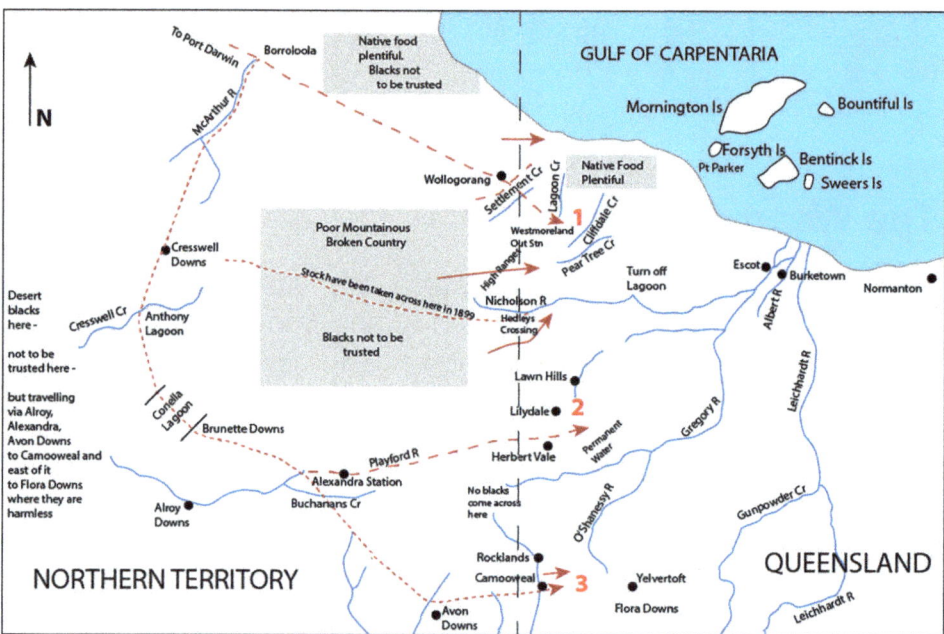

Figure 3.2 Roth sketch map (arrows and numbers show historical movement eastwards).

Source: David Trigger, based on original by Roth.

---

5   Waanyi customary succession is addressed in a sequence of available legal reasons for decisions that have been informed by this research, including Aboriginal Land Commissioner (1985), *Waanyi Peoples Native Title Determination Application* No. Qn94/9 [1995] NNTTA 51, and *Aplin on behalf of the Waanyi Peoples v State of Queensland* [2010] FCA 625. The formal recognition of Waanyi succession culminated in the decision in *Aplin on behalf of the Waanyi Peoples v State of Queensland* No. 3 [2010] FCA 1515. My research in the early 1990s was assisted by Jeannie Devitt, and from 2000 to 2002 was conducted jointly with Pauline Fietz (Trigger and Fietz 2003).

Colonial settlement, however, meant that a more permanent Waanyi territorial expansion began late in the nineteenth century. Research indicates this was due to a mix of desires on the part of Aboriginal people for commodities, such as tobacco and a secure food supply from ration depots and stations in Queensland, and to obtain protection from the extensive violence which characterised the period (Trigger 1992: 26ff; Roberts 2005). Dymock (1982, 1993), Trigger (1982, 1992) and Trigger and Devitt (1992) have presented comprehensive accounts of the effect of such historical processes on Aboriginal groups in the region. In summary, settler incursions into Waanyi country did not occur with the same level of force and disruption experienced by adjacent groups to the east and south. These latter areas, which were subsequently incorporated into Waanyi country, were the initial settings for pastoral activity due to both their relative accessibility and the perceived suitability (well-watered savannah plains country) of the land for running domestic herds. Such groups as the Nguburindi and Injilarija suffered the full brunt of these frontier displacements of Aboriginal people from the land.

The scholarly anthropological and linguistic literature indicates Nguburindi and Injilarija languages were distinct from Waanyi. Nguburindi was related closely to Ganggalida (Yukulta), Mingginda (Minkin) and the languages of the Wellesley Islands (Evans 1990: 173, 190). Nevertheless, the fact that these languages were not mutually intelligible was seemingly no impediment to the speakers having shared a similar system of customary law in regard to rights in land. Multilingualism was likely to have pertained (Rumsey 1993: 195) and, as noted for the Ganggalida case, Evans, along with other researchers, finds the language groups west of the Leichhardt River sharing a broad range of cultural practices and knowledge.

One aspect of shared regional law and custom is the system of eight subsections (known in Aboriginal English as 'skins') which are categories best understood as identifying distinctive internal spiritual qualities of persons, Dreamings and country (Kirton and Timothy 1977; Trigger 1982; Bradley 2010). In the course of research in 2000, a senior Waanyi man commented that Injilarija people owned the country 'before', and while he was not certain of the actual skin names they used, he was clear that they had 'skin belong to Dreaming', i.e. a system of categories for country similar to Waanyi people. The existence of a cultural bloc extending throughout the region does not necessarily imply that all skin names were identical; e.g. Mathews (1900: 497) suggested that the 'Inchalachee' (Injilarija) language shared a somewhat different set of subsection terms with the 'Warkya' (Wagaya) language to the southwest. Breen (2002: 302–4) discusses the material reported by Mathews (1899, 1905) and acknowledges this possibility. However, Breen's work makes it clear that various languages of this region share the skin (subsection/semimoiety) *system* and hence people were able to work out social relationships with reference to different terms that may be regarded as nevertheless 'equivalent' across languages (McConvell 1985).

Senior people have commented on particular Waanyi deceased forebears whose personal skin affiliation matched parts of the country into which Waanyi people had moved historically. Typically, these individuals, and hence their descendants, were said to have connections with both ancestral estates in the west (which had been mapped for the Nicholson River land claim under the Northern Territory Land Rights Act in the early 1980s (Trigger 1982; Dymock 1982; Aboriginal Land Commissioner 1985)) and parts of the succession area in the east.[6] Coterminous with the skin significance of the succession areas was the pattern of Dreaming routes and sites. Examples include *Jumburuna* (Yellow Goana), *Bujarda* (Piebald Snake), *Bujimala* (Rainbow Snake), *Warrgi* (Dingo), *Bardagalinya* (Red Kangaroo), *Wirrigajigaji* (Catfish) and *Marrarrabana* (Water Girls).[7]

Waanyi people thus recounted the travels of mythic figures across land encompassing both the original estates in the west and the succession area in the east. Taking as illustrative *Marrarrabana* (a female Dreaming often termed in Aboriginal English 'Water Girls'), this is known to have travelled from a considerable distance to the west (where it is named *Mungamunga* (Bell 1994)). At some locations, *Marrarrabana* created ceremony grounds for women. *Marrarrabana* danced through country in the west such as Walhallow and Calvert Hills stations and then into Queensland, at times leaving significant marks in the country. It travelled across the south of Lawn Hill Station looking for Rhumburriya country (the Dreaming's skin (semimoiety) category name), stopping at a site on Riversleigh station, which is also of that skin, eventually arriving at a location on the Leichhardt River (east of Waanyi country) where a manifestation of the Dreaming is said to be at times evident.

Such Dreaming routes extending across the landscape would appear to have pre-existed the historical movements of people eastwards, and hence provided part of the traditional cultural logic for Waanyi people becoming successors to the Nguburindi and Injilarija original occupants. In some cases, it appears that physical properties of locations have been the prompts for decisions

---

6   This does not mean that all the forebears' descendants had the same skin affiliation as the succession country, as this is so only for those who inherit connection through patrifiliation (Trigger 1982, 1989; Reay 1962; Bradley 2010). However, links of matrifiliation also traditionally give rise to rights in country, and cognatic land holding groups have become significant in recent decades. As well, many individuals assert more than one skin affiliation in light of traditional marriage rules having undergone much modification (Trigger 1985: 90–2, 354–7).

7   Dymock (1993: Sections 4 and 5) presents details of Dreamings through Waanyi country that are consistent with my findings. Tacon (2008) documents a number of these Dreamings and reports the views of various Waanyi persons assisting with studies of rock art representations associated with the mythic figures.

about the presence of particular Dreamings in accordance with what has been termed 'epistemic openness' in reading the country (Merlan 1998: 72, 209–28). Examples include places with a distinctive powdery white rock interpreted as associated with Catfish Dreaming and its associated skin category, the substance understood as the spiritual manifestation of fish faeces, and known as potentially dangerous in the hands of individuals with malevolent intentions to harm others through sorcery. Similarly, red ochre sites and round-shaped waterholes were connected to Rainbow Snake Dreaming and its distinctive skin category. Hence the Waanyi knowledge connecting physical and spiritual properties of landscape is read into the succession areas that Waanyi forebears and now their descendants have assimilated into laws and customs regarding land and waters.

A small number of sites in parts of the succession country had been recorded in the 1970s from one senior woman as Yinjilaaji (Injilarija) place names.[8] In the late 1990s, these names were publicly known as Waanyi terms among older people, with some acknowledging their forebears had taken over that part of the country. In the case of the Waanyi term for catfish, known as a place name for two areas with that Dreaming's presence, it is possible that the term was the same in the Injilarija language (though we have insufficient information about the latter to know definitely). It is equally possible that some considerable time ago the Waanyi term was imposed at these two sites on the basis of the pre-existing Dreaming known to be located there. A further illustration is a site name in Breen's linguistic data (named Kudawudanngirri) which his informant said was located in the Waanyi succession area. This is the same name I had recorded as Gudawudangirri, for Border Waterhole, situated within pre-succession Waanyi territory to the west. In 1982, the meaning of this name was given during my videoed research visit to the site as a 'mob of girl together', based on a Waanyi term for a young woman (*gudangirri*). This was a reference to the 'Water Girls' (*Marrarrabana*) Dreaming at the Border Waterhole area,[9] and we have Breen's elderly informant in the early 1970s giving that same name to a place in the succession area. This may again indicate similar site names for Water Girl Dreaming places in both Waanyi country and what was previously Injilarija territory, or a Waanyi term being applied as part of that group's succession eastwards and associated cultural assimilation of the landscape.

---

8    This information was documented as part of Gavan Breen's linguistic research with Ivy George (personal communication, G. Breen, November 2000), an elderly woman whose mother in my genealogical research was recorded as 'Injilarija/Waanyi mix'. Ivy George (deceased by the time of the Waanyi native title claim) was a senior woman who had lived much of her life on a cattle station that had been subject to Waanyi succession.
9    Mary Laughren's linguistic research similarly recorded a senior man recounting this Dreaming travelling to a site some 30 kilometres to the east of Border Waterhole. Laughren comments (personal communication, 30 October 2014) that *kudawudanngirri* is a plural form of a Waanyi word for 'young woman'.

Table 3.1 Waanyi families by pre-succession estates and post-succession areas (area A = Pastoral Station 1 Country; area B = Old Market Garden Country; area C = Three Rivers Country; area D = Pastoral Station 2 Country; area E = River Country).

| Family # | Pre-succession estates in the west | | | | | | | | | Post-succession areas in the east | | | | |
|---|---|---|---|---|---|---|---|---|---|---|---|---|---|---|
| | Estate1 | Estate2 | Estate3 | Estate4 | Estate5 | Estate6 | Estate7 | Estate8 | Estate9 | Area A | Area B | Area C | Area D | Area E |
| 1 | ■ | | | | | | | | | | | | | |
| 2 | | ■ | | | | | | | | | | | | |
| 3 | | | ■ | | | | | | | | | | | |
| 4 | | | | | ■ | | | | | ■ | | | | |
| 5 | | | | | | ■ | | | | ■ | | | | |
| 6 | | | | ■ | | | | | | ■ | | | ■ | ■ |
| 7A | | | | | | | | | ■ | ■ | | | ■ | ■ |
| 7B | | | | | | | | ■ | ■ | ■ | | | | ■ |
| 7C | | | | | | | | | | ■ | | | | |
| 8 | | | | | | | | | | | | ■ | ■ | |
| 9 | | | | | | | ■ | | | | | | | ■ |
| 10 | | | | | | | | | | ■ | | | ■ | ■ |
| 11 | | | | | | | | | | ■ | | | ■ | |
| 12 | | | | | | | | | | | ■ | | | |
| 13 | | | | | | | | | | | | | | |

Individual and family connections to the succession areas were thus the product of both the skin system and its implications of Dreamings across the landscape. This aspect of tradition-based law and custom operated in the context of the fundamental influences of physical residence and occupation of the succession areas that had been historically produced and enabled by the locations of pastoral stations, ration depots and police bases. The descendants of known deceased Waanyi forebears asserted a connection to both the pre-succession estates in the west and the identifiable areas (which we might term transformed versions of traditional estates) in the east. Both sorts of connection have come to be held on the basis of cognatic descent from either male or female forebears. Features of the country that Waanyi have taken over have clearly been interpreted to fit the system of deduced skins and Dreamings. Table 3.1 shows schematically how nine families (cognatic groups) asserted connections both to a pre-succession estate in the west and a section of the succession area in the east. Two families claimed only pre-succession estates and a further four only succession areas. My conclusion was that the Waanyi research, in the context of the native title claim, indicated a completed case of adaptation and succession according to tradition-based law and custom in relation to land and waters.[10]

## Conclusion

Building upon Peterson, Keen and Sansom's (1977) short but seminal report written during the early phases of Northern Territory land claim research, Sutton's (2003: 6) subsequent writing about native title claims considers succession that involves 'whole language groups' as 'conjoint'. This is distinguished from, and yet also based upon, the processes whereby individuals or families *within* a group assume primary interests in estates to which they may previously have held secondary rights. In the Gulf Country cases presented here, both kinds of succession can be said to 'rely on territorial proximity and pre-existing systemic grounds for territorial amalgamation' (Sutton 2003: 6). Just as Keen (1994b: 124–31) showed how succession between estate groups in Arnhem Land involved an extension of rights in expanded domains of land and waters, Sutton comments that conjoint, or perhaps 'collective', succession does not involve 'the extinguishment of pre-colonial rights of surviving groups so much as their transformation—usually involving considerable simplification—and their generalisation to wider "tribal" areas' (p. 6).

---

10  The legal decision in *Aplin on behalf of the Waanyi Peoples v State of Queensland* [2010] FCA 625, paragraph 89, discusses David Martin's anthropological opinions based on Trigger and Fietz's (2003) documentation of these relationships between particular extended families and areas across Waanyi country. The legal decision names the post-succession estates or 'countries' which are given pseudonyms in Table 1 presented here.

We might question whether the nature of either Ganggalida or Waanyi rights to country once east of that of their forebears involves any form of 'simplification', given the evident complexity of the networks of individual and family ties to the succession areas in both cases. The process has encompassed spatial movement and demographic changes driven by modified Indigenous cultural traditions in the context of colonial and postcolonial law enforcement, work in the pastoral industry, liaisons and marriages between Aboriginal women and men of European, Chinese and Afghan ancestries, Christian evangelism and establishment of a residential mission (Trigger 1992), and so on. However, Sutton's analysis would seem to fit the southern Gulf Country fairly well. Importantly, in terms of the argument that these forms of change are tradition-based, he points out (2003: 6) that we cannot exclude the possibility that this type of collective language group succession may have occurred prior to European disruption; while perhaps unusual, parallel 'similar population losses' to those following colonisation 'may have occurred before the colonial era, where epidemics could have wiped people out in big numbers from time to time'.

In his discussion of cultural continuity and native title claims in light of broad social theory, Keen (1999: 2) noted significant anthropological research between the 1950s and 1970s, particularly in the southeast and southwest of Australia, finding that people 'had lost their distinctively Aboriginal culture'. Both at the time of his writing (particularly in the Yorta Yorta case in the southeast), and subsequently (notably the Noongar case in the southwest), this 'culture-loss model' has been stressed by some native title researchers (see Keen 1999: 7, footnote 7; Brunton 2007). However, Keen also notes (pp. 2–3) findings of continuity of aspects of kinship, ways of speaking and spiritual beliefs, as well as complex processes of consecutive rejection and then reassertion and revival of cultural forms over several generations. Whether in the north or south of the continent, native title claims typically reveal often-impressive Indigenous strategies to maintain a distinct cultural heritage, as a form of self-conscious resistance to assimilationist pressures. While this may at times entail evidence that 'recently formed beliefs become ancient truths' (Keen 1999: 4–5), the Gulf Country cases indicate that Keen is also correct to qualify such analyses. Both Ganggalida and Waanyi processes of succession and change are best understood to a significant degree as developments of 'emergent cultural forms' rather than the formation of solely symbolic or strategic identifications with land and waters occupied through the impacts of (post)colonialism (Keen 1999: 5).

While the Gulf cases exhibit greater richness of traditional connections to land and waters than the settings Keen had in mind in southern Australia, they simultaneously offer broadly indicative principles by which changing rights to country may be documented and potentially recognised by the Australian legal system. Substantial change has occurred, yet forms of contemporary connection with country are also continuous with adaptations in the previously operating system. Tradition-based connections in the succession areas have developed alongside Ganggalida and Waanyi people's routine participation in many of the regional institutions of the wider Australian society, including considerable processes of cultural assimilation. Given the obvious tensions of changing belief and lifestyle practices involved, the process of adaptation of customary law in relation to country affiliations is not always articulated unanimously among the relevant families and individuals.

Where disagreement emerges between contesting Aboriginal parties about whether or not succession has been licit in terms of law and custom, or whether it is a completed process, it can be difficult to determine a resolution. This can involve quite bitter disputes that continue over decades, as in the Finniss River area of the Northern Territory, where an historically incoming group was seen as seeking to displace the descendants of those who had been in occupation at the time of European arrival (Layton 1985: 162–5). New names had become attached to local sites and Dreamings from the incoming group's country to the south had been imposed. Yet this process of succession was contested as there remained Aboriginal people who, while articulating less traditional knowledge of the country, nevertheless continued to argue that they inherited legitimate rights from forebears who had been historically displaced. Similar disputes over whether change has been coexistent with traditional succession have been evident in a number of other land claims and native title applications (Sutton 2003: 5).

In the Gulf cases my conclusions are that succession has been completed legitimately as understood in traditional law and custom. At times, respondent parties have argued against this analysis, as with a Waanyi matter where the mining company CRA, as well as the Queensland government, 'submitted that there was no evidence of transmission or transfer of native title from the Injilarija to the Waanyi in accordance with traditional laws and customs of the Injilarija' (Waanyi Peoples Native Title Determination Application. No. Qn94/9 [1995] NNTTA 51, paragraph 41). The issue can thus be whether evidence of one or more particular 'transmission or transfer' *events* can be identified. However, I have depicted here a more informal process that has been accepted in legal cases, whereby tradition-based succession has occurred as demographic and historical change is prompted by engagements with the wider Australian society and economy. I have described how succession becomes assumed over time in the context of a regional body of broadly shared traditional law and custom, rather than any form of institutionalised decision-making about 'take over' of country occurring through discrete recounted events.

Nevertheless, particularly given the increasing access among Aboriginal people to written records about pre-existing 'tribal' groups, there may emerge possible new assertions from individuals and families that they believe they constitute depleted segments of landowning groups as they existed at the time of European arrival. In the Ganggalida case, there are occasional suggestions that the coastal succession area is still Mingginda, and individuals among one or two families who assert a distinctive connection to inland parts of what was once Mingginda country. In the Waanyi case, there was an unsuccessful attempt by a family based far away in southern Queensland to argue descent from an allegedly Nguburindi forebear and consequent rights to country, based on their reading of certain historical records.[11] There has also been legal argument in the Waanyi case in relation to who may legitimately be regarded as a member of the group holding rights in the succession area (*Aplin on behalf of the Waanyi Peoples v State of Queensland* [2010] FCA 625), and some disagreement between Waanyi and Ganggalida people over their territorial boundary in light of the historical changes and succession processes over the past 100 years or more.

The material presented indicates the importance of substantial and historically informed research in addressing such complexities. Anthropologists or other researchers cannot be expected to necessarily resolve clear outcomes in cases of tension or dispute (Keen 1994a). However, in the Gulf Country, it has been significant that my research in native title has come after many years of academic work. This has enabled my findings to apprehend systemic adaptations in traditional law and custom. In light of the adaptive capacity of Indigenous cultural traditions evident from the Gulf cases presented here, it would seem important that researchers bring a sophisticated approach to both ethnographic studies of changing relations with country, and the legal requirements for the recognition of Indigenous rights. To the extent that native title requires evidence of a 'grounded' and 'systemic' connection to land and waters (Keen 1999: 6), one that exhibits customary beliefs and practices as derived from a continuing 'society', the concept of succession is a powerful analytical tool. Its sensible application may be both intellectually productive and practically useful in many regions. The cases show that through the concept of succession, Aboriginal rights can be acknowledged as arising from a dynamic body of customary law that coexists with complex and changing Indigenous lives in modern Australian society.

---

11  A researcher was engaged to prepare a confidential anthropological report for this family.

## Acknowledgements

Thanks to the Ganggalida and Waanyi people for their participation in my research over many years. I wish to acknowledge particularly Lizzy Daylight (Ganggalida) and Tommy George (Waanyi) for their patient tutelage in developing my understanding of Aboriginal relations with country. Thanks to Jeannie Devitt, Pauline Cook (née Fietz) and Lorna Gregory for collaboration with research on Waanyi relations with country, to Sandra Barkla, Peter Maden and Rachel Siddall for assistance in our studies of traditional Ganggalida connections with coastal areas and seas, and to Richard Martin for collegial collaboration on research across the Gulf Country in recent years. Thanks to Matt Whincop and Andrew Sneddon for preparation of maps. Peter Toner's comments, together with those of two anonymous reviewers, have been helpful in finalising this chapter.

## References

Aboriginal Land Commissioner (W. Kearney). 1985. Nicholson River (Waanyi/Garawa) land claim. Report to the Minister for Aboriginal Affairs. Canberra: Australian Government Printer.

Babidge, S. 2011. The proof of native title connection in absentia. In T. Bauman and G. Macdonald (eds), *Unsettling Anthropology: The Demands of Native Title on Worn Concepts and Changing Lives*, pp. 82–99. Canberra: Australian Institute of Aboriginal and Torres Strait Islander Studies.

Behrendt, J. 2004. *Lardil Peoples v State of Queensland* [2004] FCA 298, *Indigenous Law Bulletin* 6(2). Available at: www.austlii.edu.au/au/journals/ILB/2004/37.html#fn17.

Bell, D. 1994. The tracks of the MungaMunga. In M. Joy and P. Magee (eds), *Claiming Our Rites: Studies in Religion by Australian Women Scholars*, pp. 213–46. Adelaide: Australian Association for the Study of Religions.

Bradley, J. 2010. *Singing Saltwater Country: Journey to the Songlines of Carpentaria*. Crows Nest, NSW: Allen and Unwin.

Breen, G. 2002. Making your skin fit properly: displaced equivalence in skin systems in the Barkly. In J. Henderson and D. Nash (eds), *Language in Native Title*, pp. 291–310. Canberra: Aboriginal Studies Press.

Brunton, R. 2007. 'A bombshell in the centre of Perth': an anthropologist considers the single Noongar judgement. Occasional paper. Sydney: The Bennelong Society.

Curr, E.M. 1886. *The Australian Race*. Melbourne: Government Printer.

Dymock, J. 1977. The first Whitemen. *Journal of Anthropological Society of South Australia* 15(2): 4–10.

Dymock, J. 1982. Historical material relevant to the Nicholson River land claim. Report to the Northern Land Council, Darwin.

Dymock, J. 1993. Something deep and rich: indigenous and post contact environment and heritage materials relevant to the Lawn Hill/Riversleigh District of Queensland. Unpublished report prepared for Queensland Government Department of Environment and Heritage.

Evans, N. 1990. The Minkin language of the Burketown region. In G. O'Grady and D. Tryon (eds), *Studies in Comparative Pama-Nyungan*, Pacific Linguistics C-111, pp. 173–207. Canberra: The Australian National University.

Evans, N. 1995. *A Grammar of Kayardilt, with Historical-Comparative notes on Tangkic*. Berlin: Mouton de Gruyter.

Keen, I. 1994a. Conflict in Aboriginal land tenure. In J. Fingleton, M. Edmunds and P. McRandle (eds), *Proof and Management of Native Title*, pp. 26–31. Canberra: Australian Institute of Aboriginal and Torres Strait Islander Studies.

Keen, I. 1994b. *Knowledge and Secrecy in an Aboriginal Religion: Yolngu of North-East Arnhem Land*. Melbourne: Oxford University Press.

Keen, I. 1999. Cultural continuity and native title claims. *Land, Rights, Laws: Issues of Native Title*, Issues paper No. 28. Canberra: Australian Institute of Aboriginal and Torres Strait Islander Studies.

Keen, S. 1983. Yukulta. In R. Dixon and B. Blake (eds), *Handbook of Australian Languages*, vol. 3, pp. 191–304. Canberra: Australian National University Press.

Kirton, J. and N. Timothy. 1977. Yanyuwa concepts relating to 'skin'. *Oceania* 67(4): 320–2.

Langton, M. 2013. *The Quiet Revolution: Indigenous People and the Resources Boom*. Boyer Lectures 2012. Sydney: Harper Collins.

Layton, R. 1985. Anthropology and the Australian Aboriginal Land Rights Act in northern Australia. In R. Grillo and A. Rew (eds), *Social Anthropology and Development Policy*, pp. 148–67. London: Tavistock.

Macdonald, G. and T. Bauman. 2011. Concepts, hegemony, and analysis: unsettling native title anthropology. In T. Bauman and G. Macdonald (eds), *Unsettling Anthropology: The Demands of Native Title on Worn Concepts and Changing Lives*, pp. 1–18. Canberra: Australian Institute of Aboriginal and Torres Strait Islander Studies.

Mathews, R.M. 1899. Divisions of north Australian tribes. *American Philosophical Society Proceedings* 38: 75–9.

Mathews, R.M. 1900. The Wombya organization of the Australian Aborigines. *American Anthropologist* 2: 494–501.

Mathews, R.M. 1905. Ethnological notes on the Aboriginal tribes of Queensland. *Queensland Geographical Journal* 20: 49–75.

McConvell, P. 1985. The origin of subsections in northern Australia. *Oceania* 56: 1–33.

Merlan, F. 1998. *Caging the Rainbow: Places, Politics and Aborigines in a North Australian Town*. Honolulu: University of Hawai'i Press.

Merlan, F. 2007. Indigeneity as relational identity: the construction of Australian land rights. In M. de la Cadena and O. Starn (eds), *Indigenous Experience Today*, pp. 125–49. Oxford and New York: Berg.

Old, J. 1899. (Acting Sergeant, Police Station Burketown) 25.5.1889. Extracts from correspondence, Burketown Police Station, compiled by P. Memmott (1975), Aboriginal Data Archive, University of Queensland.

Palmer, E. 1883. Notes of some Australian tribes. *Royal Anthropological Institute Journal* 13: 276–346.

Pearson, N. 2009. Land is susceptible to ownership. In N. Pearson, *Up from the Mission: Selected Writings*, pp. 100–32. Melbourne: Black Inc.

Peterson, N., I. Keen and B. Sansom. 1977. Succession to land: primary and secondary rights to Aboriginal estates. (A submission to the Ranger Uranium Environmental Inquiry.) In Joint Select Committee on Aboriginal land rights in the Northern Territory, *Official Hansard Report*, pp. 1002–14.

Reay, M. 1962. Subsections at Borroloola. *Oceania* 33: 90–115.

Roberts, T. 2005. *Frontier Justice: A History of the Gulf Country to 1900*. St Lucia: University of Queensland Press.

Roth, W.E. 1901. Sketch map showing Aboriginal movements into Queensland. 'The Northern Territory – Queensland Border north of Urandangie'. 14 August 1901. Qld State Archives A/45400.

Rumsey, A. 1993. Language and territoriality in Aboriginal Australia. In M. Walsh and C. Yallop (eds), *Language and Culture in Aboriginal Australia*, pp. 191–206. Canberra: Aboriginal Studies Press.

Sansom, B. 2001. Irruptions of the Dreaming in postcolonial Australia. *Oceania* 72: 1–32.

Sharp, R.L. 1939. Tribes and totemism in north-east Australia. *Oceania* 9(3): 254–75; 9(4): 439–61.

Strelein, L.M. 2006. From Mabo to Yorta Yorta: native title law in Australia. *Journal of Law and Policy* 19 (Spring 2006): 225–71.

Sutton, P. 2003. *Native Title in Australia: An Ethnographic Perspective*. Cambridge: Cambridge University Press.

Tacon, P. 2008. Rainbow colour and power among the Waanyi of northwest Queensland. *Cambridge Archaeological Journal* 18(2): 163–76.

Tindale, N. 1974. *Aboriginal Tribes of Australia*. Canberra: Australian National University Press.

Trigger, D. 1982. Nicholson River (Waanyi/Garawa) Land Claim book. Darwin: Northern Land Council.

Trigger, D. 1983. Land rights legislation in Queensland: the issue of historical association. In N. Peterson and M. Langton (eds), *Aborigines, Land and Land Rights*, pp. 192–201. Canberra: Australian Institute of Aboriginal Studies.

Trigger, D. 1985. Doomadgee: A Study of Power Relations and Social Action at Doomadgee Aboriginal Settlement, Northwest Queensland. PhD Thesis, University of Queensland, Brisbane.

Trigger, D. 1989. Garawa/Mugularrangu (Robinson River) Land Claim. Senior Anthropologist's Report prepared for Northern Land Council, Darwin.

Trigger, D. 1992. *Whitefella Comin': Aboriginal Responses to Colonialism in Northern Australia*. Cambridge: Cambridge University Press.

Trigger, D. 2011. Anthropology and the resolution of native title claims: presentation to the Federal Court Judicial Education Forum. In T. Bauman and G. Macdonald (eds), *Unsettling Anthropology: The Demands of Native Title on Worn Concepts and Changing Lives*, pp. 142–60. Canberra: Australian Institute of Aboriginal and Torres Strait Islander Studies.

Trigger, D. and J. Devitt. 1992. A brief history of Aboriginal associations with the Lawn Hill area. Report prepared for Doomadgee Aboriginal Community Council.

Trigger, D. and P. Fietz. 2003. Anthropological report: Waanyi native title claim (QC 99/23). Prepared for Carpentaria Land Council.

Turnbull, W. 1896. [Word lists of Aboriginal languages], *Australian Anthrop. Journal* 1(1): 13.

# 4 From Skills to Stories: Land Rights, Life Histories and the Terms of Engagement

Robert Levitus
The Australian National University

## Introduction: Ian Keen and the Alligator Rivers Land Claims

In the 1970s, in the Alligator Rivers region of the Northern Territory, things changed. From being a region of small-scale economic activity that had only recently achieved a modest level of significance even within the Territory, it became a national political hotspot, as the contentious policy discourses of uranium development, Aboriginal land rights and environmental conservation converged and collided over the same area of ground. Saddler (1980) called it 'the battle for the Alligator Rivers'. In 1975 Ian Keen, a doctoral research student working at Milingimbi in northeast Arnhem Land, suddenly found himself in the middle—and an agent—of that transformation.

The Alligator Rivers region had become known as the Uranium Province following the major discoveries there in the years 1969 to 1973. In 1975, before any mining was allowed, the Ranger Uranium Environmental Inquiry (RUEI) was established and began taking evidence on possible future land uses in the region (RUEI 1977: 7–8). In Canberra, legislation was being drafted to introduce Aboriginal land rights into the Northern Territory, and the Australian Institute of Aboriginal Studies agreed to a request from the nascent Northern Land Council in Darwin to provide anthropologists to begin preparing land claims

(Ucko 1976: 7–8). Plainly, the vacant Crown land in the Alligator Rivers region was a priority area for the first round of claims. At the end of his first major period of field research at Milingimbi, the student Keen was contacted by the principal of the institute, Peter Ucko, and directed to go west and carry out that Alligator Rivers research. Of the seven researchers seconded into that first wave of land claim research across the NLC's region of responsibility, Ian was the only one asked to work outside his existing field area.

To prepare the claim, Ian, with the Northern Territory Museum's George Chaloupka, visited Aboriginal camps between Darwin, Oenpelli and Katherine. Then with four Aboriginal men, one of whom is discussed in this chapter, they carried out a brief period of fast and intense fieldwork within the claim area. Keen documented clan groups, their genealogies and principles of attachment to land; Chaloupka mapped sites and clan territories. Ian was familiar with patrilineal clan territories from northeast Arnhem Land, and adopted a similar model from the Berndts' (1970) work on the Kunwinjku of western Arnhem Land. There was only the proposed form of the legislation and the advice of NLC lawyers to guide them in the framing of a land claim. With these constraints, they produced a tentative account of traditional ownership over part of the area available for claim. The *Aboriginal Land Rights (Northern Territory) Act* was finally passed at the end of 1976, and in effect authorised the Ranger Inquiry to hear this first land claim (RUEI 1977: 6). Keen's and Chaloupka's reports then became a major source of the evidence considered by the inquiry (Keen 1975; Chaloupka 1975; RUEI 1977: 256–8).

In addition, Ian contributed to an argument put successfully by the Northern Land Council that extant clan groups succeeded to ownership of the territories of clans that had died out, and that that succession could take effect immediately on the death of the last previous owner (Peterson, Keen and Sansom 1977; RUEI 1977: 259–60, 265). Together, the claim evidence and the succession argument allowed the inquiry to find that traditional owners as defined by the *Act* existed over a large part of the claim area (RUEI 1977: 277–83). Ian later wrote that the inquiry's acceptance of a process of immediate succession represented the first significant extension of the category of 'traditional Aboriginal owners' beyond the orthodox anthropological model that had been adopted by the Aboriginal Land Rights Commission and imported into the *Land Rights Act* (Keen 1984: 25–9).

When two pastoral leases in the north of the region were resumed by the federal government in 1978, the NLC lodged a further claim. The Alligator Rivers Stage II Land Claim covered those former lease areas as well as that part of the first claim area that had not been granted. Ian was contracted again by the NLC to research this claim (Keen 1980), but it succeeded in winning only a small further area of land in the northeast. Ian himself later took issue with some of the positions adopted by the Aboriginal Land Commissioner that had led to such a poor outcome (Keen 1984). Nevertheless, many of the senior people who lived in or near Kakadu National Park at the time of its establishment in 1979 were recognised as traditional owners of their clan estates by one or both of these land claims.[1]

The policy revolution that occurred in Aboriginal affairs in the 1970s, and especially the advent of statutory land rights in the Northern Territory, marked a watershed in the history of engagement between a generation of Aboriginal men in the Alligator Rivers region and Australian society as represented by a succession of white interlocutors. This chapter proposes a way of understanding that watershed as a change in what those interlocutors were asking for, from skills to stories. It describes aspects of how the change occurred in the institutional and political context of the Alligator Rivers region. It then begins to address the question of how successfully those men met the changed expectations of the land rights era by considering the example of one of their number.

## Working Lives

The generation of senior men who experienced the land rights process had substantial employment histories behind them by the mid-1970s. They had worked for a number of employers in a variety of jobs, mostly in the area between Darwin, Pine Creek, and Oenpelli mission. Much of this was the buffalo country that stretched east from Darwin across floodplains and savannah woodlands, a region that from the 1880s to the 1950s was an economic backwater of buffalo-shooting camps, poorly developed cattle stations, timber camps, garden leases and small mining shows. The fossicking economy (Levitus 1995: 69) that persisted there over those decades consisted of often-transient enterprises requiring little capital, but it provided opportunities for dry-season employment of Aborigines doing bush work in return for European commodities and, mainly in the later years, some money.

Around its edges were other, more stable options. To the northeast was Oenpelli mission, to the northwest the town of Darwin, and to the southwest the small mining and servicing centre of Pine Creek. Connecting the first two were luggers that worked their way along the coast and rivers, and between the latter two were a railway line, mines and other smaller settlements. During the war there were army compounds along the railway line. Then in the 1960s,

---

1   Ian's involvement in the Alligator Rivers region did not end there. He carried out other projects, including a site survey on a proposed extension of the Arnhem Highway, a report on traditional ownership of the Koongarra mineral lease, a report for the Resource Assessment Commission on the Kakadu Conservation Zone and, much later, another land claim.

small abattoirs, buffalo domestication projects, tourist safari camps, crocodile shooters and barramundi fishermen developed new entrepreneurial niches in a region that now attracted serious policy attention from the Northern Territory administration, but still little from Canberra.

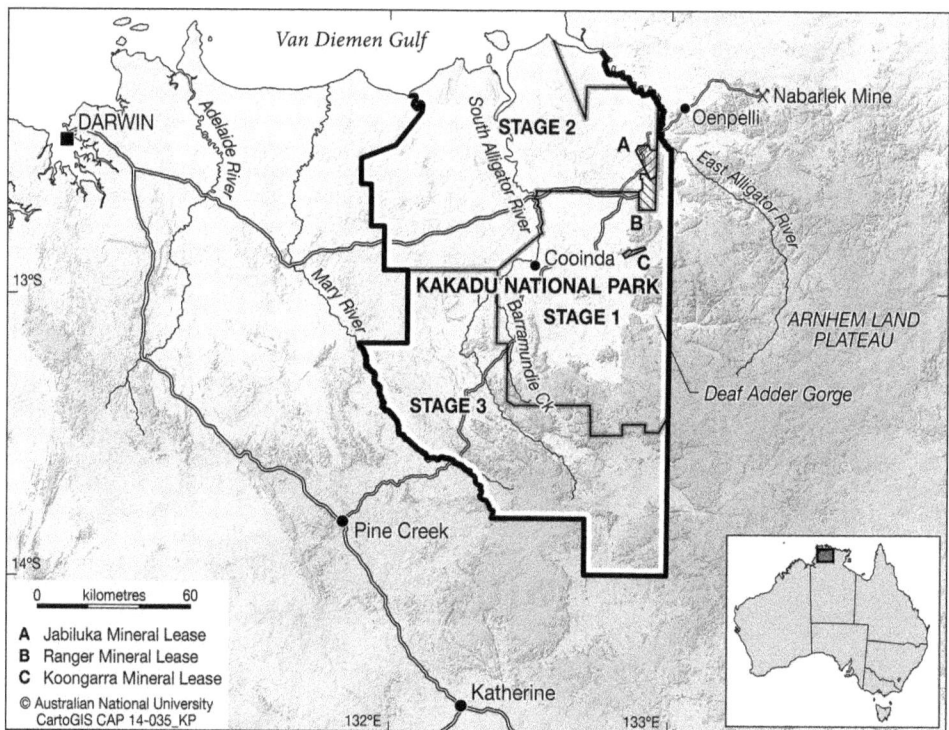

Figure 4.1 Kakadu National Park and surrounds.
Source: The Australian National University.

Aboriginal men from the Alligator Rivers region whose life histories I have researched worked widely across this region and sometimes well beyond. They often started young, around the camp, collecting wood and water, doing simple cooking and tending animals. Their various later jobs included buffalo shooter, crocodile shooter, stockman, horse breaker, pig catcher, builder, driver, fisherman, boat crewman, slaughterman, municipal worker, timber getter, safari guide, and labourer. They were mobile and versatile, they knew their own value as workers, and the skills and experiences they accumulated were often a source of pride and repute in their later years.

For most of their adult lives, it was in these capacities that they had engaged with white society. Bush entrepreneurs sought them out for their abilities at shooting buffalo from a galloping horse, skinning without damaging a hide, breaking in wild brumbies, droving over long distances, working a canoe quietly and quickly within harpooning range of a crocodile at night, or the hard hot work of providing a new station with an airstrip, abattoir and yards. The skills they offered were not only those of the introduced economy. Their native bush skills, especially a facility for navigation that their white employers sometimes found uncanny, added to their value as workers.

By the early 1970s, much of this employment had ended in the buffalo country. The buffalo hides industry ceased in 1956, the introduction of equal wages drastically reduced Aboriginal employment on stations in the late 1960s, saltwater crocodiles had been hunted out and were declared a protected species in the Territory in 1971, and many people had begun overusing alcohol. Nipper Kabirriki, whom I later discuss, was among those sitting unemployed at Pine Creek, watching a steadily growing stream of tourists passing through on their way to the bush attractions of the Alligator Rivers region in the eastern buffalo country.

# The New Regional Design and Aboriginal Power

Then, the discovery between 1969 and 1973 of the major uranium deposits of Ranger, Nabarlek, Koongarra and Jabiluka raised for the Australian government the question of how this powerful industrial interest was to be brought into some form of accommodation with the assertive new political discourses of Aboriginal rights and environmental conservation. During the remainder of that decade, the Alligator Rivers region was a consistent focus of national controversy and passed through a phase of major political, institutional and infrastructural transformation (Lawrence 2000). The first land claim was granted, the Ranger mine was approved and constructed, a town was built nearby to house the workers, and the first stage of Kakadu National Park was declared.

Critically, this transformation was effected by the Commonwealth government (Lawrence 2000: 91–5). While previously the Commonwealth had allowed the Territory to decide land use, it now refused to transfer power over Aboriginal land rights or over major land use decisions in the Alligator Rivers region to the Territory administration under the self-government package then being negotiated (Heatley 1990: 70–3, 91–2, 130). The Commonwealth instead exercised recently acquired statutory powers to determine a new regional design. Three such exercises of power are relevant here. The Ranger Uranium Environmental Inquiry was instituted by the Whitlam government under the Commonwealth's *Environment Protection (Impact of Proposals) Act* of 1974, the land claims were heard pursuant to the 1976 Commonwealth land rights legislation, and the major ultimate land use, that of national park, was vested in a new Commonwealth agency, the Australian National Parks and Wildlife Service (ANPWS; Haynes 2009: 57–62), respectively declared and created under the *National Parks and Wildlife Conservation Act* of 1975.

In the formative years of the mid to late 1970s, these intersected. The Ranger Inquiry bestowed on the region's Aboriginal population its first serious recognition as a central interest group and studied the likely impacts of development upon it (RUEI 1977: 225–33). The *Land Rights Act* transferred existing reserve lands in the region to Aboriginal ownership and empowered the inquiry to hear the first land claim (see above). The inquiry also recommended the creation of a major national park over a large part of the region, to be declared under the Commonwealth *Act* rather than the Territory *Ordinance* (ibid.: 334). It further recommended that Aboriginal participation in park planning and management should apply to the whole of the national park, including areas that were not legally Aboriginal land (ibid.: 205–6). All of this was implemented.

There had been a turnover in the incumbencies of power in the Alligator Rivers region, and the new Commonwealth incumbents professed a truth about Aborigines that was different to that of their Territorian predecessors. Acceptance of Aborigines' interests in land and their concomitant right to be consulted about its use instigated a change in their formal status from a passive, uninformed and disregarded population of onlookers to a central interest group whose participation in the affairs of the area had to be elicited. This new nationally promulgated legal and administrative regime had refigured Aborigines. People known through the years as seasonal bush workers, wards of the state and welfare recipients, could now be installed as traditional owners of land and custodians of sites, and met with as self-determining participants in consultation.

In the wake of these and other decisions relating to governance, development, land ownership and environmental management, the impact of this late 1970s multi-stranded policy process on Alligator Rivers Aborigines was the subject of much inquiry and debate (Australian Institute of Aboriginal Studies 1984; Tatz 1982; von Sturmer 1982). Much of that debate went to the question of whether the change in their legal standing had effected change in their political standing: what authority and control had passed into local Aboriginal hands. One common critical theme in these writings was that the transfer of land ownership to Aboriginal people was not accompanied by a power of determination over the new jurisdictional and institutional design being put in place over the region, or the developmental future anticipated for it.

The crucial decision in favour of mining the Ranger deposit was taken in disregard of Aboriginal opposition (RUEI 1977: 9). Accompanying this development, a complex structure of regulation and administration, which became in itself a social impact of mining, was imposed on the region (Gray 1980: 147–8; von Sturmer 1984b: 120–31). Land rights satisfied the formal preconditions for Aboriginal participation and influence, but their exercise could be smothered by a cluster of organisational mediators. Von Sturmer identified the incongruity within the Ranger Inquiry between land rights and the exercise of authority and responsibility with respect to the land. He noted the absence of direct evidence from local Aboriginal people, and the denial of a future determining voice to them, in favour of external specialists: the Northern Land Council, the director of the Australian National Parks and Wildlife Service and the Supervising Scientist (von Sturmer 1984a: 84–5, and see 53–6).

Nor did it appear, from the Ranger Inquiry's qualitative assessment of Aboriginal capacity, that it anticipated the emergence of any confident local Aboriginal determining voice. The inquiry saw a demoralised and beleaguered population (RUEI 1977: 46) for which it recommended a series of ameliorative measures that I have elsewhere summarised as a 'design for protection' (Levitus 2005: 30–1). Von Sturmer (1984a: 83) similarly remarked on the 'general air of malaise and decay and hopelessness which hovers over everything'. In the mid-1990s, the activist Jacqui Katona (personal communication), representing the Mirarr traditional owners in their opposition to development of the Jabiluka uranium deposit, remarked that land rights had not been worth a 'hill of beans' to the people of the Alligator Rivers region.

## Kakadu and Consultation

But in a region suddenly crowded with interest groups and agencies of the state, Aboriginal influence did find two institutional homes to the west of the East Alligator River. One of these, the Gagudju Association, took on an importance in the 1980s that had not been anticipated by the region's planners (Levitus 2005). The other was Kakadu National Park. It is the latter that is important to my present theme. Even as capital and the state had their way in the Alligator Rivers region, policy and politics combined in Kakadu to create new space, politically and geographically, for Aboriginal people.

Following Ranger Inquiry endorsement, the principle of Aboriginal participation in management of the entire park had been accepted by the federal government and the ANPWS from the beginning (Viner 1977: 4; Wellings 1995: 242). However, the formal settings did not look promising. The terms of the lease from the traditional owners to the Commonwealth, and the first Plan of Management, were not strong on the point (Lawrence 2000: 99–101, 180–1; Tatz 1982: 153–6), there was no board of management on which Aboriginal numbers could dominate during the first decade of the park's existence (Haynes 2013:

198), and one critic perceived a fatal ambiguity in the term 'management' itself, between high-level policy and planning, and everyday ground-level ranger work, that he thought the Parks Service was exploiting to exclude traditional owners from real control (Tatz 1982: 175–6).

But that same critic described the first ANPWS officers in Kakadu as 'excellent and admirable', 'moral and caring' (Tatz 1982: 155–6). Those first park managers tried to institute a style of relationship with the traditional owners that would give some substance to land rights. As one of these officers, Chris Haynes, later wrote, 'That was through the best dialogue we were able to imagine at the time' (Haynes 2009: 164). ANPWS began its work in the region with a principled commitment to consultation. The first three parks officers to arrive in Kakadu—Haynes, Dan Gillespie and Ian Morris—were recruited

> on the strength of our demonstrated ability and experience to relate to the traditional owners, and so we were given a free hand to do what we knew best. Although aware that the formal [park lease] agreement had made almost no direct provision for the voice of traditional owners to be heard, it seemed inconceivable to any of us that important decisions on Aboriginal land could be made without consultation with its traditional owners. And so, with the approval of an already-overworked Northern Land Council we initiated dialogue with traditional owners immediately. (Haynes 2009: 160; see also Gillespie 1984)

Here in this new institutional setting, those senior Aboriginal men with substantial working lives already behind them were invited to engage with a new set of white interlocutors who adhered to a new truth about Aborigines and wanted to hear their stories. Haynes and Gillespie shared the prior experience of witnessing John Hunter's methods of genuine engagement with the Aboriginal people of Maningrida during his tenure as superintendent (Gillespie 1982). Now in Kakadu, they shared the task of general liaison with the Aboriginal residents, spreading news and information, and raising the initial questions of park planning. Their consultation style was personal, informal and cumulative:

> Consultation did not just entail one-on-one or group meetings about the agenda of the moment. It was surrounded by hours and days of casual discussion in all sorts of locations—and just simply exchanging information. Thus when there were issues for decision-making each side had some understanding of the other's positioning. Our personal associations grew while looking at items of interest: in the field, in cars, on house verandas, under caravan annexes, and in shops and pubs. Sometimes there was a lot of note-taking but often it was just the sharing of opinions and stories. (Haynes 2009: 161)

By this communicative process, some Aborigines were refigured as actors in the public affairs of the region. Von Sturmer (1984c: 156) observed that 'of all the essentially European organisations operating in the Region, ANPWS has the greatest sensitivity to and knowledge of Aboriginal issues and politics'.

Park management was of course not the only originator of consultations, although combined with the various academic research projects pursued in the park by archaeologists, linguists and others under the aegis of ANPWS, it accounted for a large proportion. But there were also consultations with other agencies and individuals about traditional ownership issues, proposed mines, further land claims, management of royalty and lease payments, sacred site documentation, popular films and books, commercial developments and social programs. Not all these consultations were of the same quality as those of the early Kakadu years (von Sturmer 1981; Gundjehmi Aboriginal Corporation 1997).

## The New Terms of Engagement

The politicking of the 1970s and the settlement of new jurisdictional and institutional arrangements by the end of that decade were only the beginning. Consultation was now the standard and it operated as a two-edged sword of both a right and a burden. In the lives of the senior generation of the time, I treat this as a change in the currency of their articulation with non-Aboriginal society. Having been asked for skills in their earlier lives, they were now being asked for stories. Later, by way of an individual example, I begin to address the question of how they responded to the potentialities thrown up by that change.

By stories I mean cultural accounts: genealogies, language, life histories, myths, sites, livelihood patterns, the identities and meanings of country and people's connections to it, and judgements as to what entitlements arose from those connections and what activities might be allowable on that land. They were being asked to articulate local Aboriginal cultural values, especially values of place, and to say how those values should properly be recognised in the new regimes of management and development. In a less directly instrumental way, they were also being asked to inform and enrich the new European appreciation of Kakadu with the stories of its own people, their lives, languages and places. One prominent man, Bill Neidjie, came to recognise this new time as one that placed whites themselves under an obligation.

> This time White-European must come to Aborigine,
> listen Aborigine and understand it.
> Understand that culture, secret, what dreaming. (Neidjie 1989: 78)

But the Aboriginal people who claimed attachments to the region were often initially surprised that they should be consulted at all. That they should be asked by whites of some apparent official standing to consider the plans of whites of some apparent power (sometimes the same ones) and express judgement upon them was new in their experience, and confusing or embarrassing for some. When Keen and Chaloupka were contracted to research the first land claim in 1975 (above), they were initially asked to also ascertain the opinions of the claimants regarding the proposed uranium developments. While this task was not pursued systematically, Keen gained the impression from those people he did approach that they had no idea as to why they were being asked.

A few years later, by which time consultation had become more familiar, the invitation to participate in processes of decision and control could still be unsettling. Chris Haynes, one of the first generation of senior managers of Kakadu National Park, approached Mick Alderson, one of the central traditional owners of the park land, to contribute to the development of initial management strategies:

> When I asked his view about an issue in the first months of our association he often giggled a bit, looked at the ground embarrassed, shrugged in an exaggerated and prolonged manner, and said, 'It's up to you'. After perhaps some silence, he might continue ... 'You've got the lease. The park has gone to you mob. You're supposed to know what to do.' (Haynes 2009: 162)

Such confusion and hesitation were the responses of people discovering that the terms of the intercultural had suddenly and unaccountably changed. The transition from skills to stories presupposed that different white interlocutors were now seeing Aborigines differently and expecting different things from them. As before, their interlocutory position was a manifestation of white authority. Whites sought Aboriginal engagement with and contributions to exercises of white design, even if, in the case of the search for stories, they were designs for cultural recognition. The framework of consultation was itself always a non-Aboriginal creation, an artefact of a progressively liberalising colonialism.

Participation in these designs exposed Aborigines to the normative regimes that governed them. Those regimes proposed and then inculcated models of personhood appropriate to effective participation. We find in Judith Butler an explanation of how this operated as an instance of Foucault's 'politics of truth':

> The politics of truth pertains to those relations of power that circumscribe in advance what will and will not count as truth, which order the world in certain regular and regulatable ways, and which we come to accept as the given field of knowledge. We can understand the salience of this point when we begin to ask: What counts as a person? What counts as a coherent gender? What qualifies as a citizen? Whose world is legitimated as real? Subjectively, we ask: Who can I become in such a world where the meanings and limits of the subject are set out in advance for me? By what norms am I constrained as I begin to ask what I may become? (Butler 2002: 220–1)

So we are concerned with the 'intelligible formation of the subject within a given historical scheme of things', a 'self-crafting, which always takes place in relation to an imposed set of norms' (Butler 2005: 17, 19). The work camps that senior men had grown up around and been recruited into required that they adopt the subjectivity of the bush worker. McGrath (1987: 167–9) discusses this process as one of identity formation on the part of Aboriginal stockmen in north Australian cattle station camps. Similarly, the expectations, requirements and commitments of working lives spent in the buffalo camps and other fossicking economy sites constituted a normative environment that conditioned the emergence of certain kinds of person who understood their own narratives in terms of their relationships to that environment (Butler 2005: 7–8).

What the transition from skills to stories showed was that the narratives crafted from those relationships were not comprehensive. They did not exhaust the potential for self-narration that could be found within those life histories. To different degrees for different members of the senior land claim generation, subsisting alongside the accumulated experiences of work were items or themes of learning of precolonial origin—though sometimes acquired in the course of employment—including information about Aboriginal land relationships (see Merlan 1998: 79–96). The surprise and discomfort of people experiencing their first moments of consultation is testimony to the long-standing irrelevance of this kind of knowledge for establishing an Aboriginal subjectivity that could be viable in relations with whites. The sources of this new relevance and new viability have already been indicated.

Predominant among them was the *Land Rights Act* and the new legal status of traditional owner that it instituted. Merlan (1998: 166ff) has discussed how traditional ownership is formulated in law and tested in court as an exercise in the structured and reified imitation of precolonial relationships to land. While she emphasises the changing but persistent gap between such formulations and social reality, the important point here is that that legal imitative exercise was sufficiently successful to resonate with Aboriginal claimants and provide them with a model around which they could marshal their memories and to which their current self-representations could aim to approximate. It referred to something that they knew, or felt they should know, something about.[2]

Following that was the takeover, or withholding, of Territorian political authority by the Commonwealth in the Alligator Rivers region, and the commitment that its politicians and agencies professed to an ideology of self-determination. Finally there were those frontline personalities—Keen, Chaloupka, Haynes, Gillespie and Morris have already been named—who were experienced in recognising

---

2   Povinelli (2002) offers extensive critical discussions of this point.

Aborigines as something other than bush workers even before land rights were legislated and before any of them (except for Chaloupka) began working in the region. I mentioned earlier that the Commonwealth professed a different truth about Aborigines than had the Territory. These individuals tried to hold to that truth. That different truth, of Aborigines as participating landholders, constituted in Butler's terms a normative frame for the encounter between them.

> In asking the ethical question 'How ought I to treat another?' I am immediately caught up in a realm of social normativity, since the other only appears to me, only functions as an other for me, if there is a frame within which I can see and apprehend the other in her separateness and exteriority. So, though I might think of the ethical relation as dyadic or, indeed, as presocial, I am caught up not only in the sphere of normativity but in the problematic of power when I pose the ethical question in its directness and simplicity: 'How ought I to treat you?' If the 'I' and the 'you' must first come into being, and if a normative frame is necessary for this emergence and encounter, then norms work not only to direct my conduct but to condition the possible emergence of an encounter between myself and the other. (Butler 2005: 25)

We are dealing then with how people responded to a change in the normative frames created for their encounters with whites (cf. Batty 2005). The rest of this chapter is about how one man met the demand for skills in earlier times, and especially how he then managed the new interest in stories. It shows how someone who had felt confident of his value as a worker during an earlier era now fared when engaged by one of the land rights era's primary intended instruments of empowerment—consultation.

## Nipper Kabirriki

Kabirriki was born in a cave in the western Arnhem Land plateau, and spent his early years living an Aboriginal bush life with minimal white contact. His country, Badmardi clan territory, is centred on Deaf Adder Gorge, which straddles the Kakadu/Arnhem Land boundary. As a boy before World War II, he saw the first buffalo come into his country. It was speared by his brother and they ate the meat. His memories of his family's annual round of travel well beyond the limits of that estate provided the substance of Chaloupka's remarkable early paper 'Badmardi Year of Seasons'.[3] When talking of those areas, Kabirriki remembered place names in the order in which they would be

---

3   Later published as Chaloupka 1981.

visited, as lines of travel, whether wet season rock shelters on the plateau, or billabongs and swamp pockets along a lowland creek: 'I have to go all around, every place.'[4]

Kabirriki commented that in those old days people had moved around and camped all over, wherever they wanted. Since he had started working for whitefellers, he didn't walk around anymore. Whitefellers had quietened people down, he said. He took credit for being a reliable worker. He said he had had no bad bosses, because he had been a good man. Throughout his working life he didn't 'bad name' himself. If a white man told him to do something, he did it well. He worked on a number of cattle stations around Pine Creek and Adelaide River, and for several buffalo shooters between the Mary River and Deaf Adder Gorge. In the most distant venture from the Alligator Rivers that I recorded from that generation, he was part of a team that drove a mob of horses north from Alice Springs. He did building work on the Pine Creek pub, and worked for a butcher in Katherine, and at a gold mine near Barramundie Creek.

For Kabirriki, the transition to a regime of recognition for stories came early. The first policy response to the uranium discoveries was the Alligator Rivers Environmental Fact-Finding Study in 1972–73. It included an archaeological survey for which the researcher, Johan Kamminga, recruited him as an informant. They did two trips into Deaf Adder Gorge, within Kabirriki's own traditional estate, which he had not visited since the last years of the buffalo-shooting industry about 20 years before.

Kabirriki later spoke of the first of these trips as the means by which he, alone, had resumed contact with his country. He said that during his working years, no one had looked after his country. Then in the 1970s, people came looking for him and picked him up. His father and mother had been dead a long time, and when he went into Deaf Adder on that first trip, he went alone with the archaeologist and there was no one there. Shortly afterwards, he identified a location at a billabong outside of Deaf Adder for the establishment of an outstation, Kolondjorr, which he subsequently referred to as 'my station'. He then resumed intermittently living near and visiting his country.

The fact-finding study began Kabirriki's elevation to public status as a knowledgeable elder, perhaps the most knowledgeable, of the Kakadu area. It was a status that he enjoyed and of which he boasted. The land claims and the early phase of park management consummated the process, but it was also husbanded and sustained by another research relationship. Soon after that first field trip, he began assisting the exploratory rock art specialist George Chaloupka, and continued doing so until Kabirriki's death in 1987. For over a decade in

---

4   The statements attributed to Kabirriki are either quotes or close paraphrases taken from my field notes.

the 1970s and 1980s, the partnership between Kabirriki and Chaloupka was probably the most important single conduit for lodging the cultural significance of the Kakadu landscape in the archive and representing it in the public domain (Chaloupka 1993; Flood 1997: ii).

One of the earliest and most important projects by that partnership, in company with Ian Keen and three other informants, was the bush trip to document clan territories and sites over most of what later became the first stage of Kakadu National Park. This research, discussed earlier, was written up into two reports for what became the first land claim under the new *Land Rights Act*. Kabirriki went on to act as an important source of information, again for Ian Keen, in the Alligator Rivers Stage II Land Claim. This claim included 11 patrilineal clan territories: nine in the north of the park and two in the south (Keen 1980). Kabirriki participated in field trips to nine out of the 11 estates, easily more than any other of Keen's informants, and was the only one able to provide information about clan territories in both areas of the park. He continued to work with Chaloupka on major site documentation exercises, and in 1981 he accompanied Rhys Jones' archaeological research team when it excavated and surveyed several Kakadu sites (Jones 1985). In all of these research exercises, and especially his wide-ranging explorations of stone country areas with Chaloupka, Kabirriki was encouraged in what was mostly a single-handed project of giving names and attributing significance to country, places and paintings.

Kabirriki was well equipped to flourish in this new era. His value to researchers lay in his ability to confidently recite from what appeared to be a substantial corpus of knowledge retained from his early years of bush living. A botanist working in the area considered him clearly the most knowledgeable person for trees and landscape, and remarked that even people of the East Alligator area, well away from Kabirriki's country, deferred to his expertise (Russell-Smith personal communication). Jones (1985: 20) called him 'a man possessing profound knowledge about the traditional affairs of his culture'. These assessments reflected Kabirriki's own: 'I know all the story and law from when I was kid. My father and grandfather tell me. I remember any story.'

He was forthcoming with what he knew. On field trips he gave information abundantly. Each stop might elicit place names and their geographical order and context, the people that camped or events that took place there, methods of hunting and cooking bush foods, or the travels of dreamings and the ceremonies that they brought to different places and groups. He presented a geography of traditional ownership for areas of the park, indexing each set of place names that came to mind against patrimoiety, clan, language group or individuals. Where an area had no surviving patrilineally descended traditional owners, he might designate a proper successor: 'Paddy gotta take that country.'

Kabirriki was also one of four senior men recruited to show aspects of Aboriginal culture for Breeden and Wright's (1989: 150–75) popular book on Kakadu. The authors described him as 'the repository of the Dreamtime stories and their application to everyday life' (1989: 150). Their front dustjacket photograph (Figure 4.2) shows Kabirriki as custodian of country.

Figure 4.2 Kabirriki on the cover of *Kakadu*.
Source: Belinda Wright/National Geographic Creative.

Despite the artifice of the photograph, Kabirriki's straight and confident gaze at the camera bespeaks his comfort with that persona. Not only would the photo have appealed to him as a way of publicly disseminating his custodianship, but it also implied real capability. The picture claimed for Kabirriki a subsisting native bush competence that he could have resumed practising had it been necessary to do so. Two other photos (Figures 4.3 and 4.4) featured in other popular books. Both taken by Chaloupka, they place Kabirriki in even closer association with ancient Aboriginal culture.

Figure 4.3 Kabirriki on the cover of *Archaeology of the Dreamtime*.
Source: George Chaloupka.

Figure 4.4 Dedication page from George Chaloupka, *Journey in Time*.
Source: George Chaloupka.

Having been reinstated into a relationship with these stone country places by both a mimetic policy process and traditionalist research projects, Kabirriki nurtured and displayed that relationship through both embodiment, as shown in the photos, and story. He told once how he had been mad for two nights during which two female *mimi*, or rock country spirits, had picked him up from his station at Kolondjorr and taken him into Deaf Adder Gorge. There the *mimi* showed him two bush medicines that he could boil up and drink to cure his tuberculosis, in place of the ineffective 'white doctor medicine'. After being taught about his own wild medicine by the *mimi* he had come good.

That performative impulse extended to the tourists who arrived in Kakadu in rapidly growing numbers in the years after the land claims. Kabirriki would spontaneously introduce himself into conversation with groups seated at the Cooinda pub. He also encouraged the dissemination of stories about places as a way of discharging the responsibilities of custodianship (Gabirrigi 1984). He regarded this as a necessary means by which park rangers and traditional owners could take proper care of Kakadu and protect tourists from danger.

Kabirriki had a strongly individualistic sense of the importance of his record of fieldwork. The first trip to Deaf Adder for the fact-finding study (above) became for Kabirriki the instrument for claiming a singular pioneering role with respect to his country, despite the presence on that trip of two other Aboriginal men. He thought of his contribution to the land claims as an equally singular achievement, eclipsing the contributions of others. In recalling the seminal research trip in 1975 for the first claim, he said that 'Chaloupka and Ian Keen and me went all over', listing a series of locales—Anbangbang, Nanguluwurr, Burrunguy, Djelandjal, Djanbaldjakakodj—encompassed in their accelerated journeyings through the bush. He omitted to mention the three other senior men who participated in that trip, including his half-brother. Another time, at a casual night-time gathering in one of the Kakadu camps, Kabirriki observed how he and one of the other men present were united by a mutual life-history involvement in each other's countries, so he had come from Deaf Adder to help this man's group win their land.

There was little exaggeration in this. Keen (personal communication) himself recalled the documentation for the first land claim as being heavily reliant on Kabirriki, and I indicated above his pre-eminence in the second claim. The energy that Kabirriki had devoted to these efforts, and the kudos that he claimed from them, demonstrated his sense of what was to be gained from this new generation of white interlocutors and their projects of cultural recognition. He understood that in the era of land rights, knowledge and stories were the raw material of personal standing and authority, a potentiality that could be realised when one had a white person to 'book it down', something that he regularly instructed us to do: 'George Chaloupka, Ian Keen, Chris Haynes, Rhys Jones, Ian Morris ... they got all my word, all my story. They got it in their book. No one can cheat me now. I gotta win'.

He also grasped that behind these individual researchers was a higher institutional authority that was similarly receptive and could legitimate his claims. One such claim was to have succeeded to authority over a nearby clan estate with no remaining owners, so that he was now the boss all the way from his country to that one. He announced that he would soon be going to Canberra with Jones and Chaloupka, 'and then I'll be big boss for whole lot'.

Kabirriki's standing was widely acknowledged locally, especially among younger people. One man referred me to him with the recommendation that 'he was first man been write 'em down all the place and dreaming for land claim'. Kabirriki reciprocated with a critical eye over the claims and pretensions of his fellows. He forthrightly advised me that I was misguided in working with one very old local man who Kabirriki thought 'don't know nothing', and he gave the same evaluation of two other men who in the 1970s had purported to act as informants for his own country of Deaf Adder Gorge before Kabirriki himself had returned from Pine Creek: 'Which one proper right man? Well I'm the right man really for this country.'

He had no patience with those other Badmardi people who had failed to learn about their country, had ignored his attempts to teach, and 'only savvy beer'. His view was that if a government man or lawyer were to come, it was the responsibility of those people to prove their claim with their own knowledge. If they called for his assistance with place names, he would say he didn't know. If they didn't know and he did know, well then they should get out and he would make it his own country. He was already looking after it. But also, in the early years of widespread royalty distributions from the Ranger mine (Levitus 1991), he adopted the cause of a man whose attachments to another area Kabirriki believed entitled him to money, and declared his intention to send a paper to Canberra to right the situation.

While a personality such as Kabirriki's would have sought and achieved a measure of independent space and recognition in any context, he became a free operator by reason of a paucity of constraints upon him. Historical depletion and dislocation of the Aboriginal population of the Alligator Rivers region, and a long period in which traditional knowledge counted for little, meant that among the people who repopulated the park area in the 1970s and 1980s were only a limited number who could offer the stories needed by white interlocutors. In that context Kabirriki was a standout performer, but one whose prominence itself became problematic because his information often stood alone.

There was no rich and active traditionalist Aboriginal discourse by reference to which Kabirriki's statements could be verified; no well-populated network of similarly knowledgeable and motivated men to whom he might in the ordinary run of things be made accountable for his claims. Certainly there were some other, less assertive senior people who knew some areas well, and one could hear occasional grumblings accusing Kabirriki of taking liberties in his declarations about this or that topic, but there was no challenge and no arbitration. His knowledge came from his own memory and extrapolations, and his deployment of it was relatively unfettered by anything other than his own judgements. For those recording his information, his singular status meant there was no way to know how much of what he gave was genuine inherited knowledge. But his confidence was seductive and there was neither reason nor grounds on which to challenge what he said.

Some problems, however, became evident in time, and some of what he said was revised. In at least one instance this was of his own volition. During an early park management planning exercise, Kabirriki realised that he had previously put a place name on an incorrect location and so relocated it, blaming his mistake on Chaloupka for having made him go too fast (Haynes, personal communication). At a grander scale, the map of clan territories published in the Ranger Inquiry *Second Report* (RUEI 1977: 278) and widely reproduced thereafter had to be significantly revised, partly with the assistance of Kabirriki, in the context of later projects aimed at verifying traditional ownership of parts of the same region. Such examples leave the impression that during the first wave of consultation and documentation campaigns in the Alligator Rivers region in the 1970s, often carried out under time constraints, insistent researcher inquiries elicited from Kabirriki an overconfident response that later had to be rethought with the benefit of more careful recollection or deduction.

The public management domain, with its concern for rationale, consistency and precedent, also acted at certain moments to bring Kabirriki's views to account and limit his opportunistic deployment of stories. The area of Kakadu in the vicinity of his clan country, depleted of traditional owners, provided him with opportunity. Despite his being of opposite patrimoiety to that land, Kabirriki said he would look after the whole lot, because he knew all the places, and all those people were dead. This claim involved transgressing a categorical distinction that Kabirriki himself often invoked. But when a publicly authorised decision was needed as to who had succeeded to ownership of the Koongarra mineral lease, Kabirriki sat in conference with a few other senior men to arrive at a new determination of traditional ownership in the context of Keen's anthropological consultancy. Although there is no way of knowing who said what, it appears from the outcome that he did not persist with his private claim.

On another occasion, he agreed to assist a family that he had worked for in the buffalo camps and who were now trying to claim traditional rights in parts of Kakadu. When they visited Chris Haynes, the senior parks officer in Darwin, to press their case, he realised that Kabirriki was putting propositions concerning rights over an area of land that were different to what he had previously said. Haynes told Kabirriki that changing his story in that way would destroy his credibility as an informant. So where public land management issues arose, his excesses could be contained when an established ethnographic charter, often based to a great extent on his own previous testimony, was brought to bear by administrative action.

One other matter of succession was more personal. It was not entirely clear whether there were any young Badmardi. A few were proposed, including a woman for whom Kabirriki claimed paternity, but they stayed away. Some other younger people from other clans who he declared himself willing to teach were either not sufficiently interested or did not persevere. Ultimately Kabirriki and the other Badmardi died. Succession to a clan estate made important by its escarpment surrounds and Kabirriki's standing has only recently been settled amongst other interested family groups in Kakadu.

## Conclusion

This chapter is about how land rights changed the terms of engagement between Aboriginal and non-Aboriginal people in the Alligator Rivers region, and how one Aboriginal man responded to that change. I offer his case study as an indicator of individual particularity. With more space, other personal accounts could be given to widely different effects. Land rights were a watershed that altered the grounds of interaction and the criteria for success in the dealings that the men of Kabirriki's generation had with whites. Men who had gained access to desirable goods and found their place in the world through skilled physical labour, were now being asked to give an entirely different account of themselves.

That was not always easily or successfully done. Where once the principal question that the European world had put to such men was 'What work can you do for us?', that question had suddenly changed to 'What stories can you tell us?' Such a drastic change in the expectations they were called upon to meet required that they draw in a different way upon personal resources of memory and cross-cultural competence and confidence. It asked and allowed them to develop and project aspects of their personae, or their resources for self-narration, previously of no interest or value to their white interlocutors.

The legal status of traditional ownership thereby brought people into a revised awareness of their place and value in the world of the Alligator Rivers region because it relocated them within a new normative frame. Self-determination and land rights, as realised in Kakadu National Park in the 1980s, created new interaction frames in which Aboriginal people, upon whom the new status of traditional owner had been bestowed, were invited or required to participate. These new frames allowed them to take advantage, as well as they could, of the new officially legitimated truth about Aborigines, and to practise and test a new mode of subjectivity for its viability in relations with a new generation of white interlocutors.

Policy impacts categorically, but people live individually. When the land rights era introduced a consultation practice that took stories as its currency of recognition and prestige, Nipper Kabirriki discovered a new field of play open to him on which he could draw upon, reconstruct and elaborate the bush knowledge of his earlier life to easily accumulate status and prestige. After the land rights transition he began taking advantage of an absence of constraints and accountability which, for a personality such as his, were conditions of freedom. He was able to fully exploit the irony of a free-ranging individualist being anointed as a traditional authority. But the encounter between the imagined good of the consultative ethos, and individual Aboriginal subjectivities, had varied and unpredictable consequences. Other biographies would show that not all of Kabirriki's colleagues were able to find such advantage in the changed intercultural terms of engagement that were in play in the region.

## Acknowledgements

My thanks go to Dan Gillespie, Chris Haynes, Lisa Palmer, Peter Toner and the anonymous readers for their comments on the draft. Thanks also to Pina Chaloupka for permission to use the two George Chaloupka photos, Karina Pelling of The Australian National University who prepared the map, and the Australian Institute of Aboriginal and Torres Strait Islander Studies for assistance with the Breeden and Wright photo.

## References

Australian Institute of Aboriginal Studies. 1984. *Aborigines and Uranium.* Consolidated report to the Minister for Aboriginal Affairs on the social impact of uranium mining on the Aborigines of the Northern Territory. Canberra: Australian Government Publishing Service.

Batty, P. 2005. Private politics, public strategies: White advisers and their Aboriginal subjects [Special issue: *Figuring the Intercultural in Aboriginal Australia*, ed. M. Hinkson and B. Smith]. *Oceania* 75: 209–21.

Berndt, R.M. and C.H. Berndt. 1970. *Man, Land and Myth in North Australia: The Gunwinggu People.* Sydney: Ure Smith.

Breeden, S. and B. Wright. 1989. *Kakadu: Looking After the Country – the Gagudju Way.* Brookvale: Simon and Schuster.

Butler, J. 2002. What is critique? An essay on Foucault's virtue. In D. Ingram (ed.), *The Political*, pp. 212–26. Malden: Blackwell.

Butler, J. 2005. *Giving An Account of Oneself.* New York: Fordham University Press.

Chaloupka, G. 1975. Report on Aboriginal traditional land-ownership of the Alligator Rivers region: Part 2: The land-owning groups (clans) and their traditional territories. Darwin: Northern Land Council.

Chaloupka, G. 1981. Appendix 1: The traditional movement of a band of Aboriginals in Kakadu. In T. Stokes (ed.), *Kakadu National Park: Education Resources*, pp. 162–71. Canberra and Darwin: Australian National Parks and Wildlife Service.

Chaloupka, G. 1993. *Journey in Time*. Chatswood: Reed.

Flood, J. 1997. *Rock Art of the Dreamtime: Images of Ancient Australia*. Sydney: Angus and Robertson.

Gabirrigi, N. 1984. Back to my country. In H. Sullivan (ed.), *Visitors to Aboriginal Sites: Access, Control and Management*, p. 59. Canberra: Australian National Parks and Wildlife Service.

Gillespie, D. 1982. John Hunter and Maningrida – a chorus of alarm bells. In P. Loveday (ed.), *Service Delivery to Outstations,* pp. 1–7. Darwin: North Australia Research Unit.

Gillespie, D.A. 1984. Ubirr – a case study in compromise. In H. Sullivan (ed.), *Visitors to Aboriginal Sites: Access, Control and Management*, pp. 19–28. Canberra: Australian National Parks and Wildlife Service.

Gray, W.J. 1980. The Ranger and Nabarlek mining agreements. In S. Harris (ed.), *Social and Environmental Choice: the Impact of Uranium Mining in the Northern Territory*, pp. 136–53. Canberra: The Australian National University, Centre for Resource and Environmental Studies.

Gundjehmi Aboriginal Corporation. 1997. 'We are not talking about mining': the history of duress and the Jabiluka Project. Accessed online 19 January 2014. www.mirarr.net/resources.

Haynes, C.D. 2009. Defined by Contradiction: The Social Construction of Joint Management in Kakadu National Park. PhD Thesis, Charles Darwin University, Darwin.

Haynes, C.D. 2013. Seeking control: disentangling the difficult sociality of Kakadu National Park's joint management. *Journal of Sociology* 49(2–3): 194–209.

Heatley, A. 1990. *Almost Australians: The Politics of Northern Territory Self-Government*. Darwin: North Australia Research Unit, The Australian National University.

Jones, R. (ed.) 1985. *Archaeological Research in Kakadu National Park*. Canberra: Australian National Parks and Wildlife Service and The Australian National University.

Keen I. 1975. Report on Aboriginal traditional land-ownership of the Alligator Rivers region. Part 1: The land-owning groups (clans) and their membership. Darwin: Northern Land Council.

Keen, I. 1980. *The Alligator Rivers Stage II Land Claim*. Darwin: Northern Land Council.

Keen, I. 1984. A question of interpretation: the definition of 'traditional Aboriginal owners' in the Aboriginal Land Rights (N.T.) Act. In L.R. Hiatt (ed.), *Aboriginal Landowners: Contemporary Issues in the Determination of Traditional Aboriginal Land Ownership*, Oceania Monograph 27, pp. 24–45. Sydney: University of Sydney.

Lawrence, D. 2000. *Kakadu: The Making of a National Park*. Carlton South: Melbourne University Press.

Levitus, R. 1991. The boundaries of Gagudju Association membership: anthropology, law and public policy. In J. Connell and R. Howitt (eds), *Mining and Indigenous Peoples in Australasia*, pp. 153–68. Sydney: Sydney University Press.

Levitus, R. 1995. Social history since colonisation. In T. Press, D. Lea, A. Webb and A. Graham (eds), *Kakadu: Natural and Cultural Heritage and Management*, pp. 64–93. Darwin: Australian Nature Conservation Agency and North Australia Research Unit, The Australian National University.

Levitus, R. 2005. Land rights and local economies: the Gagudju Association and the mirage of collective self-determination. In D. Austin-Broos and G. Macdonald (eds), *Culture, Economy and Governance in Aboriginal Australia: Proceedings of a Workshop of the Academy of the Social Sciences in Australia*, pp. 29–39. Sydney: Sydney University Press.

McGrath, A. 1987. *'Born in the Cattle': Aborigines in Cattle Country*. Sydney: Allen and Unwin.

Merlan, F. 1998. *Caging the Rainbow: Places, Politics, and Aborigines in a North Australian Town*. Honolulu: University of Hawai'i Press.

Neidjie, B. 1989. *Story about Feeling* (K. Taylor ed.). Broome: Magabala Books.

Peterson, N., I. Keen and B. Sansom. 1977. Succession to land: primary and secondary rights to Aboriginal estates. In *Official Hansard Report of the Joint Select Committee on Aboriginal Land Rights in the Northern Territory*. Canberra: Australian Government Printer, 19 April: 1002–14.

Povinelli, E. 2002. *The Cunning of Recognition: Indigenous Alterities and the Making of Australian Multiculturalism*. Durham: Duke University Press.

Ranger Uranium Environmental Inquiry (RUEI). 1977. *Second Report*. Canberra: Australian Government Publishing Service.

Saddler, H. 1980. Implications of the battle for the Alligator Rivers: land use planning and environmental protection. In R. Jones (ed.), *Northern Australia: Options and Implications*, pp. 187–200. Canberra: Research School of Pacific Studies, The Australian National University.

Tatz, C. 1982. *Aborigines and Uranium and Other Essays*. Richmond: Heinemann Educational Australia.

Ucko, P. 1976. Review of A.I.A.S. activities 1975. *Australian Institute of Aboriginal Studies Newsletter* N.S. 5: 6–20.

Viner, I. 1977. Uranium—Australia's decision. Statement by the Hon. Ian Viner, Minister for Aboriginal Affairs and Minister Assisting the Treasurer. In *Uranium—Australia's Decision*, pp. 1–7. Canberra: Australian Government Publishing Service.

von Sturmer, J. 1981. Talking with Aborigines. *Australian Institute of Aboriginal Studies Newsletter* N.S. 15: 13–30.

von Sturmer, J. 1982. Aborigines in the uranium industry: toward self-management in the Alligator River region? In R.M. Berndt (ed.), *Aboriginal Sites, Rights and Resource Development*, pp. 69–116. Perth: University of Western Australia Press.

von Sturmer, J. 1984a. A critique of the Fox Report. In Australian Institute of Aboriginal Studies, *Aborigines and Uranium*, pp. 20–103. Canberra: Australian Government Publishing Service.

von Sturmer, J. 1984b. The social impact of mining: 1. The complexity of law and administration. In Australian Institute of Aboriginal Studies, *Aborigines and Uranium*, pp. 119–32. Canberra: Australian Government Publishing Service.

von Sturmer, J. 1984c. The social impact of mining: 2. Economic consequences: II Residence, resources, and inequities. In Australian Institute of Aboriginal Studies, *Aborigines and Uranium*, pp. 133–77. Canberra: Australian Government Publishing Service.

Wellings, P. 1995. Management considerations. In T. Press, D. Lea, A. Webb and A. Graham (eds), *Kakadu: Natural and Cultural Heritage and Management*, pp. 238–70. Darwin: Australian Nature Conservation Agency and North Australia Research Unit, The Australian National University.

# 5

# Conceptual Dynamism and Ambiguity in Marrangu Djinang Cosmology, North-Central Arnhem Land

Craig Elliott
Central Land Council

## Introduction

In a 1977 conference paper, 'Ambiguity in Yolngu Religious Language', Keen identified conceptual ambiguity as a critical cultural mechanism by which economies of knowledge and local group identities are reproduced in Arnhem Land thought and social life. The ethnographic interpretation of Yolngu conceptual indeterminancy produced a rich preoccupation in Keen's scholarship. This and related subjects were elaborated in his PhD thesis, 'One Ceremony, One Song' (1978), *Knowledge and Secrecy in an Aboriginal Religion* (1994) and in 'Metaphor and the Metalanguage' (1995). The 1977 paper highlighted the role of song language, within shared mythologies, in the process of creating difference amidst underlying socio-religious sameness (1977: 33). His thesis examined how a 'same song' interpretive technique both links and differentiates ownership of religious sacra in Yolngu belief and ceremonial practice (1978: 210–15; 1994: 132–64). These sources significantly contribute to understanding how constructs in the religious domain create and distribute social meanings in the Arnhem Land landscape, themes this paper pursues.

It is well recognised that cosmological and social classificatory systems routinely contain indeterminacies and ambiguities (Keen 1995: 507). In Arnhem Land cosmologies, little sociolinguistic distinction is made between corporeal and incorporeal entities (see Keen 1978: 42). Nor are sharp distinctions made about the conceptual aspects and boundaries of cosmological categories—anthropomorphic spirit beings, for example. It is therefore not surprising that many motifs convey a range of significations through analogy. Meaningful cultural interpretations are not entirely open-ended, but cued and referenced by local mythological, environmental, ceremonial and social contexts. For these reasons, while still noting that typologies exist, Keen rightly cautions against the categorisation of Arnhem Land spirit beings using 'unequivocal criteria' (1994: 45).

For Marrangu Djinang cosmology in north-central Arnhem Land, Borsboom (1978a, 1978b, 2011) and I (1991) have provided ethnographic evidence and analyses highlighting similar reservations. Specifically regarding the representation of *Merri*[1] and *Mewal*, two anthropomorphic spirit beings in Marrangu Djinang cosmology, there are richly multilayered and ambiguous significations at work. This paper first outlines Marrangu Djinang sociality, focusing on land and Arnhem Land local organisation, with reference to Keen's (1995) critique of that subject. The paper then employs a strongly local ethnographic perspective to describe and explain overlapping and ambiguous attributes of *Merri* and *Mewal*. The paper focuses on *Merri* and *Mewal*'s importance in the local environment and in Marrangu Djinang cosmology, song, ceremony, and mortality and affliction beliefs. The analysis proceeds with Keen's caution concerning unequivocal analytical categorisation of Yolngu ontological concepts firmly in mind.

## Marrangu Djinang Land and Identity

The physical environment of north-central Arnhem Land is dominated by dry eucalyptus forest and Darwin stringybark (*Eucalyptus tetradonta*) in particular. The eucalypt forests of Marrangu Djinang country are drained by two watercourses, Djimbi and Gattji Creeks. North of the forest areas are seasonally flooding and semi-tidal lowlands. Here Gattji and Djimbi Creeks peter out: the former into a series of swamps; the latter into a jungle waterhole. Mangrove-lined saltwater estuary systems, tidal plains and mud flats, and a band of paperbark swamps cut across the northern (near-coastal) part of Marrangu country.

---

1   Spelt 'Mere' by Borsboom (1978a, 1978b), who also spells Marrangu with one 'r' only.

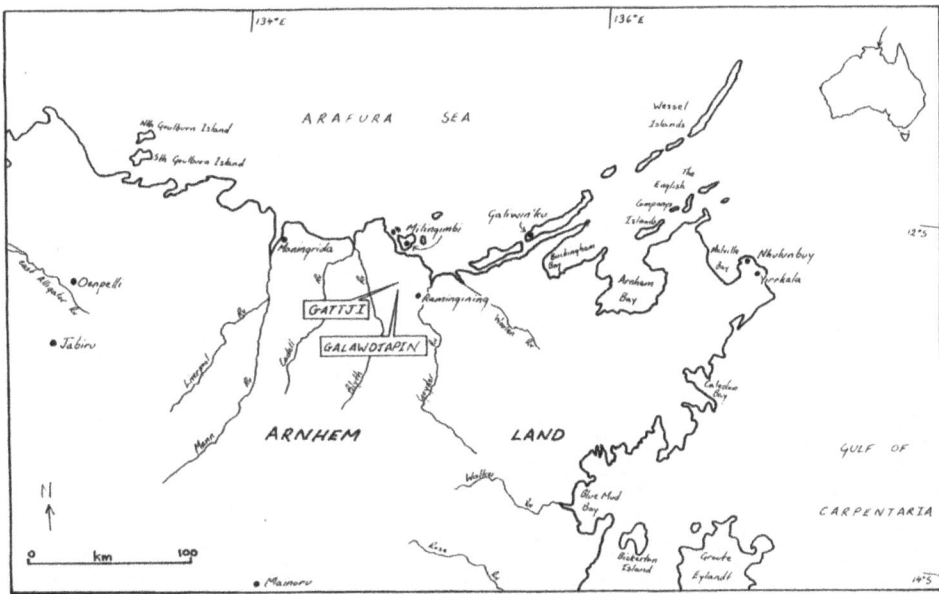

Figure 5.1 Location Map—North-central Arnhem Land, Australia.
Source: Craig Elliott.

The homelands Galawdjapin and Gattji are located beside Gattji Creek.² Gattji is a traditional Wulaki place of residence and is a 'big name' place.³ Missionaries from Milingimbi Mission visited Gattji prior to World War II, established a garden there and exchanged goods such as tea, sugar, flour, jam, cloth and tobacco for sacred objects. Gattji and another Djinang outstation, 'Gillere' (Gulidi), were visited by Donald Thomson (see Peterson 1976: 104) in 1936–37. Galawdjapin was established as a homeland much more recently, in 1974. At that time several Marrangu, Mildjingi and Ganalbingu people left Maningrida, where most had been resident since the early 1960s, and moved back to ancestral lands.

Keen (1995) has thoroughly critiqued the inadequacy of simplistic, taxonomical anthropological constructs such as 'clan', 'phratry', 'dialect' and 'tribe' to explain Arnhem Land local organisation. Keen argues much ethnographic description consists of converting conceptual metaphors viewed as 'causal' by the subjects of the ethnography, into the 'symbolic' semantic domain of the anthropological metalanguage (ibid.: 504–5). Examples of this conversion process in Arnhem Land ethnography, Keen argues, are variations of *mala* into 'clan'; *matha* as 'dialect group'; and *ba:purru* as 'phratry' (ibid.: 506–7). Comparing early and

---

2   The part of this watercourse adjacent to and south of Galawdjapin homeland is named Galawdjapin Creek.
3   While Gattji is on Wulaki country, the contemporary population there is majority Marrangu Djinang. Marrangu people live at Gattji by virtue of (generations of) intermarriage, and thereby are able to 'look after' Wulaki land, their mother's country.

later analyses, the ethnographic record of Arnhem Land contains anomalies and inconsistencies in the interpretative conversion of Yolngu concepts into anthropological categories (ibid.: 507, Table 1). As an ethnographic region, Arnhem Land is far from unique in exhibiting inconsistency between early and later ethnographers' interpretations of local concepts.

Marrangu Djinang[4] sociality exhibits layers of interconnected local organisation based on the reference points of language, land, kin and Dreaming narrative. I elucidate these layers with reference to the relevant Djinang terms and the anthropological labels with greatest continuing, albeit contested, currency in the literature. I do so mindful of the undoubted and pervasive inadequacies of the hierarchical anthropological models purporting to represent Arnhem Land concepts, as critiqued by Keen.

The Djinang-speaking Marrangu *mala* or clan belongs to the Dhuwungi patrimoiety.[5] The residential population of Galawdjapin and Gattji is made up of the local Marrangu Djinang landowners, their affines, children and individuals from adjacent clan lands who normally intermarry with Marrangu Djinang. *Mala* whose countries either border, have reciprocal food-gathering rights with Marrangu Djinang people, and/or whose country Marrangu Djinang people *djaga* ('look after')[6] are Wulaki, Yalungirri, Djadiwitjibi, Murrungun,[7] Rembarrnga,[8] Ganalbingu and Balmbi. Marrangu Djinang people have *guardianship rights* in the sense meant by Morphy (1984: 28–9) over the territory one of these groups, Rembarrnga, because the original Rembarrnga-speaking *mala* is extinct. Both Wulaki and Ganalbingu *mala* intermarry with Marrangu Djinang people, and thus 'look after' their mother's country. This means they have rights to paint their 'mother' clan's Dreamings and are obliged to perform certain ceremonial duties for their 'mother' clan. Other clan countries Marrangu Djinang people 'look after', and call 'mother', are Djadiwitjibi, Mildjingi and Murrungun (all Yirritjing moiety).

---

4   I employ the label 'Marrangu Djinang' in the paper title and throughout mindful of the history and reported inconsistencies of such labels in the ethnographic literature (for example, see Berndt 1976: 145–59; and Keen 1995: 508). The label 'Marrangu Djinang' has some similarities with Berndt's '*mada* [*matha*]-*mala* pair', in that it combines socio-religious and linguistic elements. It is only in their combination, consistent with the usage in this paper, that *Marrangu Djinang* denotes a local territory with focal sites and affiliated set of people and sacra. Each term—*Marrangu* and *Djinang*—when employed separately has potential to denote a range of additional cultural references.
5   *Dhuwungi* is the Djinang name for the patrimoiety known in northeast Arnhem Land as Dhuwa or Dua. The Djinang name for the opposite patrimoiety is *Yirritjing* (known in northeast Arnhem Land as Yirritja). For an account of the Dhuwungi moiety foundational Djang'kawu mythology, see Bagshaw (2008: 33–7).
6   See Berndt (1976: 156) and Keen (1995: 513) for comparable usages of this term.
7   This is a Wulaki-speaking, Yirritjing moiety Murrungun clan, not the Dhuwungi moiety Murrungun clan associated with the *Djareware* (Wild Honey) Dreaming.
8   'Rembarrnga' is included here in its *mala* or clan sense. 'Rembarrnga' is also a *matha* or dialect name.

*Marrangu* is also the name that identifies the group of *mala* (clans) that share a single Dreaming track or property (*baparru* or *ba:purru, babaru, bapurru*). In the Marrangu case, the shared Dreaming is *Djareware* or *Yarrpany* (Wild Honey or Sugar Bag).[9] Social and ceremonial interconnectedness through *baparru* is a feature of *mala* organisation across Arnhem Land (see Morphy 1990: 316; Keen 1995: 514–6; Bagshaw 2008: 32–3), although inclusive interrelationships based upon language (*yan*), dialect (*matha*), territoriality and intermarriage (*djungkai/djunggayi*) and reciprocal ceremonial ties are also significant.

Based on my research with Marrangu Djinang people, the term *baparru* has a number of applications. Primarily, *baparru* refers to the aggregate of same-patrimoiety *mala* that share a Dreaming (or other form of *maḏayin* or religious property) and whose countries contain sites named in that story.[10] At Galawdjapin and Gattji the word *baparru-a* is further used to denote the gathering of kin at a burial and its associated ceremonies. Others (for example, Berndt 1955: 96; Thomson 1975: 6; Hiatt 1965: 20) have noted interchangeable usages of *baparru* and *mala* elsewhere in Arnhem Land, suggesting *baparru* may mean both the Dreaming-based affiliations of several *mala* (the sense used here) *and* the patrilineal landowning group *mala*. My research at Galawdjapin and Gattji recorded the former usage of *baparru*, though the term undoubtedly has extended applications (see Keen 1995: 514).

Additional to Marrangu Djinang, the Marrangu *baparru* consists of *Dhuwungi* patrimoiety *mala* with the following names and geographical affiliations:[11] Murrungun (Raymangirr, near Lake Evella/Gapuwiyak)[12]; Djambarrpuyngu (Elcho Island, Galiwin'ku); Wagilak (Roper River); Burarra (Glyde River); Marrakulu (Trial Bay); and Kulumula (Wessel Islands[13]). According to Djinang Marrangu, all these *mala* may be identifiable as 'Marrangu' and form part of the Marrangu *baparru*. The *mala* that make up the Marrangu *baparru* are geographically widespread, located along the northwesterly journey of the *Djareware* (Wild Honey) Dreaming track. On this basis, all Marrangu *mala* are said to share 'one track' and, despite linguistic differences, 'one song'.

---

9   As is explained below, the Marrangu Djinang version of this mythology, *Mewal* and *Djareware* Dreaming, is a variation highlighting localised events and interrelationships within this more broadly shared mythology.
10  Keen (1995: 514–5) describes similar applications of the term 'ba:purru'. This kind of configuration has been called 'phratry' by Warner (1937/1958: 33) and 'totemic unions' by Shapiro (1981: 23).
11  I recognise that the labels noted here are not used in an entirely consistent way to denote a singular 'level' of social organisation. Each of the names cited here operates as a linguistic label, as well as being part of *mala* and *baparru* formations. For example, Djambarrpuyngu refers to a linguistic unit, a patrifilial group and an aggregation of several patrifilial groups (Peter Toner, personal communication). It is reasonable to say that Arnhem Landers use a range of self-referential names, and a range to refer to others. Each label can, depending on the logic of the social and geographical context, represent a more or less inclusive 'level' of group representation.
12  Clan territory locations are approximations only.
13  Ian Keen (personal communication).

*Mala* making up the Marrangu *baparru* exchange closely related and ceremonially powerful sacred property (*ma_d_ayin*), such as names, songs, ceremonial acts and objects, between each other, and direct ceremonies such as mortuary rites on each other's behalf. The high value placed upon knowledge and ownership of such property (designs, sand sculpture, ceremonies and songs) means these exchanges are an important expression of both *mala* autonomy and *baparru* interconnectedness. Taylor (1987: 381) has observed that *baparru* is a highly abstract concept with little bearing upon on-the-ground groupings, but that *baparru* relations between *mala* highlight the notion that spiritual unity transcends geographic, political and linguistic differences. *Mala* within the same *baparru* do not share in toto the same Dreaming property as each other. Along their shared Dreaming track, each *mala* highlights (in song and ceremonies) mythic aspects most relevant to themselves and their country. Marrangu Djinang emphasise that part of the *Djareware*'s journey that occurs along Djimbi Creek. Similarly, while both Djambarrpuyngu and Marrangu Djinang sing Stringybark tree *manikay,* each emphasises slightly different aspects. This custom is typically described as 'same but different'—a feature axiomatic of *baparru* relations in Arnhem Land.

Other names, all referencing local cosmology, regarded as uniquely identifying Marrangu Djinang *mala* are *Warnambi*, *Wurrkiganydjarr*,[14] *Mewal* and *Mungurrpi*. *Warnambi* and *Wurrkiganydjarr* both relate to the Stringybark tree; *Warnambi* to the tree itself while *Wurrkiganydjarr* denotes 'stringybark flower' (Borsboom 1978b: 28). Literally, '*wurrkiganydjarr*' translates as 'flower power', '*wurrki*' means flower while '*ganydjarr*' means 'power, ability, strength, stamina' (Waters 1983: 41, 114).[15] *Mewal*, the Spirit Being companion of *Djareware*, is a term used by others to address Djinang Marrangu people in public spaces, such as at nearby Ramingining. The rarely employed fourth term, *Mungurrpi*, refers to Marrangu Djinang people *at* Galawdjapin.

The Marrangu Djinang *mala* is made up of 'bottom' and 'top' parts or *companies*, known as *Nongere* (or *Mongon* or *Mongonirri*) and *Guraknere*, respectively, with roughly similar numbers.[16] Most *Nongere* individuals live at Galawdjapin and Gattji; and most *Guraknere* (or 'top') Marrangu Djinang reside at or near Ramingining. The division has a mythological foundation, when the *Djareware*

---

14   Spelt 'Wurgigandjar' by Borsboom (1978a, 1978b).
15   The name 'Wurrkiganydjarr' was given to the Djinang Marrangu people by another clan, the Djambarrpuyngu-speaking Marrangu clan (Borsboom 1978b: 28).
16   Taylor's Kunwinjku informants translated the word 'company', in the context of intra-clan division, as 'follow each other', 'mix together', 'we share' and 'all one family' (1987: 86–7). I received virtually identical glosses relating to *Nongere* and *Guraknere*. Additional to intra-clan divisions, however, 'company' is frequently used by Marrangu people to describe intermarrying clans (that is, *between* clans in a 'mother' or *djungkai* relationship). There is some crossover in these two senses of 'company', since the intra-clan *Nongere* and *Guraknere* subgroups structure marriage arrangements with *djungkai* clans. See also Keen's (1978: 214) findings concerning 'company' usage at Milingimbi.

(Honey) Being used a stone axe to cut Marrangu country into two parts, thus forming *Nongere* and *Guraknere* (Borsboom 1978b: 72). The interrelationship is further imaged in body metaphor, in that *Guraknere* means the neck or apex of the spine (hence 'top') while *Nongere* denotes the 'bottom' of the spine.[17] Both *Nongere* and *Guraknere* contain sites connected with *Djareware* Dreaming and both are considered owners of all Marrangu Djinang land and the spiritual property associated with it, but each differs in relationship to neighbouring clans. For example, *Nongere* Marrangu is adjacent to Wulaki country, whereas *Guraknere* Marrangu country, to the southeast, adjoins Ganalbingu country. *Nongere* Marrangu marry with the Wulaki-speaking *mala* named Djelaworwor, and are thus *djungkai* for Wulaki country, whereas *Guraknere* Marrangu marry with their Ganalbingu-speaking neighbours and have *djungkai* responsibilities towards Ganalbingu *mala* territory.

## *Mewal* and *Merri* in Marrangu Djinang Cosmological Landscapes

*Merri* and *Mewal* are anthropomorphic spirit beings believed to inhabit the Marrangu Djinang landscape, and are attributed significations in ceremonial practices, especially mortuary rites, and bodily experience. The local founding narrative in Marrangu Djinang belief is the *Mewal* and *Djareware* (Wild Honey) Dreaming. In this mythology, *Mewal*, imaged as part bee and part woman, collected honey in Marrangu Djinang country (as people continue to do). As a substance containing eggs, in Marrangu belief honey contains 'spirit children', and therefore conceptive power. *Mewal* is also an emblem of Marrangu Djinang origins, identity and continuity, through transformative acts such as the designation of places in Marrangu country as '*Mewal*' sites; the symbolic use of white down body decoration in Marrangu ceremonies; and in the *Mewal* ceremonies (*bunggul*), enacted during mortuary rites, where the deceased's bones become emblems of ancestral and clan regeneration. The *Djareware* Dreaming unites all Marrangu clans but *Mewal*, as an entity within this mythic tradition specific to Marrangu Djinang, highlights the clan's identity within overall *baparru* organisation.

But *Mewal* is not all 'good' in Marrangu Djinang cosmological symbolism. *Mewal* is 'bad, but him not all bad', as revered Marrangu ancestor Dick Miwirri (now deceased) once told me. In the *Mewal* and *Djareware* Dreaming, *Mewal* inhabits monsoonal jungles. These localised landscapes are both impenetrable

---

17 Body imagery as metaphors for social group constitution and reproduction are elaborate and pervasive in Arnhem Land; see Keen (1978: 281–334; 1995: 509–13).

physical environments and symbolically unsocialised, malignant realms in Marrangu cosmology. The significance of *Mewal* as founder of clan identity is thus multilayered, complicated by association with these symbolically malign cosmological 'landscapes'. *Mewal* joins *Merri*, the other Marrangu Djinang anthropomorphic spirit being, to roam in the jungle at night, making distracting sounds so people lose direction. In this form, *Mewal* is believed a corruption of the human body, ugly, deformed or skeletal only. In behaviour this *Mewal* is asocial, and, like *Merri*, evokes negative sentiments associated with the physical (and cosmological) jungle environment. Alongside this, *Mewal* is believed to have interacted congenially with the earliest human beings, teaching them and bestowing rights in songs[18] and dances (that is, *madayin* property). The belief that words in *manikay* (clan songs) are learnt from the spirits of the dead exemplifies this interaction.

There are 13 Marrangu Djinang *manikay* song subjects. The *manikay* songs celebrate the actions of Dreaming (*Wangarr*) beings including, in the present case, *Djareware*, *Mewal* and *Merri*.[19] In *manikay* performance, each song consists of formulaic recitations of name words[20] that connote interrelationships within Marrangu Djinang land and cosmology. The 13 Marrangu Djinang *manikay* songs are sung in a consistent (though, in practice, rarely identical) order and are thematically grouped, shown in Table 5.1. The left-hand column lists the 13 Marrangu Djinang *manikay* song subjects[21]; the centre column shows groupings as described to the current author; and the right-hand column shows Borsboom's 'sub-clusters' of the same song cycle.

The *manikay* subjects relate to cosmological categories and 'top to bottom' ecological sectors within Marrangu Djinang country. The '*Mewal* songs' (centre column) and Borsboom's 'Gravel sub-cluster' (right column) include subjects associated with the driest and most inland Marrangu country, dominated by stringybark trees, the flowers (*wurrki*) of which provide pollen for honeybees. The '*Gapi*' or Water group of songs cover subjects associated with wetland parts of Marrangu country—fish species and wet season rains and floodwater. My 'ungrouped' and Borsboom's 'Jungle' sub-cluster includes entities found in monsoonal thickets, or believed to inhabit parallel cosmological realms,

---

18   As Keen noted, the Liyagalawumirr clan also has a song subject named *Mewal* (author's fieldnotes).
19   See Clunies Ross (1978: 129) for an overview of the *manikay* song genre of Arnhem Land song.
20   These name or song words are often not found in everyday discourse, and therefore not all are to be found in dictionaries of the Djinang language (such as Waters 1983). This song word characteristic is typical of Arnhem Land song (see Hiatt and Hiatt 1966: 2) and indeed, of song in oral traditions worldwide (see Merriam 1964: 189).
21   The 13 *manikay* song subjects do not represent the entire corpus of Marrangu Djinang Dreamings—there are other significant Marrangu cosmological entities not represented in the *manikay* cycle. These include, for example, *Bullia* (saltwater catfish), *Dupun/Bardurru* (hollow log), *Bordjirrai* (forked stick), *Mulitji* (fish trap), *Warbalulu* or *Murla* (pelican), *Djarrka* (freshwater water goanna), *Ragi* (lily root) and several Cloud Dreamings.

in the mid-zone of Marrangu land. In these dense forest areas, such as at Djambi and Bumbaldjarri, freshwater creeks meet swampy, seasonally flooding lowlands.[22] However, the four 'ungrouped' *manikay* (Table 5.1, centre column) are not structured by any single cosmological or ecological characteristic but are transitional motifs, and thus positioned in the song cycle between '*Mewal*' and '*Gapi*' songs. The cycle abides to the 'most typical' associations (Borsboom 1978b: 74), with the less typical linkages as the transitional motifs. Marrangu people recognise the unity of the cycle overall. This is evidenced in statements that all *manikay* are 'Our Dream', reflecting an understanding that the complex interrelationships between the *manikay* songs bind the cycle together.

### Table 5.1 Groupings of Marrangu Djinang *manikay* song subjects.

| Marrangu Djinang *Manikay* song subjects | Author's sub-groupings | Borsboom's sub-clusters (1978a: 114; 1978b: 71). |
|---|---|---|
|  | ***Mewal* songs** | **'Gravel' sub-cluster** |
| 1. *Gundui* (Stringybark Tree)[a] | *Gundui* (Stringybark Tree) | *Gundui* (Stringybark Tree) |
| 2. *Djareware* (Wild Honey) | *Djareware* (Wild Honey) | *Djareware* (Wild Honey) |
| 3. *Geganggie* (Friar Bird) | *Geganggie* (Friar Bird) | *Geganggie* (Friar Bird) |
| 4. *Wak Wak* (Crow) | *Mewal* (Spirit Being) | *Wak Wak* (Crow) |
| 5. *Mewal* (Spirit Being) | *Merri* (Spirit Being) |  |
|  | **Ungrouped** | **'Jungle' sub-cluster** |
| 6. *Merri* (Spirit Being) | *Wak Wak* (Crow) | *Mewal* (Spirit Being) |
| 7. *Djudo-Djudo* (Tawny Frogmouth) | *Djudo-Djudo* (Tawny Frogmouth) | *Merri* (Spirit Being) |
| 8. *Narge Narge* (Possum) | *Narge Narge* (Possum) | *Djudo-Djudo* (Tawny Frogmouth) |
| 9. *Gulwirri* (Cabbage Palm) | *Gulwirri* (Cabbage Palm) | *Narge Narge* (Possum) |
|  | ***Gapi* songs** | **'Water' sub-cluster** |
| 10. *Morgal* (Mud Cod) | *Morgal* (Mud Cod) | *Gulwirri* (Cabbage Palm) |
| 11. *Wudurbal* (Bream) | *Wudurbal* (Bream) | *Morgal* (Mud Cod) |
| 12. *Bara* (northwest Monsoon) | *Wunggutj Gapi* (Floodwater) | *Wudurbal* (Bream) |
| 13. *Wunggutj Gapi* (Floodwater) | *Bara* (northwest Monsoon) | *Wunggutj Gapi* (Floodwater) |
|  |  | *Bara* (northwest Monsoon) |

[a] Alternate Djinang names for stringybark trees are *balatj*, *bemborlai* or *dirrka*.

---

22 As White (2003: 193–9) has observed, Arnhem Land cultural landscapes and aesthetics are complex and do not parallel Euro-Australian notions of beauty. Rather than visual appeal, it is the sacred character of a place that, in Yolngu thought, makes a place significant and memorable. In the case of Djambi and Bumbaldjarri, they are highly significant in Marrangu Djinang belief because of their centrality in *manikay* and *Djareware* mythology, despite being mosquito-infested, swampy and largely impenetrable.

The '*Mewal* songs' and '*Gapi* songs' *manikay* groupings reference two important mythic narratives in Marrangu cosmology: *Mewal* and *Djareware* Dreaming (discussed above) and *Bullia-Gapi* Dreaming. The latter mythology, *Bullia* (Saltwater Catfish) and *Gapi* (Water), references the final phase of Marrangu Djinang mortuary rites known as *Bardurru* (or *Dupun* or *Larrgan*), when crushed bones of the deceased are placed in a hollow log coffin. In *Bullia-Gapi* Dreaming, seasonal floodwaters (*Wunggutj Gapi*) inundate the coastal plains, filling fresh and saltwater creeks where fish species—*Wudurbal* (bream) and *Morgal* (mud cod)—live. These fish, which in Marrangu belief symbolise *wuguli* (*birrimbirr*) eternal spirits of the dead, are caught in *muḻitji* (fish traps) imaged as a pelican's (*warbululu*) gullet. *Muḻitji* and *warbalulu* are cosmologically associated with the northwest horizon, the direction of monsoonal rains (*Bara*) and location of Gorriba Island, spiritual home for deceased Marrangu individuals and the *Merri* Spirit Being named *Luma Luma*. *Bullia* is not a named Marrangu *manikay* song subject,[23] but is a conception Dreaming in Marrangu belief. The *Bullia-Gapi* Dreaming is thus highly significant in Marrangu eschatological beliefs and associated mortuary practices.

That *Mewal* (and *Merri*) appear in different groupings in the typologies (see Table 5.1) highlights that there are two shifting aspects to the *Mewal* spirit being: *Mewal* is the Dreaming creator allied with *Djareware*; and, additionally, a malign jungle spirit that interacts with *Merri* and spirits of the dead. Through this polysemy *Mewal* is a symbol conveying the idea of ancestral regeneration after death—a pivotal theme of the extended mortuary customs in north-central Arnhem Land. In this *Mewal* is closely analogous with *wuguli*, the immortal spirit aspect in Marrangu Djinang belief, that survives death and returns to clan country or to a spirit realm with physical referent (Gorriba Island).

While sharing a jungle landscape and some associated attributes, the *Merri* spirit (in both its 'dead body' and jungle form), and in partial contrast with *Mewal*, is a concept conveying unsettling ideas about mortality, daily human experience and bodily well-being. For example, mishaps and bad dreams are blamed on *Merri's* diffuse, unpredictable and malignant presence in the landscape, especially in local monsoonal jungle thickets and at night. As 'dead body' spirit, *Merri* is held to exist somewhere between lived and Dreaming realities. *Merri* is associated with bodily attachment and the decay of a corpse immediately after death. *Merri* spirits are thought an anathema to the continuity of social stability and individual life: they are believed to alter paths, foot tracks and landforms, cause disputation, interrupt conception processes and intercept *wuguli* spirits of the deceased, thus preventing ancestral reunion. *Merri* has

---

23  On one performance occasion during research, however, I was told that *Bullia* (or *Djikada*) was sung as a separate *manikay* subject (Elliott 1991: 100).

the further aspect of 'dead body' spirit and spirits of the longer-term dead who live at Gorriba (an 'island of the dead' off the north-central Arnhem Land coast). The cosmological significance of Gorriba Island with 'dead body' spirits parallels the association of Djambi and Bumbaldjarri, the main two monsoonal jungle sites within Marrangu country. *Mewal*, on the other hand, is not involved in unsettling daily experience and is considered more benign, independent, transcendent and intangible than *Merri*. Without overdrawing the contrast, in Morphy's (1990: 313) terms *Mewal* is closer to a Creator Being whereas *Merri* more resembles an Inheritance Being.

Figure 5.2 *Merri* and *Mewal* in Marrangu Djinang art and ceremony.

Top left: Bark painting showing (at top) the two spirit women 'Miwal' (*Mewal*) and 'Wanu-wanu' collected at Milingimbi in 1948 (in Mountford 1956: 390). The long panel in the middle is the central pole supporting the bark hut built by the two spirit women at 'Djimba' (Djimbi Creek). Inside the panel the dots represent bees and honeycomb. Top middle: Two sculptures representing *Merri* as a mother and daughter pair produced by George Putti (deceased) at Galawdjapin Homeland in 1989. The cross-hatching, termed *gumununggu*, is the Marrangu Djinang design for *Merri*. Top right: Sculpture representing *Merri* as a 'dead body' spirit produced by Andrew Margululu (deceased) at Galawdjapin Homeland in 1989. The *gumununggu* cross-hatching on stomach is complemented by skeletal 'ribs' on the chest. Bottom right: Marrangu Djinang *bunggul* (song with dance) enacting mythology where Mewal searches for *Djareware* (honey) following honeybees from Raymangirr in Marrangu Murrungun country, northeast Arnhem Land. The white line hanging above the dancers represents flying honeybees. This *bunggul* occurred during the *wirgugu* (wake) for an elder Marrangu Djinang man, Gattji, 1995. Bottom left: Marrangu Djinang perform *Mewal bunggul* at Ramingining in January 2013. This *bunggul* occurred during the *wirgugu* (wake) for a senior Marrangu Djinang man.

Sources: Bark painting: C.P. Mountford (Melbourne University Press); all photos: Craig Elliott.

As jungle spirit, *Merri* exists in various forms: in human form, usually with a deformity or as a child; in animal form (as flying fox, native cat or frog); or as an incorporeal 'ghost'. The 'dead body' *Merri* is identified with the putrefying corpse and the 'homeless' wandering spirit believed to separate from the body at death. At death this wandering spirit is thought acutely dangerous, as it hopelessly tries to return to the living community. This 'dead body' *Merri* spirit is believed to be encountered in dreams of violence and disaster, and to cause accidents, arguments and physical ailments. With the passing of time the 'dead body' spirit withdraws from the living and joins other spirits of the dead at Gorriba and in the jungle landscapes, shedding identity with the deceased individual in the process, though not entirely—the 'dead body' *Merri* spirit may withdraw but continues visiting places and people associated with the deceased.

A further significant quality of *Merri* (especially in its most 'concretely' malignant 'dead body' spirit aspect) follows from its recognised form and unique position in Marrangu ontology. *Merri* is a highly effective and valued socialising agent, orienting individuals towards sanctioned behaviours and roles from an early age. Children soon learn to fear wandering in the dark alone because when they do adults point and shout *'merri'* (or *'mokuy'*) and hold aloft a buffalo skull. Children quickly connect these actions with danger. *Merri* operates to legitimate the positive value placed on community and family bonds because emotional or mental disturbance and antisocial behaviour (e.g. eating alone, walking alone, sulkiness, silence) is accounted for as a malign predilection brought on by the agency of *Merri*. This is a culturally preferred explanation that avoids blaming an individual.

The contradictions and ambiguities in the attributions, significations and interrelationships between *Merri* and *Mewal* demonstrate the importance of these figures in Marrangu cosmology, ontology, geography and socialisation. *Mewal* and *Merri* are an important but not all-inclusive component of Marrangu Djinang thought. There are many more Dreaming beings and relationships involving different Marrangu cosmological entities.

# Accounting for Ambiguity and Form in *Mewal* and *Merri* Beliefs

The *Mewal* and *Merri* spirit beings occupy different but shifting and overlapping positions in Marrangu Djinang cosmology. There are cultural, geographical and historical demographic reasons that account for the ambiguities in the significations of *Mewal* and *Merri* in Marrangu thought. *Mewal* and *Merri* interpenetrate across aspects of cosmology, landscape, the life cycle and daily experience. *Mewal* and *Merri* do not correspond, in any singular straightforward way, with visible (or invisible) referents. *Mewal* and *Merri* are conceptually similar symbols which may at times have an acknowledged physical manifestation. At other times they do not. In these circumstances, discrepancies in the significations people attribute to them are apt to arise. People do not point to objects, in the way they can for honeybees or Stringybark trees, and say 'that is *Merri*' or 'that is *Mewal*'. Only by recognised and shared symbolic association can, for example, a corpse or a carving be called '*Merri*'; or skeletal remains or a painting of a human female collecting honey be called '*Mewal*'.

Geography and demography partially accounts for ambiguities and localised coalescence of cosmological beliefs. Galawdjapin and Gattji homelands, with predominantly Marrangu Djinang and Wulaki speakers, respectively, are two kilometres apart. The interpenetration of Marrangu Djinang and Wulaki belief systems is evident in the case of *Mewal*. Wulaki cosmology recognises a Being named *Ganingalkngalk* and Wulaki speakers sometimes use the Marrangu term '*Mewal*' to describe their Being. Like *Mewal*, *Ganingalkngalk* is both a creator Being *and* a malevolent jungle entity: for example, *Ganingalkngalk* created Gattji lagoon, an important Wulaki clan site; elsewhere in Wulaki cosmology *Ganingalkngalk* is a jungle-living '*meri*' with responsibility for the '*larkan*' hollow log coffin (see Thomson [Peterson] 1976: 103). Similarly, at Ramingining and Milingimbi, Djinang speakers use the Gupapuyngu words *mokuy* coterminously with *Merri*; and *birrimbirr* as an alternative for the Djinang term *wuguli*.

Post-war demographic change in Arnhem Land, chiefly to mission- or government-established communities, has increased the diffusion of concepts from other regional dialects and languages (interaction with Gupapuyngu at Milingimbi, Kunwinjku at Maningrida, or Rembarrnga at Beswick, for example). Borsboom cites the case of a Marrangu Djinang man who had, after years living at Bamyili on the Beswick (70 kilometres east of Katherine) acquired the Rembarrnga language word 'Bolung' which he applied, seemingly without contradiction, to both *Merri* and *Djareware* (Borsboom 1978b: 54–5). This acculturation process—aided by demographic and linguistic factors, leading to the incorporation and consolidation of names, categories and episodes, and extension of existing beliefs—has a long history in northern Australia.[24]

In part due to the introduction of Christian mission-derived oppositional ideas ('body' and 'soul', 'heaven' and 'hell') local cosmological concepts have become less internally differentiated and nuanced, with certain scenarios being truncated and consolidated with others. For example, the *Merri* being named *Luma Luma* of Gorriba Island has its own Dreaming scenarios and associated

---

24  For example, Macknight (1980: 139–40) cites the introduction of Papuan burial customs in the Tiwi Islands; and Warner describes use of Macassan designed masts in 'Murngin' mortuary rites (1937/1958: 433).

sites and ceremonies, but respondents often claimed the *Luma Luma Merri* was simply a synonym for either the 'dead body' *Merri* of the recent dead, or of the longer-term dead. Finer correlations remain existent, but the process of historical syncretism is leading to a less elaborately integrated and increasingly imprecise framework of eschatological speculations. The scope of the *Merri* figure in Marrangu eschatology has, superficially at least, been simplified as a result of assimilation with Christian notions. Marrangu people see no contradiction in the incorporation of Christian ideas within their own cosmology. In the idiom of Aboriginal English, both sets of beliefs are viewed as 'straight', containing truth and 'the Law'. People at Galawdjapin and Gattji profess their belief in Christianity to be a harmonious adjunct to Marrangu cosmology. There is no sense in which Christian ideas are seen as incompatible with local cosmological categorisations.

There is evidence from elsewhere in Aboriginal Australia that the process of systematic investigation itself has highlighted ambiguities in Indigenous beliefs that are of little concern to believers themselves. Stanner (1963: 260), in his investigation of Murinbata 'pure', 'clan' and 'creature' spirits, observed that 'there was no difficulty in getting the Murinbata to agree that their traditions left much unclear, but the conflicts were evidently of little interest to them'. He goes on, noting how systematic enquiry led to the unearthing of apparent inconsistencies in Murinbata belief:

> All the mythic personages seemed clear cut in ordinary conversation but lost outline or became shadowed by ambiguity under closer study. It seemed to me precisely that property which allowed both their mythological and ritual development ... Eventually I saw the wisdom of not forcing the ideas to a precision that was not in them. (p. 265)

Clunies Ross and Hiatt, too, in the case of mythic interpretations of a ground sculpture at a Gidjingali *Larrgan* (*Bardurru*) mortuary ceremony, found an insistence on coherent interpretations forced ambiguities to come to light where they 'might never have become overt' (1977: 139). My hosts at Galawdjapin and Gattji fielded my enquiries, though few professed an appetite to investigate the ambiguities of *Mewal* and *Merri*. The belief that *Mewal* and *Merri* exist, as evidenced by transformations in Marrangu cosmology and country, *manikay* and ceremony, was proof and knowledge enough. A closely related point here is Keen's recognition that there is a fundamental difference between objectivising anthropological analyses of concepts, on one hand, and Yolngu ontological commitment to the reality of, or living with, those concepts (1995: 505) on the other. Researchers' repeated and understandable inquiries about conceptual meaning, based on our analytical drive to explain ambiguities and generate valid generalisations, contain no ontological commitment actually to live with those concepts, rich ambiguities and all.

## Conclusion

Cosmological categorisations are an arena of human thought and practice marked by indeterminacy, interpenetration of ideas and dynamic change. This is especially so in oral traditions, but Judeo-Christian traditions exhibit similar characteristics. Consider, for example, the historical diffusion of alternate imaginings concerning angels, saints, devils and demons. In Arnhem Land, cosmological beliefs do not constitute fully integrated and harmonious encapsulations of socio-religious reality. Marrangu Djinang cosmology is not a unified, fully integrated body of beliefs. Other Yolngu clan cosmologies have been characterised as 'chunks' or 'heaps' of Dreaming scenarios 'lumped together' (Morphy 1990: 326; see also Keen 1987: 103). The aptness of these terms is arguable as they may suggest indiscriminate selection. It is true that Djinang Marrangu cosmological beliefs place profound, transformative episodes alongside seemingly inconsequential events, significant elements contrasting sharply with those of (apparently) less weight. It is not a stabilised, all-encompassing system admitting only singular, coherent or complete interpretations. Marrangu Djinang *manikay*, for instance, is a selective extrapolation of thematically linked and proximately grouped Dreaming entities, drawn from a larger and richer corpus of potential mythic scenarios and emblems.

Conceptual dynamism in belief systems engages change and active ambiguity as an explanatory device. This process produces contradictory interrelationships, not seamless integration. Conceptual ambiguity and semantic dynamism are features of Marrangu Djinang cosmological and social categories. *Mewal* and *Merri* overlap considerably in Marrangu Djinang cosmology, art, song, mortuary beliefs and practices, lifecycle beliefs and, perhaps most significantly, in the cultural landscape. The coalescence of these ideational, ceremonial, experiential and geographic realities makes finding precise contextual denotations difficult. This analysis bears out Ian Keen's findings (1977, 1978, 1994, 1995) that the creation and reproduction of Yolngu social meanings are buttressed by conceptual indeterminacy and ambiguity, features that are integral to Arnhem Land religion, and religious traditions more broadly.

## References

Bagshaw, G. 2008. The physical and cultural dimensions of the Yalangbara area. In M. West (ed.), *Yalangbara: Art of the Djang'kawu,* pp. 31–44. Darwin: Museum and Art Gallery of the Northern Territory.

Berndt, R.M. 1955. 'Murngin' (Wulamba) social organization. *American Anthropologist* 57: 84–106.

Berndt, R.M. 1976. Territoriality and the problem of demarcating sociocultural space. In N. Peterson (ed.), *Tribes and Boundaries in Australia*, pp. 131–61. Canberra: Australian Institute of Aboriginal Studies.

Borsboom, A.P. 1978a. Dreaming clusters among Marrangu clans. In L.R. Hiatt (ed.), *Australian Aboriginal Concepts*, pp. 106–20. Canberra: Australian Institute of Aboriginal Studies.

Borsboom, A.P. 1978b. Maradjiri: A Modern Ritual Complex in Arnhem Land, North Australia. PhD Thesis, Katholieke Universiteit, Nijmegen.

Borsboom, A.P. 2011. Yolngu ways of knowing country. Paper presented at 'Barks, Birds and Billabongs: An International Symposium Exploring the Legacy of the 1948 American-Australian Scientific Expedition to Arnhem Land'. Canberra: National Museum of Australia.

Clunies Ross, M. 1978. The structure of Arnhem Land song-poetry. *Oceania* 49: 128–56.

Clunies Ross, M. and L.R. Hiatt. 1977. Sand sculptures at a Gidjingali burial rite. In P.J. Ucko (ed.), *Form in Indigenous Art*, pp. 131–46. Canberra: Australian Institute of Aboriginal Studies.

Elliott, C.N. 1991. '*Mewal* is *Merri's* Name': Form and Ambiguity in Marrangu Cosmology, North Central Arnhem Land. MA Thesis, The Australian National University, Canberra.

Hiatt, L.R. 1965. *Kinship and Conflict: A Study of an Aboriginal Community in Northern Arnhem Land*. Canberra: Australian National University Press.

Hiatt, L.R. and B. Hiatt. 1966. *Notes on Songs of Arnhem Land* [accompanying booklet]. Canberra: Australian Institute of Aboriginal Studies.

Keen, I. 1977. Ambiguity in Yolngu religious language. *Canberra Anthropology* 1(1): 33–50.

Keen, I. 1978. One Ceremony, One Song: An Economy of Religious Knowledge among the Yolngu of North-East Arnhem Land. PhD Thesis, The Australian National University, Canberra.

Keen, I. 1987. Review of *Journey to the Crocodile's Nest*. *Canberra Anthropology* 10(1): 102–4.

Keen, I. 1994. *Knowledge and Secrecy in an Aboriginal Religion: Yolngu of North-East Arnhem Land*. Oxford: Clarendon Press.

Keen, I. 1995. Metaphor and the metalanguage: 'groups' in north-east Arnhem Land. *American Ethnologist* 22(3): 502–27.

Macknight, C.C. 1980. Outback to outback: the Indonesian archipelago and northern Australia. In J.J. Fox (ed.), *Indonesia: The Making of a Culture*, pp. 137–47. Canberra: Research School of Pacific Studies.

Merriam, A.P. 1964. *The Anthropology of Music*. Evanston, IL: Northwestern University Press.

Morphy, H. 1984. *Journey to the Crocodile's Nest*. Canberra: Australian Institute of Aboriginal Studies.

Morphy, H. 1990. Myth, totemism and the creation of clans. *Oceania* 60(4): 312–28.

Mountford, C.P. 1956. *Art, Myth and Symbolism: Records of the American-Australian Expedition to Arnhem Land, 1948*, vol. 1. Melbourne: Melbourne University Press.

Shapiro, W. 1981. *Miwuyt Marriage*. Philadelphia: Institute for the Study of Human Issues.

Stanner, W.E.H. 1963. On Aboriginal religion, VI: cosmos and society made correlative. *Oceania* 33(4): 239–73.

Taylor, L. 1987. 'The Same But Different': Social Reproduction and Innovation in the Art of the Kunwinjku of Western Arnhem Land. PhD Thesis, The Australian National University, Canberra.

Thomson, D. 1975. The concept of 'marr' in Arnhem Land. *Mankind* 10: 1–10.

Thomson, D. [Peterson, N.]. 1976. Mortuary customs of northeast Arnhem Land: an account compiled from Donald Thomson's fieldnotes. *Memoirs of National Museum of Victoria* 37: 97–108.

Warner, W.L. 1958. *A Black Civilization*. Revised edition. New York: Harper and Brothers. (Original work published 1937).

Waters, B. 1983. *An Interim Djinang Dictionary*. Darwin: Summer Institute of Linguistics.

White, N. 2003. Meaning and metaphor in Yolngu landscapes, Arnhem Land, northern Australia. In D. Trigger and G. Griffiths (eds), *Disputed Territories: Land, Culture and Identity in Settler Societies*, pp. 187–205. Hong Kong: Hong Kong University Press.

# 6

# Steppe Riders in the East Kimberley Contact Zone: Zoroastrianism, Apocalyptic Judeo-Christianity and Evangelical Missionaries in Australia's Colonised Periphery

Heather McDonald

## Introduction

Around 1200 BC on the Eurasian Steppe, nomadic warriors threatened to destroy the social and moral fabric of Iranian agricultural settlements. Conflicts between steppe riders and settled agriculturalists were cosmicised by Zoroastrian traditions. The concept of 'religion' as a bounded sphere of life separate from secular spheres is a Western invention. Extreme ideas develop in times of crisis—particularly, in warring societies, in the ignominy of defeat. Good/evil and heaven/hell dualisms and an apocalyptic eschatology originated in Iran. During Hellenistic and Roman persecutions (332 BC – AD 312), Jewish and Christian writers produced a flood of apocalyptic writings. In times of success and prosperity, people tend to moderate extreme ideas. In this chapter, I examine the development of Zoroastrian cosmological ideas, their adoption by post-exilic Judaisms and early Christianities, their post-Reformation revival, and their entanglements in the East Kimberley contact zone.[1]

---

1 Colonial contact zones, 'the social spaces where cultures meet … often in contexts of highly asymmetrical relations of power' (Pratt 1991: 33), have become the intercultural spaces of negotiation, translation and improvisation (Bhabha 1994: 112).

I am fortunate to have had Dr Ian Keen, an experienced supervisor of theses on Aboriginal Christianity, with a personal interest in religions that is similar to my own, as both an undergraduate lecturer and a postgraduate supervisor.[2] Aboriginal religion is one of Ian Keen's main research themes, and he writes of Yolngu/Christian syncretism in Arnhem Land. In Yolngu Christianity, God has been given the role of a cosmogonic ancestor (with the title God *wangarr* father). The ancestral Djang'kawu Sisters are likened to key biblical figures: Adam and Eve, and Moses. Yolngu people have modelled their Christian baptism ceremony on a traditional washing ceremony (Keen 1994: 284). On Arnhem Land missions and post-mission settlements, Yolngu Christian movements sought 'to establish greater unity within Yolngu social relations, to legitimise new forms of community structure and authority, and to extend relationships of amity to whites through shared sacra' (ibid.: 276). Yolngu Christianity was seen to be developing a parallel course to other universalising religious forms such as the Gunapipi ceremony, which emphasise inclusivity (ibid.: 256).

On East Kimberley pastoral stations, Christian missionisation took a different course. Early pastoralists denigrated Aboriginal ways of being as myall (ignorant) and uncivilised, and early Christian missionaries denounced traditional ritual life as Satanic. Although older Aboriginal Christians talk about *ngarranggarni* (Dreaming, ancestral) people in the Bible, and claim that Jesus Christ was walking in *ngarranggarni* time, evangelical missiologies have discouraged active syncretism.[3] Extreme religious ideas propagated by conservative evangelical churches, ideas which have been muted or discarded by liberal churches, have had adverse effects on Gija and Jaru cosmologies.[4]

---

2   Doctoral theses on Aboriginal Christianity supervised by Ian Keen include Bos (1988), Hume (1989), and Slotte (1997). Both Ian Keen's father and my father were Christian ministers of religion, though at opposite ends of the liberal-fundamentalist spectrum. Our fieldwork experiences of Christian missionisation were also at opposite ends of the liberal-fundamentalist spectrum.

3   The Assemblies of God (AOG) church espouses a missiology of radical discontinuity (i.e. there is no continuity between Aboriginal practices and Christianity and there must be no admixture of them in Aboriginal Christianity). United Aborigines' Mission (UAM) missionaries claim to follow a middle way between the fairly extreme anti-cultural stance of the AOG church and the fulfilment missiologies of Arnhem Land Christianity which claim that other religions have the same status as the Old Testament in relation to Christianity; that is, they are a preparation for the gospel, and should not be abolished but rather fulfilled in Christ (United Church 1974). For UAM missionaries, although other religions can never claim an Old Testament status in relation to Christianity, God (as well as Satan) may have been communicating with Aboriginal people through their traditions before missionaries arrived with the gospel message. For this reason, missionaries look for 'redemptive analogies' in Indigenous beliefs and practices which can be used to point people to Christ (McDonald 2001: 63–8, 186).

4   On returning to East Kimberley in 2014, I was dismayed to find that Christian missionary demonisation of Gija and Jaru spirit worlds is complete. The ancestral spirits of Gija and Jaru people are translated as 'evil spirits' in Aboriginal–English dictionaries and in texts about East Kimberley people (see Richards and Hudson 1990: 94; Hansen 1992: 53; Wrigley 1992: 63; Burke 1998: 35; Kranenbarg 2004: 3; Zucker 2005: 175; McCoy 2008: xii–xiii; McMaster 2008: 204). In 1989–91, there were Aboriginal people who knew differently, but who did not speak openly about this. They were perplexed by the constant demonisation of their practices by church pastors, especially in light of the revitalisation of Aboriginal practices in the south of the state, but they did not have the historical knowledge to confidently discuss these issues with their church pastors.

To facilitate my understanding of the Christianisation process I have adopted an (anthropologised) history of religions perspective. It makes no sense to anthropologise Aboriginal Christianity and to leave Western Christianity unexamined as an historical or cosmological given.

> [We need] to anthropologize the West: show how exotic its constitution of reality has been; emphasize those domains most taken for granted as universal (this includes epistemology and economics); make them seem as historically peculiar as possible; show how their claims to truth are linked to social practices and have hence become effective forces in the social world. (Rabinow 1986: 241)

Foucault, in his archaeological historicising, recommends treating canonical documents as monuments; that is, as unified systems of knowledge which do not reveal their power relations and discourse strategies. They must be made to speak. In applying archaeological techniques, one does not uncover universal truths. What one uncovers are the political struggles of peoples in earlier historical periods (Dean 1994: 215; Berkhofer 1995: 4–11; in McDonald 2001: 4).

Cultural amnesia renders opaque to religious believers the socially constructed nature of their concepts, texts and orders of truth. Extreme religious views take on the status of universal truths. But a careful archaeological analysis of ancient Central and Western Asian traditions can help to uncover the peculiar and particularistic antecedents of Western Christianity. In the East Kimberley contact zone, Eurasian Steppe riders (in evangelical Christian guise) have become entangled with Indigenous spirit worlds. But the first three generations of proselytised East Kimberley people interpreted evangelical Christianity according to an older, more humane (kin-based) tradition. Their land-based cosmologies and kin-based moralities blurred, and even subverted, Zoroastrian–Christian dualisms.

## Zoroastrian Literature

In the third millennium BC waves of proto-Indo-European peoples migrated east from the Black Sea. Some (later called Indo-Aryans) settled in northern India and others (later known as Iranians) moved onto the Iranian plateau. Zarathustra (the purported founder of Zoroastrianism) is said to have lived in northeast Iran around 1200 BC (Clark 1998: 18–9). Avestan *Gathic* hymns, the earliest layer of Zoroastrian literature, were composed in a very old Iranian dialect, close to Vedic Sanskrit (Foltz 1999: 27; Shaked 1984: 311). The *Old Avesta* (including the Gathas) reached its final form about 1000 BC, and the *Young Avesta* about 700–550 BC (Skjaervo 2011: 2). Although the *Vendidad* contains recent sections, it began to be written before the eighth century BC, and most of its subject matter is very old (Kellens 1989: 35).

Early Zoroastrian literature depicts an agricultural society devoted to cultivation of the land and cattle husbandry (Clark 1998: 13, 23). According to the *Old Avesta*, the gods brought irrigation and cultivation to Iran (Skjaervo 2011: 42). 'He who cultivates grain, cultivates righteousness' (*Vendidad* III.3.31, in Settegast 2005: 10). Zarathustra's world was also a world of hierarchising city-states. In the *Avesta*, the world of the gods (the 'world of thought') had already separated from the world of living beings (the 'world with bones') (Skjaervo 2011: 8). Zarathustra transformed the Iranian pantheon, elevating Ahura Mazda, the Herd-giver, to the position of Supreme Being. Iran's lesser gods were organised into Ahura Mazda's heavenly court (Clark 1998: 44–9).

## The Eurasian Steppe

> Central Asian history is defined largely by the dynamics of nomadic-sedentary relations, often hostile, even violent, but always mutually interdependent.
> (Foltz 1999: 23)

The Eurasian Steppe stretched 4,000 kilometres from the Black Sea to the frontiers of China. It supported nomadic herders driving oxen, sheep and goats in search of pasture. Herders traded with, and raided, settled agriculturalists for what they could not produce. In response, agriculturalists built defensive walls around their settlements. Nomadic pastoralists and settled agriculturalists entered into a long and difficult relationship which lasted for well over 2,500 years (Foltz 1999: 23).

Horse-mounted herding developed early in the first millennium BC (Beckwith 2009: 60). Nomadic herders developed a warrior culture, revering warrior-ancestors, and sacrificing to sky-war gods. Warrior bands made forays into agricultural settlements, seizing herds and driving them to mountain strongholds (Cohn 2001: 90; Settegast 2005: 87). Over time, nomadic warrior bands came to exercise a kind of suzerainty over the lowland cities (Beckwith 2009: 343–6; Skjaervo 2011: 16, 51–3).

## Zoroastrian World View

Extreme ideas develop in times of crisis—particularly, in warring societies, in the ignominy of defeat. Zarathustra welded nomadic–sedentary struggles into a cosmic conflict between good and evil (Nigosian 1993: 24). Creation stories involving a primal struggle between chaos and order were widespread in the ancient world. Zarathustra transformed the ancient combat myth into an absolute moral principle. The cosmos was permeated by a fundamental tension between light and darkness, good and evil (Nigosian 1993: 88). Ahura Mazda became the origin of good and Angra Mainyu the origin of evil. Angra Mainyu attacked Ahura Mazda's ordered cosmos, bringing chaos and death (Skjaervo 2011: 8, 65).

In early Iranian traditions, all the dead went to a shadowy netherworld. Later, as politico-cosmic structures hierarchised, the elite were directed to a paradise in the sky, and the rest to the netherworld (Cohn 2001: 96). The concept of a heavenly paradise derives from Old Persian *pairidaeza*, the enclosed garden of the Persian king (Russell 1997: 31). In early city-state societies, this world was a world of moral order. Moral imbalances needed to be redressed at the time they occurred for life to proceed with equanimity. But in Zarathustra's time, nomad warriors transgressed against agriculturalists and avoided punishment. In the Gathas, the netherworld was transformed into hell, a place of afterlife punishment and torment (Cohn 2001: 96–102).[5]

Zoroastrian apocalypticism is a very old tradition (Boyce 1984b). Thoughts of evil people suffering in an afterlife no longer satisfied the righteous. The forces of evil needed to be eliminated from this world. The Gathas introduced the Saoshyant, a world saviour, who will end the present era and usher in an era of righteousness (Skjaervo 2011: 29). The Saoshyant will lead the righteous against Angra Mainyu's hordes and the dead will be resurrected to face the Last Judgement. Good and evil people will be separated. In a worldwide conflagration, Angra Mainyu will be annihilated and the righteous purified to share the Kingdom of Ahuramazda. There will be no sickness, suffering or death (Boyce 1984a: 300–1; Nigosian 1993: 94–5). The Gathas convey a sense of great urgency about the coming apocalypse (Clark 1998: 15, 64; Cohn 2001: 98–101).

## Persian Empires (559 BC – AD 650)

> Jews, Christians and Moslems you are, in your system of spiritual beings, nothing but straying children of Zoroaster. (Volney 1791: 146, in Cohn 2001: 239)

In 546 BC, Cyrus II, King of Persia, invaded Asia Minor, and developed an empire which stretched from India through Mesopotamia to Syria. Zoroastrianism became the official religion of three Persian empires: Achaemenid (559–331 BC), Parthian (247 BC – AD 224), and Sasanian (AD 224–650) (Skjaervo 2011: 1).

---

5   The modern English word 'hell' derives from Old English *hel, helle* (c. AD 725) referring to a netherworld of the dead, reaching back to the Anglo-Saxon period, from Proto-Germanic *halja*, meaning 'one who covers up or hides something' (Barnhart 1995: 348). After Christianisation, Old English *hel* followed the same trajectory as Greek Hades and Hebrew Sheol, becoming a place of afterlife punishment and torment.

Monotheism is a product of empire.[6] During the Achaemenid empire, Ahura Mazda was transformed from Supreme Being to Universal God (Nigosian 1993: 71–2). If extreme ideas develop in times of crisis, we can also see that in times of success people are able to moderate extreme ideas. During the Persian empires, apocalyptic eschatology was de-emphasised (Cohn 2001: 102).[7]

After their release from Babylonian captivity, many Jews remained in the region, contributing to the Persian/Babylonian economy and east–west trade (Clark 1998: 152). The books of Daniel and Esther are set in the Persian court.[8] Persian court administration is also evident in Ezra and Nehemiah (Shaked 1984: 308–14). At the Persian court, Ezra and his scribes reworked ancient Hebrew texts and developed the 'Law of Moses' (Lee 2011). The Jews in Persia were well on the way to becoming monotheists (Clark 1998: 153).[9] Among the returnees to Judea, Persian ideas contributed to new forms of piety. The Hasidim, an exclusivist sect, developed a scrupulous observance of Zoroastrian-Jewish purity laws (White 2004: 20).

## Hellenism (c. 332 BC – AD 100)

In 332 BC, Alexander the Great defeated Persia and developed the Macedonian empire. Greek cities and temples were established in Palestine. Jewish elites benefited from Hellenisation but the Hasidim opposed it (Cohn 2001: 174). On Alexander's death (323 BC), the empire split into two, the Seleucids and Ptolemies, who fought five major wars in the third century BC with Judea as battleground and prize (Shanks 1998: xviii). In 167 BC, the Seleucid monarch, Antiochus IV, rededicated the Jerusalem Temple to Zeus, and banned study of Torah, Sabbath observance and circumcision on pain of death (Vermes 2004: 51). When resisted by the Jewish faithful, Antiochus IV destroyed Jerusalem and the temple. The Jewish Hasmonean family which drove Antiochus IV out of Jerusalem, later assumed the Judean monarchy and high priesthood (Shanks 1998: 95; Cohn 2001: 167).

---

6   Zoroastrian monotheism was not the first monotheism to be introduced in Central or Western Asia. Akhenaten (1353–1335 BC) imposed a monotheistic regime on the Egyptian empire by promoting the sun disc, Aten, to Universal God, naming himself as Aten's son, and suppressing all other deities (Silverman 1991: 81).
7   Apocalyptic ideas were reignited by Alexander the Great's conquest of Persia (332 BC) and by the later Muslim conquest (AD 633) (Cohn 2001: 102).
8   The Book of Daniel contains many Zoroastrian ideas. Nebuchadnezzar's prophetic dream mirrors a much older Zoroastrian work, the *Zand-i Vohuman Yasht* (Cohn 2001: 222–30).
9   Universal gods may outlive the empires that produced them. The hybrid (Zoroastrian-Jewish-Platonic) God of the Roman Empire became the Universal God of the Western European powers. Monotheistic regimes attempt to suppress religious pluralism in their territories. In Australia, evangelical monotheists continue to demonise and suppress Indigenous spirit worlds.

## A Changing Jewish World View

For peoples of the ancient world, this world was a world of moral order. The early Israelites had no concept of hell (Foltz 1999: 32). But Antiochus IV's persecution fell on the righteous. The Persian word for heaven—*pairidaeza* (*pardes* in Hebrew translation)—appeared in Jewish literature at this time (Clark 1998: 154). In Greek Orphic traditions (which had absorbed Zoroastrian ideas), moral imbalances in this world were resolved by afterlife retribution (Herrero de Jáuregui 2007: 306).[10] Some Jewish groups transferred retribution to the afterlife. Sheol (Hades in Greek translation) became a place of temporary punishment (Rudman 2001: 241). At some point, Gehinnom, a valley of human bones outside Jerusalem, became linked with Sheol/Hades (Papaioannou 2004).[11] Ideas about afterlife retribution were in flux in Jesus' time, and were rejected by some Jewish groups including the priestly Sadducees (Cohen 2006).

Before contact with the Persians, the Israelites did not harbour apocalyptic ideas. Temple cults functioned to maintain an ordered universe rather than eliminate disorder from the world (Cohn 2001: 114). Zoroastrian ideas were fixed in chants and temple recitations. They travelled along trade routes and were discussed in the market place (Foltz 1999). Apocalyptic ideas resonated with Jews who experienced Antiochus IV's persecution (Russell 1994: 107–9). Jewish writers developed a belief in an earthly messiah who would restore the Kingdom of David (Clark 1998: 154). By around 150 BC, the messiah had come to be seen as a heavenly figure who would usher in the Kingdom of God. This understanding is expressed in Second Temple period apocryphal literature including the Dead Sea Scrolls (Shanks 1998: 68–9, 167).

During the Hellenistic period, Jewish (and later Christian) writers produced a flood of apocalyptic writings (Russell 1994: 2). Moses, Solomon and Enoch were appropriated as intermediaries who provided safe passage to celestial realms. Satan, a *bene ha-elohim* (son of the gods) was transformed into an opponent of God and cast out of heaven (Cohn 2001: 179–85; Russell 1977: 190–204).[12] The notion of fallen angels can be traced to Orphic (and Zoroastrian) ideas

---

10  Macedonian imperial expansion (333–30 BC) destroyed the Greek city-states. The displaced Greek aristocracy sought salvation from earthly existence by initiation into mystery cults. Plato brought Orphic traditions (which had absorbed Zoroastrian ideas) into mainstream Greek thought (Collins 1998: 35; Herrero de Jáuregui 2007).
11  Gehinnom was the place where the Israelites, during the reigns of Ahaz and Manasseh, sacrificed their children to the god Moloch (Joshua 15:8; II Kings 23:10) (Kohler and Blau n.d.).
12  The term *elohim* made many shifts in meaning from 'the dead' to 'the gods' to 'God' in line with changing politico-cosmic structures. During the Babylonian exile, the Hebrew *bene ha-elohim* were transformed from sons of God to angels. Satan became a prosecutor in the heavenly court of Yahwel-El. In later apocryphal texts, he was transformed into an opponent and accuser of God, lying in court and obstructing the path of truth. He tempted humanity to sin and was cast out of heaven and bound in a pit (Russell 1977: 109–204).

(Shaked 1984: 324; Collins 1998: 35). The Qumran community, an offshoot of the Hasidim who fled to the Judean desert during Antiochus IV's reign, saw themselves as the True Israel (Vermes 2004: 46, 200–10). But Persian dualism is evident in the *Tractate of the Two Spirits* and *The Scroll of the War of the Sons of Light Against the Sons of Darkness* (Shanks 1998: 166–9).

## Zoroastrian–Christian World View

In 63 BC, Mesopotamia became a battleground between the Roman and Parthian (Persian) empires. Apocalyptic eschatology, now part of mainstream Jewish thinking, became available to early Christianities (Shanks 1998: 170). Christian groups in Syria, Asia Minor and Greece had come to see Jesus as divine. In the first three centuries of Christianity, particularly during Roman persecution, extreme religious ideas flourished, including expectations of an imminent apocalypse (Chidester 2000: 29–31). The Gospel of Matthew, most likely produced by a Syrian Jewish-Christian community around AD 80–90, contains many Zoroastrian ideas (Duling 2010: 298–302). Jesus will return as the Son of Man (a Zoroastrian term) to resurrect the dead to face the Last Judgement (King 2003: 72). In a worldwide conflagration, the wicked will be annihilated and the righteous purified to share the Kingdom of God (Cohn 2001: 228–9).

In Jesus' time, many Jewish groups believed in Sheol/Gehinnom (Hades/Gehenna in Greek translation) as a place of afterlife retribution. In the gospels, Jesus' sayings reflect these views. The early theological schools at Alexandria, Antioch, Caesarea and Edessa, established around AD 100, combined Jewish understandings of afterlife retribution with Greek metaphysics. Hades/Gehenna became a place of remedial punishment. The theology of universal restoration (the view that God will redeem all humans), was influential in the Eastern Church (Repas 2009: 16–7).

However, the bishopric see of Rome developed a different interpretation. The Roman school, influenced by Roman law, introduced the concepts of original sin, human depravity, vicarious atonement, and eternal punishment. Irenaeus, Ignatius, Justin Martyr, Athengorus and Tertullian wrote tracts on eternal punishment in hell (Repas 2009: 17). Political manoeuvring (including the claim to be in apostolic succession from the apostle Peter) allowed the Roman school to become pre-eminent (Chadwick 1990: 237–46; Repas 2009: 20).[13]

---

13  The Zoroastrian notion of purification by fire, and the Jewish (and Eastern Christian) view of Sheol/Gehinnom as a place of remedial punishment, found a place in the Roman Catholic doctrine of purgatory (Zaleski 2012).

## Allegorical versus Literalist Exegetical Traditions

The early Eastern and Western Church fathers promoted allegorical interpretations of the Hebrew scriptures. They used Middle Platonic speculation about the realm of Being, the realm of becoming and the mediating logos, to develop a Christian logos theology which subordinated Hebrew texts to the Platonic voice (Dawson 1992: 187–9, 239).[14] This allegorising tradition continued throughout the European Middle Ages. But the Protestant Reformation created a literalist turn. Lutheran emphasis on *sola scriptura* (scripture alone) and Protestant emphasis on a plain-sense reading of the Bible led to literal interpretations of biblical texts (Hannam 2009: 226). Although the European upper classes were intent on keeping the lower classes illiterate, Puritans and evangelicals encouraged literacy so that everyone could read the Bible (Graff 1991).[15]

In seventeenth- and eighteenth-century Europe, extreme religious ideas were revived in response to a new crisis. The rationalising discourses of the scientific revolution and the Enlightenment, particularly the new geological and biological sciences which contradicted biblical 'history', led to the development of pietistic religious societies in High Anglican and Calvinist circles. English Puritanism and German mystical pietism ignited in the person of John Wesley to produce the eighteenth-century evangelical revival which swept through European Christendom spawning Pentecostal experiences, millennial expectations, and missionary fervour (Turner 2002). This evangelical revival, and the American revivals which followed, paved the way for missionary enterprises in East Kimberley.

## The Concept of Religion

In the ancient world, gods, spirits and the afterlife were not features of a sphere of life called 'religion'. *Religio* in Roman culture related to a person's civic responsibilities. The term came to be synonymous with *cultus*, the proper observance of rituals, including sacrifices to city founders and military heroes,

---

14 Middle Platonism embraced features of Aristotelian physics, Pythagorean metaphysics and Stoic ethics (Dawson 1992: 189).
15 In Australia, the evangelical missionary focus on Bible translation and linguistic research can be seen as an extension of post-Reformation literacy for converts. Aboriginal–English dictionaries published by the Summer Institute of Linguistics in Darwin and the Institute for Aboriginal Development in Alice Springs reveal traces of evangelical Christian doctrine. In contrast, Catholic missionisation relied on performance rather than intellection. Liturgy, sacraments and oral traditions were given greater prominence than the (written) Word (McDonald 2001: 167).

which maintained the politico-cosmic order (White 2004: 129). After Christianity became the official *cultus* of the emperor Constantine, the concept of 'religion' developed and changed within a Christian context.

In the first three centuries AD, there were many Christianities. Rival Christian groups produced their own gospels but the questions that primarily concerned them were ones of practice, not theology (Pagels 2003: 15, 179). In AD 312, Constantine recognised only the best organised and largest group as 'the lawful and most holy catholic church' (Eusebius, *Historia Ecclesiae* 10.6, in Pagels 2003: 168). In order to create a unified Christendom, Constantine ordered Christian bishops to develop the Nicene Creed. Christianity, always a syncretism, invented itself as a 'pure form' by excluding competing groups, including Jewish Christians and Gnostic Christians as hybrids/heresies (Boyarin 2004: 28–9). Doctrine rather than practice defined true religion. However, the boundaries around Jews, Christians and pagans were not firmly established until the fifth century AD (White 2004: 297, 437).[16]

In thirteenth-century Europe, theology was the most important branch of knowledge. The Church saw moral and natural philosophy as aspects of the same unified discipline but deemed natural philosophy the servant of theology. Conflicts between science and scripture were accommodated by fitting new knowledge into the Church's interpretive framework. But in the seventeenth century, Francis Bacon, Galileo and Descartes removed science from the Church's reign over the nature of truth (Rowland 2001: 57–72, 145–9). In Western societies, religion was reinvented as a distinctive, even *sui generis*, phenomenon, separate from the secular spheres of politics, economics and science. It is conceived as a transhistorical and transcultural order of reality which (strangely) assumes a Christian soteriological guise (Asad 1993: 27–9; Fitzgerald 2000: 14, 55–6, 71).

## Hunter-Gatherer Cosmologies and Evangelical Missionaries in East Kimberley

Hunter-gatherer societies which practiced 'aggressive egalitarianism' (Woodburn 1982) did not develop a hierarchical political order or a cosmic world above/world below dualism onto which other dualisms (spirit/matter, good/evil, God/Satan) could be grafted. Cosmologies follow polities.

---

16  In the third century AD, Origin of Alexandria wrote of Jewish Christians who attended synagogue on Saturday and church on Sunday. Some Jewish Christians attended synagogue and observed Jewish laws well into the fourth century AD (King 2003: 41). And there are people who identify as Jewish Christians to this day (Boyarin 2004: 48).

> The Australian pattern is not one of celestial withdrawal, but of terrestrial transformation and continued presence ... Connection with the ancestors is on the terrestrial plane, and it is forever available ... There is no 'celestial rupture' that needs to be overcome. (Smith 1987: 5)

Reincarnation cosmologies also follow the cyclical imperatives of the living world. In East Kimberley, all the dead went to the ancestral spirit place, a place in the country invisible to ordinary people except in dreams. *Mabarn* (clever men/healers) could 'see' and visit the spirit place. *Jurnbabarlibarli* (song finders) would sleep at the spirit place in order to receive song ceremonies from their ancestors. When *mamu* and *juwarri* (spirits of the dead) became tired of living as disembodied spirits and decided that their families could manage without them, they returned to the outside world via the body of a living woman.[17] They transformed themselves into their 'totem' animal (their true Dreaming shape), entered the mother's womb, and *garaj wajarn* (became a body), that is, became a new human being. Aboriginal spirit beings are much more complex than simple dualisms allow for. In East Kimberley, humans and spirits do not subscribe to absolute moral values. Gija and Jaru people, who are able to tolerate contradictions in people and in the world, do not feel the need to totally isolate and displace bad events and people (via a good/evil dualism).

Evangelical Christian missionaries arrived in Australia's colonised periphery with concepts developed over 3,000 years of city-state development, wars and empire-building in Central and Western Asia. These concepts were refined within the Persian and Macedonian empires, and found their way into diverse scriptures. When Christianity became the official *cultus* of the Roman Empire, apocalyptic eschatology was de-emphasised. In *The City of God*, Augustine of Hippo (AD 354–430) equated the millennium with the present spiritual reign of the Church (Allis 2001: 3).[18] But after the Protestant Reformation, particularly during the seventeenth and eighteenth centuries, apocalyptic ideas were re-awakened by newly literate European and American populations (Balmer n.d.).

---

17   *Mamu* (Jaru) and *juwarri* (Gija) are ancestral life-forces which cycle between the spirit world and the outside world (the world of humans and animals) via reincarnation. As independent spirits they are most powerful because they can see, hear and travel vast distances to access knowledge-power. They can act as invisible forces in the outside world or they can make themselves visible by taking on the form of an animal or other life form.

18   In the late second and early third centuries AD, literal and allegorical interpretations of the apocalypse vied for supremacy. By the mid–fourth century, allegorical interpretations had become dominant. The apocalypse as an allegorical story dominated Eastern Orthodox and Roman Catholic churches throughout the Middle Ages (Alexander 1985).

During my initial fieldwork in Halls Creek, Assemblies of God (AOG) and United Aborigines Mission (UAM) pastors were preoccupied with apocalyptic eschatology.[19] 'When [an AOG pastor] first came to Halls Creek [in 1982], he said Jesus is coming very soon. We haven't got time for language translation work' (Jenny Summers, UAM).[20] AOG sermons frequently focused on the torments awaiting unbelievers. 'The whole earth will burn. When you've been in hell for thirty seconds you'll believe' (Pastor Phillip, AOG). The UAM pastor, presenting a series of sermons on the Book of Revelation, took a softer approach: 'During the Great Tribulation non-Christians will be given a second chance to receive Christ' (Pastor John, UAM).

In Halls Creek, Aboriginal Christians in the evangelical churches propound an eschatology which bears traces of Zoroastrianism:

> The pastors are preaching in the desert. There are seven more places in Australia to hear the word [of God]. When the word has gone right through, Jesus will come back. He's having a spell first. As soon as all the Aborigines have heard the gospel, Jesus will come back. (Laurie Jacobs, AOG)

> When Judgement Day come, everybody will wake up, even *mamu* [spirits of the dead] what got drowned in the sea or burned. They still come out. God gotta judge us now. Good person, he tell to go to his side. Satan other side with his mob. If your name not in the Book, he say, 'I don't know you. Cast into hell'. (Lizzie Tracker, AOG)

In East Kimberley, the ghost of Zoroastrianism also looms over evangelical missionaries' attempts to interpret Aboriginal cosmologies. The missionaries' favoured dualisms (God/Satan, good/evil, and heaven/hell) are unmediated by Clement's logos theology or by any other humane tradition:

> There are only two powers in this world, that of darkness and that of light, that of Satan and that of God. On Judgement Day, humanity will be separated into two groups: one will spend eternity with God. The other will spend eternity in hell. (Pastor John, UAM)

---

19  In 1989–91, I conducted research in East Kimberley for my doctoral thesis at The Australian National University. During 2002–05, I conducted research in the same region while a research fellow at the Australian Institute for Aboriginal and Torres Strait Islander Studies. I returned to East Kimberley in 2014 to assist with the recording of family histories. The preoccupation of UAM and AOG pastors with apocalyptic eschatology continues to this day.
20  The names of Kimberley people have been changed to protect their privacy.

## Good/Evil Dualism

Early missionaries to the Kimberley aligned Aboriginal spirit beings, ancestral snakes and traditional healers with Satan's realm. They recategorised *mamu* and *juwarri* (spirits of the dead) as the evil spirits or demons of Christianity. However, for Gija and Jaru people, the Devil who comes from hellfire is evil, but other devils (*mamu* and *juwarri*) are not so evil. Some are not evil at all. In East Kimberley, goodness and badness intermingle. Rather than a good/evil dichotomy, there appears to be a continuum of moral attribution which reflects a kin-based ethos. One's family spirits are good devils. Other people's spirits can be half-good devils. The spirits of traditional enemies are commonly referred to as 'half *mamu* and half cannibal' (Laurie Jacobs) or as 'the biggest Satan' (Alice Sim). In East Kimberley, family spirits assert their 'traditional' attributes of caring for country and people, and in doing so, blur cosmic dualisms.

> What person die, he come back spirit *mamu* and look after his own family. You can sleep anywhere la flat [country]. Anyone sneak up la you, he wake you up. 'Shift your blanket that way. Watch that road'. He guide you back to your camp. (Gabriel Jordon, UAM)

> *Mamu* heal people too. If I sick, I got my *mamu*. Just like Jesus Christ. My mother [deceased] hang on to me. I ask him, 'I feel headache, Mum. Just feel my head'. I go to sleep. In the morning I feel better. That's mother mine, that *mamu*. (Tracker Dinggul, AOG)

Family spirits have well-developed nurturing qualities, and according to some Christians, even take on Logos-Jesus roles of identifying with and sharing the human condition. But they do not follow God's way. They follow the traditional way. They are bound by kin-based loyalties, prejudices and emotions. Sometimes they want everyone to be friends; at other times they incite hatred and division. This is a problem for middle-aged Aboriginal Christians who, as children, received a mission education at Moola Bulla government settlement or Fitzroy Crossing UAM mission, and have assimilated Christian moral values:

> *Juwarri* haven't got Christian love. They jealous. They tempt people to fight and swear. God don't like *juwarri* because they doing the wrong things. I wouldn't say that *juwarri* hate God. (Alice Sim, UAM)

> My granny tell us, 'We'll be *juwarri* for you mob kid [when we're dead]. We'll be here, all the spirit'. They look after their own family. Nother way round, *juwarri* can make people *wangala* [mad, witless]. You'll climb up the hill. You'll walk bush and die. (Sarah Peters, AOG)

For AOG pastors in Halls Creek, all representations of serpents in all cultures symbolise Satan. In East Kimberley, *Garluruny* (ancestral snakes) are powerful generative forces which are locally exclusive to the point of extreme jealousy.

When confronted by strange presences or behaviours, they may become violent, generating storms and floods to sweep the intruders away. However, East Kimberley people emphasise the importance of ancestral snakes to the health of country and people. 'Every place gotta living water. *Garluruny* hold that water. If *Garluruny* leave that place, water will dry up' (Laurie Jacobs, AOG). Middle-aged and older Christians exempt their ancestral snakes from connection with Satan, and claim their connection with God. 'God made *Garluruny*. *Garluruny* belongs to God. When Christians swim in the waterhole, he can't hurt them. When we swim in the healing waterhole, *Garluruny* heal us' (Alice Sim, UAM).[21]

Although evangelical pastors categorise *mabarn* healing as witchcraft, many Aboriginal people take a more considered view. Some Aboriginal Christians say God endowed Aboriginal healers with *mabarn* power at a time when there were no *gardiya* (whitefella) doctors or hospitals in Australia. Others claim that '*mabarn* [healers] are the same as Jesus and God'. Their role is one of reconciliation and restoration of social order. When people have been 'jealousing and fighting', *mabarn* tell them, 'You fella gotta friend up now' (Alice Sim, UAM). For older Aboriginal people, 'God can't say nothing [about *mabarn* healing]. White doctor is *mabarn* too' (Saddleman, UAM).

## Christian/Sinner Dualism

AOG pastors in Halls Creek make an absolute moral distinction between Christians and non-Christians:

> The Bible says there are two kinds of people in the world: the children of God and the children of the Devil. The children of God do righteousness and love the Christians. The children of the Devil do unrighteousness and hate the Christians. (Pastor Daniel, AOG)

AOG pastors counsel their adherents not to associate with people (including relatives) who are not AOG members. A pastor told Sally Wilmirr not to 'have that sinful woman [a close relative] in your house'. He advised Paddy Ejay not to talk to his brother who was applying for land by pastoral excision. AOG adherents are instructed to avoid Aboriginal community-controlled organisations and government departments involved in Aboriginal affairs. Vinni Manday, an East Jaru speaker, was counselled not to 'get mixed up with that language mob [Kimberley Language Centre] or any kind of business

---

21   Caroline Pool, the baptising water for the UAM mob, is also the home of a well-known *Garluruny*. According to UAM adherents, he was initially frightened by Christian baptisms and swallowed a horse in retaliation. Today he favours the Christian mob and tends mainly to swallow sinners (McDonald 2001: 167).

[Aboriginal cultural activity]. Those places are full of devils' (Pastor Phillip). Kelly Jangala was told to stop making boomerangs for the Yarliyil Art Centre. 'It will drag you down' (Pastor Daniel).

Aboriginal people in Halls Creek also make a clear divide between Christians and sinners. Sinners 'drink, swear and fight, play cards, chew tobacco, dance corroboree' (Gabi Cousins, AOG). Christians 'go to church, pray for people, heal people, love everybody' (Hilda Saddleman, UAM). 'Card places' (places where card games are held) and 'grog places' (places where drinkers congregate) are sinner places, as are the race course and the circus which comes to Halls Creek at race time. The licensed store on the corner of the main street where drinkers congregate is referred to by AOG adherents as 'that Devil corner'. When Christians drive past the Devil corner at night they are vulnerable to having a tyre puncture.

However, in Halls Creek the Christian/sinner divide is blurred by a kin-based morality. There is a constant flow of people and resources between Christian and sinner domains. Aboriginal Christians ask sinner relatives for their winnings from card games to fund church travel. Christians join card games when they are away from Halls Creek or when the pastor is away. When Christians experience 'too much trouble' in their daily lives, particularly constant demands or failure of obligation from relatives, government, or church pastors, they frequently 'fall back' to card playing, drinking and fighting.

Some Aboriginal members of the evangelical churches pressure family members to give up drinking and come to church. At church, they cajole their kin to go forward to the altar to 'give their heart to the Lord'. If they do not do this, the churchgoers will no longer look after them. They may throw close family members out of the house when they revert to a drinking lifestyle. 'Bessie threw [her drunk sister] out like rubbish' (Gabriel Jordan, UAM). Other church members are tolerant of sinners and backsliders and do not follow their pastors' directives. Families with large numbers of adult children are unable to achieve the ideal state of all family members being sober and churchgoing at the same time. These church members find that their pastors frequently fail to demonstrate Christian love. On one occasion, a young woman opened her well-underlined Bible and read, 'If anyone says, "I love God", yet hates his brother, he is a liar, for he who does not love his brother whom he has seen cannot love God whom he has not seen' (1 John 4:20). On other occasions, church members threaten to, and do, take their families out of the churches.

In Halls Creek, half-Christians straddle the divide between Christians and sinners. They enjoy the benefits of churchgoing, particularly the perceived benefits of prayer and healing, but insist that they 'can't be perfect all the time' (Sarah Fielder, AOG). Half-Christians practice 'sin sneaking', that is, they engage in sinful activities behind the pastor's back. They tap into different kin networks according to whether they are in churchgoing or backsliding mode. Like sinners, half-Christians frequently become sick as a result of their sinful activities and lack of concern for their physical welfare. When they need respite from the treadmill of drinking, lock-up and injury, they utilise their churchgoing kin and return to church for healing. When their health is sufficiently restored, and they become bored with church activities, they utilise their sinner kin networks to return to a drinking lifestyle. At death, the destination of half-Christians is neither heaven nor hell, but reincarnation:

> Spirit for Jimilu [deceased] always hang around our camp. Two-ways bloke, playing card, swearing and fight, he don't go up [to heaven]. He hang around here. Then he come back to mother and father [as a human being]. (Laurie Jacobs, AOG)

## Heaven/Hell Dualism

In Halls Creek, all but the oldest Aboriginal people accept the Zoroastrian-Christian heaven/hell divide. This dualism is clearly a very old feature of missionary evangelism in East Kimberley. Gehenna's flames feature in Aboriginal people's descriptions of hell: 'Hell is hot and burning and smell. The rivers and waterholes are boiling. Devil standing up gotta biggest fork' (Gabi Cousins, AOG). Young people's reasons for joining the evangelical churches frequently include the fear of hell: 'I became a Christian because [an AOG pastor] preached about hell and fire. I was frightened. I went to the front [at the altar call] and gave my heart to the Lord' (Danny Hawk, AOG).

But the heaven/hell distinction is blurred by a number of factors. Gija and Jaru spirits are not individualised immortal souls. Spirit is a stream of life which manifests itself in different forms. When a life form dies, the spirit is reincarnated in a new form. According to some Aboriginal people, even Christian spirits are reincarnated. When Christian spirits go to heaven, God sends them back to be reincarnated. Some Aboriginal Christians are not prepared to consign their living or dead relatives to hell. Spirits of the dead in caves and graveyards are waiting for the Second Coming of Jesus. On Judgement Day, Jesus will take everyone to heaven because he loves all sinners (Sadie James, AOG). Hell, the abode of Satan and his demons, is uninhabited (and will always be uninhabited) by Aboriginal spirits (McDonald 2010: 62). Sadie James, who has access to an older, more humane (kin-based) tradition, has modified AOG doctrines about heaven and hell. In her theologising, she has unwittingly stumbled upon the Alexandrian school's theology of universal restoration. Clement of Alexandria would not tolerate the thought that any soul would forever resist the force of redeeming love. Sadie's views are closer to Greek metaphysics than to the punitive Roman concepts that inform AOG doctrines.

## Younger Aboriginal Christians

Younger Aboriginal Christians in Halls Creek, many of whom have been recipients of missionary teaching since childhood, appear to have adopted extreme evangelical views which denigrate Gija and Jaru cosmologies.

> Dad reckon little *rayi* was good, but I don't.[22] Little *rayi* and little demon, I reckon it's all evil. (Liby Sheeran, UAM)

*Mamu* and *juwarri* (spirits of the dead) are the Devil disguising himself as a person who died.

> *Mabarn* [healing] power comes from Satan. Satan can form any miracle because he's the Prince of Darkness. (Louis Jabul, UAM)

> Snake represents Satan. I used to believe in *Garluruny* Snake. Now I believe in one Creator. (Jimmy Esau, UAM)

> Some corroborees get tangled up with evil spirits. They singing songs like spirits. You gotta be careful because Satan can use these things. (Louis Jabul)

> When we die, our spirit can't come back again, walking around. Christian spirit goes to heaven. Lost people that don't know the Lord, their spirit just floating around. They don't come back and walk around like a dog or cat. They gotta wait for Judgement Day. If they die with sin in their heart, they'll be heading for hell. (Liby Sheeran)

However, rejection of local cosmologies does not translate into freedom from land and kin-based protocols. In East Kimberley, countries are held by landholding kin groups and Aboriginal Christians who reject traditional ritual life continue to adhere to protocols of country. Sherry Magill, a young AOG adherent, told me that *gardiya* (white people), but not Aboriginal people, could ignore kin-based protocols without shame and without fear of retribution. When travelling through other people's countries, Sherry's behaviour was always watchful and circumspect. She told me, 'You're all right. You're a *gardiya*' (McDonald 2010: 61).

And when younger Christians encounter unendurable stress in their lives such as the murder of a close relative, they look for, and find, comfort not in Christian doctrine or in church activities, but in kin relationships and family solidarity.

---

22   *Rayi* = ancestral spirit (West Kimberley languages).

In Halls Creek this includes sitting down in the main street park, participating in card games, and listening to Gija and Jaru storytelling which links the present with the past, the living with the dead, and contemporary events with the Dreaming.

## Conclusion

Extreme religious views, developing on the Eurasian Steppe and cosmicised by Zoroastrianism have, in Jewish and Christian traditions, taken on the status of universal truths. Cultural amnesia renders opaque to religious believers the socially constructed nature of their concepts, texts and orders of truth. The cultural amnesiac (spirit of forgetting) which was hard at work in the Persian period, erasing particularistic antecedents of Judaism, is at work today silencing and suppressing peculiar and particularistic hunter-gatherer cosmologies.

A Foucauldian archaeological analysis reveals parallels in the development of Western Christianity and Aboriginal Christianity in East Kimberley. In both cases, particularistic traditions are denigrated and suppressed by a universalising world view. Rather than following Christian missionaries' attempts to demonise and suppress hunter-gatherer cosmologies (see Richards and Hudson 1990: 94; Hansen 1992: 53; Burke 1998: 35; Zucker 2005: 175; McCoy 2008: xii–xiii; McMaster 2008: 204), students of Aboriginal Christianity can consider Ian Keen's understandings of Yolngu Christianity as an attempt by Yolngu people to develop a 'common moral order' (Keen 1994: 287). They can recognise and work with postcolonial theologians' attempts to develop a theology of religious pluralism and a pneumatology of 'many spirits' (Kim 2007).

## Postscript

On my return to East Kimberley in 2014, I was surprised to find some major shifts in church affiliation and in Christian/sinner alignment. Some Christians who were fiercely loyal to the new AOG church have returned to the UAM church of their youth. Some of the most strident Holy Spirit Christians, including a prominent church leader, have returned, permanently it would seem, to a drinking lifestyle.[23] Others continue the endless churchgoer/backslider cycles of

---

23   One woman who attended the AOG church because her brother-in-law refused to maintain her vehicle otherwise, has (on her brother-in-law's death) returned to the UAM church. Another woman who, as a result of a dream which she attributed to God, changed from heavy drinker to enthusiastic UAM member, has (after the premature death of her husband), returned to a seemingly permanent drinking lifestyle.

half-Christianity. Extreme religious ideas (particularly apocalyptic eschatologies and unmediated dualisms) continue to be engaged with, blurred and subverted according to older, more humane (kin-based) traditions.

## Acknowledgements

I thank Ngoonjuwah Aboriginal Council for permission to conduct research with East Kimberley people in the Halls Creek region. I especially thank Vera Cox, Mona Green, Doris Fletcher, Jugarie, Bill and Bessie Matthews, Ruth Mills, Barbara Sturt, Janice Hargraves, Kathy Ryder and Donald Cox for contributing their cultural knowledge to this chapter. Many thanks to Peter Toner for his careful reading of earlier drafts of this chapter and for his helpful comments and advice. Thanks to the two anonymous reviewers for their comments on an earlier draft of this chapter.

## References

Alexander, P.J. 1985. *The Byzantine Apocalyptic Tradition*. Berkeley: University of California Press.

Allis, O.T. 2001. *Prophecy and the Church*. Eugene, OR: Wipf and Stock.

Asad, T. 1993. *Genealogies of Religion: Discipline and Reasons of Power in Christianity and Islam*. Baltimore: John Hopkins University Press.

Balmer, R. n.d. Apocalypticism in American Culture. National Humanities Center. Accessed online 20 January 2015. nationalhumanitiescenter.org/tserve/twenty/tkeyinfo/apocal.htm.

Barnhart, R.K. 1995. *The Barnhart Concise Dictionary of Etymology*. New York: Harper Collins.

Beckwith, C. 2009. *Empires of the Silk Road: A History of Central Eurasia from the Bronze Age to the Present*. Princeton: Princeton University Press.

Bhabha, H. 1994. *The Location of Culture*. London: Routledge.

Berkhofer, R.F. 1995. *Beyond the Great Story: History as Text and Discourse*. Cambridge, MA: Harvard University Press.

Bos, R. 1988. Jesus and the Dreaming: Religion and Social Change in Arnhem Land. PhD Thesis, University of Queensland, Brisbane.

Boyarin, D. 2004. The Christian invention of Judaism: the Theodosian Empire and the Rabbinic refusal of religion. *Representations* 85: 21–57.

Boyce, M. 1984a. Persian religion in the Achemenid age. In W.D. Davies and L. Finkelstein (eds), *The Cambridge History of Judaism Volume 1: Introduction: The Persian Period*, pp. 279–307. Cambridge: Cambridge University Press.

Boyce, M. 1984b. On the antiquity of Zoroastrian Apocalyptic. *Bulletin of the School of Oriental and African Studies* 47: 57–75.

Burke, D. 1998. *Dreaming of the Resurrection: A Resurrection Story*. Sydney: Mary MacKillop Foundation.

Chadwick, H. 1990. *The Early Church*. London: Penguin.

Chidester, D. 2000. *Christianity: A Global History*. San Francisco: HarperCollins.

Clark, P. 1998. *Zoroastrianism: An Introduction to an Ancient Faith*. East Sussex, UK: Sussex Academic Press.

Cohen, S. 2006. *From the Maccabees to the Mishnah*. Louisville: Westminster John Knox Press.

Cohn, N. 2001. *Cosmos, Chaos, and the World to Come: The Ancient Roots of Apocalyptic Faith*. Second edition. New Haven/London: Yale University Press.

Collins, J.J. 1998. *The Apocalyptic Imagination: An Introduction to Jewish Apocalyptic Literature*. Second edition. Grand Rapids, MI/Cambridge, UK: William B. Eerdmans.

Dawson, D. 1992. *Allegorical Readers and Cultural Revision in Ancient Alexandria*. Berkeley: University of California Press.

Dean, M. 1994. *Critical and Effective Histories: Foucault's Methods and Historical Sociology*. London/New York: Routledge.

Duling, D.C. 2010. The Gospel of Matthew. In D.E. Aune (ed.), *The Blackwell Companion to the New Testament*, pp. 296–318. Oxford: Wiley-Blackwell.

Fitzgerald, T. 2000. *The Ideology of Religious Studies*. New York: Oxford University Press.

Foltz, R. 1999. *Religions of the Silk Road: Overland Trade and Cultural Exchange from Antiquity to the Fifteenth Century*. New York: St Martin's Press.

Graff, H. 1991. *The Legacies of Literacy: Continuities and Contradictions in Western Culture and Society*. Bloomington, IN: Indiana University Press.

Hannam, J. 2009. *God's Philosophers: How the Medieval World Laid the Foundations of Modern Science*. London: Icon Books.

Hansen, K.C. and L.E. 1992. *Pintupi/Luritja Dictionary*. Third edition. Alice Springs: Institute for Aboriginal Development.

Herrero de Jáuregui, M. 2007. Orphic ideas of immortality: traditional Greek images and a new eschatological thought. In M. Labahn and M. Lang (eds), *Lebendige Hoffnung—Ewiger Tod?! Jenseitsvorstellungen im Hellenismus, Judentum und Christentum*, pp. 247–73. Leipzig: Evangelische Verlagsanstalt.

Hume. L. 1989. Yarrabah: Christian Phoenix: Christianity and Social Change on an Australian Aboriginal Reserve. PhD Thesis, University of Queensland, Brisbane.

Keen, I. 1994. *Knowledge and Secrecy in an Aboriginal Religion*. Oxford: Clarendon Press.

Kellens, J. 1989. Avesta. *Encyclopedia Iranica* 3, pp. 35–44. New York: Routledge and Kegan Paul.

Kim, K. 2007. *The Holy Spirit in the World: A Global Conversation*. Maryknoll, NY: Orbis.

King, K. 2003. *What Is Gnosticism?* Cambridge, MA: Harvard University Press.

Kohler, K. and L. Blau n.d. Gehenna. *Jewish Encyclopedia*. Accessed online 20 January 2015: www.jewishencyclopedia.com/articles/6558-gehenna.

Kranenbarg, M. 2004. Painting Authenticity: Aboriginal Art and Knowledge in an Intercultural Space (Warmun, Western Australia). MA Thesis, University of Nijmegen, Netherlands.

Lee, K.J. 2011. *The Authority and Authorisation of Torah in the Persian Period*. Leuven: Peeters.

McCoy, B.F. 2008. *Holding Men: Kanyirninpa and the Health of Aboriginal Men*. Canberra: Aboriginal Studies Press.

McDonald, H. 2001. *Blood, Bones and Spirit: Aboriginal Christianity in an East Kimberley Town*. Melbourne: Melbourne University Press.

McDonald, H. 2010. Universalising the particular? God and Indigenous spirit beings in East Kimberley. *The Australian Journal of Anthropology* 21: 51–70.

McMaster, N. 2008. *The Catholic Church in Jaru and Gija Country: Reworking a Context of Evangelisation in the Kimberley*. Melbourne: David Lovell Publishing.

Nigosian, S.A. 1993. *The Zoroastrian Faith: Tradition and Modern Research*. Montreal and Kingston: McGill-Queen's University Press.

Pagels, E. 2003. *Beyond Belief: The Secret Gospel of Thomas*. New York: Random House.

Papaioannou, K.G. 2004. Places of Punishment in the Synoptic Gospels. PhD Thesis, Durham University, UK.

Pratt, M.L. 1991. Arts of the contact zone. *Profession* 91: 33–40.

Rabinow, P. 1986. Representations are social facts: modernity and post-modernity in anthropology. In J. Clifford and G.E. Marcus (eds), *Writing Culture: The Poetics and Politics of Ethnography*, pp. 234–61. Berkeley: University of California Press.

Repas, M.A. 2009. From Gehinnom to Hell: An etymological and conceptual history. Rothberg International School, The Hebrew University of Jerusalem. Accessed online 20 January 2015: exploratorius.files.wordpress.com/2009/05/from-gehinnom-to-hell1.pdf.

Richards, E. and J. Hudson 1990. *Walmajarri-English Dictionary*. Darwin, NT: Summer Institute of Linguistics.

Rowland, W. 2001. *Galileo's Mistake: A New Look at the Epic Confrontation between Galileo and the Church*. New York: Arcade Publishing.

Rudman, D. 2001. The use of watery imagery in descriptions of Sheol. *Zeitschrift für die Alttestamentliche Wissenschaft* 113(2): 240–4.

Russell, D.S. 1994. *Prophecy and the Apocalyptic Dream: Protest and Promise*. Peabody, MA: Hendrickson Publishers.

Russell, J.B. 1977. *The Devil: Perceptions of Evil from Antiquity to Primitive Christianity*. Ithaca, NY: Cornell University Press.

Russell, J.B. 1997. *A History of Heaven*. Princeton: Princeton University Press.

Settegast, M. 2005. *When Zarathustra Spoke: The Reformation of Neolithic Culture and Religion*. Costa Mesa, CA: Mazda Publishers.

Shaked, S. 1984. Iranian influence on Judaism. In W.D. Davies and L. Finkelstein (eds), *The Cambridge History of Judaism*, vol. 1, pp. 308–25. Cambridge: Cambridge University Press.

Shanks, H. 1998. *The Mystery and Meaning of the Dead Sea Scrolls*. New York: Random House.

Silverman, D.P. 1991. Divinity and deities in ancient Egypt. In B.E. Shafer (ed.), *Religion in Ancient Egypt: Gods, Myths, and Personal Practice*, pp. 7–81. Ithaca, NY: Cornell University Press.

Skjaervo, P.O. 2011. *The Spirit of Zoroastrianism*. New Haven and London: Yale University Press.

Slotte, I. 1997. We Are Family, We Are One: An Aboriginal Christian Movement in Arnhem Land, Australia. PhD Thesis, The Australian National University, Canberra.

Smith, J.Z. 1987. *To Take Place: Toward Theory in Ritual*. Chicago: University of Chicago Press.

Turner, J.M. 2002. *John Wesley: The Evangelical Revival and the Rise of Methodism in England*. London: Epworth Press.

United Church. 1974. Free to Decide: The United Church in North Australia Commission of Enquiry, Arnhem Land. Darwin: The United Church.

Vermes, G. 2004. *The Complete Dead Sea Scrolls in English*. Fifth edition. London: Penguin Books.

Volney, C.F. de. 1791. *Les Ruines, ou Meditations sur les Revolutions des Empires*, vol 1. Paris.

Woodburn, J. 1982. Egalitarian societies. *Man* 17(3): 431–51.

White, L.M. 2004. *From Jesus to Christianity*. New York: HarperCollins.

Wrigley, M. 1992. *Jaru Dictionary*. Draft edition. Halls Creek, WA: Kimberley Language Resource Centre.

Zaleski, C. 2012. Purgatory. *Encyclopædia Britannica Online*. Encyclopædia Britannica Inc. Accessed online 20 January 2015: www.britannica.com/EBchecked/topic/483923/purgatory/.

Zucker, M. 2005. *From Patrons to Partners: A History of the Catholic Church in the Kimberley, WA*. Second edition. Fremantle: University of Notre Dame Australia Press.

# 7  The Failures of Translation across Incommensurable Knowledge Systems: A Case Study of Arabic Grammar Instruction

Allon J. Uhlmann
School of Archaeology and Anthropology,
The Australian National University

In a 1995 paper, Ian Keen took on the issue of incommensurability between systems of knowledge, demonstrating the power of ethnographically grounded analysis to move beyond the abstractions that have dominated debates over cognitive universality and variability. Keen juxtaposes two different terminological systems that seek to capture a particular behavioural reality. One system is the analytic conceptual framework that anthropologists have applied to Yolngu kinship and social organisation. The other is the very conceptual system that Yolngu draw on in living out that sphere of life which anthropologists designate as kinship.

The metaphorical and metonymic logic of these two conceptual systems are incommensurable, leading to 'anomalies', as it were, in translation. The anthropological conceptual framework is heir to a long historical tradition that harks back to formal Aristotelian logic, and is predicated on an ontology of distinct, bounded entities embodied in the European notions of person and property (cf. Uhlmann 2006: 49ff). The application of this conceptual framework to Yolngu realities imposes that specific logics on Yolngu concepts.

The Yolngu conceptual framework is different for various reasons. Unlike the anthropological framework, it is a lived or 'enacted' conceptual framework whose application and use is quite different from the analytic, descriptive, external position that the anthropological conceptual framework adopts. Moreover, the underlying metaphors and metonyms that inhere in the Yolngu conceptual framework are quite different (Keen 1995: 504–5). As Keen writes,

> Concepts such as lineage, clan, descent group, and corporate group depend on images of segmentary structure, external boundaries, and taxonomic hierarchy. These constructs go hand in hand with concepts of land and country, which also entail spatial metaphors of enclosure and boundaries and which imply hierarchies of small bounded places contained in larger ones of a different type. None of these tropes fit Yolngu modes of 'group' identity and relations, which involve images drawn from the human body and plants, and beliefs about ancestral journeys and traces. Far from being constituted by enclosure within boundaries, Yolngu 'group' identities, like those of place, extend outward from foci. Connections among such identities are not those of enclosing sets but open and extendible 'strings' of connectedness. (Keen 1995: 502)

The result is a series of anomalies, whereby Yolngu usage would seem to violate the basic rules of logic when reconstituted in anthropological terms. For example, several *malas* are said by Yolngu to make a *mala*, and groups with distinct *ba:purru* identities may also have a common *ba:purru* identity (Keen 1995: 519–20). Keen argues that such offences against Aristotelian logic are a product of the imposition of an anthropological conceptual framework—a discourse which is external to social reality and steeped in implicit European tropes—on the Yolngu lived logic of practice.

Such grounded analyses of specific cultural clashes in lived systems of logic can advance our understanding of the sociocultural influence of logic past the abstract and all-too-often moralistic debates that ensued after Lucien Lévy-Bruhl first posed the question of cognitive variability well over a century ago. But instances in which the differences between conceptual systems can be observed in detail are not easily found. They would typically require a contrast of two culturally or historically distinct conceptual frameworks that seek to conceptualise the same phenomenon. Keen's paper contrasted Indigenous and anthropological conceptualisations of Yolngu society. In what follows I will describe another case study which draws on two historically distinct sciences of the same phenomenon. The conceptualised phenomenon is Arabic grammar, and the two contrasting systems are the Orientalist and the Arab sciences of grammar as they are manifest in Arabic instruction.

University Arabic grammar instruction in Israel offers a particularly instructive instance of systemic incommensurability because it brings together students who have been schooled in the two different approaches to grammar, and enacts a veritable cultural clash in cognition and knowledge. Arabic grammar instruction resembles the case study analysed by Keen in that in both studies the contrasted systems are ontologically different and are animated by different tropes. Furthermore, in both studies the two systems are entangled in an unequal power relationship in which the indigenous system of knowledge is in the subordinate position. And in both studies, indigenous practice, when observed through the prism of the dominant system, inevitably emerges as deficient, inconsistent or incomprehensible.

This paper relies on several years of ongoing ethnographic research in Israeli schools and universities[1] to analyse an instance where translation obscures the true meaning of the translated terms and camouflages the incommensurability between two alternative systems of knowledge. This case study points to the problematic nature of translation across different systems of knowledge. The scholarly investigation into Arabic grammar has been pursued in different historical and cultural settings. This paper discusses translation between the modern manifestations of two of these distinct scholarly traditions. One is the Arabic grammatical tradition, that is, the tradition of grammatical scholarship that was written in Arabic within the Islamic world. The other is the European, Orientalist tradition of Arabic grammatical analysis. Notwithstanding some mutual influences between the two traditions, they remain distinct intellectual enterprises that have evolved in different contexts striving to achieve different goals. Nominally, however, they appear equivalent in that both traditions seek to make sense of Arabic grammar (Suleiman 1989; Bohas et al. 1990/2006).

The Arabic tradition can be seen as a project of an Islamic theology of language that relies on metaphors of social action and social justice in order to establish the inherent logic of a canonical corpus of texts. This tradition also strives to emphasise the uniqueness of Arabic which it sees as epitomised in Arabic's desinential inflection[2], or as it is called in Arabic— $)i^{(}r\bar{a}b$—which literally translates as Arabisation. The Orientalist tradition is rooted in Latin grammar and adopts a comparative approach striving to identify the underlying structures of relationships into which words and parts of words can be inserted to form meaning. The two traditions are motivated by different imperatives, have evolved at different times, were produced and propagated with different

---

1   The formal ethnographic research began in 2004 and spanned over several periods of fieldwork which included observations of classroom instruction at schools and universities, participation in teacher seminars, interviews, open-ended discussions and a fair amount of library work. The analysis, however, is very much informed by other experiences as well, mostly my own academic trajectory having gone through the system myself several decades beforehand. In other words, this is as much a work of observant participation as it is of participant observation.

2   Desinential inflection is inflection that commonly modifies the end of words and varies inter alia according to the word's syntactic function.

technologies of knowledge production, and were learnt and taught in vastly different educational milieux. Not surprisingly, perhaps, the two are radically different bodies of knowledge.

The Arabic grammatical tradition forms the basis for Arabic instruction in the Arab public school system in Israel. Jewish schools, where instruction is conducted in Hebrew, follow the Orientalist tradition of Arabic grammar. This very Orientalist approach carries through to universities' advanced grammar instruction in departments of Arabic language and literature. Significantly, these departments assume prior Arabic proficiency on the part of students and are not intended as programs of Arabic language acquisition. Rather, they are advanced programs in Arabic language and culture, and their students are both Arab and Jewish.

The cognitive significance of the radical alterity between the two systems of knowledge becomes apparent in university Arabic grammar classes. The fact that these advanced classes rely on the European tradition in their instruction suits the learning experience of Jewish students who come to university having studied Arabic and Hebrew grammars at school in ways that draw upon the Orientalist tradition of grammar. Arab students, by contrast, having undergone their primary and secondary school instruction in Arabic grammar in a modern variety of the Arabic grammatical tradition, encounter a new approach at university, with fateful consequences. Notwithstanding the fact that Arab students learn Arabic throughout their schooling while Jews learn Arabic as a second foreign language at high school—and notwithstanding the fact that Arab university students are proficient at Arabic while Jewish university students are not—the Arab students struggle greatly and flounder in Arabic grammar classes at university.

Elsewhere I analysed this loaded educational context (Uhlmann 2012).[3] A crucial aspect precipitating Arab underachievement in these courses is the profound incommensurability between, on the one hand, the grammatical common sense

---

3    In Uhlmann 2012 I also discuss the broad problematic relationship between Arabs and Arabic grammar—a relationship that is beset by Arabic's diglossia and the social relations of knowledge production and reproduction in the Arab world. The issue here is different, though, and more specific, namely a clash in the area of formal grammatical analysis. In other words, it is not the mastery of Arabic that is at issue here but rather the mastery of the formal elaboration of the grammar of Arabic. There is no question that Arab students are immeasurably superior to Jewish students in their practical mastery of Arabic grammar. Jewish students are rarely able to compose any independent prose in Arabic. Arab university students invariably can, albeit to varying degrees of grammatical competence. Yet while Arab students' mastery of Arabic prose construction and decoding—uneven though it may be—is superior to Jews', this mastery fails to translate into an advantage in the formal grammatical analysis of Arabic. The fact that Arabs spend years of school instruction learning a formal grammar of Arabic further accentuates this perverse reality whereby, notwithstanding their superior mastery of grammar in practice, and notwithstanding the greater time and effort they had spent at school on a formal grammar of Arabic, Arab undergraduate students are outperformed by Jews at university Arabic grammar.

that Israeli university instruction assumes, and, on the other hand, the grammar that Arab students actually learn at school. Crucially, the extent of this difference remains largely invisible to all parties to this educational exchange, be it Arab students, Jewish students, or university grammar instructors who are almost always Jewish graduates of the Jewish school system. This misrecognition hinders Arab students from understanding their incomprehension in systemic ways, and their instructors from effectively addressing this incomprehension. Consequently, Arab students experience their underperformance as personal failure. This has the pernicious effect of reconstituting social power relations as an individualised difference in learning capacity. A social difference in knowledge construction is transformed into individual failure of Arabs. What is more, this happens in a field of knowledge that is central to Arab identity and being.

The political implications of this situation are clearly significant, but I will not dwell on them here. Rather, I would like to focus on one of several mechanisms that seem to camouflage the profound incommensurability in knowledge systems, namely the translation of concepts between the two systems of grammatical knowledge.

A common practice in Arabic grammar instruction at Israeli universities is to render Arabic grammatical concepts in equivalent Hebrew concepts which are part of the contemporary Orientalist grammar of Arabic. These translations seem to work in that they generally designate the same objects as the original Arab term. But being rooted in a different system of knowledge, this sense of translatability is misleading. In fact, the original concept is not translated in any way. And the fact that the translation seems to 'work' makes it all too easy to mistake the two systems as somehow similar conceptual frameworks that are merely rendered in different languages. They are not.

In fact, the translation does not even 'work' as well as participants might think. The inevitable anomalies are kept invisible by several mechanisms. Israeli university instructors and educators in the Jewish school streams translate concepts from Arabic opportunistically and haphazardly. There is not a systematic translation of terms from Arabic to Hebrew which would inevitably stumble over refractory terms. But even when the translation of a particular term seems to succeed, this sense of success may be false. In the example I will discuss below a term in Hebrew is taken to be equivalent to an Arabic term. But this equivalence is an illusion. The Arabic term denotes a set of phenomena that is merely a subset of what is taken to be its equivalent Hebrew term. Because the instructional power relations are such that terms need to be translated from Arabic into Hebrew, but not vice versa, a false sense of equivalence between the two terms can emerge. What the Arabic term designates is also designated by the seemingly equivalent Hebrew term. The fact that the opposite direction of translation would run into contradictions passes unnoticed.⁴

The seeming equivalence of the terms in the two systems is deceptive. People on both sides of the language/knowledge divide operate as if the two systems are somehow compatible. This false sense of commensurability then makes it impossible for stakeholders—most significantly baffled Arab university students of Arabic—to make sense of the difficulty that Arabs have with university Arabic grammar.

The areas of basic syntax and verb morphology are useful illustrations of these underappreciated limits on translatability. For example, Jewish students learn that the Arabic terms *fiʕl* and *fāʕil* are, respectively, the predicate and subject of a verbal sentence, and that the former normally precedes the latter in standard Arabic.

This might seem a reasonable equivalent to Arab constructions, such as 'every sentence that is made up of a *fiʕl* and a *fāʕil* is called a verbal sentence (*jumla fiʕliyya*)' (*alnaḥw alwāḍiḥ*, elementary, book 1, p. 28).⁵ But note the lack of mention of word order in this quote. We shall return to the issue of word order below.

---

4   It would be an interesting intellectual exercise to think what would happen if an anthropological textbook on kinship, or a specific anthropological construct like segmentary kinship, were to be translated into Yolngu language in a way that would strive to be relevant to Yolngu concerns and to make sense to a Yolngu person of different kinship practices or what Latin grammar would look like if rendered in terms of the Arabic grammatical tradition. Readers familiar with Hebrew grammar might wish to juxtapose the contemporary grammar of Hebrew with the Qara'ite grammar of Hebrew that was produced in the Islamic world in the eleventh century (cf. Vidro 2011).

5   The discussion draws on the major Arabic textbooks used in Israel in both Arab and Jewish schools and at universities until 2010. For instruction on the Arab side I rely on three main texts. The first is the two volumes of the textbook by ʕAli al-Jārim and Muṣṭafā ʔAmīn, *alnaḥw alwāḍiḥ fī qawāʕid allugha alʕarabiyya*. This textbook, which was written in Egypt in the early twentieth century, was the main text used in Arab schools in Israel until the 1990s, and is still used in some Arab schools. The second textbook source is the series of *al-jadīd fī al-lugha*—the textbooks that are part of Israel's Ministry of Education's new curriculum for Arab schools. This series was introduced in the 1990s to replace the outmoded books by Jārim and ʔAmīn, and is nominally used throughout Arab schools, although the extent to which it has transformed instruction in practice is not very clear. The third textbook to form the basis for the analysis that follows is volume 4 of *mabādiʔ al-ʕarabiyya* by Rashīd al-Shartūniyy, which is universally used as a reference book by teachers and often inspires class preparation by teachers, although I have not heard of it actually being used as a textbook in class. While clearly each of the textbooks exhibits a unique approach, the commonalities among them are profound when contrasted with the textbooks that are used in the Jewish sector.

For Arabic instruction in the Jewish sector and at universities I draw primarily on the following books. Yaʕaqov Landaʔu, *madrikh bishvilei hapoʕal haʕaravī* is the standard textbook for verb conjugation instruction beyond the very basic forms. It is used in both schools and universities. Dov ʕIrōn, *taḥbīr halashōn haʕaravīt* remains a standard of Arabic syntax which is used at universities, and relied on by school teachers in the Jewish sector for specialised exercises and for explanations more generally. Yishai Peled's *Written Arabic Syntax: In Theory and Practice* (in Hebrew) is a recently published university-level textbook that is used at Tel Aviv University.

Another pair of terms—*mubtadaʾ* and *khabar*—are taken by Arabic instructors in the Jewish streams and universities to be the terms that are used to designate the subject and predicate of a nominal sentence.[6] This seems close to the terms' definition in Arab Arabic instruction, but there is an almost imperceptible yet significant difference. Consider 'Every sentence that is composed of a *mubtadaʾ* and a *khabar* is called a nominal sentence' (*alnaḥw alwāḍiḥ*, elementary, book 1, p. 30); or 'The verbal sentence begins with a verb, while the nominal sentence does not begin with a verb but rather usually begins with a noun'; and 'The nominal sentence is a sentence that is headed by a noun (*ʾism*) and is composed of a *mubtadaʾ* and a *khabar*' (*aljadīd*, grade 7, pp. 24, 110, respectively).

What the Arab textbooks say is that nominal sentences are sentences that contain a *mubtadaʾ* and a *khabar*. Significantly, the textbooks do not say that *mubtadaʾ* and *khabar* are the subject and predicate of a nominal sentence. (Below I will return to the question of what the two terms are.)

And from here an almost imperceptible departure in the systemic logic of the two doctrines begins. Jewish students are presented with the observation that Arab grammarians distinguish between nominal sentences and verbal sentences according to the first word in the sentence. If the first word is a verb, the sentence is called a verbal sentence and Arabs use the terms *fiʿl* and *fāʿil* to denote subject and predicate. If the first word is not a verb, usually a noun, then the sentence is called a nominal sentence and the terms *mubtadaʾ* and *khabar* are used to indicate the same terms, namely subject and predicate. And together these two sentence structures form the universe of sentences in Arabic.

Jewish students see this as an interesting contrast with the syntax of Hebrew grammar, where the differences between nominal and verbal sentences depends on the nature of the predicate and not its position in the sentence in relation to the subject. If the predicate is a verb, the sentence is verbal. If the predicate is not a verb, the sentence is nominal.

That Arab grammarians should base their syntactic typology on something trivial like which word begins the sentence, while grammarians of Hebrew should focus on something systemic and complex like the nature of the predicate, confirms to many Jewish students and their Jewish Arabic school teachers a prejudicial sense of the relative simplicity of Arab scholarship.

---

6  For example:

"הנושא במשפט השמני נקרא מֻבְתָדָא (مُبْتَدَأ) כלומר המלה שבה מתחיל המשפט), ואילו הנשוא במשפט זה נקרא خَبَر – ידיעה, ידיעה על הנושא), כגון: زَيْدٌ حَكِيمٌ, זַיְד הוא ה מֻבְתָדָא: حَكِيمٌ – خَبَر." (עירון כרך א' עמ' 1).

These are, however, misconstructions based on mistranslation. *Mubtadaʾ* is a concept rooted in the syntactic theory of ʿ*amal*, (which is normally translated in the historiographic research into the Arabic linguistic tradition as 'the theory of governance' or 'the theory of dependency'), and is not at all a subject (see below). But once translated as subject, classroom instruction continues using the terms of subject and predicate in Hebrew, even in areas where Arab terminology differs. This consistent (mis)translation of the Arabic term *mubtadaʾ* as subject of a nominal sentence creates a false sense of security in Jewish students of Arabic and their teachers that they understand the Arabic term and that they are dealing with equivalent concepts, when in fact they are not.[7]

And so, when discussing two groups of prepositions and auxiliary verbs that lead nominal construction with abnormal desinential inflections, the conscientious Jewish-sector teacher might also present the seemingly relevant Arabic terms for the subject and the predicate. The groups are named in both Arab and Jewish-sector instruction after their prototypical member and are called ʾ*inna* and her sisters (i.e. ʾ*inna* and the prepositions that behave similarly) and *kāna* and her sisters (i.e. *kāna* and the auxiliaries that behave similarly). The terms that are normally presented by Jewish-sector teachers as the subject and predicate are the ʾ*ism* of ʾ*inna* or *kāna* and the *khabar* of ʾ*inna* or *kāna*. The term *khabar* seems familiar. It is the same term that is translated as predicate of a normal nominal sentence. This gives a reassuring sense of parallel between the Arabic and the Hebrew terms, but what happened to *mubtadaʾ*? It is no longer used here to denote the word that functions as subject, and is replaced by the term ʾ*ism*—literally 'noun'—to create the construct of 'the noun of ʾ*inna*' and 'the noun of *kāna*'. The significance of the fact that in this context the term *mubtadaʾ* is no longer used to denote the word that functions as subject is overlooked by such teachers, or shrugged off as an unnecessary terminological infelicity of Arab grammarians.

With this little bit of oversight, the mistranslations of *mubtadaʾ* and *khabar* seem to work in that the translated terms seem to designate the same instances as the original ones. But conceptual cracks keep appearing, demanding some patching up.

---

7   As the discussion below will clarify, a more accurate way of rendering the relationship between the concepts would be to point out that the word which is the *mubtadaʾ* in the nominal sentence functions as the subject of the sentence. But this would only beg the question of what a *mubtadaʾ* actually is. And because the concept has no equivalent in the Orientalist grammar, because it is part of a heuristic system that is completely different from the European system—the two differ in their structure, their function, and the role they play within the broader intellectual culture—the only way to explain it would be to acknowledge the radical conceptual alterity between the two systems, and start presenting the alternative system of knowledge.

Topicalised sentences—in particular those where the subject of the predicative clause is topicalised—are usually classed in the Jewish-sector schools and university classrooms as normal nominal sentences. Dov ʿIron's book, the most advanced text on syntax that is used at schools, does discuss topicalisation as a complex sentence in which the *khabar* may be a verbal sentence (vol. 1, pp. 2–3). But it focuses on sentences in which the subject of the topicalised sentence is an object of the verbal sentence. The example given is 'زيدٌ مَرِضَ أَبُوهُ' (*zaydun mariḍa ʾabūhu*)—literally, 'Zayd, his father fell ill'. Significantly, the concept of topicalisation is exemplified with sentences whose verbatim translation into Hebrew inevitably produces a sentence that is topicalised too. This further reinforces the false sense of conceptual compatibility between the two systems of grammatical theory. ʿIron does not canvass sentences that to Arab grammarians are topicalised, yet may be translated as simple Hebrew sentences (see below). This further confuses things as Jewish students assume that their intuitive notion of topicalisation applies to Arabic topicalisation. By the same token, Arab university students are also led to believe that when they discuss topicalisation they mean, in fact, the same thing as their instructors and fellow Jewish students.

The problems would become apparent if instructors chose to foreground topicalised Arabic sentences in which the subject is identical in both the topicalised sentence and its predicative clause. The sentence 'زيدٌ مَرِضَ' (*zaydun mariḍa*) would appear to the Jewish student as 'Zayd fell ill', where in fact it is best translated as a topicalised construction, something like 'Zayd, he fell ill'. This construction may be used to indicate meanings that are constructed in English as 'It is Zayd who fell ill' or any number of alternative constructions that foreground and emphasise the fact that the person who fell ill was Zayd. By contrast, 'Zayd fell ill' would be conveyed in standard Arabic by the simple verbal sentence 'مَرِضَ زيدٌ' (*mariḍa zaydun*) with the verb preceding its subject.

Sentences like 'زيدٌ مَرِضَ' (*zaydun mariḍa*) which I glossed as 'Zayd, he fell ill' are presented in the Israeli-Jewish classroom as inverted simple sentences, a kind of unusual construction that is reserved for specific stylistic contexts like newspaper headlines. Students learn that, notwithstanding such unusual constructions, Arabic generally prefers to have the verb appear before its subject. The latter point needs to be emphasised to Jewish students because contemporary Hebrew stylistic preferences would have the subject precede the predicate in contrast with the preferred construction in standard Arabic. Hence the need to reiterate to students the practice of putting the verb first.

However, when instructors at Israeli universities and in Jewish schools identify such topicalised sentences as nominal sentences, they open up a new can of worms for the teachers and students of Arabic, namely the problem of inconsistency in agreement in number between verb and subject.

Strings of Connectedness

This involves another mistranslation, as it were, of the conceptual framework of Arabic grammar into the Orientalist grammar of Arabic. Or rather, in this case, it involves ignoring the difference between the two scholastic traditions in the designation of the analytic boundaries of verb morphology. In contrast with the Arab construction of syntax, the dominant approach in Jewish schools and in Israeli universities sees the pronominal suffixes of verbs as part of the verb conjugation as a matter of morphology rather than a matter of syntax. And so, those schooled in Israeli-Jewish grammar of Arabic treat the pronominal affixes of conjugated verbs as an integral part of verb morphology, that is, as one of the dimensions along which verbs are conjugated.

This leaves us with the following anomaly. When the subject seemingly precedes the verb, as in the topicalised sentence 'الاولاد مرضوا' (al'awlād mariḍu) 'the children, they fell ill', the verb appears to agree in pluralisation with the subject. The 'u' sound at the end of the verb 'mariḍu' is a pronominal suffix that indicates masculine, third-person plural. In other words, when the subject is plural, dual, or singular, the affixes of the verbs will indicate plural, dual or singular, respectively. But when the subject is stated explicitly after the verb, as in 'مرض الاولاد' (mariḍa al'awlād) 'the children fell ill', the verb lacks a pronominal affix, seemingly appearing in the singular.[8]

So from the perspective of Jewish students and instructors in university Arabic grammar classes, Zayd and his friends can fall ill in grammatically variable ways. One of these ways, مرض الاولاد (mariḍa al'awlād) 'the children fell ill', appears to have a verb in the singular preceding a plural subject; while the other, الاولاد مرضوا (al'awlād mariḍu), appears to convey the same meaning, but with the verb, now following the subject, appearing in the plural.

And so, Jewish students of Arabic learn that a verb that precedes its subject will always come in the singular, but a verb that follows its subject will agree with the subject in duality and pluralisation.

These syntactic irritants, namely the preference to begin a sentence with a verb and the inconsistent agreement between subject and verb, are major hurdles for Jewish students. The paucity of composition and free-writing exercises that Jewish students are required to undergo throughout their academic careers both hides the extent of the problem and hinders them from internalising proper syntactic style in Arabic writing.

---

8   Strictly speaking, from the perspective of Arabic grammar that will be briefly described below, the verb here is not in the singular. It is a verb without any indication of person. This very same structure, however, in appropriate syntactical contexts can also indicate both the verb and an implicit pronominal referent indicating a subject in the third-person singular.

Still, this construction of Arabic syntax and grammar seems basic to Jewish teachers and students of Arabic. Academic instruction in Arabic assumes that students are already familiar with these aspects of Arabic, yet they are completely bewildering to Arab students, many of whom had never encountered the conditional statement about the verb's erratic agreement with the subject. Their bewilderment is no less bewildering to the few Jews who are made privy to their bewilderment.

It would have been much less bewildering all round if it were recognised that the seeming translation of syntactic terms, although it appears to work, is a mistranslation. The syntax that Jews acquire during their schooling—a contemporary variety of Orientalist grammar—is fundamentally different from the grammar that Arabs learn at school.

For their part, Arab students arrive at university having learnt a set of observations that are rooted in a science of dynamic relations between words and particles that produce specific desinential inflections and structures in specific contexts. The systemic logic of the grammar that Arab students learn is fundamentally different from that which is taught at Jewish schools or at universities.

At its core, the Arab science is constructed around a theory of *ʿamal*, a word that is normally translated in this context as 'governance' or 'dependency'. This theory is effectively a social science of words and parts of words, and it underpins the conceptualisation and instruction of desinential inflection. Syntax and grammar in this approach are predicated on a notion of words and parts of words as entities which enter into relationships to form and modify meanings. This is rather different from the conceptual framework that operates in the European approach to grammar, including subject and predicate, or in their more appropriate Arabic translations of *musnad ʾilayhi* and *musnad*. The field of desinential inflection is perceived as the heart of Arabic grammar in the Arab tradition, and the theory of *ʿamal* is the core of that field, and is fixed in its position by the inertia of tradition, along with the stylised declamation of the analysis of desinential inflection.

According to this theory, the verb always precedes its subject and acts upon it in such a way that it produces the *rafʿ*, or what European grammarians have construed as the desinential inflection that marks the nominative.

Ironically, perhaps, for Arab grammarians no less than for grammarians of Hebrew, a verbal sentence is a sentence whose predicate is a verb. Word order as such is not what defines the type of a sentence. This is in contrast with the understanding that is propagated among Jewish students of Arabic according to which Arab grammarians define the sentence by the nature of its first word (see above).

As far as the canonical Arab grammarians are concerned, verbs always precede their subject. The subject can take the form of a separate word (noun or pronoun), e.g. 'مرض الاولاد' (*mariḍa alʔawlād*—'the children fell ill'); a pronominal suffix, e.g. 'مرضوا' (*mariḍu*—'they fell ill'); or be implied in the verb, e.g. 'مرض' (*mariḍa*—'he fell ill') which can strictly speaking form a complete sentence entirely on its own (see e.g. *aljadīd*, grade 7, p. 163).[9]

Significantly, in the Arabic grammatical tradition the pronominal suffixes are not part of the verb, and verb morphology does not include a dimension of plurality. Rather, pronominal suffixes that indicate pluralisation are elements of syntax. They are but one of the three ways mentioned above (along with implicit pronouns and explicit nouns) to connect subject to predicate in order to render a potentially complete sentence. Not surprisingly, then, when verb conjugations are discussed in Arab texts, pluralisation is not emphasised, and often not even included in systematic discussions of conjugation tables.

Now, some sentences have no verbs. These are nominal sentences. In these sentences subjects are not preceded by verbs. Instances where a subject is not preceded by a verb posed a theoretical challenge to theorists of *ʿamal*, namely the need to explain what gives such a subject the inflection of the *rafʿ*. According to the theory, the governing element must precede the word it governs. In a verbal sentence the verb precedes its subject and produces the *rafʿ*. But in nominal sentences the opening words are not preceded by the verb that would normally put its subject in the *rafʿ* in a verbal sentence. How can the fact that such words have the mark of the *rafʿ* be explained? The explanation that emerged was that it is the principle of *ʔibtidāʔ*—of initiation, of beginning—that governs these words and inflects them with a mark of *rafʿ*.

So the term *mubtadaʔ* does not mean a subject in a nominal sentence. Rather, what the term *mubtadaʔ* designates is a word in the *rafʿ* (i.e. nominative according to European grammarians) whose desinential inflection is governed by the principle of initiation for lack of an apparent alternative governor.

---

9   Within the European approach the verb 'مَرِضَ' (*mariḍa*) is a past tense in the third-person singular regardless of whether it appears in the sentence 'the children fell ill' (*mariḍa al'awlād*) or 'he fell ill' (*mariḍa*). Instructors within the Arabic grammatical tradition would interpret the former instance as a verb stripped of any indication of subject (because the subject is explicitly indicated following the verb), and the latter instance as a verb plus the implicit third-person singular subject.

## 7 The Failures of Translation across Incommensurable Knowledge Systems

Arab educators have traditionally avoided explicitly elaborating on the theory of ꜥamal in treatises and works that were aimed at the general public, or textbooks aimed at the general population of school pupils. Their definitions tend to be rather laconic, as in 'the *mubtadaʾ* is a noun in the *rafʿ* at the beginning of a sentence' (*alnaḥw alwāḍiḥ*, elementary, book 1, p. 25). This reluctance to elaborate on the underlying logic of grammar—the preference to keep instruction on a 'need-to-know' basis—is also a significant contributing factor to the invisibility of the incommensurability between the Arab and Orientalist approaches to grammar.

Not surprisingly, then, if a nominal sentence should be preceded by ʾ*inna* or *kāna*—using ꜥIron's examples[10] we have 'كَانَ زَيْدٌ مَرِيضًا' (*kāna zaydun marīḍan*—'Zayd was ill', p. 80) and 'إِنَّ زَيْدًا عَالِمٌ' (ʾ*inna zaydan* ꜥ*āliman*—'Zayd is indeed a scholar', p. 98)—the word that had been *mubtadaʾ* is no longer referred to as *mubtadaʾ* but rather as ʾ*ism* ʾ*inna* or ʾ*ism kāna* (the noun of ʾ*inna* or the noun of *kāna* respectively), because now its desinential inflection is governed by ʾ*inna* or *kāna*, respectively, and not by the principle of *ibtidāʾ*.

The way the *khabar* is defined fits in this scheme and differs fundamentally from the approach that prevails in Israeli-Jewish instruction. 'The *khabar* is a noun desinentially inflected in the *rafʿ* [defined in European syntax of Arabic as the nominative case] that together with the *mubtadaʾ* form a complete sentence' (*alnaḥw alwāḍiḥ*, elementary, book 1, p. 25). *Khabar* according to this quote is a noun and not a verb, and if a nominal sentence is one that has a *mubtadaʾ* and a *khabar*, then a sentence with a subject followed by a verb cannot possibly be a simple nominal sentence. (This is in contrast with the way Arabic grammar is presented in Jewish education, whereby if a sentence begins with a noun it is nominal.)

Clearly, then, from an Arab perspective topicalised sentences like 'زَيْدٌ مَرِضَ' (*zaydun mariḍa*) 'Zayd, he fell ill' cannot be defined as sentences with a subject followed by its verb. Rather, they are complex sentences with a subject followed by a clause, which may itself be a verbal sentence, in which case it requires its own subject and this will follow the verb (e.g. *aljadīd*, grade 7, p. 111).

A topicalised sentence is classed as a *jumla* ʾ*ismiyya kubra* (literally 'a great nominal sentence'). The first word is the nominal subject that is also a *mubtadaʾ*. The *khabar* that follows in such a sentence is itself a sentence, or a clause, composed of one word or more. When the *khabar* is a verb, the verb is in fact a

---

10  I include ꜥIron's vocalisation marks. These are not quite the way standard Arabic textbooks would have them, but that is a different issue which I will not raise here.

full verbal sentence that can be decomposed into a subject (be it a pronominal affix or an implicit subject) following its verbal predicate, in a way totally consistent with the fundamental rule that a verb always precedes its subject.

Thus, 'الاولاد مرضوا' (al'awlād mariḍu—'the children, they fell ill') has a topicalised subject 'الاولاد' (al'awlād—'the children') followed by a complete sentence, namely 'مَرِضُوا' (mariḍu—'they fell ill'), which in turn is composed of the verb 'مرض' (mariḍa—'fell ill') and its following subject, the pronominal suffix u which indicates 'they'. By contrast, 'مرض الاولاد' (mariḍa al'awlād—'the children fell ill') is again a sentence with the verb 'مرض' (mariḍa—'fell ill') and its following subject, in this case an explicit noun, namely 'الاولاد' (al'awlād—'the children').

But the clause that to Arab grammarians is a complete sentence composed of a verb and its pronominal subject ('مرضوا'—mariḍu—'they fell ill') would be approached by a person schooled in European grammar as a conjugated verb ('fell ill' third-person masculine plural), which appears to be a straightforward predicate to the subject that precedes it. This is why it is so easy to confuse it as a verb that is pluralised in agreement with its preceding subject.

In the Arab grammatical interpretation of topicalised sentences, then, the main sentence has no independent verb; the inconsistency in agreement between verb and subject never arises; verbs always precede their subjects; and verbs have no inherent quantity and do not conjugate along dimensions of quantity or number.

What is an elementary syntactical rule to Israeli-Jewish students—namely, that if a verb precedes its subject it is rendered in the singular, and if a verb follows its subject it agrees with its pluralisation—makes no sense in this scheme of things. The closest Arab equivalent I found in the Arabic textbooks is 'The *khabar* agrees with the *mubtada'* in number and gender' (*alnaḥw alwāḍiḥ*, elementary, book 3, p. 4) which is quite a different way of rendering this (see Table 7.1 for a schematic approximation of the differences between the two systems).

These differences are radical in that elements of one system cannot be reconstituted in terms of the other system. The two systems cannot be reconciled. These differences are therefore bewildering. They are shrouded in metacognitive blindness. None of the students, Arab or Jewish, that I spoke with was aware of the extent of the incommensurability of the two approaches on this particular issue. These differences, precisely because they pass unnoticed, are quite insidious.

Table 7.1 A schematic approximation of some differences between the two systems.

| The Arab perspective | The sentence | The Jewish-sector perspective |
|---|---|---|
| Meaning: The children fell ill. | مرض الاولاد<br>mariḍa al-ʾawlādu | Meaning: The children fell ill. |
| A verbal sentence because it contains a verb. | | A verbal sentence because it opens with a verb. |
| The verb (which never conjugates by number), mariḍa, precedes a noun, al-ʾawlād, which is a plural noun. | | The verb, mariḍa, precedes its subject, al-ʾawlād and is therefore in the singular in disagreement with the plural verb. |
| The preceding verb governs the noun al-ʾawlād and puts it in the rafʿ which is marked by u. | | The noun al-ʾawlād has the mark u of the nominative case[a] because it is a subject of the sentence. |
| Meaning: The children, they fell ill. | الاولاد مرضوا<br>al-ʾawlādu mariḍū | Meaning: The children fell ill. |
| A topicalised sentence without a verb (and therefore not a verbal sentence) where the predicate is a clause, which is itself a verbal sentence. | | A nominal sentence because it begins with a noun (which is followed by a verb). |
| The verb (which never conjugates by number) mariḍa is followed by its subject, the suffix ū, to construct a full sentence, mariḍū (they fell ill), which serves as a clause in the topicalised construction where it is preceded by an explicit noun. | | The subject is al-ʾawlād and its predicate is mariḍū. The verb follows its subject and therefore agrees with it in number. |
| The principle of ʾibtidāʾ governs the noun al-ʾawlād and puts it in the rafʿ which is marked by u. | | The noun al-ʾawlād has the mark u of the nominative case because it is the subject of the sentence. |

[a] Normally glossed as 'the first case'—ḥayaḥsa harishona (היחסה הראשונה).

A fundamental reason why these limits in translatability escape the consciousness of participants in educational exchanges has to do with the direction of the translation, which is itself a reflection of power politics of language in general and the educational arena of Arabic in particular. The significant translation goes from Arabic to Hebrew, Hebrew being the language that is usually used in university educational exchanges. Moreover, the grammatical theory and knowledge that underlies Arabic instruction at Israeli universities—a variety of the Orientalist linguistics of Arabic—is written about, discussed and thought of in Hebrew, English, and to a lesser degree German, but not usually in Arabic.

The instances that are classed as *mubtadaʾ* in Arabic are a subset of the instances that are classed as subjects of nominal sentences in Hebrew, and in Orientalist grammar of Arabic more generally. This is why translating the term *mubtadaʾ* as subject of a nominal sentence seems to consistently work, but translating a subject of a nominal sentence into Arabic as *mubtadaʾ* does not always work (as happened with the noun of *ʾinna* and the noun of *kāna*). And because in the context of university grammar instruction it is the Orientalist perspective that is the dominant structure, in that Arab students need to adapt to it rather than Jewish students needing to adapt to the Arabic grammatical approach, the mistranslation remains impervious to these anomalies and further reinforces the false sense of commensurability between the systems.

Such camouflaged mistranslations are among the normally invisible elements that make up the systemic incommensurability between the two grammars. The other mechanisms include differences in the organisation of the material, in the patterns and styles of reasoning, in the intellectual priorities, in the underlying analytical projects, and in the underlying metaphors and other tropes that animate the disparate grammatical and syntactical imagination. The cumulative effect of these mechanisms is a perverse situation whereby Arab students, who are far superior to their Jewish counterparts in Arabic proficiency and in the active application of Arabic grammar and syntax, are nonetheless outperformed and experience inexplicable difficulties in following and assimilating the material taught in Arabic grammar classes at university.

This becomes, then, yet another mechanism whereby formal education turns social disadvantage into personal failure, a situation made particularly acute by the fact that members of the subaltern group—Arabs—become alienated from a key component of their very cultural identity, namely Arabic.

It is possible that an instructional strategy that emphasises metacognitive awareness, where students realise that theirs is but one grammar of Arabic, not *the* grammar of Arabic, would go a considerable way towards addressing the pedagogical challenge of a student body schooled in incommensurable grammars of Arabic. In fact, by relying on the incommensurability as a point of departure, and highlighting the historic specificity of systems of knowledge, grammatical instruction could lead both Jewish and Arab students to a deeper understanding of the grammatical nature of the Arabic language.

More generally, I would suggest that close ethnographic studies of incommensurability—like the one offered here, and like Keen's earlier work—may thus be immensely significant, well beyond the narrow confines of theoretical reflection. They can support a metacognitively informed rehabilitation of subaltern systems of knowledge. In other words, where members of disenfranchised groups find their knowledge is judged in terms of dominant knowledge, such analyses can allow for the integrity of the subaltern knowledge to be defended without it being collapsed into a variant of the dominant knowledge.

And as for the field of theoretical reflection, this case study, like Keen's work before it, attests to the possible depths of incommensurability in systems of knowledge, the mechanisms that hide it, and how the incommensurability, embedded as it is in power structures, inevitably renders deficient both the subaltern and his or her knowledge.

## References

Bohas, G., J.-P. Guillaume, and D. Kouloughli. 2006. *The Arabic Linguistic Tradition*. Washington, DC: Georgetown University Press. (Original work published 1990)

Keen, I. 1995. Metaphor and the metalanguage: 'groups' in northeast Arnhem Land. *American Anthropologist* 22(3): 502–27.

Suleiman, M.Y.I.H. 1989. On the underlying foundations of Arabic grammar: a preliminary investigation. *British Society for Middle Eastern Studies* 16(2): 176–85.

Uhlmann, A.J. 2006. *Family, Gender And Kinship in Australia: The Social And Cultural Logic of Practice And Subjectivity*. Aldershot: Ashgate.

Uhlmann, A.J. 2012. Arabs and Arabic grammar instruction in Israeli universities: alterity, alienation and dislocation. *Middle East Critique* 21(1): 101–16.

Vidro, N. 2011. *Verbal Morphology in the Karaite Treatise on Hebrew Grammar* Kitāb al-ʾUqūd fī Taṣārīf al-Luġa al-ʿIbrāniyya. Amsterdam: Brill.

## Textbooks Cited

ʾAbu Khadra, F. et al. 2000. *Aljadīd fī qawāʿid allugha alʿarabiyya* [six volumes; grades 7 through 12]. Second edition. Jerusalem: Ministry of Education and Culture, Pedagogical Administration, Curriculum section.

ʿIron, D. n.d. *Taḥbīr halashon haʿaravit* [two volumes]. Expanded edition. Tel Aviv: Dyonon.

Aljārim, ʿA. and M. ʾAmīn. 2005. *alnaḥw alwāḍiḥ fī qawāʿid allugha alʿarabiyya* [two volumes; one for elementary and one for secondary schools, each volume containing three books]. Beirut: Almaktaba Allughwiyya.

# 8  Bakhtin's Theory of the Utterance and Dhaḻwangu *Manikay*[1]

Peter Toner
St Thomas University

Ian Keen's groundbreaking work on Yolngu sociality is based on the fundamental premise of indeterminacy and heterogeneity in culture and practice, the idea that there is no sense of a singular 'Yolngu identity'. Yolngu social practices exhibited 'a mosaic distribution of variant forms' (Keen 1994: 4), and Keen emphasised that a 'relativity of perspectives was at the heart of Yolngu religious and other practices' (ibid.: 6). Although Yolngu people across northeast Arnhem Land developed shared forms of religious and social practice, these shared forms were interpreted differently, groups were distinguished by deliberately created differences, and 'systematic ambiguity was one basis for the constitution of religious mystery and secret knowledge' (ibid.: 7). Keen goes on to write:

> The enactment of practices, institutions, and relations thus entails a constant interplay of utterance and interpretation, misinterpretation as judged by a speaker (or bystander), and deceit. Forms of expression and application of expressions are constantly subject to new, inventive, ill-informed, or aberrant recombination and extension ... But more fundamentally, perhaps no linguistic expression has an invariant interpretation; its 'fit' with the world is to a degree uncertain and contestable among users. (ibid.: 12)

---

[1]  My first introduction to Bakhtin came at the suggestion of the anthropologist Alan Mason, who supervised my honours thesis before I came under Ian Keen's tutelage. I had sent Alan a draft of some of my writing while I was conducting my fieldwork in Gapuwiyak, and his very perceptive comments included a suggestion that Bakhtin's work might prove to be useful. This chapter is dedicated to him.

Keen has made these premises the basis for much of his writing on Yolngu society: first, in an extended analysis of Yolngu religious practice, whereby ambiguity allows for the control of religious knowledge; and second, in his important reconceptualisation of Yolngu sociality (1995), which resists the unitary interpretations of Yolngu social forms that characterise much of the ethnographic literature.

In an otherwise favourable review of *Knowledge and Secrecy in an Aboriginal Religion*, Fred Myers calls for greater attention to the work of linguistic anthropologists working on communication and interaction as a way of furthering these analytical aims, and he specifically mentions Bakhtin's theory of the utterance in this connection (Myers 1995: 160). In my own research and writing, I have been interested in extending Keen's insights into Yolngu sociality, and have also seen Bakhtin's ideas as a possible way forward. Elsewhere I have written that Bakhtin's ideas on dialogism and heteroglossia have many significant parallels with Keen's analysis of the negotiation of shared religious forms (Toner 2005a: 41–2). In this chapter I would like to continue down that path that was inspired by Keen's work, and focus specifically on the theory of the utterance developed by Bakhtin and his contemporaries. Taking Keen's emphasis on heterogeneity and indeterminacy as a starting point for my analysis of Yolngu society, I argue that the ritual music of the Dhaḻwangu people of Gapuwiyak is best understood through the framework of the Bakhtinian utterance.[2] Not only are Dhaḻwangu *manikay* best understood as utterances in Bakhtin's sense, but the prominent place of *manikay* in Dhaḻwangu ritual life can be construed as one of the building blocks for social life more generally, in a manner consistent with Keen's own interpretation.

## The Bakhtin Circle[3]

At the very heart of much of the work of the 'Bakhtin Circle' is an attempt to transcend subjectivism and objectivism in the study of language and, by extension, in the study of literature and of social life. As Gary Saul Morson has written:

> Most of the social sciences have been plagued, before Bakhtin and since, with a recurring problem: Which is the fundamental unit, the individual or the group?

---

2   I am not the first scholar to make use of the work of the Bakhtin Circle in analysing Yolngu culture; in his analysis of Yolngu bark painting, Howard Morphy (1991: 126) drew upon Vološinov's distinction between meaning and theme.

3   On the question of the 'disputed texts' attributed by some scholars to Bakhtin but published under the names of Vološinov and Medvedev, I adopt the position outlined by Dentith (1995: 8–10) that it is sensible to group these three writers together because of the important similarities in their thought, but that the evidence is not conclusive enough simply to attribute those texts to Bakhtin.

Whichever you choose, you tend to resolve the other into it. One choice leads to an enormous underestimation of the role of individual action, as with most Marxists; the other, to an insufficient appreciation of the manifold social factors which really make us who we are. Bakhtin's idea was to find a new minimal unit of social analysis ... from which both the social and the individual, the macro- and the micro-, the systematic and the unsystematic could be derived ... The double-voiced word, the dialogic utterance, would be such a unit and could form the basis for the general science of culture and for its constituent disciplines. (1986: 7–8)

The Bakhtinian position on language and language philosophy is perhaps best articulated in Vološinov's *Marxism and the Philosophy of Language*. As with practice theorists like Bourdieu and Giddens who came after him (and whom I discuss later in this chapter), Vološinov is critical of both 'idealism', which locates consciousness somewhere above existence, and 'psychological positivism', which locates it in psychophysiological reactions. He writes that the real place of existence of the ideological 'is in the special, social material of signs created by man. Its specificity consists precisely in its being located between organised individuals, in its being the medium of their communication' (Vološinov 1973: 12). Continuing in a vein that is germane to Keen's analysis of Yolngu sociality, Vološinov writes that the interpretation of the sign within its social situation may help to resolve debates concerning the primacy of either the psyche or ideology:

Each word, as we know, is a little arena for the clash and criss-crossing of differently oriented social accents. A word in the mouth of a particular individual person is a product of the living interaction of social forces ... Thus, the psyche and ideology dialectically interpenetrate in the unitary and objective process of social intercourse. (ibid.: 41)

Vološinov carries on a sustained critique of both extremes of the debate on language, each of which ignores the value of the social. In individualistic subjectivism, typified for Vološinov by Wilhelm von Humboldt, 'the laws of language creativity are the laws of individual psychology' (ibid.: 48), whereas in abstract objectivism, typified by Ferdinand de Saussure, language is based on a ready-made system of grammatical, phonetic, and lexical forms (ibid.: 52). For Vološinov, neither perspective does justice to language as a complex system that is social at its core. He seems to regard abstract objectivism as the greater threat as he devotes more time to its critique, in particular its view of language as a synchronic system. Vološinov writes that such a synchronic system of language can only exist in 'the subjective consciousness of an individual speaker belonging to some particular language group at some particular moment of historical time' (ibid.: 66) and not in any objective sense; likewise, Vološinov states that systems of social norms occupy an analogous position (ibid.).

These views are particularly important in the reassessment of Yolngu sociality along the lines suggested by Ian Keen in his critique of more systematic models of Yolngu society, and so I will quote Vološinov at some length:

> The speaker's subjective consciousness does not in the least operate with language as a system of normatively identical forms. That system is merely an abstraction arrived [at] with a good deal of trouble and with a definite cognitive and practical focus of attention. The system of language is the product of deliberation on language, and deliberation of a kind by no means carried out by the consciousness of the native speaker himself and by no means carried out for the immediate purpose of speaking.
>
> In point of fact, the speaker's focus of attention is brought about in line with the particular, concrete utterance he is making. What matters to him is applying a normatively identical form (let us grant there is such a thing for the time being) in some particular, concrete context. For him, the center of gravity lies not in the identity of the form but in that new and concrete meaning it acquires in the particular context. What the speaker values is not that aspect of the form which is invariably identical in all instances of its usage, despite the nature of those instances, but that aspect of the linguistic form because of which it can figure in the given, concrete context, because of which it becomes a sign adequate to the conditions of the given, concrete situation.
>
> We can express it this way: what is important for the speaker about a linguistic form is not that it is a stable and always self-equivalent signal, but that it is an always changeable and adaptable sign.
>
> The task of understanding does not basically amount to recognizing the form used, but rather to understanding it in a particular, concrete context, to understanding its meaning in a particular utterance, i.e. it amounts to understanding its novelty and not to recognizing its identity.
>
> In other words, the understander, belonging to the same language community, also is attuned to the linguistic form not as a fixed, self-identical signal, but as a changeable and adaptable sign. (ibid.: 67–8)

This passage seems admirably well-suited to the perspective on Yolngu sociality that I have tried to develop elsewhere (Toner 2003a) and which I am trying to advance here, providing that we are willing, with Vološinov, to extend the consideration of language to a broader discussion of sociality. An individual's self-conception is partly influenced by ideas about the persistence and regularity of social groups and other 'systemic' or 'structural' aspects of society, but we must also recognise that named groups and ideas about them do not determine individual social practice in any absolute way. What is significant in a ritual context like a funeral, for example, is not the participation of 'the Dhaḻwangu' or 'the Munyuku' in an abstract sense, but rather in the participation of particular Dhaḻwangu or Munyuku people, related to the deceased and to each other in particular ways, and articulating their sociality through particular songs, melodies, and rhythms. What is significant to a person in this situation is not the formal qualities or structures of the Dhaḻwangu as one group in 'a system of normatively identical forms', but the meaning that being Dhaḻwangu takes on in that ritual context. The key is to focus our attention on sociality in use, as it is in use that both the systemic and individual aspects of sociality come together (cf. Dentith 1995: 28). Yolngu sociality does have a systematic character, but it must be completed, refuted, or altered in social practice.

An important point discussed by Vološinov is the evaluative orientation taken towards another's utterance, which is an essential feature of dialogic understanding. Vološinov writes that the process of understanding another's words involves 'lay[ing] down a set of our own answering words' (Vološinov 1973: 102). He continues:

> Everything vital in the evaluative reception of another's utterance, everything of any ideological value, is expressed in the material of inner speech. After all, it is not a mute, wordless creature that receives such an utterance, but a human being full of inner words. All his experiences—his so-called apperceptive background—exist coded in his inner speech, and only to that extent do they come into contact with speech received from the outside. Word comes into contact with word. The context of this inner speech is the locale in which another's utterance is received, comprehended, and evaluated; it is where the speaker's active orientation takes place. (ibid.: 118)

To extend this insight to the study of Yolngu sociality, we might say that every individual's inner speech includes his or her 'apperceptive background' of previous social experience: previous rituals, social situations, and of course statements about sociality—what one might call a person's 'conceptual' social structure. New social acts—statements, songs, rituals—are received against this background and evaluated against it, and a reply is generated, whether of agreement, disagreement, cooperation, or conflict.

For many making use of Bakhtin, the classic text is the long essay 'Discourse in the Novel' (1981), written in 1934–35. The 'social diversity of speech types' (1981: 263) is one of the key themes of the essay—for Bakhtin, any language is broken down into social dialects and languages used by different professions, age groups, and classes, and the novel itself is organised according to this diversity (ibid.: 262–3). Bakhtin refers to such linguistic and social diversity by the term *heteroglossia*, and states that it is 'the basic distinguishing feature of the stylistics of the novel' (ibid.: 263). The heteroglossia of the novel stands in contrast to the unitary language system represented by, for instance, poetic genres (ibid.: 264). Bakhtin posits that the philosophy of language and traditional stylistics, based on unitary language and the individual monologic utterance, is inadequate for the understanding of both language as a heteroglossic phenomenon and of the novel as a heteroglossic artistic genre.

The philosophy of language oriented toward a centralising view of language, such as Saussure's, ignored the dialogic nature of language, 'which was a struggle among sociolinguistic points of view' (ibid.: 273), preferring instead to seek 'unity in diversity' (ibid.: 274). Of much anthropological theory concerning the nature of social groups, we might write with Bakhtin:

> This exclusive 'orientation toward unity' in the present and past life of languages has concentrated the attention of philosophical and linguistic thought on the firmest, most stable, least changeable and most mono-semic aspects of discourse—on the phonetic aspects first of all—that are furthest removed from the changing socio-semantic spheres of discourse. Real ideologically saturated 'language consciousness', one that participates in actual heteroglossia and multi-languagedness, has remained outside its field of vision. (ibid.: 274)

This is reminiscent of Keen's critique of the 'orthodox model' of Australian Aboriginal social organisation, in that there has been a similar orientation toward the stable features of sociality to the exclusion of a dynamic social heteroglossia. As Keen writes, 'It has long been unsafe to assume a fundamental uniformity in Aboriginal social arrangements' (Keen 2000: 39).

In treating language as a unitary system, Saussurian linguistics views the word as neutral and as belonging to nobody in particular. Bakhtin, in contrast, points out that 'no word relates to its object in a singular way' (Bakhtin 1981: 276) but rather exists in a dynamic environment of other words about the same object. In this context of active engagement with other words, an utterance may enter into all manner of diverse relationships with them: agreement, disagreement, merging, resistance (ibid.). Yolngu social utterances may take a wide variety of forms, from actual statements about sociality, to social action in a ritual context, to the 'text' of a ritual (the sequence of songs, dances, and ritual episodes), to individual musical performances. Each of these can be understood as an utterance whose object is Yolngu sociality itself, and which contributes to a continually emerging Yolngu social theory—after all, anthropologists aren't the only social theorists around. These utterances concerning Yolngu sociality enter 'a dialogically agitated and tension-filled environment' (ibid.: 276) of other utterances by other Yolngu. None of these is definitive, but each makes a unique contribution to an unfolding social dialogue.

Let us suppose that a Yolngu person passes away and his or her funeral is organised. The deceased occupies a node in a social network that indicates the potential involvement of a range of people. Some of these people will decide to participate in the ritual, and they themselves will mobilise a social network of particular kin to join them. Others will decline to participate for a range of reasons and thus fail to mobilise other portions of the social network; still others will step in to fill the void. Once involved, senior men and women will discuss the overall structure of the ritual and how different groups will be involved. For instance, moving the body, painting the coffin, marking the grave, building a shelter in which to keep the body, and many other facets of the ritual all involve performances that will involve particular people. During each of these performances, particular songs and dances will be chosen, and each individual song will be performed using particular musical features, such as melody and rhythm, and using particular words and phrases in their song texts. At every stage and level of organisation, and in every aspect of performance, Yolngu are making social utterances, statements (whether verbal or not) about the nature of the social world and their place in it. These are not mere 'expressions' of an underlying 'social structure', but strategic orientations in an interminable social dialogue. When a singer names the people and places associated with a particular patrifilial identity in a song, or uses a distinctive melody associated with that identity (cf. Toner 2003a), he is in effect positing a relationship between those people and himself. This utterance enters an ongoing dialogue about the relations between those identities, and it may reinforce some utterances and contradict others. Other singers present may contribute to this conception of sociality through their song texts, or they may put forward alternatives. This social dialogue continues during the performance, and in other performances during the same ritual, and in other rituals. At no point is a definitive version established, but these events feed into each person's conception about the Yolngu social universe and their place in it.

A Bakhtinian approach to Yolngu sociality, then, is one that requires striking a new balance between structure and agency. While recognising the undeniable fact that certain features of Yolngu social life have a systemic and persistent nature, such an approach must also resist the kind of centralising, structuralist interpretation that has also been applied to language. Sociality can only be thought of as unitary when it is treated as an abstract social system of normative forms taken in isolation from concrete social life. An abstract social system—such as a system of Yolngu 'clans'—is, in actual social life, a multitude of social identities which each have their own semantic and ideological content. The language of Yolngu sociality is not neutral; it exists 'in other people's mouths, in other people's contexts, serving other people's intentions' (Bakhtin 1981: 294), and it must be appropriated by each individual to be put to their own ends. Social action, in ritual, musical, and other contexts, is the site of intersubjective struggles over meaning.

A view of Yolngu sociality which accepts in an uncritical way the 'clan' as the main unit of social organisation is one which seeks, or accepts, 'fixed and specific socially typical ... traits' (Bakhtin 1984: 47); in this view, the 'clan' becomes the focus of 'unambiguous and objective features' (ibid.) which define a person's social identity in a normative way.[4] One alternative is to examine the ways in which individual social agents develop their perspectives on the social world around them, and on their own sense of self, through an unending dialogue with others. When individual agents make decisions in social or ritual life, those decisions are shot through with the words of others; other people's ideas about sociality inevitably permeate one's thinking, meaning that social action is inherently intersubjective. Thus dialogue is an essential aspect of human being. Bakhtin writes that, for Dostoevsky, dialogue is not a means but an end in itself, and is not a threshold to action but action itself (ibid.: 252). He writes that dialogue

> is not a means for revealing, for bringing to the surface the already ready-made character of a person; no, in dialogue a person not only shows himself outwardly, but he becomes for the first time that which he is—and, we repeat, not only for others but for himself as well. To be means to communicate dialogically. When dialogue ends, everything ends. (ibid.)

So the crux of the matter is that Yolngu social dialogue, or the musical dialogue that I am particularly interested in, is not a coming together of completed social identities; rather, it is through these dialogues that those social identities are actually generated. This is an ongoing process in Yolngu social life, but one that is especially notable in musical performances.

An important distinction in Bakhtin's writing, which he elaborates in detail in his essay 'The Problem of Speech Genres', is the difference between sentences and utterances. Bakhtin writes that there is no neutral, passive listener who simply receives another person's words; rather, listeners always take an active, responsive attitude, agreeing with or disagreeing with, acting on or not acting on what was said (Bakhtin 1986: 68). What is more, the speaker is oriented toward that responsiveness and fully expects it (ibid.: 69). The speaker is also a respondent to previous words, not 'the one who disturbs the eternal silence of the universe' (ibid.). It is this dynamic theory of language which leads Bakhtin to define the utterance as 'the real unit of speech communication' (ibid.: 71). The utterance has boundaries that are determined by a change of speaker, preceded by other people's utterances, and followed by other people's utterances (ibid.). In contrast, the sentence is a unit of language, and 'as a language unit is

---

4   It is certainly possible to develop a critical, dynamic, and ethnographically informed view of the Yolngu 'clan' while continuing to use that term. Howard Morphy, for example, grapples in a very productive way with the nature of Yolngu sociality and how best to understand it, but he opts in the end to continue to use the term 'clan' (Morphy 1990, 1997).

grammatical in nature' (ibid.: 74). This distinction between language as a system and language in use is helpful in considering the interplay between systematic and practical aspects of Yolngu sociality. Bakhtin writes:

> The sentence, like the word, has a finality of meaning and a finality of grammatical form, but this finality of meaning is abstract by nature and this is precisely why it is so clear-cut: this is the finality of an element, but not of the whole. The sentence as a unit of language, like the word, has no author. Like the word, it belongs to nobody, and only by functioning as a whole utterance does it become an expression of the position of someone speaking individually in a concrete situation of speech communication. (ibid.: 83–4)

Again, we can rework the principles of Bakhtin's thought to think about the way Yolngu people interrelate. It is possible for anthropologists to think about Yolngu sociality in terms of abstract, neutral groups and their 'grammatical' interrelations, to construct *sentences* about Yolngu social life. In concrete social situations, however, Yolngu people construct *utterances* that are positioned, responsive, and part of an ongoing give-and-take of other utterances. The persistent and systemic features of Yolngu sociality are utterances that have been perpetuated more successfully, more widely, more influentially, and over a greater period of time, such that they are reiterated and reinforced by others in their own utterances. As Bakhtin writes, 'When we select words in the process of constructing an utterance, we by no means always take them from the system of language in their neutral, dictionary form. We usually take them from other utterances' (ibid.: 87). In other words, Yolngu sociality is profoundly influenced by the social utterances of other Yolngu people: the actions and words of others feed into the sense of self of every individual, subtly changing their concept of the Yolngu social world and influencing their responding social utterances. Bakhtin writes: 'Our speech ... is filled with others' words, varying degrees of otherness or varying degrees of "our-own-ness", varying degrees of awareness and detachment. These words of others carry with them their own expression, their own evaluative tone, which we assimilate, rework, and re-accentuate' (ibid.: 89).

Although they are not identical, Bakhtin's intellectual project covers some of the same ground as practice theory, a point that deserves some discussion here. Numerous scholars have noted important points of comparison between Bakhtin and Bourdieu (Hanks 1987; Holton 2000: 92; Holland, Lachicotte, Skinner, and Cain 2001; Myles 2010: 49–50; Myles 2013). Among its aims, practice theory also seeks to transcend the opposition between subjectivism and objectivism. As I have written elsewhere, Bourdieu's notion of *habitus* and Giddens' theory of structuration both investigate the ways in which social actors work within the confines of particular structures, but whose social action itself plays a part in reinforcing or reconfiguring those structures—in other words, social systems and individuals exist in a dynamic relationship in which neither can be said to determine the other (Toner 2003a: 79–81). More recently, Anthony King has criticised both Giddens and Bourdieu for lapsing into the objectivism they set out to critique: Giddens by continuing to draw upon a notion of structure (as in his concept of 'duality of structure') that is incompatible with his theoretically important idea of 'practical consciousness' (King 2000a); and Bourdieu by moving beyond his very useful concept of 'practical theory' into the a priori and deterministic structures of the *habitus* (King 2000b).

In both cases, King feels that Giddens and Bourdieu have developed genuinely important strategies for addressing the agency-structure debate, but have undermined those insights by recourse to notions of 'structure' that he feels are unnecessary. Giddens' 'practical consciousness' emphasises the shared understandings between individuals that allow people to know 'how to go on' in social life because, like Wittgenstein, he recognises that 'the final tribunal for action is not abstract reason but other individuals, engaged in a form of life, who mutually decide, given certain self-understandings, what constitutes appropriate practice' (King 2000a: 366). Similarly, although the concept of the *habitus* represents a relapse into structure and objectivism, Bourdieu's 'practical theory' emphasises the idea that 'social agents are "virtuosos" ... who are not dominated by some abstract social principles but who know the script so well that they can elaborate and improvise upon the themes which it provides and in the light of their relations to others' (King 2000b: 419). In both cases, the meaning of social practices is generated intersubjectively, which is why King concludes that their social theories have much to offer despite certain problems. Writing of Bourdieu's 'practical theory' King concludes:

> Social life is the mutually negotiated network of interactions and practices between individuals which is always necessarily open to strategic transformation ... All individual practice and the understandings which inform that practice are always social; they are always learnt from others and performed in reference to others, requiring the understanding of other individuals, even if a particular individual might reject and ignore that interpretation ... The intersubjective social context in which we are always already thrown constrains our practices and ensures that any practice we perform is social—it is always derived from shared understandings—but that context does not determine exactly what we will do or exactly what it is appropriate to do under any circumstance. We can never perform a pristine, individual act (as Sartre's existentialism wrongly demands), but there is always indeterminacy in the relations between individuals, which allows for intersubjectively meaningful but creative social action. (King 2000b: 431)

This passage is very reminiscent of a number of important features of Bakhtinian thought outlined above, and points to some productive links between Bakhtin and practice theory in the reinterpretation of social life.

So to summarise the position that I am adopting: the features of Yolngu social organisation that we may recognise as persistent, systemic, or 'structural' are those that have been reiterated and reinforced by a large number of utterances over a long period of time, and which consequently may have considerable influence over subsequent utterances. The Yolngu term *bäpurru*, to consider just one type of social identity, is used in conjunction with proper names to refer to an individual's concept of his or her social world and the kinds of people that are in it; at any point in time, an agent responds to pre-existing utterances about named *bäpurru* like 'Dhaḻwangu' with his or her own utterances about that identity, how it is constituted, how it relates to other identities, and what it means to partake of such an identity. Clearly, a certain degree of consensus in utterances over time by different people produces a systemic effect that plays an important part in shaping how individuals go about their lives and interact with others, especially under the guidance of the powerful and influential—another point emphasised by Keen (1994: 11–2). The key point is that both structure and agency are meaningfully understood in the intersubjectivity of actual social situations. Individuals base their concept of society and their place in it largely on the utterances of other people, such as their elders or contemporaries, and especially members of previous generations. These utterances are sometimes verbal, but may often take the form of what we might call 'social utterances' such as marriages or ritual performances. When individuals go into social situations such as musical performances, their own utterances respond to all those which came before, and they anticipate the active responsive understanding of those around them. These others may, through their own utterances, agree with their point of view, or disagree, or effect subtle alterations. So Yolngu sociality is neither an objective all-determining structure nor a subjective creation of an isolated individual, but a robust dialogical interaction.

Sociality thus constructed is not a singular thing but a multiple one. Yolngu people go into social situations with a variety of different ways of conceiving of their place in the world, and all of these different ways exist simultaneously, although in particular contexts one identity may take temporary precedence over the others. But in ritual musical performances, it is often the case that many identities are articulated almost at once.

## The Utterance in Yolngu Ritual Music: *Manikay* as a Speech Genre

In what ways can we construe Bakhtin's utterance as an appropriate analytical unit in better understanding Yolngu music? As stated above, for Bakhtin the utterance is where language is realised in various aspects of human activity;

he writes, 'Language enters life through concrete utterances (which manifest language) and life enters language through concrete utterances as well' (Bakhtin 1986: 63). He identifies three aspects of the utterance for focused attention—thematic content, style, and compositional structure—noting that all three are linked to the whole of the utterance. Furthermore, although every individual utterance is unique, there are relatively stable (although extremely heterogeneous) forms of utterance associated with different spheres of language use, which he calls speech genres (ibid.: 60). He distinguishes between primary (simple) and secondary (complex) speech genres, noting that the latter (including the novel) 'arise in more complex and comparatively highly developed and organised cultural communication' and are made up of various primary genres 'that have taken form in unmediated speech communication' (ibid.: 62). He notes further that primary speech genres 'are altered and assume a special character when they enter into complex ones' (ibid.), such as the difference between a rejoinder of everyday dialogue in the context of as novel and the same rejoinder in real life.

Bakhtin notes the important relationship between style and the utterance in its typical form as manifested in different speech genres. The individual style of a speaker or writer is characteristic of individual utterances, especially in artistic speech genres that do not require standard forms; indeed, in artistic speech genres, style enters into the very intent of the utterance. Bakhtin notes that style is also operative at the level of language styles (or functional styles) that correspond to particular genres and their generic unity, and indicates further that we must also consider historical changes in language styles as complex systems. Bakhtin also states that, although grammar can be considered separately from style, at the level of the individual utterance the two converge, as a speaker's choice of grammatical form is also a stylistic choice (ibid.: 63–6).

The form of song performed in the context of most public rituals in Yolngu society is known as *manikay*. Performed by one or more (sometimes many more) vocalists accompanying themselves with hardwood clapsticks called *bilma*, together with a single didjeridu (*yidaki*) player, *manikay* recount activities and events which occurred in a long-ago creative era known as the *wangarr*, when ancestral beings (also known as *wangarr*) walked the earth, gave it its particular features, gave birth to human groups, and created social institutions. Individual performances of songs (song items) are quite short, usually 20 to 30 seconds in length but sometimes up to around two minutes, and are separated from other song items by periods of talking, drinking a beverage, or smoking a cigarette. Each song item uses short and elliptical phrases to describe some particular aspect of an ancestral being or its activities in a particular place. Sets of three to six song items (song versions) focus on similar poetic themes and use the same clapstick rhythm, and from two to five different song versions are almost always performed in the poetic description of some ancestral animal, plant, human, or meteorological phenomenon (the song subject). So, for example, a song subject about a particular freshwater stream may be performed in four different rhythmic settings (song versions), each developing some particular poetic theme pertaining to those waters (first bubbling up from underground springs, then beginning to flow, then swirling, and finally becoming calm); each of these song versions may be performed four or five times before moving on to the next. An entire performance of a song series can consist of perhaps 15 to 20 song subjects, and can take three to four hours to complete.

*Manikay* are well described as a type of secondary (complex) speech genre in Bakhtin's sense. They are composed of words and phrases often used in everyday life (primary speech genres), although they can also include certain words and phrases that only occur in ritual musical contexts. As a type of speech genre, *manikay* exhibit thematic content in their articulation of ancestral narratives (albeit in a more elliptical form than spoken narratives about the same ancestral beings and events); they consist of specific compositional structures that are unique to this artistic form, namely image, modal, formal, contiguity, and analogical tropes (Friedrich 1991, Toner 2005b); and they display elements of style at both the individual and generic level. Most importantly, performances of *manikay* display those dialogical elements that are so important to Bakhtin's overall scholarly and philosophical project: an active, responsive attitude on the part of the listener; the orientation of the singer toward the expectation of such a responsive listener; and the recognition that the singer is responding to utterances that came before him, both as individual utterances and in terms of the language system as a whole (Bakhtin 1986: 68–9). Individual singers of *manikay* use utterances consisting of strings of words and phrases to articulate some particular aspect of the song subject, and these concrete utterances have definite boundaries marked by a change in singer (ibid.: 71), although in *manikay* the utterances of different singers often overlap as strict turn-taking is not a feature of Yolngu singing. The utterances of *manikay* also display a second constitutive feature of the utterance, its finalisation that indicates that a speaker has said all that he wishes to at that moment (ibid.: 76). In the case of *manikay*, that finalisation is most often signalled musically by the end of a distinctive melodic phrase (see Toner 2003a). And these utterances are all linked to one another and to the extraverbal context of the performance (Bakhtin 1986: 72–3). Additionally, not only are a singer's individual phrases to be understood as utterances with these features, but also performances of song series as wholes are utterances at a broader and more complex level—these 'work-utterances' (ibid.: 76) respond to previous performances of the 'same' song series ('same' in the sense of bearing the same name and relating to the same ancestrally significant place), and anticipate the responses of future performances.

Bakhtin writes that the finalised wholeness of the utterance, which guarantees the possibility of a response, is determined by three factors linked in the utterance as a whole. The first is 'the referential or semantic exhaustiveness of the theme of the utterance' (ibid.: 77) which, in artistic genres like *manikay*, is only relative, 'a certain minimum of finalisation making it possible to occupy a responsive position' (ibid.). The second factor, necessarily linked to the first, is the speaker's 'speech plan' or 'speech will' that determines its length and boundaries and marks 'what the speaker *wishes* to say' (ibid.). The third factor is the choice of a particular speech genre, in this case *manikay*, which gives shape to the speaker's (singer's) speech plan and which has 'definite and relatively stable typical *forms of construction of the whole*' (ibid.: 78). In other words, Yolngu singers articulate their understanding of ancestral and social realities in particular generically stable ways in performances of *manikay*, recognising that the same ancestral and social realities can also be articulated in other stable generic forms (oral narrative, painting, dance, etc.).

## Utterances in the Gurrumuru *Wängangur* Song Series

It remains to demonstrate exactly how performances of *manikay* can be understood as utterances. To do this, I will examine selected song texts from a 1996 performance of a song series called Gurrumuru *Wängangur*. Gurrumuru is one of the most significant places in the cosmology of the Dhaḻwangu people of Gapuwiyak, and the word *wängangur* ('at the camp') refers to ancestral events that took place right at the place where Dhaḻwangu ancestors lived during the *wangarr* era. The song subjects making up this song series consist of a range of ancestral activities (talking, walking, sitting, sleeping, fighting) and naturally occurring phenomena (flies, bush fowl, the north wind), but most notably items of material culture used by Dhaḻwangu ancestors (knives, tobacco, cloth, drums, mouth organs, cards, alcohol, rice, and flags). These objects were first introduced by Indonesian seafarers who visited the north coast of Arnhem Land searching for trepang, or sea cucumber, but they have become 'mythologised' and now are considered to 'belong' to the Yolngu ancestral being Birrinydji (Toner 2000). The overarching narrative on which this song series (and a number of others as well) is based describes an ancestral ship travelling from Numbulwar, to the south of the Yolngu region, along the coast to the north, around the Gove Peninsula, into Arnhem Bay, and down the Gurrumuru River, where it dropped its anchor.

Song textual utterances in this performance certainly demonstrate the features that Bakhtin posited for utterances generally. When individual phrases of different song items are analysed carefully, one can identify responsiveness on the part of each singer as he[5] listens to the phrases of others singers and formulates his own phrases in response. There are at least four types of responsiveness evident in this performance, which I will designate by the terms repetition, expansion, elaboration, and contestation.

In repetition, a singer hears another man using a particular word or phrase before him, and decides to incorporate the same word or phrase into his own song textual utterance. In one song item of the song subject *ngarali* (tobacco), for example, an initial phrase by the first singer was repeated by a second singer (which the first singer also repeated):

| *gatjala* | *Bambangbuy* | *gatjala* | *Bambangbuy* |
|---|---|---|---|
|  | ah | *gatjala* | *Bambangbuy* |
| tobacco | from Bambang[6] | tobacco | from Bambang |
|  | ah | tobacco | from Bambang |

In another example, two singers initially sang at the same time but using different phrases, but the second singer continued by repeating the initial phrase of the first singer:

| *marrngur* | *ditjburrkngur* |  | *murraygamanytja* |  |  |
|---|---|---|---|---|---|
| *dhiyala* | *ngali* | *wurruku* | *marrngur* | *ditjburrkngur* | *murraygam* |
| at | at the home of the knives |  | sleep |  |  |
| here | we | will | at | at the home of the knives | sleep |

More common is expansion, in which a singer will use another singer's utterance as a springboard for a poetically similar but expanded utterance using the same poetic form. In the song *matha* (talking), one singer's utterance was:

| *dhiwilyun* | *dhiwilyun* | *lamutja* |
|---|---|---|
| talking | talking | talking |

followed immediately by a second singer:

| *marrtjila* | *dhiwil* | *dhiwilyun* | *nyilbum* | *wanga* | *Dharulya* |
|---|---|---|---|---|---|
| talking | talking | talking | talking | talk | people of Gurrumuru |

---

5   Singers of *manikay* are always men, although women perform a poetically very similar but a cappella form called *ngäthi*.
6   This is an alternate name for Gurrumuru.

In this case, the word *dhiwiḻyun* (talking), used twice by the first singer, was then used by the second singer in the same form and in a grammatically altered form, in addition to a number of different words with the same meaning. In another example, a singer performing the song subject *dhamburru* (drum) used the phrase:

| *djingarra* | *miwurryun* | *miḏay* | *miḏay* |
|---|---|---|---|
| the sound | the sound | drum | drum |

followed immediately by a second singer's expansion upon his imagery:

| *djingarra* | *miwurryun* | *guywuyun* | *wagalwuy* | *binydjan* | *liyawinydjan* | *Mayarra* |
|---|---|---|---|---|---|---|
| the sound | the sound | the sound | for fun | at | at | Mayarra[7] |

In this case, the first singer's emphasis on the sound of the drum was expanded upon by the second singer's indication of the purpose and the location of the drumming.

Very often, a number of singers will build upon each other's utterances, each adding a new and unique dimension to the narrative, but nevertheless attempting to fit in with the previous singers' 'speech plan', which can be referred to as elaboration. In one song item of the song subject *yiki* (knife), the first singer's utterance was:

| *Gubanytji* | *Gubanytji* | *lirrbum* | *dhangatjayan* |
|---|---|---|---|
| Gubanytji[8] | Gubanytji | clearing[9] | clearing |

responded to and elaborated upon by the second singer:

| *Gunirima* | *Dharrwalawal* | *lirrbum* | *nganya* | *yuwukurr* |
|---|---|---|---|---|
| Gunurima[10] | Dharrwalawal[11] | clearing | that | while talking |

In this case, only one word used by the first singer was repeated by the second. However, it is clear that the basic poetic theme of 'clearing the camp at Gurrumuru' was elaborated upon by the second singer in his use of two additional alternate names for that place, a deictic word, and an additional image of the ancestors not only clearing the camp, but talking while they did so.

---

7    Another alternate name for Gurrumuru.
8    Another alternate name for Gurrumuru.
9    i.e. using the knife to clear away the brush in the camp.
10   Another alternate name for Gurrumuru.
11   Another alternate name for Gurrumuru.

In another example from the *ngarali* (tobacco) song, the first singer's phrase

| *warali* | *gatjala* | *warali* | *Bambangbuy* | *warali* | *warali* | *Mayarra* |
|---|---|---|---|---|---|---|
| tobacco | tobacco | tobacco | from Bambang | tobacco | tobacco | Mayarra |

was followed by a second singer:

| *gatjala* | *warali* | *wikun* | *marrtji* | *bulutjuwurr* | *warali* | *waralinyga* |
|---|---|---|---|---|---|---|
| tobacco | tobacco | smoking | smoking | through the beard | tobacco | tobacco |

Again, some compelling additional imagery allowed the second singer to take the basic idea of Dhaḻwangu ancestors smoking tobacco at Gurrumuru, and to develop the elaborated visual image of the smoke from the tobacco appearing to come out through the men's beards.

In the *nhina* (sitting) song subject, one singer's phrase

| *wayuklil* | *nhinanytja* | *madaywal* | *narrpiya* | *garrathawal* | *ganburrkwudhun* |
|---|---|---|---|---|---|
| on the arm | we sit | octopus | octopus | octopus | sit down |

was matched by a second singer's contrasting imagery:

| *nhina* | *bukman* | *ngamangamayun* | *marrlil* | *lukuwurrngulil* |
|---|---|---|---|---|
| sit | properly | properly | sit on | on the anchor |

In this case, both singers are referring to 'the foundations' of Gurrumuru as an ancestrally significant place by indicating the most sacred ancestral beings associated with that place. The river mouth of Gurrumuru, on the coast of Arnhem Bay, is the subject of a separate song series known as Yikari (the name of that place), and the subjects of that song series (including *narrpiya*, the octopus) describe animals, objects, and other beings that exist in that part of the river and the associated coastline. *Narrpiya* is among the most important subjects of that song series, and is considered to be an icon of Dhaḻwangu identity. The anchor, *lukuwurrngu* or *djalkiri*, is another centrally important and sacred symbol of Dhaḻwangu identity, referring to the ship's anchor, believed to lie beneath the soil of Gurrumuru. The first singer's reference to one important symbol of Dhaḻwangu identity led to an elaborated response on the part of the second singer in his reference to a second important symbol. The centrality of these two particular symbols is confirmed by imagery used in Dhaḻwangu funerals, in which flags decorating the shade in which a dead body is kept lying in state may depict images of octopuses or anchors, among other symbols.

Sometimes, a singer's utterance is a form of contestation, in the sense that personal rivalries can result in one singer either trying to displace the imagery of another singer by replacing it with quite different tropes, or else ignoring that singer completely. In the case of this performance, two of the singers had a rather tense relationship, one being an older, more experienced, but arguably less talented singer, and the other being a younger, up-and-coming talent. In this particular performance, there were a number of occasions where the younger singer was developing a particular set of poetic images, only to have the older singer come in over the top of him with a forceful delivery of quite different and incompatible imagery. On example comes from the *yiki* (knife) song:

| *nyarkun* | *yukurr* | *bilaram* | *nyarkirrirrngu* | |
| | *nhathin* | *dhay'yi* | *dharrumbanytja* | *lingulingu* |
| sound | is | sound | sound | |
| | how | this | clearing | clearing |

In this case, the older singer cannot be said to be expanding upon the younger singer's phrase: not only is the second set of images quite different from the first (which focused on the sound of the knives clashing together), but the delivery itself was rather overpowering and not attentive to the younger singer's phrasing—in other words, he barged in and asserted his own utterance as an aggressive form of contrast or contestation with the immediately previous utterance. And in case there was any doubt of this interpretation, the younger singer pointed it out to me repeatedly when we later listened to the recording. However, even contestation is a form of responsiveness, as Bakhtin never implied that speakers always agree with one another.

With these different forms of responsiveness in mind, we can better appreciate the various ways in which *manikay* can be understood to be composed of many different utterances, interconnected with one another in the midst of performance. Far from being a musical and poetic tradition in which singers are shackled to fixed poetic forms, performances of *manikay* display in a condensed form the dialogic nature of Yolngu sociality that exists more generally. The following transcription of one entire song item of the *garrurru* (flag) song is highly elaborated, but representative of Dhal̲wangu musical interactions. This performance was somewhat more 'staged' than others, with the singers organising in advance who would sing and in what order, because they were going to give the recording to a visiting relative as a gift. The different singers are each designated with a letter.

a. *garrurru Balawarrwarrngur garrurru ngarrakunytja Mitjbaralngur Garruburrangur*

*ngubar ngarra lalanga dhananytja wilirr dhananytja ngarra lalangur ngunhunytja dutjunmarang*

*garrurru ngarrakunytja wuyupun marrtji dhanggala mariwuy minytjinytja bundabunda warrgariny*

b. *ngarranydja warwuyun bingur buwapungal mathamirr dhangarrurru Gundjiwundji Wurindiwuy*

c. *mathamirrdhan gunarangmirr miwatjdhan galawangmirr miwatjdhan garrurru Ngulpurrngur Dhaparawungur*

d. *buwapum djalawa buwapum djalawa bingur ngarra buwapum Bambangur bili Bambang dhay'yi manydjarrka*

e. *balandi ngangunytja garrayiltjilyunar dhanggala wurrandjuna*

chorus: *ya gutharra warwu ngarra yawugay ya gutharra warwu ngarra laka marrilaka dhalalalalalala marrangmadji*

f. *wanggayngunytja ngurukuy ganygulba dhanytja ngalimurr marrtji djalaywu nhathin dhay'yi minytjinytja*

b. *gilung buwapungalwu dhanggala wananirrpu*

e. *ngarrakunytja gunarrangmirr wupuy galawangmirr gilung ngarra Burrulul Wangguwanggu djalay ngarra gunda Bathulumbu*

a. *ngupar ngarra Yikamula dhananytja Mitjbaral ngarra ngupar Mungurru Lirrinmatji*

f. *bayun dhanytja Warrunmatji Yandhala Mawuyul Walarrnga dhiyangga gurrurruri djalay marrtji ngalimurrung*

d. *yakumirr Gurrumurumirr manydjarrkanydja maripuydhan barrngbarrngdja yakumirr Gurrumurumirr maripuya Barrthanakawuy Mayarrawuy*

e. *gilung ngayiyun warwuyun*

Chorus: *ya gutharra warwu ngarra yawugay ya gutharra warwu ngarra yawugay dhalalalalalala garrurru*

a. flag/ from Warramiri country/ flag/ for me/ from Warramiri country/ from Warramiri country

sailed/ I/ [from] Birrkili country/ that/ Birrkili country/ that/ I/ from Birrkili country/ that/ take it back flag/ for me/ away/ moving/ flag/ of the war/ colour/ of the plains/ of the plains

b. I [am]/ worrying/ from/ sailing/ with language/ that flag/ Nundhirribala country/ of Nundhirribala country

c. with that language/ with Nundhirribala language/ [that is] different/ with Nundhirribala language/ [that is] different/ flag/ from Nundhirribala country/ from Nundhirribala country

d. sailing/ sailing/ sailing/ sailing/ from/ I [am]/ sailing/ from Bambang/ because/ Bambang /this flag

e. ropes/ see/ disappearing/ flag/ flag

Chorus: ya/ 'grandson' [ZDS]/ worry/ I/ worry/ ya/ grandson/ worry/ I/ flag/ flag/ flag flying in the wind/ flag

f. another/ from/ Wangurri country/ this/ we [are]/ sailing/ sailing/ how/ this/ colour

b. sailing/ sailing/ flag/ flag

e. for me/ with Nundhirribala language/ Nundhirribala language/ with Nundhirribala language/ sail/ I/ Nundhirribala country/ Nundhirribala country/ sail/ I/ rock in the ocean/ in Wurramarrba country

a. sailed/ I/ [from] Munyuku country/ that/ Munyuku country/ I/ sailed [past]/ ocean at Garrapara/ ocean at Garrapara

f. leaving/ this/ Birrkili country/ Birrkili country/ Birrkili country/ Birrkili country/ with this/ this flag/ sail/ sail/ for us

d. with a name/ with Gurrumuru/ this flag /of the war/ this torn one/ with a name/ with Gurrumuru/ of the war/ from Gurrumuru/ from Gurrumuru

e. sailing/ sailing/ worrying

Chorus: ya/ 'grandson' [ZDS]/ worry/ I/ worry/ ya/ 'grandson'/ worry/ I/ worry/ flag flying in the wind/ flag

This version of the *garrurru* (flag) song is known as a *yuṯa manikay* (new song), which makes use of both traditional song texts and a unison chorus section that refers to contemporary events (see Knopoff 1992; Toner 2000). The composer was trying to heal his sick 'grandson' (ZDS) at Numbulwar (located near the country of the Nundhirribala people) and was worried about him. As a Dhaḻwangu man, however, his own ancestral country was at Gurrumuru. In composing this song version, he used the song subject *garrurru* (flag), specifically the idea of the flag flying from the mast of the ship that travelled around the coast from Numbulwar to Gurrumuru during the *wangarr* era. The majority of the song texts used here are also found in other versions of *garrurru*, with the exception of the unison chorus that refers to contemporary events.

This song item clearly demonstrates that Dhalwangu singers are highly responsive to one another, attending to the poetic utterances which preceded their own and anticipating the responses of others. Each singer's utterances develop the central image of the ship and its travels to Gurrumuru, making particular reference to where it came from, where it was going, and the places belonging to other people who also have rights in this cosmology (Warramiri, Wangurri, Birrkili, Munyuku, Nundhirribala; and, in other song items in this performance, Gumatj). These various place references can be understood as examples of expansion. Each singer also uses forms of elaboration, consistent with the overall theme but developing unique images: the colour of the flag, the association of the torn flag with war, or the image of the halyards disappearing up the mast of the ship as the flag is hoisted. These poetic techniques illustrate that the central element of Bakhtin's utterance, the responsiveness that is essential for true dialogism, is unquestionably present in Dhalwangu *manikay*.

The above discussion demonstrates two of the key elements of the Bakhtinian utterance, thematic content and compositional structures. The third element, that of style at the generic and the individual level, remains to be commented upon. At the broadest level, the poetics of Dhalwangu *manikay* are centred around the evocation of ancestrally significant places, with singers 'painting a picture' of those places in the mind's eye of the listener (and, in keeping with Bakhtin's ideas about the utterance, anticipating the listeners' responses to that picture). They do so through a generic poetic style that is reminiscent of imagist poetry, making use of strings of names and images to evoke ancestral places in a minimalist and sometimes esoteric way; it is only through the combination of the utterances of a number of singers over several hours of performance that a kind of narrative structure emerges. Also characteristic of Dhalwangu *manikay* as a distinctive speech genre is the use of a variety of poetic devices for evoking the ancestral past in the present of performance, such as the use of the first-person singular and present-tense verb forms (e.g. referring to the ancestral flag flying atop the mast of the ship by the phrase 'I sail'), as well as deictics or 'pointers' (e.g. 'this flag', 'over there'). These poetic devices are powerful ways of conveying to listeners the idea that ancestral activity happened in the past, but also has a sense of ongoing occurrence in the present. The widespread use of parallelism is evident in the use of place names referring to the country of many different groups; not only do groups sharing the same cosmology believe that ancestral places are linked by ancestral journeys (cf. Keen 1994), but there is also a sense that the same events played out in their entirety in each place (i.e. other groups sharing this cosmology may sing the same songs, but locate the activity in their own country). These and other stylistic elements seem to be characteristic of *manikay* as a type of speech genre.

At the level of individual style, we can see how broader elements of generic style are personalised for particular singers. An analysis of all 21 song items of the *garrurru* song subject in this performance (consisting of five different song versions) revealed a great deal of diversity in how individual singers interpreted this particular song subject and what range of poetic devices they used. Only a handful of words and phrases were used by all or most of the singers involved in this performance, and indeed each individual singer was notable for using certain words and phrases that were not used by anyone else. This somewhat unexpected poetic diversity may be accounted for by a combination of age and experience (more experienced singers come to know more alternate names for objects and places), pedagogy (who the singer learned from), personal motivation (a desire to develop an individual style), and talent. At any rate, it is certainly possible to identify individual style in Dhaḻwangu *manikay*, even though the song subjects themselves impose certain generic constraints on individual creativity.

The analysis above also shows that singers have a well-developed method of marking boundaries by changing singers, which is one constitutive feature of the utterance. The second constitutive feature, finalisation, is best recognised through the distinctive melodies to which song texts are set. All Yolngu *bäpurru* identities are associated with distinctive melodies; Dhaḻwangu people have four (see Toner 2003a). A singer's 'speech plan' for any utterance is partly based on the imagery on which he wants to focus, but also must be based on the physical limitations of how many words can be fit into a melodic phrase. Other performers are able to make educated guesses about how long a given singer will make an utterance, based on the words he is using, on gestures, but especially on the melody itself and how far the melodic phrase has progressed. In anticipating the end of an utterance based on melody, a singer is able to prepare for his own utterance with a calculated amount of overlap (usually quite small).

Take, for example, the *garrurru* song subject analysed above. This song was performed using a Dhaḻwangu melody referred to as the '*yuṯa* A' (*yuṯa* meaning 'new', and the 'A' distinguishing this melody from the '*yuṯa* B'). A graphic representation of this melody (Figure 8.1) shows that it consists of three pitches: a high note held for half of the melody; and two alternating lower notes, the first almost eight semitones[12] below the top note, and the second a further two semitones lower.

---

12  Each semitone in the scale can be divided into 100 equal increments called 'cents'.

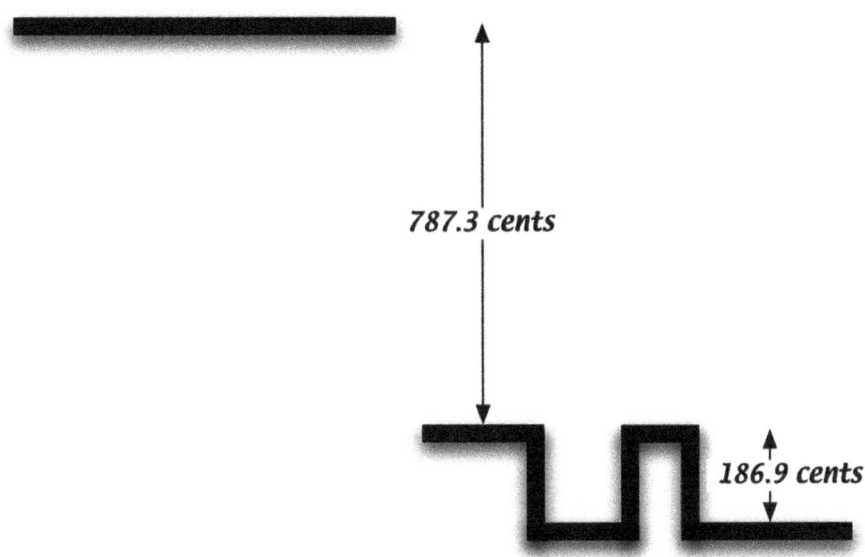

Figure 8.1 The Dhalwangu *yuṯa* A melody.
Source: Peter Toner.

In practice, this melody is usually performed across two vocal phrases, with a breath after the end of the high note. The length of the two vocal phrases is about the same, although singers tend to prolong the second phrase as they complete the 'speech plan' of their utterance. It is during this short period of prolongation that another singer could join in with his own utterance with minimal disruption. It needs to be stated, however, that strict turn-taking is by no means a customary feature of *manikay* as a speech genre, and it is common for singers to overlap each other considerably. As a method of finalisation, however, the use of melody is a clear marker. As Bakhtin writes, 'When hearing … we clearly sense the end of the utterance, as if we hear the speaker's [singer's] concluding *dixi*' (Bakhtin 1986: 76).

## Conclusions

Bakhtin's utterance is evidently a useful analytical tool for better understanding the dialogism inherent in *manikay* as a creative form that meets the criteria of a speech genre. Space limitations prevent me from elaborating further, but it bears mentioning that the notion of the utterance is well suited to other levels of Yolngu ritual practice as well. The features of the utterance examined above (responsiveness, dialogism, style, boundary marking, finalisation) are also evident when rituals as wholes are examined, as evidenced by the most detailed accounts of Yolngu rituals in the literature (Keen 1978; Morphy 1984). Indeed, the highly political nature of Yolngu ritual (Keen 1994) stands as a testimony to how carefully Yolngu consider the previous and future utterances of others concerning the depiction of Yolngu society and connections to country that rituals entail. Additionally, research conducted on the repatriation of archival audio recordings back to their Yolngu communities of origin indicates that Yolngu singers are clearly concerned with (and nostalgic about) the utterances of previous generations of Yolngu singers, and craft their contemporary performances accordingly (Toner 2003b).

For the purposes of this volume, what is most significant is that the challenges laid down by Ian Keen in his analyses of Yolngu social and ritual life are well responded to by a turn toward Bakhtin's thought. Keen encourages us to shed the orthodoxies of established analytical frameworks, to the extent that they accept the systematic and structured aspects of Yolngu sociality, in favour of greater attention to heterogeneity and contingency. Keen's perspectives have encouraged me to examine Yolngu social life as it is lived on the ground, even if that life does not fit easily within established analytical frameworks. Bakhtin also called for a focus on living language, on the utterance, as opposed to the more abstract formal structures that were prevalent in the language scholarship of his day. Bakhtin's notions of dialogism and heteroglossia are well suited to an analysis of Yolngu social and ritual life. There is no neutral word, nor any first speaker, in Yolngu life, and all Yolngu discourses and practices are shot through and inflected with the discourses and practices of others. Understanding Yolngu *manikay* as a distinctive speech genre, and Yolngu song texts as utterances, provides a coherent analytical framework that speaks to these larger social processes.

# References

Bakhtin, M.M. 1981. Discourse in the novel. In M. Holquist (ed.), C. Emerson and M. Holquist (trans.), *The Dialogic Imagination: Four Essays*, pp. 259–422. Austin: University of Texas Press.

Bakhtin, M.M. 1984. *Problems of Dostoevsky's Poetics*. C. Emerson (ed. and trans.). Manchester: Manchester University Press.

Bakhtin, M.M. 1986. The problem of speech genres. In C. Emerson and M. Holquist (eds), V.W. McGee (trans.), *Speech Genres and Other Late Essays*, pp. 60–102. Austin: University of Texas Press.

Dentith, S. 1995. *Bakhtinian Thought: An Introductory Reader*. London and New York: Routledge.

Friedrich, P. 1991. Polytropy. In J.W. Fernandez (ed.), *Beyond Metaphor: The Theory of Tropes in Anthropology*, pp. 17–55. Stanford: Stanford University Press.

Hanks, W.F. 1987. Discourse genres in a theory of practice. *American Ethnologist* 14(4): 668–92.

Holland, D., W. Lachicotte, D. Skinner, and C. Cain. 2001. *Identity and Agency in Cultural Worlds*. Cambridge, MA: Harvard University Press.

Holton, R. 2000. Bourdieu and common sense. In N. Brown and I. Szeman (eds.), *Pierre Bourdieu: Fieldwork in Culture*. Lanham, MD: Rowman and Littlefield.

Keen, I. 1978. One Ceremony, One Song: An Economy of Religious Knowledge among the Yolngu of North-East Arnhem Land. PhD Thesis, The Australian National University, Canberra.

Keen, I. 1994. *Knowledge and Secrecy in an Aboriginal Religion*. Oxford: Clarendon Press.

Keen, I. 2000. The debate over Yolngu clans. *Anthropological Forum* 10(1): 31–41.

King, A. 2000a. The Accidental Derogation of the Lay Actor: A Critique of Giddens's Concept of Structure. *Philosophy of the Social Sciences* 30(3): 362–83.

King, A. 2000b. Thinking with Bourdieu Against Bourdieu: A 'Practical' Critique of the Habitus. *Sociological Theory* 18(3): 417–33.

Knopoff, S. 1992. *Yuṯa manikay*: juxtaposition of ancestral and contemporary elements in the performance of Yolngu clan songs. *Yearbook for Traditional Music* 24: 138–53.

Morphy, H. 1984. *Journey to the Crocodile's Nest*. Canberra: Australian Institute of Aboriginal Studies.

Morphy, H. 1990. Myth, totemism, and the creation of clans. *Oceania* 60(4): 312–29.

Morphy, H. 1991. *Ancestral Connections: Art and an Aboriginal System of Knowledge*. Chicago: The University of Chicago Press.

Morphy, H. 1997. Death, exchange, and the reproduction of Yolngu society. In F. Merlan, J. Morton, and A. Rumsey (eds), *Scholar and Sceptic: Australian Aboriginal Studies in Honour of L.R. Hiatt*, pp. 123–50. Canberra: Aboriginal Studies Press.

Morson, G.S. 1986. *Bakhtin: Essays and Dialogues on his Work*. Chicago: The University of Chicago Press.

Myers, F. 1995. Review of *Knowledge and Secrecy in an Aboriginal Religion*. *Oceania* 66(2): 159–61.

Myles, J. 2010. *Bourdieu, Language and the Media*. London: Palgrave MacMillan.

Myles, J. 2013. Instrumentalizing voice: applying Bakhtin and Bourdieu to analyze interactive voice response services. *Journal of Communication Inquiry* 37(3): 233–48.

Toner, P. 2000. Ideology, influence and innovation: the impact of Macassan contact on Yolngu music. *Perfect Beat—The Pacific Journal of Research into Contemporary Music and Popular Culture* 5(1): 22–41.

Toner, P. 2003a. Melody and the musical articulation of Yolngu identities. *Yearbook for Traditional Music* 35: 69–95.

Toner, P. 2003b. History, memory and music: the repatriation of digital audio to Yolngu communities, or, memory as metadata. In L. Barwick, J. Simpson, and A. Harris (eds), *Researchers, Communities, Institutions, Sound Recordings*, pp. 1–17. Sydney: University of Sydney. ses.library.usyd.edu.au/bitstream/2123/1518/1/Toner%20rev1.pdf.

Toner, P. 2005a. Home among the gum trees: an ethnography of Yolngu musical performance in mainstream contexts. In F. Magowan and K. Neuenfeldt (eds), *Landscapes of Indigenous Performance: Music, Song and Dance of the Torres Strait and Arnhem Land*, pp. 29–45. Canberra: Aboriginal Studies Press.

Toner, P. 2005b. Tropes of longing and belonging: nostalgia and musical instruments in northeast Arnhem Land. *Yearbook for Traditional Music* 37: 1–24.

Vološinov, V.N. 1973. *Marxism and the Philosophy of Language*. Cambridge, MA: Harvard University Press.

# 9  Development of Collecting at the Milingimbi Mission

Louise Hamby with Dr Gumbula
The Australian National University

By the time Ian Keen purchased a few bark paintings there in the mid-1970s, the collection of material culture at Milingimbi had already been underway for half a century, from its very earliest days as a Methodist mission. It has hosted a steady stream of visitors, art collectors, anthropologists, and others since those early days. They went to Milingimbi with a wide variety of purposes, but the collections they made integrate them together into the story of Milingimbi. Some of these collections remained together and others were dispersed immediately; some are relatively small and private and others are prominent parts of internationally recognised museums. As Satterthwait notes, 'In essence, the process by which museum collections come into being reflects the outcome of a sequence of selective events, some deliberate and systematic and others opportunistic and highly contingent' (Satterthwait 2008: 42). Perhaps most importantly, the meanings of collections and their objects are not fixed, and are interpreted differently in different historical periods and by members of different cultures. A critical examination of the collection of material culture from Milingimbi, then, can reveal a great deal not only about Yolngu society and how it has changed over the last century, but also about the shifting impulses and motivations of the collectors themselves.

Satterthwait notes that collections are themselves artefacts even as they are composed of them, and the associations linking things together give collections a meaning beyond their individual elements (ibid.: 29). He also notes that all collections are structured in a variety of ways, which could include type of object, techniques of production, function, place of origin, and contextual meanings (ibid.: 31). Importantly, Satterthwait also asks what degree of spatial proximity is necessary for objects to be considered a 'collection', given that widely dispersed materials located in museums around the world may form a 'distributed collection' (ibid.: 46–7), especially in the Internet age. Given all of these considerations, we may define collections as 'social artefacts consisting of individual elements connected by webs of socially engendered meanings' (ibid.: 48).

With this in mind, recent engagement by Aboriginal people with ethnographic collections may be seen to represent a new kind of collection-making, in a process of cultural reclamation spanning material objects dispersed in museums around the world. In contemporary life in Arnhem Land today, Yolngu are seeking ways of reaffirming their identity and taking an active role in how they are perceived by others, and the reinterpretation of items collected by others over the past century plays an important role. Paintings and other objects not only 'tell people who they are' (Corn and Gumbula 2006: 190), but are key to the mediation and transmission of knowledge to younger generations today and to *balanda* (outsiders). In the broad sense outlined by Satterthwait above, these acts of examining, reclaiming, and reinterpreting material objects relevant to Yolngu cultural identity constitute Yolngu collection-making, regardless of the physical location of the objects themselves or who collected them.

This chapter will focus on collections from Milingimbi as a means of investigating the motivations behind collecting and other issues concerning identity, agency and power relations. Ethnographic collecting as an activity has changed over time in Australia, and five collecting periods have been classified based primarily on the motivations behind their formation: unsystematic collecting (contact to c. 1880); collecting under the influence of social evolutionary theory (c. 1880 – c. 1920); collecting under the influence of a philosophy of obtaining materials 'before it is too late' (c. 1920–40); research adjunct collecting (c. 1940–80); and predominantly secondary collecting (c. 1980 – present) (Peterson, Allen, and Hamby 2008: 8–10). Milingimbi enters into this type of classification in the third period of salvage ethnography influenced by structural functionalism, and accounts for a significant amount of the material from Milingimbi. The collections examined in this chapter end with the fourth period, c. 1940–80, even though the last period of collecting extends to the present day. Collections made in all periods are now in the process of critical reassessment, and there is a shift in museum practice that gives recognition to the authority of the original makers and their descendants that shifts the power balance. Importantly, we can also recognise that, regardless of the time frame and motivations for the original collecting activities, the resulting collections of material culture may be interpreted according to a radically different set of culturally specific criteria which may convey previously unrecognised meanings.

9  Development of Collecting at the Milingimbi Mission

Figure 9.1 Djäwa and Wulili from Goulburn Island, c. 1926–39.
Source: Rev. T.T. Webb. Courtesy University of Sydney Archives.

The idea that some objects of material culture may be subject to contested and shifting interpretations may be relatively new in museum studies, but it is not for Yolngu people, a point that Ian Keen's scholarship has demonstrated time and again. From his first article, 'Ambiguity in Yolngu Religious Language' (Keen 1977) to *Knowledge and Secrecy in an Aboriginal Religion* (1994) and beyond, Keen has argued that systematic ambiguity is an inherent feature of Yolngu myth and religious practice, and that the interpretation of *maḏayin* is a political act. It was fitting, then, that Dr Gumbula[1] (1954–2015), the son of one of Keen's main informants, Djäwa Daygurrgurr (1905–80), was a key player in the Yolngu reinterpretation of materials collected by his forebears. In his extended study of Yolngu cultural materials in museum collections around the world, especially those pertaining to his own Gupapuyngu group, we can see the active and politically empowering process of forming new 'legacy collections' by linking items through Yolngu 'webs of socially engendered meanings'.

---

1  In accordance with the wishes of his family, and in recognition of Yolngu cultural protocols concerning the recently deceased, 'Dr Gumbula' will be used as a term of reference throughout this chapter in place of the co-author's Yolngu name.

## Milingimbi the Place

The decision by missionaries to start a mission at Milingimbi proved to be the pivotal point in time for the formation of legacy collections of material culture, that is, collections handed down by previous generations. Also known as Yurruwi, Milingimbi is one of the largest islands in the Crocodile Islands group, and at the time of missionisation 'had a reputation as a meeting ground for the preparation and ultimate staging of great Aboriginal ceremonial rituals' (E. Wells 1982: 5). Its physical nature is quite different from the Methodist mission stations of Elcho Island and Goulburn Island, being quite flat. It is off the mainland of Arnhem Land between the Glyde and Blyth Rivers, approximately 25 kilometres away from the closest mainland Arnhem Land community, Ramingining. Mangrove and tidal mud flats divide the island into many sections. In addition to the mangroves, there are a great number of tamarind trees, an inheritance from Maccassan trepangers who found Milingimbi to be an excellent place for their activities.

> Milingimbi was a centre for Macassan trepang gatherers because of its permanent waterhole and fine beach. For similar reasons Milingimbi was a ceremonial centre for the Yolngu; several hundred could gather at the permanent waterhole towards the end of the dry season to exploit the abundant cycad-palm nuts in the forest, and rush-corms and long-necked turtles from the plains and lakes. (Keen 1978: 16)

Figure 9.2 Beach at Top Camp, Milingimbi, 2013.
Source: Louise Hamby.

In addition to the flat low country that was ideal for collecting trepang, the presence of the Macassan visitors was important for Yolngu in the selection of a mission site. Different Yolngu groups had established a pattern of engagement and trade with the Macassans for items that they wanted. The exchange of labour for the processing of trepang was matched with cloth, tobacco, rice and other goods. Yolngu familiarity with this process of trading made it easier to come to an understanding with mission ways of dealing with people with respect to their work for the mission. The Macassan background engagement with Milingimbi was a cultural reason for the establishment of the mission.

Rev. James Watson (1865–1946), who was appointed as the first missionary to Milingimbi in 1923, described it in a positive manner: 'It is an emerald set in a sapphire sea' (McKenzie 1976: 28). Later people were not so positive in their description. The missionary T.T. Webb's opinion, recounted by Gracie McKenzie, was quite different.

> He saw the rivers as 'winding channels, cut through the primaeval mud and slime, swarming with crocodiles, and walled in all the way by dense mangrove swamps, with a tidal rise and fall of from 15 to 20 feet … Altogether depressing, beyond all description' (McKenzie 1976: 43)

Aboriginal people from many clans have lived for a long time on the main island and surrounding islands, including nearby Murrunga Island in the Arafura Sea. The establishment of the mission brought with it things that people desired, such as rations and tobacco, and thus brought together people who were not always at peace with each other. The main Dhuwa-moiety tribal and clan groups are L̲iyagalawumirri, Manarrngu, Ngaymil, Buyugulmirri, Djambarrpuyngu, Gälpu, Marrangu, Gamalangga, Gorryindi, and Mal̲arra. Yirritja-moiety groups are Gupapuyngu, Warramiri, Wangurri, Wubulgarra and Birrkili (ALPA 2009).

## Collectors in the Third Phase of Collecting, c. 1920–40

The first collector in the third phase of collecting, characterised by the philosophy of obtaining materials 'before it is too late', was Sir Hubert Wilkins (1888–1958). He was commissioned by the British Museum of Natural History to make a collection of flora and fauna from the northern portion of Australia during 1923–25 to fill in the gaps in the museum's collection. Although not part of his brief, and although salvage ethnography was not an explicitly stated aim, he collected objects of material culture from Queensland, Groote Eylandt and from Milingimbi. While at Milingimbi (August to December 1924) he accompanied James Watson on the mission lugger. On nearing Elcho Island, a group of Aboriginal men paddled out to the lugger and 'traded turtle-shell for tobacco, cloth, and blue glass beads' (Wilkins 1929: 130). His collection of ethnographic items in the British Museum contains 30 labelled objects, one being a large group of armbands. Other items include bodywear, containers, clapsticks and *yidaki*. His material culture collecting followed his scientific approach to the extent that he used the same labels for objects as he did for animals. Wilkins's photographs from Arnhem Land through this period are significant to contemporary Yolngu, and some of these photographs appear in his book *Undiscovered Australia* (1929).

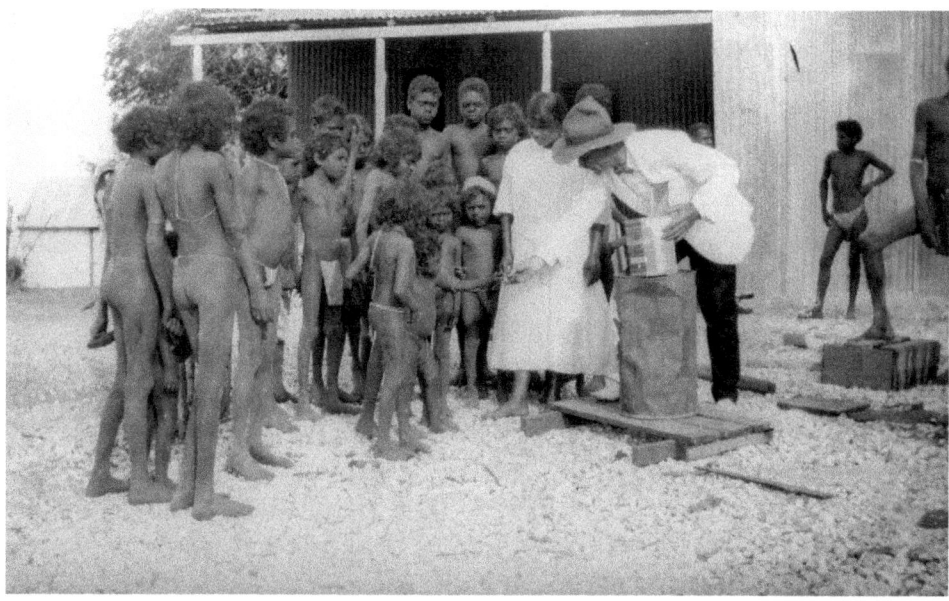

Figure 9.3 Rev. James Watson distributing food to children assisted by Rosie from Goulburn Island, wife of Andrew Birrinydjawuy Garawirrtja, Milingimbi, 1924.
Source: Hubert Wilkins, Courtesy of Byrd Polar Research Center, The Ohio State University. Wilkins32_14_39.

Thomas Theodor Webb (1885–1948) arrived in 1926 with his wife, Evelyn Mary, to replace James Watson, who retired a sick man in January 1926 (McKenzie 1976: 1). The Methodist Missionary Society of Australasia had made Webb superintendent of Milingimbi station, and chairman of the North Australia District. In 1928 the Milingimbi team grew with the addition of the lay missionaries Harold (1903–2000) and Ella Shepherdson, who arrived in the Northern Territory in 1927. The Shepherdsons were to become the longest-serving husband-and-wife team in Arnhem Land: they stayed at Milingimbi until World War II intervened, and on 22 June 1942 they moved to Elcho Island and remained there until they left Arnhem Land in 1977 (Shepherdson 1981).

In addition to their primary tasks as missionaries, Webb and Shepherdson also made collections of material culture while they were at Milingimbi. As was the case with Wilkins, collecting was not their primary purpose for being at Milingimbi. Webb was a strong leader and advocated for Aboriginal people to maintain most of their cultural practices, and was an unusual missionary in that he was very interested in anthropology and had a desire to understand Yolngu culture. 'Webb would accept the preservation of Yolngu customs not deemed intrinsically oppositional to the missionary way of life' (Risemen 2008: 249–50). This attitude helped considerably in the collection of material culture items. By being allowed to maintain their ceremonial life, Yolngu people produced objects that were sought after by museums in the south, and were also a means for Webb to understand cultural practices. He was more interested in objects than art, as demonstrated by the fact that only two bark paintings were sent to Museum Victoria. Webb also paid people for everyday items that he collected and sold as well. He was considered to be 'the most profound thinker of the mission in his era, and the most anthropologically informed' (Kadiba n.d.). He contributed many articles to the journals *Missionary Review* and *Oceania* and published two books about his experiences in Arnhem Land. Webb made a substantial collection from Milingimbi. The majority of this work is held in Museum Victoria in Melbourne (around 400 objects), while another significant portion is at the Museum der Kulturen in Basel.

Shepherdson had a vision of Aborigines living on their own country away from the large mission settlements, and flew his own plane to these small settlements to collect artefacts and deliver rations. He could be called 'the prophet of the homelands movement' (Cole 1979: 113). He and his wife were not as prolific as Webb in their documentation of events, but as a team they produced photographs and Ella wrote a diary that was developed later into the book *Half a Century in Arnhem Land* (1981). Although the Shepherdsons were not academically inclined, they had the welfare of Yolngu at the heart of what they did. The rationale for their collecting must have been in a great part to generate income for both the artists and for the mission, very much like that of Webb. Yolngu were paid for making objects, and the mission also received a percentage of the sale of these items to museums. The Shepherdson Collection numbers over 700 items acquired during their time in Arnhem Land, and is now located in the South Australian Museum. The group of objects contains items both from their time at Milingimbi and their years spent on Elcho Island. Many items that were collected by the missionaries and sold to museums were of a ceremonial nature, used in practices about which the missionaries were ambivalent: the missionaries tolerated these ceremonies as long as they did not directly contradict their teaching and they were able to obtain the items to boost income for the mission.

Figure 9.4 *Murayana* by Djäwa Daygurrgurr.
Source: Collected by Edgar Wells. Courtesy of Museum Victoria.

The American anthropologist William Lloyd Warner (1898–1970) arrived in 1927 to conduct research centred around the social structure and totemic beliefs of the people in Milingimbi and the surrounding area (Warner 1969). In the process of this work, and secondary to his prime objectives, he made a collection of artefacts. At Berkeley, Warner had been surrounded by and taught by students of Franz Boas, including Robert H. Lowie and Alfred Kroeber. Warner made a substantial collection that was dispersed across nine institutions and two countries, and which includes containers, mats, paintings, weapons, ceremonial objects, items worn on the body, photographs, objects and sound recordings. The time of Warner's research was a transition between diffusionism and functionalism in anthropological theory that saw a decline in the significance of artefacts as data. Warner's mentors, Malinowski and Radcliffe-Brown, did not view objects as an important part of the social order. It is not certain if Warner was motivated by salvage ethnography, collecting before the items were no longer made; more likely, he collected as part of his obligations to the University of Sydney and his grant. In the functionalist view advocated by Lowie and others, artefacts were relevant mainly to the anthropologist's local findings. He did not write about any particular motivations for his collecting practices; it appears that he did not seek out particular examples of material culture, but rather obtained what was at hand.

After Warner left Milingimbi another famous anthropologist who worked across Arnhem Land visited the island. Donald Thomson first trained as a scientist before studying anthropology at the University of Sydney. Thomson went to Milingimbi several times, the first visit being in July 1935 when he stayed for two months, and then going back for similar periods in 1936 and 1937. Thomson was skilled in many areas, including photography and languages. These abilities, coupled with his successful working relationships with Yolngu, enabled him to collect over 5,000 objects and 2,500 photographs from across Arnhem Land. The Thomson Collection has 240 items specifically identified as being from Milingimbi. Beyond the desire to amass materials, he sought to collect a representative selection of both everyday and ceremonial objects at the time; perhaps, according to Allen, it was an attempt to preserve the culture (Allen 2008: 400), and in that respect he was collecting 'before it was too late'. His background as a scientist influenced his collecting practices in that he would be very familiar with characteristics that would help to classify a specific object.

# Collectors in the Fourth Phase of Collecting, c. 1940–80

The fourth phase of collecting is primarily known as adjunct collecting, meaning that it was usually undertaken alongside another major area of research or activity. This was the kind of collecting practised by missionaries, whose primary focus was not collecting. Rev. Arthur F. Ellemor (1906–80) was at Milingimbi from 1939 to 1949, including during the war years when Ellemor remained at Milingimbi while Shepherdson went to Elcho Island. Keeping people alive during the war was a primary concern, but Ellemor also collected some objects, 19 of which are at the University of Queensland Anthropology Museum. The majority of these entered the collection after the war.

Edgar Wells, superintendent from 1949 to 1959, was known as a patron of the arts at Milingimbi. His collecting may have been adjunct to his role of being a missionary, but he was strongly motivated to collect art, as he had a personal interest in art as well as an anthropological one that involved drawing people to the mission. Wells not only collected paintings for the mission to sell to museums, but also made a personal collection of bark paintings. He comments about bark painting at the time:

> Encouragement of the arts attracted interest over a very wide area of Arnhem Land and Djawa, at that time manoeuvring to become ceremonial leader at Milingimbi, used this interest to his own advantage and invited clan leaders from other areas to visit Milingimbi and take part in various ritual activities. (E. Wells 1982: 69)

Djäwa was an accomplished artist and produced many paintings that attracted the interest of Wells. The personal collection of Edgar Wells from his time as a missionary during the 1950s now resides at Museum Victoria. On reflection, Ann Wells saw this relationship with the men as being formative in many ways at the mission:

> The trade that really became the channel for understanding between my husband and the adult men was their art work. He became so interested in it that he procured books and read widely on the subject of primitive art. He soon grew able to meet the men on a common ground when they were interpreting their beautiful paintings for him. I wish now I had some photographs of his Saturday morning 'native affairs' as we called them. Dainanan and Yilgari, Jawa, Dawawangulili and Magani, and other artists as they moved in and out of the station, would meet in the dim coolness and sanctuary of the store. (A. Wells 1963: 136)

Figure 9.5 Djäwa Daygurrgurr and Edgar Wells at Milingimbi, c. 1955.
Source: Beulah Lowe. Courtesy Kluge-Ruhe Collection, The University of Virginia. 6.01.09.002.

The material culture collecting of Ronald (1916–90) and Catherine Berndt (1918–94) supported their primary research on religious and social organisation. When they were in Milingimbi in May–June 1950 they collected paintings. In addition to Milingimbi itself, they also collected work from the mission store in Darwin, particularly in 1961 and 1964. Objects were collected later from their many visits to Darwin, and directly from Milingimbi Crafts when it was established (John Stanton, personal communication, 13 November 2012).

For some scholars during this period, collecting was not an adjunct activity but rather a primary one. When Helen Groger-Wurm came to Milingimbi in June 1967, her main purpose was to collect and document paintings. Included in her book *Australian Aboriginal Bark Paintings and their Mythological Interpretation* are a selection of Daygurrgurr Gupapuyngu paintings: three of Djäwa's paintings, one from Bonguwuy and seven belonging to Lipundja (Groger-Wurm 1973). Similarly, the collecting of Frederick McCarthy from the Australian Museum and Frank Setzler in July 1948 was not adjunct collecting at all (Setzler 1948). They were part of the American–Australian Scientific Expedition to Arnhem Land that had the collection of everything as its primary objective. McCarthy and Setzler had different ideas about collecting than the expedition leader, Charles Mountford, who was probably more in tune with the collecting aims of the previous phase of salvage ethnography 'before it was too late'. While Mountford often directed people what objects to make based on an idea of 'real' artefacts (those from the past), the Milingimbi team collected what was made or was available for use in everyday life rather than commissioned objects (Hamby 2011: 222). More than 130 items were collected at Milingimbi, and are now in the following institutions: the Australian Museum, the National Museum of Australia, the South Australian Museum and the National Museum of Natural History, part of the Smithsonian Institution in Washington, DC.

During the 1960s the marketing of the art work was done by the missionaries in addition to their other duties. Alan Fidock was the main person involved in this type of work at the time, arriving in Milingimbi in 1961 as a teacher, and staying on the island until 1970 when he took an active role as an arts manager, locating the first art centre shop underneath his house (Mundine 2004: 40). In 1967 a mud brick building was built as an art centre by the beach (McCulloch 2011). Many changes came about in 1972 that also saw a greater interest in collecting art. Ken Nowland was superintendent at the time, when the Methodist Overseas Missions was handed over to the Northern Synod of the Uniting Church. The government transferred its administration to Milingimbi Community Incorporated, transforming it from a mission station into a township.

During Nowland's time on the island the American collector Edward Lehman Ruhe (1923–89) first became interested in Aboriginal art. In 1965 he visited Australia as a Fulbright scholar, during which time he was a visiting lecturer in English at the University of Adelaide (Ruhe 1971a). Although he did not go to Milingimbi at that time, he did make almost daily visits to the collection of Geoffrey Spence, which was housed in a municipal building within the Botanical Gardens in Darwin (Smith 2008: 560). He subsequently continued his research on bark paintings and communicated with many people in Australia, including previous staff at the Milingimbi mission. In 1966, Ruhe organised the purchase of half of Spence's collection, 130 paintings and more than 350 artefacts, some of which were from Milingimbi. Ruhe wrote many letters to B.A. Clarke, the assistant, and G.F. Symond, the chairman of the Methodist church in Darwin during 1971 to gain permission to work in Arnhem Land on his collection. In his letters he offered to volunteer:

> It makes good sense to me to pay my own way and offer my services as a temporary mission worker with special interests and qualifications—the latter bound to be debatable, although I have supporters—and an additional willingness to accept any kind of mission chores for the sake of living close to the native community. (Ruhe 1971b)

For the Methodist church, the greatest problem for accepting Ruhe was a lack of accommodation. Permission was granted for him to spend two months at Milingimbi for purposes 'of scientific investigation of Aboriginal art and associated anthropological, sociological and individual patterns', as noted on his permit (Milliken 1972). He returned to Australia in 1972 to undertake this work at Milingimbi, meeting the artists, buying paintings, and taking photographs and film footage that he later made into a short documentary about bark painting.

Some of the footage, which was later transferred to videotape, shows five artists painting in a grove of trees. Ruhe's notes identify the 'atelier of artists' as 'Burrungurr' (painting five Julungul in log), 'Boyun' (lily, snake, diver bird), 'Malangi' (two fish), 'Binyinyiwuy' (lizard and totem object) and 'Bonguwoi' (wurrpan and murayana, emu and ancestor spearing). (Smith 2008: 568)

Included in this sequence of film is Djäwa, wearing a purple T-shirt and sitting with these artists as the 'headman'. We also learn from this film that Djäwa adopted Ruhe (Herzmark 1972); indeed, it was a powerful relationship, one of *märr mirri*, having sacred power and carrying with it ceremonial obligations. This relationship had an impact on the work collected, influencing Ruhe to collect work from Djäwa and other Gupapuyngu painters. We can only assume this was a combination of the nature of the social relationship and the aesthetic appeal of the works themselves.

After the 1967 referendum, which recognised Aboriginal people as citizens, changes started to be made. In 1972 the Uniting Church appointed David Morgan as art and craft advisor, the first such dedicated position at Milingimbi. In 1973 the Australian Council for the Arts established positions of craft advisers in Arnhem Land communities. This position was held by Jurgen Groneberg during the mid-1970s. This title was later changed to art adviser. Djon Mundine came to this position at Milingimbi in 1979 before moving to Ramingining (Mundine 2000: 73). The system of having funded art centres with staff certainly had an impact on production of work and its appropriate attribution but is the topic of a much larger discussion.

## Yolngu Motivations and Reinterpretations

The distinctive periods of collecting for the Milingimbi material represent Western ideas about the making of the collections and the intentions of outsiders. The Yolngu responses to collecting activities were probably quite different. It seems clear that Yolngu involvement in producing material culture for Western collections was motivated, at least in large part, by economic considerations. For example, James Watson was an exceptional man who gained the trust of the Yolngu, and whose relationship with Yolngu would play an important part in future dealings with other missionaries relating to collecting. This trust was achieved not only in his belief in a 'Great Creator Spirit' but by paying the artists for their work, first at Goulburn and then at Milingimbi. Richard Trudgen has observed that Watson's mission became a place where fair trade was practised, and men would travel for months with goods to trade. 'They could see that Bäpa (father/Reverend) Watson was a fair trader' (Trudgen 2000: 29).

Yolngu motivations in being involved in the activities of Western missionaries, collectors, and scholars also revolved around the propagation and maintenance of specific Yolngu languages. The Methodist missionaries had to select one of the local languages in which to teach and to spread the gospel, one that would be widely understood in the region. The choice of Gupapuyngu satisfied this criterion, but also reflected the language affiliations of individuals who were prominent in community affairs and who had close relationships with the missionaries. Harry Makarwalla, who had been Warner's main informant in the late 1920s, was also the main helper at the mission and must have exerted some influence on the choice of Gupapuyngu, even though it was not the language originally spoken in Milingimbi before the mission was established. After his father died in the Wessel Islands, Makarwalla had been adopted by two of his *märi* (MMB), the Gupapuyngu brothers Narritjnarritj (father of Djäwa) and Waltjamirr, and so he would have supported the use of Gupapuyngu at the mission. This language choice continued with the work of the teacher and linguist Beulah Lowe (1927–2005), who came to Milingimbi in 1951. During her time she worked both with Baraldja, son of Harry Makarwalla, and with Djäwa, father of Dr Gumbula (Wearing 2007: 23, 87). Although Gupapuyngu is still widely spoken, Djambarrpuyngu, one of the languages of the Dhuwa moiety, has become the lingua franca in the community (Tamisari and Milmilany 2003: 2).

Edgar Wells also benefited from the fact that Makarwalla decided to work with him, bringing some continuity to the mission assistance. As noted earlier Makarwalla was assisted to this position of power by his Gupapuyngu supporters and because of his *märi-pulu* connection to country.

> It was my very good fortune to have on Milingimbi as my first Aboriginal headman and general guide in Aboriginal affairs, Warner's principal informant, Mahkarolla, whom we came to know as Makawalla, and from him and his companions we learned to appreciate a little of the patterns of mind influencing the Aboriginal men of the area. (E. Wells 1982: 5)

Another important Yolngu motivation was educating outsiders about Yolngu life, a motivation that became more important as time passed in Milingimbi, often through performances and ceremonies that were filmed or photographed. A visit in 1954 by the Queen of England to Toowoomba highlighted this aspect involving performance. Betsy Wearing describes who from Milingimbi attended that event:

> The following year when the Queen visited Australia a troupe of six men, including Djawa, Baraltja, Yipidi and Bungawui went to Toowoomba to dance for the Queen. Beulah was on furlough; she and her parents were proudly present. (Wearing 2007: 180)

Figure 9.6 Arnhem Land dancers performing for Queen Elizabeth II and the Duke of Edinburgh at Toowoomba, 1954.
Source: Courtesy National Archives of Australia, A1773, RV1105.

Ann Wells writes about this event in terms of the preparation given to the men who were going; for the men it was a disquieting experience to see that many white people and to see the luxurious way of life, 'but for Jawa it was a treasured and instructive journey into a new world' (A. Wells 1963: 209). As with the contemporary reinterpretation of collections of material culture, this event is of importance to Gupapuyngu people today, particularly Djäwa's family. In July 2011 Zanette Kahler, manager at Milingimbi Art and Culture, brought a group of artists including John Damarrwura, Raymond Bulumbula, Wilson Manydjarri Ganambarr, and two of Djäwa's sons, Joe Dhamanydji and Dr Gumbula, to Brisbane for the Buku-Manupanmirr Exhibition and Bunggul. Afterwards, they went to Toowoomba to the showground to perform the same series of dances that Djäwa performed for the Queen ('Yolngu follow father's footsteps', 2011). Gumbula said, 'We could feel that by our imagination we were part of the story of Djäwa'.

The dances performed at Toowoomba both in 1954 and in 2011 were also held at Milingimbi in 1997 when the announcement was made of the death of Princess Diana. Daisy Baker (granddaughter of Makarwalla) and other Yolngu from the Gupapuyngu group danced white cockatoo, emu and brown hawk. These Gupapuyngu people were reasserting their position as leaders in the community by agreeing to perform. This type of performance had a history in the community with Djäwa holding leading roles in two documentary films directed by Cecil Holmes, *Faces in the Sun* (1963) and *Djalambu* (1964) (Corn and Gumbula 2007: 118). These performances concur with Tamisari's ideas about performance; as she writes, 'Dancing is one of the most effective ways of claiming, affirming and legitimising one's knowledge and authority in ceremonial contexts' (Tamisari 2005: 49).

The same objects, documents and photographs, used by collectors for particular purposes, are viewed by Yolngu today with different perspectives and put to dissimilar uses. One example of this was Ruhe's use of catalogue cards. On his return to America, Ruhe worked diligently on his catalogue of bark painters, starting with the Milingimbi ones. On the cards he kept all the relevant information about each painter, and he communicated with people at Milingimbi, including Edgar Wells and Beulah Lowe, about appropriate spellings and correct information (Smith 2008: 569). In order to publish biographical information about the artists in his catalogue of works he collected as much data as possible on the cards from many sources. Indeed, these cards and other relevant documentation were of great interest to Dr Gumbula when he visited the collection in 2010. Gumbula was most concerned about the information that Ruhe had included on the card about his father, Djäwa. Gumbula wanted to know all the information gathered by Ruhe about his father; for him, the reading of the information reaffirmed Djäwa's position not only within the Gupapuyngu clan, but in the Milingimbi community and beyond.

A photograph taken by Donald Thomson was a key item in the reconstructing of the Daygurrgurr Gupapuyngu legacy and highlights the different intentions of 'collection makers' and the repurposing of collections by collection users. Thomson was interested in documenting life at the time; it was impossible to 'collect' everything, and photographs provided much information not only about objects, but about everyday and ceremonial life. Gumbula was seeking a photograph of Djäwa that depicted him with his famous shock of white hair, which is how he was remembered by most people of Gumbula's generation. The photo confirmed the identity of his father, but more importantly the place of his clan in ceremonial activity, as Thomson selected this Gupapuyngu activity to photograph. Eventually Djäwa was found in a photograph of a group of people, including Djäwa's father, Narritjnarritj, who were in the final stages of burial of Djäwa's grandfather. The *Djalumbu* film made in 1963, in which Djäwa stars, is a re-enactment of the Djalumbu ceremony for the final burial of Narritjnarritj (Corn and Gumbula 2007: 118). Gumbula's rationale for wanting the photograph was quite different than Donald Thomson's rationale for taking it, but he still appreciated the documentation of the ceremony.

When Ian Keen arrived in Milingimbi in 1974, it was a time of transition of authority, and Yolngu were determining their position in this new order. Keen worked with two leaders, one from each moiety, Djäwa and Bäriya. Djäwa was the accepted Daygurrgurr leader (*liya-ngärra'mirri*) at that time, and was also influential over others. 'A senior power-man like Djäwa has a measure of control over several clans' ceremonial life' (Keen 1978: 234). Indeed, Djäwa was the *dalkarramirri* song leader as well. In a description of a circumcision ceremony linked with the Daygurrgurr estate at Djiliwirri, Keen gives us another view of the person Djäwa. He quotes Djäwa: 'I have a lot of power, no one gets the better of me, white or black. I have the law for everyone. I am the elbow. I have the *dalkarra*, the power' (ibid.: 53). In a recent interview Keen reflected on leadership roles then and now and agreed that Gumbula was taking on that role. 'Djäwa was very much like [Dr Gumbula], very energetic and very similar in character' (Ian Keen, personal communication, 21 June 2012). Keen remembers that Djäwa and his brothers painted sacred work and would not let him look at those paintings, demonstrating a desire to control what items would be collected and by whom. Keen recalled that there was some carving of birds at the workshop. The mission was still in control of art at that time and they sometimes 'bumped up production when they were short of funds—to get money to eat' (ibid.) From this scenario it is easy to see that one motivation for the production of work was clearly an economic one on the part of Yolngu.

Figure 9.7 George Milaybuma, Matthew Baltha, Ian Keen and Dr Gumbula at Djiliwirri, 2005.
Source: Louise Hamby.

For contemporary Yolngu, collections of artefacts are integrally linked to the ancestral estates to which they are connected, and the reinterpretation of such materials may be most meaningfully done on those estates. In July 2005, many of Djäwa's descendants (including Dr Gumbula), along with a number of researchers, visited the Daygurrgurr Gupapuyngu estate at Djiliwirri. Lindy Allen, senior curator from Museum Victoria, and Louise Hamby documented aspects of the Donald Thomson Collection. Aaron Corn and Ian Keen recorded a Gupapuyngu song cycle, Baripuy, over a one-week period. This *manikay* recounted the original observations of Murayana, a *wangarr* of the *mokuy* (ghost) class, who is also a subject in the series. These songs are also about the paperbark trees and the freshwater of Djiliwirri (Corn and Gumbula 2007: 117). Corn commented: 'From the earliest photograph of Thomson's shown to the youngest visitor among us, the family's presence at Djiliwirri spanned seven decades and six generations' (ibid.: 119). The visit highlighted the importance of the early collections like Donald Thomson's, but also demonstrated the continuing presence of the Gupapuyngu in the collecting practices and knowledge of *balanda*. The occasion was not merely one for *balanda* research, but was essential for the Gupapuyngu to reaffirm their position on their own country.

Figure 9.8 Gupapuyngu family and researchers including Ian Keen, Aaron Corn and Louise Hamby at Djilwirri, 2005.
Source: Lindy Allen.

In 2010 Dr Gumbula, Pip Deveson and Louise Hamby embarked on a trip to the United States to document Gupapuyngu material culture in four museums: the Phoebe Apperson Hearst Museum of Anthropology at the University of California, Berkeley; the Peabody Museum of Archaeology and Ethnology at Harvard University in Cambridge, Massachusetts; the Smithsonian Museum of Natural History in Washington, DC; and the Kluge-Ruhe Aboriginal Art Collection at the University of Virginia in Charlottesville. Hamby had previously undertaken research at each of these institutions and knew what material would be of particular interest for the Gupapuyngu project. It is from the last institution particularly, the Kluge-Ruhe Collection, that we drew on some more recent examples, mainly those made in Gumbula's lifetime when he was a teenager or in his early 20s. As discussed above, Ruhe's collection contains many items from Milingimbi, ones which he collected himself in 1972 plus others bought from people such as Geoffrey Spence and Jim Davidson in the 1960s.

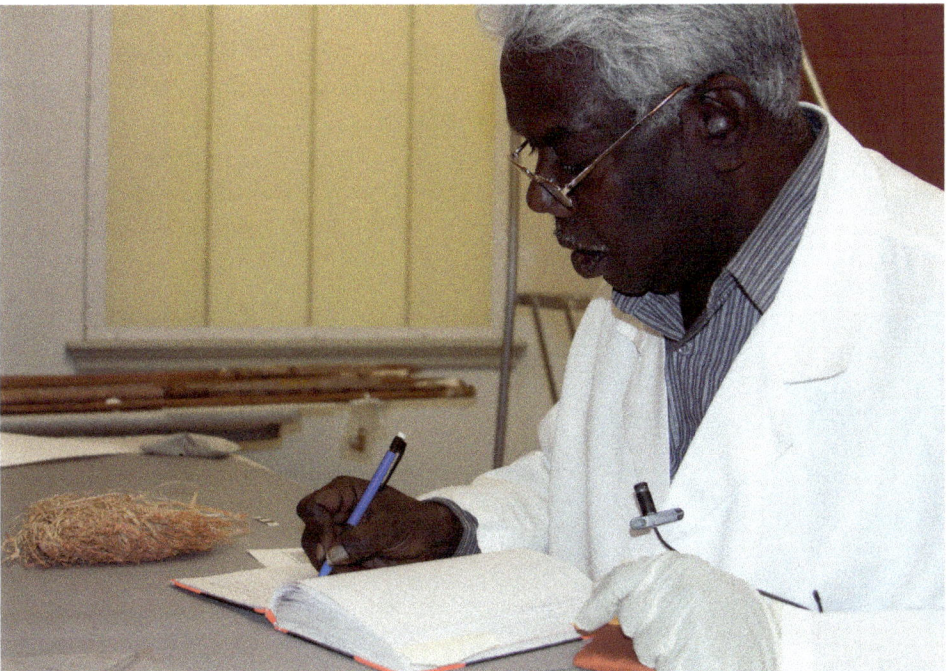

Figure 9.9 Dr Gumbula in a storeroom at The Peabody Museum of Archaeology and Ethnology, Harvard University, 2010.
Source: Louise Hamby.

Included in the items we examined in the collection were extensive archival materials, consisting of photographs, letters and mission records. Much time was spent looking at the Mission Register of Wards of all the people on the island in 1957. Djäwa's name was found on page 7, 'Jawa, born in 1905'. Many smiles came later when Gumbula said, 'I am here. That's me!' as he found himself listed on page 11 as Nibarnga, born in 1954. He was not so lucky when he saw a photo (11.03.02.019) of a man and child eating ice cream in wafer cones. 'The first ice cream; I remember this ice cream but my photo is not here.' Finding oneself or a relative either in a record or a photograph is always a satisfying moment and triggers many other memories. The absence of oneself in a documented event can show that the affiliation of the photographer may have belonged to another group of people that were captured on film. These records, and the paintings and objects, helped to fix a Gupapuyngu identity during the later years of the mission. Today the presence and absence of individuals in photographs or of particular works is often a source of concern for Yolngu, who may ask: 'Why wasn't my family depicted at this event?' Some groups may be represented partly on the basis of their relationship to the collector rather than the overall importance of an event or an object. During these early times representation in a collection was seen by some to be important and is manifested today. Being correctly documented provides a position in history. The importance of Djäwa as headman was reinforced with two photos (11.03.02.023 and 11.03.02.024) in the Ruhe Collection of what Gumbula described as an open court case in the community. In one photograph, the accused person, Ngalandirr, was seated on the ground. Seated on chairs at a table in front of him were Edgar Wells with Jacky Badaltja, son of Harry Makarrwala, on one side and Djäwa on the other as the headman. From discussions with Gumbula we learned that Jacky Badaltja is acting as the translator. Ngalandirr is on trial for murder.

Figure 9.10 Court case for Ngalandir; Djäwa, Edgar Wells and Jacky Badaltja seated at table at Milingimbi, 1955.
Source: Frank Clune. Courtesy Kluge-Ruhe Collection, The University of Virginia. 11.03.02.023.

> It was an open meeting in the open court in the community with the missionaries and the elders sitting down. They are hearing what Wells is saying. I know the story of this one but I had not seen the photos. *Manymak* [good] history!

The rediscovery and reinterpretation of objects like this photograph by contemporary Yolngu demonstrates the importance of kinship ties in Yolngu collection-making. For Daygurrgurr people, collected materials reaffirm the central place of Djäwa not only as an ancestor, but also as one of Milingimbi's most important leaders.

Djäwa painted four bark paintings in the Ruhe Collection, two purchased at Milingimbi by Ruhe and two from Geoff Spence in the 1960s. Gumbula explained that Djäwa, although Yirritja, had rights to paint the Dhuwa painting of the Morning Star (1993.004.124) because it was from his mother's people, the Guyula Djambarrpuyngu family from the Barge Landing outstation at Gapuwiyak. This relationship, according to Gumbula, relates to the fact that Djäwa was a *wayirri watangu,* hereditary owner in Yolngu law, for Milingimbi. His mother was Djambarrpuyngu and his grandmother was Walamangu. This was a contributing factor to Djäwa remaining at Milingimbi and partially a rationale for his accepted leadership. The painting *Hammerhead Shark and Stingrays* (1993.0004.018), in addition to its titular animals, also depicted small fish that Dr Gumbula did not know the English names for, nor did he think his father knew at the time. However it was important for Gumbula to find this information out for the painting in order to 'make sure we have a true story for this'.

The last two paintings linked to Murayana, the malevolent ghost who, according to Ian Keen's information, 'collected honey, hunts kangaroo, eats its raw flesh, spits out blood which becomes the sunset and "its power"' (Keen 1978: 60) are *Murayana—Spirit of the Dead* (1993.0004.067) and *The Burala Rite* (1993.005.865). *Spirit of the Dead* is a depiction of Murayana with yams, much like the body paintings painted on Gupapuyngu men in ceremony.

*The Burala Rite* is a painting that has more than one story to tell. The middle of the painting contains a *djalumbu,* or hollow log, surrounded by *burala* or bull roarers; there is also a *manbiri* or catfish and a long-neck turtle *yangara.* Gumbula told us (Pip Deveson, Louise Hamby and Margo Smith) about the story of the painting that is most obvious by looking at the figurative elements:

Figure 9.11 *Burala Rite* by Djäwa Daygurrgurr, 1972, collected by Ed Ruhe at Milingimbi.

Courtesy Kluge-Ruhe Collection, The University of Virginia. 1993.0004.865.

We call it *burala* and you call it bull roarer. To represent these *burala* are thrown in the film that he made in 1963; that film called, titled, *Djalumbu*. It was in the movie thrown or done by various elders. The *burala* sound is like a *burala* diving bird coming down to the water. As they make that noise coming down with their wings. That is the significance of the sound that they do with the *burala*, making the sound of the bird going diving into the lake. The ancestors being giving for this side of work is Murayana; side to the Gupapuyngu nation, people.

When Smith asked Gumbula about the herringbone design on the *burala* she was told that it represented the bones of the catfish depicted in the painting. While contemplating the design he said: 'We got a club, *bäḻatha*. Where did we see that club? Oh, at the Smithsonian, that was painted with the same design, *bäḻatha*'. On 8 November 2010, we did look at a club (E387533) or *bäḻatha* in the Smithsonian storeroom in Maryland. Gumbula told us at the time it was made of ironwood and was a Gupapuyngu design. 'This a catfish painting, catfish bones. This is like an X-ray. I paint this. It is *mambiri*.' This memory and contemplation of the bones prompted Gumbula to provide us with another interpretation of the painting:

> Another story was in the catfish. That was ceremony ground. This Murayana he had a lot of catfish for the day and it was piling up. So when he was eating the fish he was piling lots and lots of bones. So what he had done with the bones; he had to do something with the bones. It was storing this high. Ate a lot, and feed the family as well. There were two Murayanas, their wives and children. It was stored in a heap of bones so what Murayana recommended something about making a ceremony which was happening at the garma ground at that billabong. He went over bush and got the hollow log and took it back and disturbed the human remains. They put the bones to the fish in the entrance of the *djalumbu*. And they dance along the bunggul that goes with it so every time they dance they put every piece of bone through the bunggul ceremony inside.

> [It] remains as a true thing what happened before. There was a ceremony like this. This is like a monument for the Gupapuyngu nation, people. When they put the bone inside somebody, so their spirit does not go dead looking through the two eyes the eyes of the deceased looking out.

Gumbula, having a great knowledge of Gupapuyngu styles, motifs and people, was able to attribute names to two painted boomerangs in the collection (1993.0004.0389 and 1993.0004.0390). He said, 'This is my detective work.' The two boomerangs, collected by Spence in 1966, were completely covered in *rrark* and other designs on both sides. According to Gumbula, Spence did not come to Milingimbi but collected from people when they went to Darwin. There was no documentation about the painter of the objects, but there was a note stating that they were used in ceremony. Gumbula compared these to a painting (1993.004.664) about the Wagilag Sisters by Lipundja #1, his uncle. The thickness of the line in the *rrark* and the colour combinations were very similar. His conclusion was that the boomerangs were also painted by Lipundja.

## Conclusion

The examples presented from the Kluge-Ruhe Collection are Gupapuyngu ones from the 1970s, a continuation in the long history of collecting from Milingimbi. There are others documented in this chapter that make substantial links to Gupapuyngu past history. The insights that emerged from Gumbula's engagement with his cultural patrimony in museums are that Yolngu played important roles in the formation of these collections, particularly his Daygurrgurr Gupapuyngu family, and that they reaffirm the identity of the descendants of the makers and point towards future roles they can play. As few official records exist of the roles of Yolngu at the mission, other than in employment and census records, the important relationships developed with missionaries, anthropologists and collectors, and the application of a cross-cultural research model to the materials these people collected and to their writing, has the potential to contribute significantly to the dialogue around Indigenous agency in mission history. Art, anthropology and museology present different interpretations of the same objects. At the end of the American trip Gumbula asked for a commentary for people at Milingimbi to be filmed. It sums up much of the importance of this work.

> I want to explain the story as a Yolngu person. I'm talking about Yolngu things—how we look at things ... how we want to look at the past—the Yolngu Law and stories. And it's going to take our memories back ... so we can bring the Yolngu Law into the present ... looking at it from different angles ... what information the anthropologists and researchers recorded ... about the art—the paintings—and why Yolngu gave this to them [the researchers]. So we'll see. And how our elders were doing this work. Most of this has been forgotten but some is kept by elders who are living today ... and by the *balanda* [Europeans]. But according to the field notes the elders didn't give much information ... when the researchers were collecting Yolngu history and information.
>
> We have to stand on that foundation, restoring all the information about the clans. So that it will make things easier for later researchers. We have to go through the guidelines ... so people will know the correct information. If they see Djäwa's painting ... they have to put down that it was Djäwa's work, with a photograph of Djäwa. Or if it's Lipundja's painting, they'll do the same. And Mungunu—the same thing—they'll put his names. They are the sons of Narritjnarritj. So we'll be checking more information ... We have to check everything to put some things in the open access category. Like the bark paintings that were done just to get some smokes! We have to respect and recognise the elders and the people who

worked with the researchers ... because we have to acknowledge their work—
to give some acknowledgement in writing for their hard work. And that's all.
(Deveson 2010)

There has been a significant change in attitudes about material culture and collecting in the late twentieth century, particularly in museum practice. More emphasis has been placed on Indigenous knowledge and authority from source communities, showing that the meanings of collections are more open. The same objects can have significance in different ways. Yolngu are seeking ways of reaffirming their identity and taking an active role in how they are perceived by others. Gumbula, for example, made (with his *balanda* co-researchers) a virtual legacy collection of his clan and others from Milingimbi.

Time is bringing new interpretations of old materials, but in this case it is paired with relationships built over time. Ian Keen worked with Djäwa Daygurrgurr in the 1970s, examining how he and other Yolngu interpreted religious practice into political statements about their authority, and Louise Hamby worked with Dr Gumbula, the son of Djäwa, who reinterpreted materials. This work is a translation of agency—Djäwa asserting the terms of collection of objects and Dr Gumbula embedding those into the collections. In Dr Gumbula's study of Yolngu cultural materials in museum collections around the world, especially those pertaining to his own Gupapuyngu group, one can see the active and politically empowering process of forming new 'legacy collections'.

# References

Arnhem Land Progress Aboriginal Corporation. 2009. Milingimbi Community.

Allen, L. 2008. Tons and tons of valuable material: the Donald Thomson collection. In N. Peterson, L. Allen and L. Hamby (eds), *The Makers and Making of Indigenous Australian Museum Collections*, pp.387–418. Melbourne: Melbourne University Press.

Cole, K. 1979. *The Aborigines of Arnhem Land*. Adelaide: Rigby.

Corn, A. and J.N. Gumbula. 2006. Rom and the academy repositioned: binary models in Yolngu intellectual traditions and their application to wider intercultural dialogues. In L. Russell (ed.), *Boundary Writing : An Exploration of Race, Culture, and Gender Binaries in Contemporary Australia,* pp. 170–97. Honolulu: University of Hawai'i Press.

Corn, A. and J.N. Gumbula. 2007. *Budutthun ratja wiyinymirri*: formal flexibility in the Yolngu *manikay* tradition and the challenge of recording a complete repertoire. *Australian Aboriginal Studies* 2: 116–26.

Deveson, P. 2010. Gumbula commentary to Yolngu from film footage.

Groger-Wurm, H. 1973. *Australian Aboriginal Bark Paintings and their Mythological Interpretation.* Canberra: Australian Institute of Aboriginal Studies.

Hamby, L. 2011. The forgotten collection: baskets reveal histories. In M. Thomas and M. Neale (eds), *Exploring the Legacy of the 1948 Arnhem Land Expedition*, pp. 213–38. Canberra: ANU E Press.

Herzmark, M. 1972. *The Arnhem Land Painters.* Television Services.

Kadiba, J. n.d. Webb, Thomas Theodor (1885–1948). *Australian Dictionary of Biography Online Edition.* Retrieved from adb.anu.edu.au/biography/webb-thomas-theodor-11990.

Keen, I. 1977. Ambiguity in Yolngu religious language. *Canberra Anthropology* 1: 33–50.

Keen, I. 1978. One Ceremony, One Song: An Economy of Religious Knowledge among the Yolngu of North-East Arnhem Land. PhD Thesis, The Australian National University, Canberra.

McCulloch, S. 2011. Buku-manapanmirr: Meeting Together and Sharing Yolngu Knowledge and Culture. Exhibition brochure, Woolloongabba Art Gallery.

McKenzie, M. 1976. *Mission to Arnhem Land.* Adelaide: Rigby.

Milliken, E.P. 1972. Permit to enter Arnhem Land. 7 April.

Mundine, D. 2000. The native born. In B. Murphy (ed.), *The Native Born: Objects and Representations from Ramingining, Arnhem Land*, pp. 29–111. Sydney: Museum of Contemporary Art.

Mundine, D. 2004. Some people are stories. In S. Jenkins (ed.), *No Ordinary Place: The Art of David Malangi*, pp. 29–41. Canberra: National Gallery of Australia.

Peterson, N., L. Allen and L. Hamby. 2008. Introduction. In N. Peterson, L. Allen and L. Hamby (eds), *The Makers and Making of Indigenous Australian Museum Collections*, pp. 1–26. Melbourne: Melbourne University Press.

Risemen, N. 2008. Disrupting assimilation: soldiers, missionaries and Aboriginal people in Arnhem Land during World War II. In A. Barry, J. Cruikshank, A. Brown-May and P. Grimshaw (eds), *Evangelists of Empire? Missionaries in Colonial History*, pp. 245–62. Melbourne: University of Melbourne eScholarship Research Centre.

Ruhe, E. 1971a. Letter to Ted Milliken. Kluge-Ruhe Archives, University of Virginia.

Ruhe, E. 1971b. Letter to B.A. Clarke, 13 December. Kluge-Ruhe Archives, University of Virginia.

Satterthwait, L. 2008. Collections as artefacts: the making and thinking of anthropological museum collections. In N. Peterson, L. Allen and L. Hamby (eds), *The Makers and Making of Indigenous Australian Museum Collections*, pp. 29–60. Melbourne: Melbourne University Press.

Setzler, F. 1948. *Groote Eylandt to Yirrkala to Milingimbi* [Diary, vol. 2]. Canberra: National Library of Australia.

Shepherdson, E. 1981. *Half A Century in Arnhem Land*. One Tree Hill, SA: Ella and Harold Shepherdson.

Smith, M. 2008. Aesthete and scholar: two complementary influences on the Kluge-Ruhe Aboriginal Art Collection of the University of Virginia. In N. Peterson, L. Allen, and L. Hamby (eds), *The Makers and Making of Indigenous Australian Collections*, pp. 556–79. Melbourne: Melbourne University Press.

Tamisari, F. and E. Milmilany. 2003. *Dhinthun wayawu*—looking for a pathway to knowledge: towards a vision of Yolngu education in Milingimbi. *The Australian Journal of Indigenous Education* 32: 1–10.

Tamisari, F. 2005. The responsibility of performance: the interweaving of politics and aesthetics in intercultural contexts. *Visual Anthropology Review* 21(1–2): 47–62.

Trudgen, R. 2000. *Why Warriors Lie Down and Die: Towards an Understanding of Why the Aboriginal People of Arnhem Land Face the Greatest Crisis in Health and Education Since European Contact*. Darwin: Aboriginal Resource and Development Services Inc.

Warner, W. L. 1969. *A Black Civilization: A Social Study of an Australian Tribe*. Revised edition. New York: Harper and Brothers.

Wearing, B. 2007. *Beulah Lowe and the Yolngu People*. Glenning Valley, NSW: Betsy Wearing.

Wells, A. 1963. *Milingimbi: Ten Years in the Crocodile Islands of Arnhem Land*. Sydney: Angus and Robertson.

Wells, E. 1982. *Reward and Punishment in Arnhem Land 1962–1963*. Canberra: Australian Institute of Aboriginal Studies.

Wilkins, C.S.G.H. 1929. *Undiscovered Australia*. London: G.P. Putman's Sons.

Yolngu follow father's footsteps. (2011, July 12). *The Chronicle*. Toowoomba, NSW. Retrieved from www.thechronicle.com.au/news/yolngu-follow-fathers-footsteps/903562.

# 10 Rupture and Readjustment of Tradition: Personal Autonomy in the Feminised Warlpiri Diaspora in Australia

Paul Burke
The Australian National University

## Introduction

I am very happy to be a part of this festschrift for Ian Keen. Although there is no straightforward connection between this chapter and his intellectual interests, there is a strong connection via his supervision of my doctoral research and the general inspiration of his approach to anthropology. This approach could be summarised as empirically grounded, open to a critical engagement with theoretical developments (neither knee-jerk rejection nor discipleship, more often the deflating of pretensions through open-minded evaluation) and a commitment to a clear style of writing. These elements continue to guide and challenge my own research.

The discovery of a largely feminised Warlpiri diaspora in Australia during 2009–12 has prompted a further reconsideration of Diane Bell's support in the 1970s and 80s for the project of increasing the status and independence of Aboriginal women via a return to traditionalism and traditional country. Many doubts were raised at the time about her characterisation of the relatively high pre-contact status of Aboriginal women (Berndt 1989: 14; Hamilton 1986: 9; Keen 1989: 29–30; Merlan 1988: 26–30; Tonkinson 1990: 141–3), but the present chapter looks instead at the homogeneity of her reported responses to declining settlement conditions and her underemphasising of personal autonomy as a break with the constraining relationships that traditionalism entailed. The Warlpiri women of the diaspora decided to leave the remote settlements and make a life for themselves at a distance from the home settlements and their traditional country. This chapter outlines a variety of their projects of personal autonomy: escape from promised marriages, becoming an itinerant camper, being a leader of a Pentecostal church, being the matriarch of a Christian *jilimi* (widows' camp) in a town camp, being a semi-professional artist in Adelaide, and being a house mother for settlement children attending school in Adelaide. All involved a variety of relationships to tradition ranging from outright hostility to more subtle readjustment.

Although there was an early signal coming from Beckett's account of the Torres Strait Islander diaspora in the 1970s that the position of women would be an issue in other indigenous diasporas (Beckett 1983: 214), that signal became a blinding light in the Warlpiri diaspora research project (2009–12).[1] I found a largely feminised Warlpiri diaspora throughout Australia. Of the total Warlpiri population of 3,600, I estimated that about one-quarter (900) lived permanently beyond the main Warlpiri settlements in other Aboriginal settlements and in more distant towns and cities, and many other Warlpiri travellers moved between these locations following networks of kin and drinking camps. Among the permanent diaspora the stable households were overwhelmingly run by mature Warlpiri women. Moreover, the Warlpiri women's stories of 'getting away' from their home settlements, strongly infused with the themes of escape and the assertion of their personal autonomy, including the marrying of non-Aboriginal men completely outside of their kinship universe, necessitated the thematisation of Warlpiri women as actors in intercultural history. In the same diaspora locations there were also Warlpiri women who had not made decisive choices but drifted to their present locations along seemingly circuitous and haphazard routes. Yet others asserted the prerogatives of personal autonomy, but became dependent upon alcohol or romantically entangled in abusive or exploitative relationships with white men. All of them, however, had made some sort of life for themselves permanently residing away from their home settlements and traditional country.

Thirty years before my research, during the high point of anthropology's response to second-wave feminism, Diane Bell, among others, had presented a quite different model of Aboriginal women's autonomy, one with a decidedly traditionalist orientation towards the *jilimi* (widows'/ single women's camp), *yawulyu* (women's ritual) and *Jukurrpa* (the Dreaming, land-based religion)

---

1   Australian Research Council Discovery Project (DP0987357) 2009–2012, Indigenous Diaspora: A New Direction in the Study of the Migration of Australian Aboriginal People Leaving Remote Areas.

(Bell 1978, 1980, 1983, 1985; Bell and Ditton 1980; Bell and Nelson 1989). She characterised the alleviation of Aboriginal women's subordination in contemporary settlement life as a return to what she controversially argued was Aboriginal women's greater autonomy and more equal status in the pre-contact past.[2] This characterisation allowed for a propitious alignment of a feminist critique of Aboriginal women's contemporary circumstances, the traditionalist predilections of her main informants and recuperative government projects of land rights, the outstation/homelands movement and the recognition of some aspects of customary law. Baldly stated, Bell's work presented an ideal of Aboriginal women's liberation as following Aboriginal law and the sustaining values of service to kin on a family outstation/homeland on traditional country with secure title.

The juxtaposition of orientations I have outlined here—to homeland outstation versus to the diaspora—therefore raises many issues of historical transformation over the contact period, particularly since the 1970s, but also variation in the capacity to exercise autonomy and the variety of Aboriginal women's projects aimed at achieving greater personal autonomy. In this chapter, I want to explore in some detail the diversity of Warlpiri women's projects of diaspora, that is, the various ways they have found to sustain a life permanently at a distance from the homeland settlements. In this way I hope to develop a greater understanding of the nature of Warlpiri women's active and constructive agency (and its opposites) in the Warlpiri diaspora. This will initially involve an examination of the variety of ways Warlpiri women have taken their leave of the home settlements, something that was beyond the achievable horizon of most of Bell's informants, like Warlpiri ritual leader Topsy Napurrula Nelson, who was deeply embedded in settlement life and in her mature years worried about who would look after her father's traditional country in a more remote area beyond her home settlement (Bell 1985; cf. Nelson 1990).

In addition to the sometimes dramatic action of leave-taking, the Warlpiri women of a later era sometimes entered a period of precarious, free-form living among the 'long-grassers' of Darwin (dwellers in makeshift camps on secluded vacant land near the city), or in the unofficial camps of Katherine and Alice Springs or the parklands of Adelaide. Of those who survived this period and regained

---

2   For reasons of limited space I do not wish to rehearse the evidence presented to challenge Bell's most disputed claims about the relative autonomy and equality of Aboriginal women in the pre-contact era and the mostly sceptical reactions of other regional specialists (see, for example, Berndt 1989: 14; Hamilton 1986: 9; Keen 1989: 29–30; Merlan 1988: 26–30; Tonkinson 1990: 141–3). Merlan has provided a balanced and scholarly review of the issue and has been at pains to untangle the conflation of homosociality and equality (Merlan 1988, 1992). Bell has never made a detailed or convincing reply to the critiques of her view of the pre-contact era (but see her more general reply to her critics, Bell 1993: 273–306). To be clear, I am not trying to engage with all of Bell's arguments about the marginalisation of Aboriginal women in Australianist anthropology, many of which were justified.

their sobriety, some became the matriarchs of households in the town camps. In Bagot Camp in Darwin some of these matriarchs became the cornerstone of a Pentecostal church. In Alice Springs some of them recreated a *jilimi* (widows'/single women's camp) in new circumstances. The other projects described will be the maintenance of relationships with a white art wholesaler in the diaspora and an unusual project of fostering children from the home settlements for schooling in the city. Before describing those projects, however, it is necessary to attempt some conceptual clarification about the terms 'agency' and 'personal autonomy'.

## Conceptual Clarification

In suggesting 'personal autonomy' and 'active and constructive agency' as relevant categories of analysis I am aware of the pitfall of naïve voluntarism creeping in. I am, however, encouraged by recent clarifications of philosophers, including feminist philosophers, conceptualising personal autonomy as a particular kind of competency of a fully socialised individual and as a matter of degree (see, for example, Friedman 2003; Kühler and Jelinek 2013; Meyers 1989, 1997). Friedman, for example, in defining personal autonomy in terms of 'reflecting on one's deeper wants, values and commitments, reaffirming them and behaving and living in accordance with them even in the face of at least minimal resistance from others' (Friedman 2003: 99) acknowledges varying individual capacities and social spaces for such reflection. In the same way, adopting the idea of non-routine actions that strive to create something, what I have called active and constructive agency (or, more succinctly, 'a project'), does not deny that such agency is always part of the making and remaking of larger social and cultural formations (Ortner 2006: 129–53).

In using these concepts in the analysis of intercultural history, one does not have to deny that personal autonomy may be viewed as a peculiar development of Occidental modernity with its pressures on everyone to be a distinct person, an individual capable of moral judgement and a citizen with legally recognised rights and responsibilities. Giddens also suggests a further development of this trajectory is the rise in late modernity of 'the project of the self' (Giddens 1991). Taken at face value, therefore, the rise of personal autonomy among an encapsulated indigenous population could be seen as an index of transformation to modern subjectivities. Such overgeneralised characterisations are challenged by accounts of what could be called constrained personal autonomy, most influentially by Myers (1986). While his insistence upon autonomy and relatedness as central tensions in Aboriginal desert society has sometimes been inaccurately portrayed as a cultural trait of respect for personal autonomy, Myers himself was careful to identify certain inherent contradictions.

He conceived of personal autonomy as an achievement of the final stage of the maturation of men who, because of the extension of their network of relations and the growth of their traditional knowledge, could become someone who was recognised as being able to look after others. Interestingly, Bell presents a similar model of Aboriginal women's autonomy increasing with age, for example, in the lack of choice of the first marriage partner followed by a greater choice in subsequent marriages (Bell 1980).

Both would appear to be aligned with the concept of personal autonomy as competent performance of social relationships. Yet, especially for feminist philosophers, there is also a sense in which personal relationships can be a hindrance to personal autonomy which, for someone wishing to question basic presuppositions or norms, can only be achieved through the severing of social ties. It is this dual-aspect personal autonomy—escape from constraining relationships/mastery of social relationships—which has been most apposite for the following case studies.

## Background to the Ethnographic Examples

Since most of the Warlpiri women mentioned in the ethnographic examples left their home settlements after the period of Bell's most intensive period of interaction with the women of Ali Curung between the mid-1970s and the mid-1980s, questions of generational change arise. Perhaps the most significant thing to register is that despite the great successes of the Warlpiri in achieving land rights and the initial success of the outstation movement through the 1980s, seemingly intransigent problems of unemployment, alcohol abuse and violence against women have meant a continuing decline in social conditions on settlements, notwithstanding that liquor restrictions made them more liveable than the towns, at least for the non-drinkers. Occupation of the outstations has dramatically declined partly due to funding restrictions and policy changes (Kerins 2009) but also, I suspect, because the knowledgeable old men and women who were their most ardent supporters have been passing away. The rate of such deaths seems to have accelerated with epidemics of diabetes, heart disease and substance abuse. Mortuary rituals are now the most frequent ceremony performed (Glaskin et al. 2008). Fundamental demographic changes have been taking place which mean that there are now fewer older people to care for and socialise the growing percentage of the young. The passing of the generation who grew up in the desert has also revealed problems of the transmission of detailed knowledge about the country and associated rituals (Curran 2010; Peterson 2008). Initiation ceremonies continue but in a somewhat truncated form. At the same time there has been a rise in Western Desert-style painting as fine art in the international art market (Myers 2002) and, as we shall see below, this has influenced other art markets providing a supplementary economic basis for the diaspora, which is otherwise predominantly sustained by portable welfare payments and public housing. As we shall also see, the continuing government project of education on the settlements, while now hobbled by widespread disengagement, was for some the inspiration and means of their diaspora lives.

## Ethnographic Examples of Warlpiri Women's Diaspora Projects

### 1. 'Getting Away'

The first set of examples covers the dramatic escape from promised marriage at the remote settlement of Lajamanu. They provide the clearest cases of projects of personal autonomy as focused action to avoid conforming to norms on the settlement and resisting the exercise of power over them. These will be contrasted with other forms of leave-taking which did not have the character of resistance; rather, they demonstrated mastery of prevailing cultural constraints and the successful calibration of action to manoeuvre around constraining forces. Finally, the focused action of escape will be contrasted with the more diffuse negotiation of life as a long-grasser.

I should make it clear that my informants were middle-aged women who were recalling their youth in the late 1960s to 1980s when community support for the fulfilment of marriage promises, including the sanction of physical violence against the reluctant girl, was still very much in evidence. Generally speaking, today there is a different balance of forces that has resulted in a much looser attitude to enforcement of promises, a movement away from the traditionally most preferred kinship categories for spouses and the weakening of the ideal of long-term relationship (Bell 1980; Burbank 1988; Musharbash 2010). It was in fact the early pioneers of the Warlpiri diaspora who had opened up the possibility of escape to geographically and socially distant places like Alice Springs, Katherine and Darwin.

Perhaps the most dramatic story was of two young women, who secretly saved up their wages from teacher assistant jobs (or, according to another version of the story, the winnings from card games) and booked a direct flight from Lajamanu to Darwin, a distance of 890 kilometres. In the execution of the plan they had enlisted the help of their school principal and the settlement bookkeeper, who were sympathetic to them as the victims of fairly sustained physical violence from the promised husbands, particularly when drunk. One of them had sheltered in the principal's house more than once. The secrecy of the plan, the lack of direct involvement of their Aboriginal kin and the swiftness of its execution was intended to limit any retaliation against their kin and also to avoid alerting those whom they knew would not support them.

The brutality of the beatings typically played a part in arousing the sympathy and support of key kin, usually a mother or sister, and also the support of white settlement staff. A relevant broader context for the white staff was probably the slowly changing attitudes to domestic violence in the broader community during the 1970s and 1980s (Laing 2000). This meant that in one case, after a long series of violent incidents, one young woman at Lajamanu was given a police escort to a waiting plane then flown to Darwin and delivered to a women's shelter there. Other stories revealed more opportunistic and zigzagging routes to the diaspora location involving things like a lift with a sympathetic visiting truck driver, hitchhiking with white strangers or sympathetic young Aboriginal men heading for a Darwin adventure, short stays with relations along the way and sometimes repeated attempts after recapture by relations.

Another form of 'getting away' for a few in the late 1970s was elopement with a white partner. Two of these cases involved white male teachers who had arrived in the settlement with their own white partners. Similarly careful planning for a sudden departure was involved and in one case there were heightened concerns about taking a young Aboriginal son with the eloping couple. The anticipated strong negative reaction from the in-laws of the Warlpiri woman was partly because of the strength of the Warlpiri husband's family who would not only have to endure the breakup of the relationship but the taking of the young boy without their approval. In the other case, the Warlpiri woman left her young children behind when she went to Darwin to be with the white teacher. This case was viewed rather bitterly by her kin as abandonment.

Other instances of 'getting away' involved a Yuendumu woman leaving after a beating inflicted by her in-laws who accused her of 'running around' (having adulterous affairs), and a Willowra woman who left after her husband took a second, younger wife. Sometimes the women simply wanted to end a constraining relationship and pursue other more exciting possibilities. These separations tended to be the most difficult to achieve because, like the younger escapees, they required a degree of boldness, orchestration of support, tenacity and, ideally, having close kin already established in the diaspora location who would be willing to receive them. One woman's departure to Alice Springs from Yuendumu followed her husband's non-attendance at her brother's funeral, an unforgivable solecism in the view of her kin thus ensuring their support for her. Another moderated a potential backlash for leaving a husband by attaching herself to her daughter's household in Alice Springs and helping her look after her young children, her own grandchildren.

The dual notion of personal autonomy was nowhere more apparent than when those who had escaped their promised husbands in Lajamanu arrived in Darwin. The accomplishment of their escape plan was typically not matched by any detailed plan about how they would live in Darwin. Instead, they sought out the few kin who were already there. One was a Warlpiri man who had stayed on in Darwin after working for the Aboriginal Army Corps in the Second World War and married a Tiwi Island woman. This Warlpiri pioneer appeared in many of the stories about the Warlpiri in Darwin, sometimes offering shelter in his own modest house at Bagot Camp and, critically, transforming the visitors from strangers into quasi-kin by introducing them to his in-laws—a potentially momentous joining of two separate kin networks. A number of young Warlpiri women, attracted to the life of long-grassers, with their free attitude to sexual partners and liquor, made a precarious life for themselves, in true bricouleur fashion, out of the bits and pieces that were around: the drinking partner who became a 'husband', whose relations in Darwin shared food and liquor with them when they could; the YMCA where one could shower; the friendly taxi driver who might give credit; a scrounged scrap of plastic for a tarpaulin; a second-hand mattress; the occasional gift of fresh fish from anonymous white people; lunch at the soup kitchen; wild drinking and dancing nights at the club favoured by Aboriginal people; the occasional sale of a painting. In other words, this was a much less ordered existence than the one described by Sansom at a different unofficial camp on the outskirts of Darwin in an earlier era (Sansom 1980, 1988, 2010).

Although drinking partners and 'husbands' changed often, some of the intertribal relationships did endure and part-Warlpiri children would grow up back on the father's settlement in Arnhem Land. Generally, though, among the long-grassers relationships seemed to be more negotiable. The whole raison d'être of the long-grass camps was to be free of all sorts of inhibiting restrictions, although some traditional prohibitions die hard. One Warlpiri woman enjoying her newfound freedom of selecting her own partners could not quite bring herself to have a permanent relationship with an unrelated man from another desert tribe who happened to have the same subsection name as her, in theory a possible brother.

## 2. The Pentecostal Churchgoers at Bagot Camp, Darwin

A number of Warlpiri women did not survive as long-grassers. Some died prematurely because of the rigours of the lifestyle, others died in violent incidents and another spent 10 years in jail for a homicide. The middle-aged Warlpiri women I found at Bagot Camp in 2009–12 were the survivors who, through emotional exhaustion or health crises or religious conversion, had regained their sobriety and some control over their lives and now ran functioning households in the camps (cf. Brady 1995). A few had joined forces with two white Assemblies of God missionaries and had become elders in the local Pentecostal church in the camp. They became partners in the project of sustaining the church against all the odds: the congregation was relatively small (I would say less than 100) putting pressure on the same core group, the pace of conversions seem to be fairly sedate and moreover, their functioning households in camp continued to be a destination for hard-core drinkers and a reception centre for kin visiting Darwin for business or pleasure or just passing through. I estimated the core group to be about five Aboriginal and five non-Aboriginal people. During the week they would organise Bible study groups, band and choir practice, informal prayer meetings at people's houses and good works such as prison visits. The climax of the week would be the Sunday service at the meeting centre in the camp.

It was during the testimonials at the Sunday service that I heard the most dramatic and forthright challenge to Aboriginal traditions. The three middle-aged Warlpiri women I saw at the service had belonged to the Baptist church back on the Warlpiri settlements, and that church had generally taken a non-confrontational attitude to traditional rituals and had taken on some indigenised modes of evangelisation (see, for example, Jordan 2003). Two of the women had been on a long journey since then. One, on becoming a widow in Lajamanu, had taken up the drinking life first in Top Springs, then Katherine and then at Bagot in Darwin before being 'saved'. The dramatic change in her life to become the sober elder in the church and head of a functioning household still seemed something of a surprise to her. Another had left Ali Curung after the unsettling premature death of her adult daughter and had taken some of the grandchildren with her to put them through school in suburban Darwin. She had first attended a Baptist church in Darwin but was shocked when no one in the unfamiliar congregation spoke to her. She then joined the more intimate and welcoming Assemblies of God congregation at Bagot where she found other settlement women like her. One of these women in her testimony specifically denounced the prototypical male Aboriginal sorcerer: 'He did not heal me. He is a liar and a thief. I got out of that system, praise the Lord.'

This was not an aberration, but reflected the doctrinal approach of all Pentecostal churches including the Assemblies of God (McDonald 2001: 66; Ono 2007; Robbins 2004: 127–30). Occasionally, a drunken Aboriginal man wandering past the open service would briefly remonstrate with the women for expressing such views. In that moment the women, with the support of each other and of their congregation and church, were undeterred. In one sense, the form of their challenge to traditional law represented the most radical statement of rejection of traditional male authority (in favour of the authority of the Lord). In other respects, however, the Warlpiri women involved in the church retained aspects of homeland settlement traditionalism: they maintained their Warlpiri language, they participated in the continual testing of kin relations through making demands and responding to demands for generosity (demand sharing), they retained traditional knowledge of their own traditional country beyond the homeland settlements and they organised traditional mortuary rituals in the town camps.

Their defiance of sorcery, though, placed them well outside the vast majority of contemporary Warlpiri people who continued to believe in the ubiquity and efficacy of sorcery. It seems unthinkable that someone like Topsy Nelson would ever have embraced such a religion. Their denunciation of Aboriginal law in the context of the service was in some ways a competent enactment of social relations since it met the expected format and mode of expression favoured by the church. Indeed, it is the relatively simple formulations and lack of extended training that some anthropologists see as easing the spread of Pentecostalism (Robbins 2004: 130). But in the broader context of Warlpiri society, their denunciations marked a dramatic challenge to well-entrenched social norms and a defiance of the powerful interests of senior male ritual leaders.

## 3. The *Jilimi* in the Alice Springs Town Camp

While there were a surprising number of commonalities between the matrifocal households in Bagot and in the town camps of Alice Springs, I labelled one of those households in Alice Springs a *jilimi* (the name for the traditional widows'/single women's camp) because its matriarchs seemed to be more self-consciously attempting to establish a women's space and to use their traditional prowess in hunting and gathering, Warlpiri language and traditional culture to extend their social networks and differentiate themselves from the local Arrernte people. The fact that the leading matriarch was an elder in the Alice Springs Baptist church allowed them to avoid the overtly confrontational approach to Aboriginal law required by the Pentecostals. Rather than confrontation, her Christian beliefs would sometimes disappoint expectations of her kin, for example to be involved in violently prosecuting family feuds. Instead they prayed outside the courthouse during the associated criminal proceedings. At other times their Christianity provided a means of avoiding direct confrontation, as in praying for the drinkers who sometimes congregated outside their yard, that they would drink quietly and not become violent during the night.

Despite the difficulties of life in the town camp, the core Warlpiri women of the *jilimi* had all given up thoughts of returning permanently to Yuendumu or of marrying again (they were in their late 50s and early 60s). And, although the course of their pre-conversion lives had been subject to some common vicissitudes (violent relationships, alcohol abuse, jail, motor vehicle accidents) and continually encroaching family dramas, I interpreted their *jilimi* as a new kind of Warlpiri project: to live out the greater autonomy, bequeathed by their mature age, in Alice Springs rather than at Yuendumu or some remote outstation. Emblematic of this project was their cultivation of a friendly Indian taxi driver who would take them out to their favourite hunting grounds just south of Alice Springs. There, they could escape the immediate pressures of the town camp, have a picnic, go hunting for goanna and collect bush medicine which was still familiar to them from their own traditional country hundreds of kilometres to the northwest. They converted the Baptist congregation to their love of hunting and persuaded church members to provide transport for hunting trips to the northwest of Alice Springs after the Sunday morning service. The hunting trips become part of the established Sunday routine. The Warlpiri women's involvement with the overwhelmingly non-Aboriginal Baptist congregation, some of whom had strong links to Yuendumu from its very beginning in 1946, was in my view highly significant in sustaining the Warlpiri women. In particular, the matriarch of the *jilimi*, who was also an elder in the church, had many supportive friends and acquaintances and undertook official church work of visiting Warlpiri hospital patients and prisoners and praying over them. The core women of the *jilimi* also rode the wave of the self-determination policy which resulted in the 1980s in a proliferation of Aboriginal organisations in Alice Springs in which they became valued participants, for example, as students in literacy courses at the Institute for Aboriginal Development, producing traditional paintings at Jukurrpa Artists and in providing Warlpiri content for the Warlpiri students in the new 'two-way' Aboriginal primary school (Yipirinya School).

They were not alone. There were a number of middle-aged Warlpiri women and their children in Alice Springs at the same time enabling them to provide support at critical times such as the various stages of mortuary rituals and to take advantage of opportunities to assert their traditional cultural repertoire, for example, traditional dancing at cultural festivals in Alice Springs. In these activities and in their hunting they occasionally exhibited a somewhat chauvinistic attitude towards the local Arrernte people whom they pitied because, they said, unlike the Baptists, the Catholic missionaries had stopped their traditional women's dancing. They did not bother consulting the local Arrernte people about where they could hunt near Alice Springs, reasoning that the Arrernte were now focused exclusively on store-bought food. Indeed, resurgent Arrernte pride following a successful native title claim to the land around Alice Springs had begun to provoke retaliative calls for badly behaving 'visitors' to return to their own country.[3]

---

3   See, for example, comments by Darryl Pearce, then CEO of Lhere Artepe, the Arrernte native title corporation, quoted in *The Australian* newspaper 24 May 2009 and a series of TV community service announcements produced by Lhere Artepe and broadcast on local TV in 2009 (available on YouTube as Lhere Artepe Respect 1, 2 and 3 TVC by Bellettemedia).

The cultural assertiveness and self-direction of the Warlpiri matriarchs in the town camp *jilimi* are similar to that described in Bell's account of the Kaytej *jilimi* at Ali Curung in the 1970s (Bell 1983). What seemed to be missing in Alice Springs were the career 'businesswomen' (ritual specialists) who, when freed of child-minding duties in their middle age, would pursue the advancement of their knowledge of and ability to perform *yawulyu* ceremonies. The competitive efflorescence of such ceremonies, described by Bell and later by Dussart at Yuendumu (Dussart 2000), was absent in Alice Springs. The relative stability of the *jilimi* household attracted near-senile parents, dialysis patients and Warlpiri visitors who were passing through and looking for a relatively safe place to stay. It also became a contact place for child welfare workers looking for foster parents for neglected Warlpiri children. In this respect, they remained very much part of a kin-based service economy described by Merlan and others (Merlan 1991; Sansom 1988) and had to cope with the relentless challenges of provisioning their immediate needs in the lean week following their fortnightly welfare payment.

## 4. The Warlpiri Children's House in Adelaide

In Adelaide I met a Warlpiri woman from Ali Curung who had been living in Adelaide for about 20 years. She had known and revered Topsy Nelson and had known Diane Bell when she was doing her fieldwork in Ali Curung. Her story, while exceptional, provides a dramatic counterpoint to Bell's account, for despite her respect for the traditionalism of Topsy Nelson and the traditionalism of her own fathers and other legendary figures such as Engineer Jack, she decided to leave.

She had no children of her own and over a period of 20 years she and her white husband from Adelaide hosted 65 Aboriginal children from Ali Curung for varying periods of time so that they could attend school in Adelaide. This remarkable project was conceived and operated outside of any targeted government program.[4] It was the labour of love of four key individuals: the 'mother' (stepmother) who was an Aboriginal police aide back in Ali Curung, her daughter (stepdaughter) who had gone to Adelaide to further her education, the daughter's non-Aboriginal husband who supported the project (cf. Batty 2005) and, quite fortuitously, the white ex-principal of Ali Curung school who had retired to Adelaide. The education project could alternatively be conceptualised as one of sustaining long-term relationships with significant non-Aboriginal people (see below).

---

4  It was funded unofficially by virtue of the payment of carer's benefit for looking after the children concerned. Other major sources of income for the project included the private income of the non-Aboriginal husband and the ex–Ali Curung school principal.

The ex-principal's extraordinary generosity in devoting his time and a high percentage of his financial resources to helping his grown-up ex-pupil settle into Adelaide means that he could be seen as the midwife of the Ali Curung diaspora in Adelaide. More accurately though, this small corner of the Warlpiri diaspora was the result of the confluence of a number of factors, including a very different range of responses of the young woman to the circumstances of Ali Curung in the 1980s. She was alarmed at the promised marriage prospects she was facing as she grew up at Ali Curung. While her own respected father, who was a leader in the land rights and outstation movements, was a non-drinker, her prospective promised husband had become a hopeless alcoholic. I doubt whether she would have been moved by Bell's balancing comments about the system as a whole—that in subsequent marriages there would be a greater degree of personal choice involved (Bell 1980). Moreover, with the support of her family, she had succeeded in the education available on the settlement and to an unusual degree had adopted the message of education as her own. It is now difficult to reconstruct the sequence of her leave-taking. Critically, however, she had the support of her influential father to postpone her promised marriage and further her education in Adelaide where she linked up again with her old school principal.

There is no written manifesto of the school education project but it was expressed in 'two laws talk' (cf. Austin-Broos 1996; Harris 1990) and it was clear that they aspired to produce bicultural individuals (cf. Pearson 2009: 292–300). It was always envisaged that following the completion of their school education the visiting children would return permanently to Ali Curung. They all visited Ali Curung on a yearly basis. Sometimes included in that visit would be spending time at the deceased father's outstation where they received some instruction in traditional culture from his widow. The non-Aboriginal husband had been increasingly drawn into the ceremonial life of the settlement over the course of these return visits. The emblem of this group, with its frequent orbiting back to the settlement and ferrying children to school, could be its small bus purchased via a personal loan that stretched the resources of the household.

## 5. The Adelaide Warlpiri Women Artists

In this example the project of sustaining a long-term relationship with a significant non-Aboriginal person, their art wholesaler, is bound up with a project of economic independence as semi-professional Warlpiri artists. The relationship began rather fortuitously when they were introduced by a former settlement art adviser who was not himself in a position to help. From humble beginnings the art wholesaler had developed a relationship with four Warlpiri women artists and in 2009–12 that relationship had become one of the dual economic foundations of those Warlpiri women's existence in Adelaide.

The other economic foundation was the welfare system, which they continued to rely upon for housing and other necessities. They received a few hundred dollars for each canvas they completed, typically one or two a week, thereby doubling their welfare income. This allowed them to buy food and clothes they liked, even during the lean week after the fortnightly welfare payment, to purchase motor vehicles, to send money to relatives and occasionally to indulge their favoured vices. Their physical distance from most of their relations enabled some circumvention of opportunistic demand sharing, although the increasing incidence of mobile phone ownership was encroaching upon that. Even so, it seemed to me that their circumstances in Adelaide enabled unprecedented personal autonomy which I observed first-hand when one of the four artists arrived back from Melbourne, having broken up with her partner, with literally no possessions. Ill and penniless and without access to welfare payments, which she had diverted to paying off a car (long since broken down), she commenced painting in a small spare bedroom of a Warlpiri relation in Adelaide. By the end of the week she had replenished her wardrobe with the proceeds of one painting and purchased a car with another painting.

The relationship with the art wholesaler endured primarily because their project of relative economic independence coincided with their art wholesaler's own project of economic independence. Both were reliant on the fickle flows of changing tastes in the international and national art market and cyclical fluctuations in the disposable income of art purchasers. Critically, the wholesaler had chosen to deal with artists whose work he thought he could sell and had developed a niche of affordable Aboriginal art which was to some extent insulated from the wilder fluctuations of the high-end fine art market. His relationship with one of the most successful artists, a former Aboriginal teacher assistant, sometimes came under strain when she tried to enlarge their relationship into advancing loans and assisting with sundry everyday problems and family crises. He resisted these pressures and relied instead upon his consistent payment, honest dealing and a much appreciated annual artist residency he organised for some of them to spend time in an art gallery at Yulara in the Northern Territory. From there they could more easily visit their relations in Alice Springs and back at Mount Allen, their home settlement. For their part, the Warlpiri artists were broadly loyal to the art wholesaler, but to varying degrees. Their immediate needs sometimes overrode the logic of maximising price by having an exclusive agent, and they seemed to enjoy the flexibility that such occasional freelancing gave them.

## 6. Those with Little Personal Autonomy or Constructive Agency

Thus far I have been describing those women in the diaspora who have taken some positive action in various projects of personal autonomy and self-direction. In this section I wish to briefly outline the other side of the Warlpiri diaspora: those who are drifting or stuck or who have entered into such controlling relationships or drug dependency as to severely limit any capacity for personal autonomy or active and constructive agency. There are those already mentioned who gather around the functioning households of the matriarchs in town camps and the suburbs of towns and cities: the alcoholic relations, the frail elderly, unemployed adult children and adopted grandchildren. There are also the committed drinkers who have their own network of drinking camps and drinking households around Australia. They sometimes move in and out of the networks of their kin in more functioning households, but are more likely to be found in the long grass of Darwin, the unofficial camps around Katherine, Tennant Creek, Alice Springs, Mount Isa and Cairns and the parklands of Adelaide.

The idea of sustaining a household to enable its residents to drink is still a project of minimal agency for the few who occasionally have to deal with welfare housing authorities and NGOs specifically established to support fragile tenancies. Even that minimal agency broke down in the case of those whose health problems become severe because of their years of drinking and self-neglect. They were sometimes given priority for welfare housing, notwithstanding a background of damaged and abandoned houses. On reflection, it is not always easy to clearly separate the sober projects of personal autonomy described previously and dissolute dependency. In some instances these worlds overlap, for example, when independently derived income from jobs or from painting is channelled exclusively into drinking parties or poker machine addictions. There are also inherently problematic cases of dependency in projects of sustaining intimate relationships with non-Aboriginal men, since some of them seem to have involved unfulfilled aspirations for romantic love intertwined with the surrendering of independent income from painting.

# Conclusion

I commenced this chapter by asserting a contemporary heterogeneity of Warlpiri women's approaches to projects of personal autonomy, especially against the return to traditionalism and traditional country advocated by Bell and her key informants. Looking back at the momentous era of the 1970s and early 1980s it is now easier to see how the neat alignment of Bell's view of the pre-contact era and the policy agenda of land rights and outstations would obscure the variety of ways Warlpiri women would respond to the challenges of deteriorating settlement life. Bell was, of course, well aware of the extraordinary pressures on Aboriginal women and courageously brought to the surface issues of drunken violence against women and intra-racial rape (Bell and Ditton 1980; Bell and Nelson 1989). But the predilections of her key informants and relatively sedentary fieldwork predisposed her account (along with all accounts based on community studies) towards those Aboriginal women who sought out the available degrees of personal autonomy locally rather than by leaving.[5] Locating those women who did leave the settlements has not only enabled the enlarging of our knowledge of the kinds of Aboriginal women's responses to their circumstances; it has also provoked a closer examination of the concepts of personal autonomy and of active and constructive agency.

In identifying the Janus face of personal autonomy as both the competent performance of social relationships and sometimes the deliberate fracturing of constraining relationships, it becomes clear that Bell's general orientation underplayed the latter. In the Warlpiri diaspora this kind of assertion of personal autonomy was most commonly exemplified in the many stories of escape from promised marriage. Once the immediate infringement of their intimate personal autonomy had been avoided they assumed a different mode of action, more spontaneously responding to quotidian necessities. There were certainly no grand plans of disappearing into white society. In most cases, the rejection of a particular promised husband did not involve a more general rejection of all aspects of traditional life (just of some aspects as they applied to them).

All of the projects described had the character of a repositioning with regard to some traditional norms and the creation of a new mix (like choosing from a menu) of elements that make up their contemporary Warlpiri life. In the case of the Warlpiri artists of Adelaide, the distant location of their project of economic independence and less constrained consumption moderated the immediate impact of demand sharing. The schoolchildren's household gave prominence to Western-style education and the continuing development of a 'two laws' or bicultural project, which had started on the settlements but the required discipline of the children was easier to maintain in a supportive household in the city. The Alice Springs *jilimi* brought the idiom of Christianity to the operation of a traditionally sanctioned women's space. It can be noted that all

---

5   I should make it clear that even in the 1970s there were some Aboriginal women known to Bell who had married white husbands, although her focus on settlement life and its ritual would have precluded her making their acquaintance and obtaining their perspective. Also, the limits of Bell's traditionalist focus became a theme in the initial reception of her work. Hamilton, for example, wondered why the implications of the broader societal revaluation of traditional culture in the post-assimilationist period, including women's ritual, was not more explicitly thematised (Hamilton 1986: 13–15).

of these projects have their counterparts on the settlements. But for a variety of reasons the women involved have found their projects easier to sustain away from their home settlements and traditional country.

The denunciation of some key aspects of tradition and male authority by the Warlpiri Pentecostal women, at least in their testimonies during Sunday services, represents the most extreme version of personal autonomy in rejection mode. In the boldness of their self-assertion I see them as the diaspora counterpart to some of the separatist elements of Bell's account of the personal autonomy of mature Aboriginal women organising their own lives in the *jilimi* or on the outstation, conducting their own healing ceremonies and rituals sustaining the sacred local landscape without the mediation of men. The appearance of the Warlpiri Pentecostal women as a thoroughgoing, modernising women's liberation movement must, however, be tempered with their continued embeddedness in a domestic moral economy of the service mode and the paradoxical preservation within Pentecostalism of beliefs about the reality and power of a spiritual realm. As Robbins has pointed out, it is the preservation of such beliefs that distinguishes Pentecostalism sharply from other modernising projects such as development (Robbins 2004: 128–9).

# References

Austin-Broos, D. 1996. 'Two Laws', ontologies, histories: ways of being Aranda today. *The Australian Journal of Anthropology* 7: 1–20.

Batty, P. 2005. Private politics, public strategies: white advisers and their Aboriginal subjects. *Oceania* 75: 209–21.

Beckett, J.R. 1983. Ownership of land in the Torres Strait Islands. In N. Peterson and M. Langton (eds), *Aborigines, Land and Land Rights*, pp. 202–10. Canberra: Australian Institute of Aboriginal Studies.

Bell, D. 1978. For our families: the Kurundi walk off and the Ngurrantiji venture. *Aboriginal History* 2: 32–62.

Bell, D. 1980. Desert politics: choices in the 'marriage market'. In M. Etienne and E. Leacock (eds), *Women and Colonisation: Anthropological Perspectives*, pp. 239–69. New York: Praeger.

Bell, D. 1983. *Daughters of the Dreaming*. Sydney: McPhee Gribble/George Allen and Unwin.

Bell, D. 1985. Topsy Napurrula Nelson: teacher, philosopher and friend. In I. White, D. Barwick, and B. Meehan (eds), *Fighters and Singers: The Lives of Some Australian Aboriginal Women*, pp. 1–18. Sydney: Allen and Unwin.

Bell, D. 1993. *Daughters of the Dreaming*. Second edition. St Leonards, NSW: Allen and Unwin.

Bell, D. and P. Ditton. 1980. *Law: The Old and the New: Aboriginal Women in Central Australia Speak Out*. Canberra, ACT: Published for Central Australian Aboriginal Legal Aid Service by Aboriginal History.

Bell, D. and T.N. Nelson. 1989. Speaking about rape is everyone's business. *Women's Studies International Forum* 12: 403–16.

Berndt, C.H. 1989. Retrospect, and prospect: looking back over 50 years. In P. Brock (ed.), *Women, Rites and Sites: Aboriginal Women's Cultural Knowledge*, pp. 1–20. Sydney: Allen and Unwin.

Brady, M. (ed.). 1995. *Giving Away the Grog: Aboriginal Accounts of Drinking and Not Drinking*. Canberra: Drug Offensive, Commonwealth Department of Human Services and Health.

Burbank, V.K. 1988. *Aboriginal Adolescence: Maidenhood in an Aboriginal Community*. New Brunswick: Rutgers University Press.

Curran, G. 2010. Contemporary Ritual Practice in an Aboriginal Settlement: The Warlpiri Kurdiji Ceremony. PhD Thesis, The Australian National University, Canberra.

Dussart, F. 2000. *The Politics of Ritual in an Aboriginal Settlement: Kinship, Gender, and the Currency of Knowledge*. Smithsonian Series in the Ethnographic Inquiry. Washington, DC: Smithsonian Institution Press.

Friedman, M. 2003. *Autonomy, Gender, Politics*. Oxford: Oxford University Press.

Giddens, A. 1991. *Modernity and Self-Identity: Self and Society in the Late Modern Age*. Cambridge: Polity.

Glaskin, K., M. Tonkinson, Y. Musharbash, and V. Burbank (eds). 2008. *Mortality, Mourning and Mortuary Practices in Indigenous Australia*. Surrey: Ashgate.

Hamilton, A. 1986. Daughters of the imaginary. *Canberra Anthropology* 9: 1–25.

Harris, S. 1990. *Two-Way Aboriginal Schooling: Education and Cultural Survival*. Canberra: Aboriginal Studies Press.

Jordan, I. 2003. *Their Way: Towards an Indigenous Warlpiri Christianity*. Darwin: Charles Darwin University Press.

Keen, I. 1989. Aboriginal governance. In J.C. Altman (ed.), *Emergent Inequalities in Aboriginal Australia*, pp. 17–42. Sydney: Oceania Monographs, University of Sydney.

Kerins, S. 2009. *The First-Ever Northern Territory Homelands/Outstation Policy*. CAEPR Topical Issue No. 9/2009. Canberra: Centre for Aboriginal Economic Policy Research, The Australian National University.

Kühler, M. and N. Jelinek. 2013. *Autonomy and the Self*. Philosophical Studies Series. Dordrecht and London: Springer.

Laing, L. 2000. Progress, trends and challenges in Australian responses to domestic violence. Issues Paper 1. Sydney: Australian Domestic and Family Violence Clearinghouse, University of New South Wales.

McDonald, H. 2001. *Blood, Bones and Spirit: Aboriginal Christianity in an East Kimberley Town*. Melbourne: Melbourne University Press.

Merlan, F. 1988. Gender in Aboriginal social life: a review. In R.M. Berndt and R. Tonkinson (eds), *Social Anthropology and Australian Aboriginal Studies: A Contemporary Overview*, pp. 17–76. Canberra: Aboriginal Studies Press.

Merlan, F. 1991. Women, productive roles, and monetisation of the 'service mode' in Aboriginal Australia: perspectives from Katherine, Northern Territory. *The Australian Journal of Anthropology* 2: 259–92.

Merlan, F. 1992. Male-female separation and forms of society in Aboriginal Australia. *Cultural Anthropology* 7: 169–93.

Meyers, D.T. 1989. *Self, Society, and Personal Choice*. New York: Columbia University Press.

Meyers, D.T. 1997. *Feminists Rethink the Self: Feminist Theory and Politics*. Boulder, CO: Westview Press.

Musharbash, Y. 2010. Marriage, love magic, and adultery: Warlpiri relationships as seen by three generations of anthropologists. *Oceania* 80: 272–88.

Myers, F.R. 1986. *Pintupi Country, Pintupi Self: Sentiment, Place, and Politics among Western Desert Aborigines*. Washington: Smithsonian Institution Press; Canberra: Australian Institute of Aboriginal Studies.

Myers, F.R. 2002. *Painting Culture: The Making of an Aboriginal High Art*. Durham: Duke University Press.

Nelson, T.N. 1990. My story. In S. Schreiner and D. Bell (eds), *This Is My Story*, pp. 18–27. Geelong: Centre for Aboriginal Studies, Deakin University.

Ono, A. 2007. Pentecostalism Among the Bundjalung Revisited: The Rejection of Culture by Aboriginal Christians in Northern New South Wales, Australia. PhD Thesis, The Australian National University, Canberra.

Ortner, S.B. 2006. *Anthropology and Social Theory: Culture, Power and the Acting Subject*. Durham and London: Duke University Press.

Pearson, N. 2009. *Up From the Mission: Selected Writings*. Melbourne: Black Inc.

Peterson, N. 2008. Just humming: the consequences of the decline of learning contexts among the Warlpiri. In J. Kommers and E. Venbrux (eds), *Cultural Styles of Knowledge Transmission: Essays in Honour of Ad Borsboom*, pp. 114–8. Amsterdam: Aksant.

Robbins, J. 2004. The globalization of Pentecostal and charismatic Christianity. *Annual Review of Anthropology* 33: 117–43.

Sansom, B. 1980. *The Camp at Wallaby Cross: Aboriginal Fringe Dwellers in Darwin*. Canberra: Australian Institute of Aboriginal Studies.

Sansom, B. 1988. A grammar of exchange. In I. Keen (ed.), *Being Black: Aboriginal Cultures in 'Settled' Australia*, pp. 159–77. Canberra: Aboriginal Studies Press.

Sansom, B. 2010. The refusal of holy engagement: how man-making can fail. *Oceania* 80: 24–57.

Tonkinson, R. 1990. The changing status of Aboriginal women: 'free agents' at Jigalong. In R. Tonkinson and M. Howard (eds), *Going It Alone? Prospects for Aboriginal Autonomy: Essays in Honour of Ronald and Catherine Berndt*, pp. 125–47. Canberra: Aboriginal Studies Press.

# 11 The Language of 'Spiritual Power': From *Mana* to *Märr* on the Crocodile Islands

Bentley James
North Australian Indigenous Land and Sea Management Alliance Ltd

## A Brief History of Spiritual Power

When the earliest ethnographers and ethnographically minded missionaries arrived in the Crocodile Islands in northeast Arnhem Land in the 1920s, they brought with them an anthropological metalanguage that included the concept of *mana* as 'spiritual power' (Keesing 1984: 137). The nature of 'primitive religion' was still genuinely at issue among students of Oceania, and questions of religion, magic, and 'spiritual power' were matters of deep anthropological concern. W. Lloyd Warner, in his 1937 classic *A Black Civilization*, found 'spiritual power' to be a fundamental principle among the people of northeast Arnhem Land, and used the term *mana*, as developed by Bishop Codrington in Melanesia, to describe the concept known to the Yolngu[1] as *märr*.

Ethnographic research and writing in the Pacific since the early 1980s have demonstrated that earlier interpretations of *mana* have been problematic, and have overturned any simple translation of the concept. I have found the same holds true for the Yolngu concept of *märr* on the Crocodile Islands.

---

1   'Yolngu' is a term used widely by Yolngu people and researchers since the 1970s to describe the Indigenous people of northeast Arnhem Land speaking languages collectively called Yolngu *matha* (lit. 'people's tongue'). Earlier anthropological literature has referred to these people as Murngin (Warner 1937), Wulamba (Berndt 1951, 1952, 1955) and Miwuyt (Shapiro 1981). According to Schebeck (1968), the term was introduced into the linguistics literature by O'Grady et al. (1966).

Recent scholarship, including that of Ian Keen (who himself conducted research there in the mid-1970s), provides a framework for undertaking this kind of re-analysis and reinterpretation. Warner's rendering of 'spiritual power' as *mana* on the Crocodile Islands highlights the potential conflict between an anthropological metalanguage and the ideational categories as conceived by members of the society itself.[2] Writing of *mana*, Keesing calls for 'a critical hermeneutics in which cultural translation is cast deeply in doubt' (Keesing 1984: 138). Closer to home, Ian Keen has argued that ethnographic description 'often involves the substitution in an anthropological metalanguage of expressions embedding one set of metaphors for indigenous expressions that incorporate quite different tropes' (Keen 1995: 502). Both call for greater attention to local tropes, idioms, and meanings. In light of this approach I reanalyse the language of *märr*, especially in everyday social life, as the key to unlocking this complex Yolngu concept.[3]

In this chapter, I argue that rendering *märr* as a generalised 'spiritual power' is misleading as it is a highly polysemous term. Within a Yolngu worldview *märr* as 'spiritual power' is best understood as a kind of ancestral essence. This distinctive view conceives of consubstantial connections linking kinds of ancestors, people, languages, and particular places as fundamental, and a key aspect of a Yolngu site-based ontology. This chapter begins with an examination of Codrington's interpretation of *mana* and Keesing's reinterpretation, so as to illustrate the utility of comparative geo-lexical data and attention to cultural context. I will then subject the concept of *märr* to a similar process, embracing Keen's call for greater attention to local tropes and idioms, first examining the early interpretations of Warner, Thomson and others, before providing my own ethnolinguistic reinterpretation.

## Codrington's *Mana*

The concept of *mana* associated with maritime-agrarian cultures originated in southeast Asia and spread eastward throughout Pacific Melanesia, Micronesia and Polynesia over the last 10,000 years.[4] Bishop Codrington was the first to attempt an ethnographic description of *mana* in his studies of Melanesian society in the late 1800s. Codrington conceived of *mana* as a kind of magical power that existed in the world like an invisible substance or principle inhering

---

2   See also Schneider (1965: 453).
3   This paper arises from conversations with Ian and colleague Ferg Ferguson working on the far eastern side of northeast Arnhem Land.
4   This maritime/farming culture travelled southeast from continental Asia and then sailed eastward to the islands of Melanesia and Micronesia between 1200 BC and AD 500, having settled most of the Pacific islands as far as Easter Island by AD 300 (see Capelli et al. 2001).

in nature, objects and the natural world, invoked by the 'natives' through ceremony. Codrington (1891: 191) says: 'By means of [*mana*] men are able to direct and control the forces of nature, to make rain or sunshine, wind or calm, to cause sickness or remove it, to know what is far off in time or space, or to blast and curse'. The bishop's powerful imagery invokes the forces of nature, and comprises a sermon on the dangers of the unrestrained spiritual power of the 'natives'. In hindsight, it is apparent that Codrington's impression of the concept of *mana* provided direction for later constructions by missionaries and ethnologists alike.

Following Codrington's lead, later ethnologists of Polynesia such as Hocart (1914), Speiser (1923), Fox (1924), Humphreys (1926) and Hogbin (1936), assumed that *mana* was a kind of invisible medium of spiritual power discernible in sacred objects, and manifest as some kind of potency radiated by humans. Anthropological understanding of this concept and its place in Polynesian society appeared to be following the predilections of Codrington. For example, C.E. Fox, an Anglican missionary working on San Cristobal in the southeast Solomons, some distance downwind of Codrington, wrote of the Arosi concept of *mena*:

> Mena ... seems to be conceived of as an invisible spiritual substance in which objects may be immersed ... A great warrior is seen to have mena and all his possessions are soaked in it, so his club is treasured and handed down ... Certain places are impregnated with mena. (Fox 1924: 251–2).

The impression one gets of Arosi 'mena', as that of an invisible liquid in which objects are immersed, uses imagery that recalls the immersion of baptism or the impregnation of holy religious relics. The missionary Fox, writing at a period in which the European mind was captivated with Christian thematics, hydraulics and mechanical models, presents the kind of ethnocentric formulation common in the ethnological accounts of the day (see also Humphreys 1926: 70, 167; Speiser 1923/1990; cf. Oliver 1974: 55; Keesing 1984: 151; MacClancy 1986: 142). In the 1940s Raymond Firth responded to such formulations by replying that 'interpretation in terms of such abstraction can only be the work of the anthropologist' (Firth 1940: 498). Later, Jørgen Prytz-Johansen articulates the critical need for thorough and grounded linguistic examination in the case of *mana* in Maori religious practice:

> What seems to me to be missing is the simple recognition of the view that the core of the investigations must be philological, thus the use of the word mana by a definite people. Only in this way may we be sure of speaking about something real and not a compromise between a scientific technical term, mana, and more or less corresponding notions of mana in various peoples. (Prytz-Johansen 1954: 76)

Prytz-Johansen's call for a 'philological' approach here resonates with Keesing's proposition that cultural translation may 'more or less carefully, more or less faithfully' report the configuration of the conceptual schemes of native peoples through 'rigorous linguistic analysis' (Keesing 1987: 174). In this light Keesing (1984: 137) criticises the Codringtonian view of *mana*, saying it lacks solid understandings of the cultural context, and is based on insecure ethnographic evidence. He concludes:

> With few exceptions, Pacific Islanders have been unsuccessful in explaining that to theologically minded Europeans ... We have not understood that mana-ness represented a common *quality* of efficacy or success, retrospectively interpreted, not a universal *medium* of it. (Keesing 1984: 149–50)

His idea of a 'critical hermeneutic', with a greater sensitivity to the rendering of local categories, lexicon and local context, adds a new dimension to his reinterpretation of *mana* as 'spiritual power'. *Mana*, Keesing declares, is more adequately expressed as an abstract verbal noun meaning 'efficacy', 'success' and 'potency' (Keesing 1984: 137). His method of comparative reinterpretation of lexical and geographical data and close attention to cultural context are key aspects of his 'critical hermeneutics'. By dint of these methods Keesing suggests that Proto-Oceanic *mana* is a stative verb meaning 'be efficacious, be successful, be realized, "work"' (ibid.). Further, he posits, where *mana* was used as a noun, it was an abstract verbal noun.[5] *Mana*, he says, has suffered a pervasive translation error in its description as a medium of power, where as it is most widely understood as a condition. In those specific geographical locations in parts of eastern Polynesia and Melanesia, where it was referred to as a medium of power, it accompanied very distinctive hierarchical political cultural contexts (ibid.: 137). Keesing's attempt to remain in rigorous ethnographic harmony with emic understandings provides new depth of insight about the meanings of *mana*.

Similarly but more recently, Blust (2007) and Blevins (2008) have paid profitable attention to the etymology of *mana* in comparing lexical and geographical data. Blevins' work supports the reconstruction of a Proto-Central-Eastern Malayo-Polynesian that casts *mana* as a 'supernatural power, associated with spirits of the ancestors and the forces of nature' (Blevins 2008: 253). Not too distantly Blust (2007) revisits cognates of Proto-Oceanic *mana* to find it a power possessed by 'forces of nature' like 'thunder' and 'wind'. Over time, he says, notions of its 'unseen supernatural agency' became detached from such forces as '*mana* assumed a life of its own' (Blust 2007: 404). As such, he concludes, the

---

5   A verbal noun is a kind of noun derived from a verb (usually by adding the suffix '-ing' in English), and sharing noun-like properties, and also partly sharing verb-like constructions, for example, 'learning' in the expression 'a show of learning'.

meaning of *mana* can be seen as part of the wider processes of man's attempt to understand the forces of nature, and in so doing provides us with a deeper appreciation of *mana* and perhaps something about the precarious nature of the human condition.

Key among these ethnolinguistic pathways to greater insight are the comparative analysis of geo-lexical data and close attention to language and cultural context, to which I would add Keen's call for greater attention to local tropes, idioms, and meanings. If indeed the end of ethnography is to 'more or less carefully, more or less faithfully' report the 'configuration of the conceptual schemes of native peoples', then this approach affords some more fruitful ethnographic avenues of investigation (Keesing 1987: 174). Similarly I wish to begin by examining William Lloyd Warner's use of the term *mana* in the Crocodile Islands, as a prelude to a more nuanced examination of the Yolngu notion of *märr*.

## Warner's *Mana* in the Crocodile Islands

W. Lloyd Warner made two trips to the Crocodile group, first in 1927 and again in 1928, including Milingimbi and Murrungga, largest of the outer Crocodile Islands. His landmark ethnography, *A Black Civilization: A Social Study of an Australian Tribe* (1937/1969), is an anthropological classic of remarkable scope and detail. For decades the centrepiece of Australian ethnography, it stimulated commentary across disciplines influencing scholars from Lévi-Strauss to Jung and Freud. The young Warner, student of R.H. Lowie and A.L. Kroeber, was himself influenced by Malinowski, Boas and Radcliffe-Brown.

On his arrival to the islands Warner found a ubiquitous notion of 'spiritual power' he called *mana*. One may speculate as to why he chose to use the term *mana* rather than the local term *märr* given the availability of the local concept.[6] Was the term *mana* so widespread in Warner's day that it was customary for anthropologists to use it generically, much like 'potlatch' or 'totem'? Could it have been his unfamiliarity with the local language? Despite Warner's meticulous ethnography it seems possible that the term *märr*, referring specifically to 'spiritual power', may simply have eluded him. Or perhaps, given its frequency in everyday discourse, and complex multiple layered usages, it may have appeared to be a term that was too imprecise, too hard to define simply. Nevertheless, naming the local concept *mana* seems to have created inappropriate comparison with the Oceanic notion and its ethnographic entailments, offering general correspondences that may well have obscured some distinctive local questions.

---

6   On the Crocodile Islands speakers of the Yan-nhangu language use the word *mana* to mean 'is' or the progressive continuous 'still (is doing)'; for example, *nhani nhang'ku bayipi mana nyena* 'she is still living there'.

Regardless of these shortcomings, in other respects his analysis touches on some important issues for the anthropological understanding of Yolngu people. Warner explains that 'the mana of the Murngin well is due not to any mundane biological value its water may have for the group, but rather to the spiritual power of the water' (Warner 1969: 381). The sacred clan well is the origin from which each member has his or her beginning and end, the very centre of the 'spiritual life' of the clan, containing the 'souls of the dead and those who are to be born' (ibid.: 381). Warner portrays an essential ancestral nature in his picture of this *mana* and its bonds with people, place (well) and the group (clan), most particularly in his casting of the sacred totemic well as the site of the clan's *mana*. He continues:

> The clansmen are identified with the totemic well by the fact that they come from it and are allowed to be born by the action of the totem spirit that resides within the well; they are identified with the well because at death they will go back to it and because all of their kin who have died and those living, with whom they have had all of their social relations, are or will be either in this well into which their own soul returns or in other like clan wells; and finally, their wellbeing and that of their fellow clansmen and of other clans are dependent upon the proper enactment of the seasonal rituals which demonstrate the mana or power of the totem. (ibid.: 380)

In Warner's description, the linkages between *mana*, the well, ancestors, the living, the dead, religious icons (totems), and ritual life come into much clearer focus. He is describing the underpinnings of the fundamentals from which a Yolngu site-based ontology arises. The 'totemic well' is indeed a site from which members of the clan draw their spiritual identity, but some key connections are yet to be made.

With great ethnographic skill Warner develops a description of the invisible threads linking members of the clan, well, totems and ancestral powers and their shared *mana*. He then takes a Durkheimian turn, however, pronouncing that 'the mana of the ceremonial leader comes from his oral and ceremonial ritual, which in turn gains its power ultimately from a society or church, viz., the clan' (Warner 1969: 233). This Durkheimian direction sees *mana* as the 'totemic principle'; as Durkheim himself writes, 'The god of the clan, the totemic principle, must therefore be the clan itself, but transfigured and imagined ... as totems' (Durkheim 1912: 154). Perhaps the questions that need to be asked here should be: How closely do these associated constructions reflect Yolngu ideas about *märr*? Or are they manifestations of a Durkheimian metalanguage and its notion of *mana*?[7] Warner astutely identifies key elements of the distinctive Yolngu concept *märr*, despite referring to them by the generic term *mana*, but

---

7    Clifford Geertz observed wryly of Durkheim's ethnography of the Arunta that 'What one finds among the Arunta are the beliefs and practices of the Arunta' (Geertz 1973: 22).

then changes direction and opts for a generalising Durkheimian interpretation that owes more to the anthropological metalanguage than to specifically Yolngu ideas. It is not until the work of Donald Thomson, who was far more skilled in local languages, that an understanding of the Yolngu of concept of *märr* was developed more fully.

## Thomson's *Märr* and *Mana*

The first recorded usage of *märr* in the literature was by the Rev. Theodore. T. Webb (Webb 1933: 36). Webb lived at Milingimbi from 1926 to 1939 and as a keen amateur ethnologist and linguist he hosted, at different times, both Warner and Thomson. Webb, theologically trained, used the term *märr* in much the same generic way as Warner had *mana*. Thomson, who arrived in 1935, trained as a structural functionalist under Radcliffe-Brown and travelled widely throughout northeast Arnhem Land with his friend Rraywala (Raiwala).[8] Thomson's paper on the concept of *märr* in Arnhem Land, compiled from his field notes by Nicolas Peterson, refers to and extends a critique of both Codrington's and Warner's *mana*. Thomson's use of local languages develops the subtlety of his definition of the term *märr*. In a letter to Thomson in June 1948, Radcliffe-Brown remarked that 'it is valuable from the point of view of scientific scholarship to have some of the more significant statements in the native language' (Thomson 1975: 1). Thomson translated and characterised *märr* in part thus:

> *Marr* as a spiritual force underlies all ritual ceremonial life in Arnhem Land, and finds expression most forcibly in the attitude toward totemic increase ceremonies which are carried out regularly at certain of the totem centres, notably at Mooroonga Island in the Crocodile Group. (Thomson 1975: 6)

Here Thomson explicitly links *märr* to sites he called 'totem centres'. He proclaims that 'in Arnhem Land the concept of a spiritual force very like *mana* is even more strongly developed ... People ... call it *marr*, a term known or used throughout eastern Arnhem Land' (Thomson 1975: 2). Thomson recognises the likeness of *märr* to *mana*, but distinguishes the distinctive site-based quality of *märr*. He echoes Yolngu understanding that *märr* exists not only in the clan waterhole, but in sites throughout the clan estate. Furthermore, he makes us aware that the clan's totems (ritual icons), ceremonies, and associated stories,

---

8   I was told by old people that Thomson's Mildjingi informant, Raiwala (Mildjingi *bäpurru*; Djinang language) was one of four Djinang men alleged to have speared Laindjurra (Mälarra *bäpurru*; Yan-nhangu language), the lethal sorcerer of Mooroonga (Murrungga) made famous in Warner's ethnography (author's field notes, Murrungga Island, 1999).

songs, dances and paintings contain the clan's *märr*. These features of the clan's religious property are referred to by Howard Morphy as the clan's sacred *mardayin*.[9]

Thomson's work proved to be very influential on subsequent generations of Arnhem Land ethnographers. In his article 'From Dull to Brilliant: The Aesthetics of Spiritual Power among the Yolngu' (1989), Morphy credits Thomson for first noting the term *bir'yun* and its connection to *märr*. Morphy situates Yolngu paintings (*mardayin miny'tji*) within the Yolngu ritual framework and tells us that in *mardayin miny'tji* the aspect known as *bir'yun* (brilliance or shimmering) is a signifier of 'ancestral power' (ibid.: 24–5). Noting that the most important aspects of *miny'tji* refer to design and colour (ibid.: 25), he interprets *mardayin* or the clan's sacred property more fully, drawing important connections:

> The *mardayin* consists of sets of songs, dances, paintings, sacred objects and ritual incantations associated with Ancestral beings. The *mardayin* refers to the actions of Ancestral beings in creating the land and in instituting the practices of Yolngu life ... To the Yolngu the *mardayin* are not only the means of expressing Ancestral events, but also part of the essence of the Ancestral beings themselves. (Morphy 1989: 25)

Morphy makes explicit the connections between ancestors, *mardayin*, and *bir'yun* as aspects of ancestral law (or property) connected to *märr* as a 'source of ancestral power for use in ritual' (ibid.: 25). He brings out the pervasiveness of ancestral essences in Yolngu life, linking ritual, *mardayin*, and the 'ownership of land conditional on maintaining the rituals associated with the land' (ibid.). He says '*Ma:rr* is a positive force associated with happiness, strength, health and fertility, but it is also associated with death and can always have a dangerous dimension' (ibid.: 30). Morphy's descriptions afford standpoints closely reflecting Yolngu perspectives on *märr* as an ancestral essence.

Thomson points to the negative dimension of *märr* in *miringu ma:rr*, (lit. 'enemy spiritual power'), 'the power of vengeance' in paintings of the 'shark ancestor' (Morphy 1989: 30).[10] Outside the ritual framework, Yolngu elder Joanne Garnggulkpuy reaffirms how positive Yolngu social behaviours are directed by collective knowledge linked to 'places, species and practices' using the expression *märryu-dapmaram* (Garnggulkpuy and Christie 2002: 6). Garnggulkpuy and Christie have re-interpreted *märr* as 'ancestral connections'. They translate *märryu-dapmaram* as 'faith/trust/confidence/good will-instrument-clench' (ibid.). The power of *märr* as 'ancestral connections' is said to control social situations by 'appealing to people's strength through identity

---

9   *Madayin* (*madayin/mardayin/marrayin/mu-dayan*): sacred, secret, holy, taboo including objects or species containing consubstantial ancestor essence; synonym: *dhuyu* and *dharrpal* (see Zorc 1986: 204).
10  *Miringu*: enemy; soldier, warrior; battle, war, armed conflict (Zorc 1986: 235).

and kinship' (ibid.) This notion of *märr* articulating contemporary social identities and kinship relations points resoundingly to profound continuities in the foundational assumptions of spiritual power underlying the Yolngu cosmos.

So far the literature points towards a broad understanding of *märr* as a connection between ancestors and the living. 'Ancestral connections' are seen linking the living, dead and yet to be born, glimpsed in Warner's 'clan well', in Thomson's notion of 'spiritual force' and more recently in Morphy's ancestral essence of 'fertility', 'happiness' and 'death'. Garnggulkpuy provides a perspective on *märr* in *märryu-dapmaram* from her standpoint as a member of Yolngu society itself. Taken altogether these accounts describe a broad range of categories and metaphysical phenomena composed of *märr*. I want to turn now to ask, what kind of *märr*? Is it all the same everywhere, a generalised, universal *märr*, or are there different kinds of *märr*? To answer these questions it is necessary to examine briefly the cultural context that gives rise to this notion *märr*.

## Invisible Links of People, Places and Language

Yolngu cosmology posits the existence of ancestral *wangarr* (creator/spirits). These moiety-specific *wangarr* created the known universe in two halves, either Dhuwa or Yirritja.[11] This is the origin or genesis of the law (*rom*), the instantiation of the laws of cosmic order. These laws are contained in myths recounting the distinctive cosmogonic acts of the *wangarr*. Forming the world they left traces, imprints and procreative powers in the land, seas, phenomena, and names imbued with their essence. Each distinctive group, or *bäpurru*, inherit their sites, laws and myths from a particular ensemble of *wangarr*.[12] The laws, myths and acts of this ensemble of site-specific connections constitute the distinctive consubstantial ancestral inheritance of each discrete and named *bäpurru*.[13] These locality-based and site-specific myths, powers and laws comprise a worldview that provides the blueprint for the reproduction of the precepts and practices of the respective *bäpurru* and society as a whole. The *bäpurru*, their sites, *madayin*, iconic species, dances, paintings and ritual icons (*rangga*) share

---

11  Dhuwa and Yirritja are two halves, or moieties, of the Yolngu system of thought that divide the world into two categories, classifying every aspect of the physical and spiritual world. These moieties are characterised by complementary reciprocal relations understood to create the fundamental conditions for life.
12  The term clan is now usually replaced by the term *bäpurru* as it denotes a more complex meaning closer to Yolngu conceptions. *Bäpurru* have been described as complex, multilayered, focal social categories with a common identity, existing in shared ancestral essences (See Keen 1978, 1994, 1995; Toner 2001).
13  To be consubstantial with something is to be identified with it at the elemental level, to be of identical substance. Consubstantial identification constitutes the principal ontological basis of ownership of the elements of the *bäpurru*, sites, *madayin* and the ancestral essences of their living descendants (see also Bagshaw 1998: 162).

the inalienable consubstantial links of ancestral essence that distinguish their identity. These ancestral essences are the *märr* of the *bäpurru* and a key element in the overarching architecture of a Yolngu site-based ontology.

According to the laws of this site-based ontology people believe that the languages of their respective *bäpurru, madayin* and countries were simultaneously endowed to them by the *wangarr* (creator/ ancestor spirits). The mechanism of this linguistic endowment is important and described here by Nancy Williams (1999):

> The spirit beings/ancestral beings/creator beings vested land in particular groups of people in a time long past. Both the beings and the time are locally distinctive, as are the acts of vesting. They all, however, include descriptions of flora and fauna as well as topographical features of the particular land and sea, and most importantly they gave names to them. Usually the language in which these acts are done is also distinctive and pertains to the specific locality. (Williams 1999: 57)

What are of conspicuous significance are the links between the creation of, and endowment of, specific locality, sites, language, and *bäpurru*. Each *bäpurru* has its own distinctive language, as endowed by the ancestors, and conceived of as a signifier of their unique ancestral inheritance.[14] This language of the *bäpurru* is imbued with the same consubstantial ancestral essences as the land, sites, and all other aspects of the *bäpurru*. This characteristically Yolngu scheme of ancestral endowment of language is not just associative, but a fundamental ontological truth. As a consequence, the words of each *bäpurru* language are understood to be imbued with the same, particular ancestral essences or *märr* as all the other elements of the *bäpurru*. Put another way, the words of the language of the *bäpurru* contain the *märr* of the *bäpurru*. This is a feature that will re-emerge in geo-lexical analysis.[15]

This emblematic relationship of the *bäpurru*, country, and language has an enormous significance for the Yan-nhangu people and their sites in the Crocodile Islands. People share their names with sites, ancestors and their cosmogonic acts, in the language, rituals and everyday practices. People often spoke of the signs of *märr*, the signifiers of 'spiritual powers' present in the country, in the movement of the seas, in the changing seasons, everywhere manifest in

---

14  Some researchers have played down this Yolngu perspective on the distinctiveness of *bäpurru* languages citing statistical evidence of mutual intelligibility; however, in this examination, attention to emic categories of cultural context aims to render the ideational categories as conceived by members of the society itself and not the technical orthodoxy.

15  Outside the ritual sphere, decline in the significance of linguistic identification impacts more directly a younger generation unfamiliar with their *bäpurru* lands. Homeland life provides strong links of language to country, although now most homelands have been dismantled by concerted settler state policies to undermine them.

the living world. Today this sense is less apparent in the modern community setting. Also, today this idea of language ownership has a far greater significance for an older generation, those having grown up in close connection with their *bäpurru* country, or living on the homelands. Nevertheless, the idea of language connections to ancestral power persists strongly in the ritual sphere.[16]

## The Yan-nhangu People of the Crocodile Islands

My interest in Yan-nhangu began at Murrungga, largest of the outer islands, where I first began working with speakers of the Yan-nhangu language. At that time (1993), fewer than 300 words of the Yan-nhangu language had been recorded and almost nothing of their maritime way of life was known. Over the last two decades we have documented some 4,000 words from this language, giving new insights into life on the islands. While documenting patterns of everyday discourse, the profound significance of the notion of consubstantial ancestral essences linking language, sites, people and names began to emerge, a pattern that underlies the poetry, music, songs, ritual and incantations of the islands. It is here in the language of the Crocodile Islands that I first came across the term *märr*.

The Yan-nhangu people are the traditional owners of the Crocodile Islands. They are known as (and refer to themselves as) the Yan-nhangu because they own, and notionally speak, the Yan-nhangu language. Yan-nhangu is the western-most of nine distinct sociolinguistic varieties of the Yolngu language family (Schebeck 1968: 10–11; Waters 1989; Zorc 1986; cf. Christie 1994). Made up of six *bäpurru*-centric dialects or *bäpurru* languages, it is a distinct language but related to the northern Nhangu-mi language variety of the Wessel Islands (for more complete explanation see James 2009: 170–9; James and Baymarrwanga 2014: 532–8; cf. en.wikipedia.org/wiki/Nhangu_language).

The Yan-nhangu are an exclusively island-dwelling people with no mainland estates. It is the ancestral endowment of marine and island sites, together with their language, that is a fundamental dimension of their identity. This endowment at once distinguishes them from and simultaneously incorporates them into the body of their Yolngu kin, from surrounding *bäpurru* with mainland estates and languages. Yan-nhangu people are made up of six *bäpurru*, three of the Dhuwa moiety (Gamalangga, Malarra, and Gurryindi) and three Yirritja (Walamangu, Bindarra, and Ngurruwula) (James 2009; James forthcoming). Numbering about

---

16  Notably, Yan-nhangu rituals, initiations and funerals rites on the Crocodile Islands are still carried out in the Yan-nhangu language.

200 people, they live on their islands and the nearby mainland. Today most Yan-nhangu speak a variety of ex-mission Yolngu language called Yolngu *matha* (lit. 'people's tongue'). The sociolinguistic roots of this Yolngu *matha* variety arise out of conditions brought on by colonial missionisation.

The establishment of the mission at Milingimbi in 1921 brought conflict between Yan-nhangu and Yolngu groups who had migrated west from their *bäpurru* estates on the mainland to live permanently at the mission and access its resources. This influx created the need for a commonly understood code of communications between members of *bäpurru* speaking some nine different languages. These circumstances saw the creation of a new amalgamated linguistic style, Yolngu *matha*, based largely on two closely related *bäpurru* languages, Djambarrpuyngu (Dhuwa moiety) and Gupapuyngu (Yirrijta moiety). Comprising a large portion of the new community polity, kin from these *bäpurru,* speaking mainland languages, came to dominate affairs on the Yan-nhangu Island of Milingimbi. Mission routines, away from the father's *bäpurru* estates, began to undermine the significance of the father's *bäpurru* language inheritances (Devlin 1986).[17] But for the Yan-nhangu, this meant the everyday use of their language declined to the point of near extinction. Today there are only 10 full speakers of Yan-nhangu left, living with their kin in ex-mission communities and homelands, largely speaking Yolngu *matha*.

In summary, then, for the Yan-nhangu people, just as for their Yolngu kin from mainland estates, their site-based, *bäpurru*-centric views hold that their language establishes an ontological link between their identity, ancestors and the sites of their estates. A corollary of this is that the words of their language contain the *märr* of their *bäpurru*. I want to examine the effect of this belief in some of the linguistic and geo-lexical peculiarities of Yolngu languages more broadly, firstly with reference to *märr* in everyday discourse and then with reference to body-part initial verbal idioms, returning later to the Crocodile Islands and the Yan-nhangu language.

## *Märr* in Language and the Language of *Märr*

The term *märr* is unusual for many reasons. Among these is the fact that it is shared across the entire Yolngu language family. Of the nine distinct varieties of the Yolngu languages, and the 60 *bäpurru* patrilectal varieties (depending

---

17   The earlier norm of transmission of the father's *bäpurru* patrilect after learning the mother's tongue declined because the majority of people at Milingimbi mission were women speaking closely related Dhuwal languages, so most children grew up speaking these Dhuwal languages without learning father's language.

on who is counting), each uses the word *märr*.[18] In all these languages *märr* has a number of meanings, making it a kind of homonym.[19] In one sense *märr* functions as an adverb. In this sense it is used to mean 'moderately', 'a bit', 'somewhat' (like), 'relatively' or 'quite'. In this very common usage *märr* is the opposite of 'very', 'intensely' or 'extremely'—*mirithirr(i), wirrka, wirrki gurrku* (Zorc 1986: 226; James and Baymarrwanga 2014: 361–2). For example, *märr* the adverb can be used to modify an adjective, as in *märr-gorrmur* (a bit hot) or another adverb, as in *märr-gangga* (relatively slowly).

A second common usage of *märr* is as a conjunction. *Märr* is often used to introduce an independent clause. In this usage *märr* can be translated as 'because', 'so that' or 'that'. For example, as a conjunction *märr* is found in the following Gupapuyngu expression:

*Gunggayurru ngapurrrunha märr (ga) nganapurr dhu ngayathama nhunngu romnha.*
Help us so that we will/keep your law. (Lowe 1957: 155)

Another example is the Gupapuyngu phrase:

*Dhiyala limurru yurru nhina märr (ga) mulk'ngura.*
We'll sit here because it is dry. (Lowe 1957: 155)[20]

These two very common usages of *märr*, as an adverb and as a conjunction, give it a high frequency in everyday discourse. Other meanings of *märr* are recorded as dispositional nouns including strength, faith, personality, nature, emotional state, and other nouns including 'spiritual power'. David Zorc (1986: 226) mentions the Burarra, a nearby mainland indigenous language group with whom the Yan-nhangu intermarry, who translate *märr* as 'inner being' or 'essence' and at times also synonymously with *ganydjarr* 'strength' (Zorc 1986: 219). As a noun, then, *märr* is extremely variable. As a verb, Zorc (1986) records other forms of *märr*, such as *märrthirri* [verb group 3a, intransitive], as to 'want' and or to 'love'.

Many Yolngu expressions and everyday words incorporate or are derivative of *märr* and are worthy of careful semantic examination. As noted above, Thomson recorded *ma:rr miringu,* 'the power of vengeance', and the commonly heard *märr miriw* (lit. 'power-without') might well be understood to mean exhausted, but has an idiomatic meaning of 'indebted'.

---

18 In the eastern Yolngu languages, Dhangu and Djangu, '*mä*' without the '*rr*' is a potential alternate pronunciation for *märr* as spiritual power (see also Zorc 1986: 219).
19 *Märr* the homonym has identical spelling (homograph) and pronunciation (homophone) and a number of different meanings.
20 The bracketed (*ga*) may be omitted and is not used at Yirrkala (Lowe 1957: 155).

## *Märr* in Idioms: Idioms of *Märr*

The idioms of a language are a recognisable trove of culturally specific notions that in some interesting ways point to or reflect the unexamined assumptions and underlying ideas of a society. Keen reminds us of the Yolngu predisposition for drawing metaphors from natural forms (Keen 1995). And idioms, as we know, are those elements of speech in which the literal meaning may not always reflect the commonly understood meaning; for example, 'kick the bucket' has little to do with buckets. A predilection for idioms using body part names and the contours of landscape are characteristic of Yolngu languages.[21]

Another distinctive Yolngu style idiom is the body part initial verbal compound drawing its metaphorical power from the category of body parts. The kinds of idioms that *märr* appears in most commonly are these verbal compounds or body part initial verbal idioms.[22] These idioms deploying *märr* focus on human dispositional, emotional and psychological states. It may at first appear odd to use *märr* as a body part and so some further explanation is in order.

As in many societies, and depending on kin relations, among Yolngu, humorous, and otherwise intentioned verbal sledging using body parts, including genitals, is common practice and often a source of delight and sometimes conflict. Body part initial metaphors like *dhumi lalkal* (lit. 'posterior greedy', meaning 'always hungry'), *moku wanga* (lit. 'anus speak', meaning 'speaking nonsense'), and *gurrka djulngi* (lit. 'penis good', meaning 'darling' or 'adorable'), are amusing and commonly used for humorous effect. Some body part initial compounds may be very tricky to translate outside of their cultural framework. This case may be accentuated given the pervasiveness of a significant body of secret knowledge. Local styles of communication err on the side of vagueness and less direct verbal interaction. The patent opacity of some metaphors helps to sustain the local conventions of ambiguity demonstrated to be a characteristic feature of Yolngu communication styles (Keen 1995). As Wilkinson explains:

> As the body part term is associated with both literal and non-literal meanings there is much scope for ambiguity. In many contexts it seems that only knowledge of the specialised meaning of the particular collocation permits the construction to be disambiguated. (Wilkinson 1991: 533)

---

21  Body parts are regularly used to denote a wide range of phenomena, such as kin categories (*yangarra* [calf] = 'sister') and time of day (*riya* [head] *walirr* [sun] = 'noon'), etc. (see also Galpagalpa et al. 1984).
22  Wilkinson indicates a likely 'cline between true compounds and common collocations or idioms' in Djambarrpuyngu, a related Yolngu language (Wilkinson 1991: 539).

11  The Language of 'Spiritual Power'

The meanings of body part initial verbal idioms can be hard to fathom given their often tenuous relationships between body part, literal and idiomatic meanings. It is nevertheless intriguing to attempt to work out the possible layers of meaning locked within their structures. It is in these deeply convoluted twists of meaning that some of the most extraordinary insights appear.

Without an exhaustive search I have found some 300 or more such body part initial verbal compounds in Yan-nhangu, a number consistent with other Yolngu languages, including Djambarrpuyngu (Wilkinson 1991: 539). There is no systematic or formal model into which such body part idioms may be categorised, but there is a large subgroup that describe what in English we might call human dispositional, emotional and psychological characteristics. Common within this group of body part initial verbal compounds are idioms of the head, nose, mouth, eyes, skin, stomach and chest, as well as *märr*. Idioms beginning with *märr* are numerically in the top six body part initial verbal compounds, with more than two dozen instances, making them very common.

In some cases *märr* and a named body part can be substituted with no change to the meaning of the idiom. This is a limited group so I will list them all. For example, *galnga* (skin) and *ngoy* (seat of the emotions, or lower stomach) can be substituted in the expression *galnga/ngoy/märr-ngamathirri,* all having the meaning 'to be happy'. So too, *dhä* (mouth) and *märr* in *dhä/märr-bandany* (honestly), *l̲iya* (head) in *l̲iya/märr-garrpin* (to worry) and *buku* (forehead) in *buku/märr-ngal'yun* (worship). Although these are the only cases that will allow such substitution, it does appear to lend some weight to the argument for *märr* initial verbal idioms to be categorised among body part initial idioms.

These body part initial idioms have a conventional structure. The first part is necessarily a body part, like 'head', 'nose' or 'foot'. The second part, or lexeme, is usually a verb like 'put', 'see', or 'poke'. In Table 11.1 the literal meaning of the second lexeme is given in English, and in the last column the idiomatic meaning is translated. I have chosen to demonstrate these body part initial verbal idioms in the Gupapuyngu language as it is one of the common Dhuwala Yolngu *matha* varieties now spoken in communities on and around the Crocodile Islands. The examples in Table 11.1 of body part initial verbal idioms are broadly representative of the sorts of things to which such idioms refer.

Table 11.1 Body part initial verbal idioms in Gupapuyngu.

| Body Part | Second Lexeme | Literal Meaning | Idiomatic Meaning |
|---|---|---|---|
| **forehead** | | | |
| *buku* | *ngal'yun* | raise | respect |
| *buku* | *moma* | forget | misunderstand |
| *buku* | *nhäma* | see | dislike |
| **skin** | | | |
| *galnga* | *däl* | hard | obdurate |
| *galnga* | *marimirri* | trouble (possessing) | angry |
| *galnga* | *ngonungdhirri* | heavy (becoming) | sorrowful |
| **eyes** | | | |
| *mel* | *de'yun* | poke | jealous |
| *mel* | *dharangan* | recognise | covetousness |
| *mel* | *däl* | hard | unsympathetic |
| **stomach** | | | |
| *ngoy* | *badarratjun* | twinge of pain | guilty |
| *ngoy* | *badupadumirr* | erase | anxious |
| *ngoy* | *nhärra* | burn | angry |
| **chest** | | | |
| *gumurr* | *maram* | obtain | adopt |
| *gumurr* | *gumurryun* | chest (verbaliser) | meet |
| *gumurr* | *däl* | hard | unsympathetic |

As an element in body part initial expressions *märr* has a general focus on human emotional and psychological states. As previously mentioned, these body part initial constructions are a very distinctive kind of idiom that make up a large part of the corpus of conventional Yolngu metaphor. Among the 300 or so most common body part initial idioms, *märr* is the only member of the class that has no physical site in the body. Table 11.2 shows a brief selection of *märr* idioms in Gupapuyngu constructed in the same manner and similarly focusing on human dispositional characteristics, emotional and psychological states.

*Märr* in these idioms is deployed to express the qualities of emotions, demeanour and dispositions that are a part of the whole person. The sense that *märr* pervades the whole body lends it a seemingly general quality. This general quality is further augmented by the fact that *märr* is the only body part in all the body part initial idioms that is present in every language, giving it a very widespread geographical distribution.

## Table 11.2 *Märr* initial verbal idioms.

| Body Part | Second Lexeme | Literal Meaning | Idiomatic Meaning |
|---|---|---|---|
| märr | dälthirri | become hard | trusting |
| märr | dhumbal'yun | confused | ignorant |
| märr | djulkthun | pass | disbelieve |
| märr | ganggathirri | reduce | prepare |
| märr | garrpin | tie up | worry |
| märr | ngal'yun | raise up | praise |
| märr | ngamathanmirr | good | love |
| märr | wanangguma | imitate | antagonise |
| märr | yal'yun | becoming cool | calm |
| märr | bandany | drying | honest |

From a comparative lexical and geographical perspective *märr is* distinctive in these body part initial verbal compounds in that it appears in all Yolngu languages. These mutually unintelligible languages, although with many cognate or shared terms, possess their own distinctive words for body parts, and each also has a distinctive verb for the second lexeme. It is interesting that *märr* is shared by all. Further, these body part initial idioms retain their idiomatic meanings across languages (Waters 1989: 126; Wilkinson 1991). This shared meaning is hardly surprising given the very high levels of multilingualism and shared *habitus* of community life.[23] What is more interesting is the paradox that lies in the widespread and apparently general usage of the term *märr*, juxtaposed with a very *bäpurru*-specific ownership of the 'ancestral essences' of *märr*, implied in the *bäpurru* language used. Table 11.3 shows how *märr* initial idioms in Yan-nhangu and in Gupapuyngu keep their semantic meaning across the two languages.

*Märr* in these idioms is representative of its widely shared meaning, broad geographical distribution, but also another feature. Because of the language type used, it refers to its membership of a *bäpurru*-specific language. It is not a general *märr* in this sense, but a specific *märr*. As previously mentioned, it is axiomatic that the words of the language of the *bäpurru* are imbued with the *märr* of the *bäpurru*. From the perspective of the *bäpurru* language *märr* is spoken in, it always refers to the inalienable relationships of the *bäpurru*, to its

---

23   Keen (1995) and Toner (2001) have discussed shared meaning in songs sung in different languages. In ritual, as in discourse, the idea of *dhakay nhama* (tasting a piece) is a convention of performing/singing/speaking in another *bäpurru's* music/song/language to show respect/relatedness/closeness (Toner 2001).

sites, language and ancestral essences. Today, this *bäpurru*-centric interpretation is more properly present on the homelands and in religious life and the ritual context.

Table 11.3 *Märr* initial verbal idioms in two different Yolngu languages.

| Yan-nhangu Compound | Gupapuyngu Compound | Literal Meaning Second Lexeme | Idiomatic Meaning |
| --- | --- | --- | --- |
| märr-barrathalanguyirri | märr-dälthirri | become hard | trusting |
| märr-bambuma | märr-dhumbal'yun | confused | ignorant |
| märr-duwalkthun | märr-djulkthun | pass | disbelieve |
| märr-ganggayirri | märr-ganggathirri | reduce | prepare |
| märr-dät'thun | märr-garrpin | tie up | worry |
| märr-ngal'thun | märr-ngal'yun | raise up | praise |
| märr-mitthu | märr-ngamathanmirr | good | love |
| märr-wanangugumarabu | märr-wanangguma | imitate | antagonise |
| märr-dalkalyirri | märr-yal'yun | becoming cool | calm |
| märr-wirripalyirri | märr-bandany | drying | honest |

Life on the homelands is focused around people's links to country, ritual, ancestors, names and languages. This stands in contrast to the missions, founded on the colonial project to settle people, to discipline nomadism and so distance them from their land and dislocate the yearly rounds of ceremonial activity. The significance of *märr*, as links to the *bäpurru*, as ancestral essences inhering in the words themselves, is much less obvious in everyday community discourse nowadays. The routines and dialogue of contemporary ex-mission communities are no longer focused on links to country. Today, for the most part, more uniform linguistic styles result from the constant pressures of the settler state, enforced English monolingualism in schools, and the workaday clock, resulting in fewer opportunities for invoking *märr* in reference to the inalienable relationships of the *bäpurru*, ancestral essences, sites and language.

Nevertheless, *märr* retains its distinctive ancestral connotations in the ritual context. Here, in the words of the incantations, of ritual, sung in the language of the *bäpurru*, the implications of ancestral essence inhering in language are re-ignited. In light of this more metaphysical quality of *märr*, I want now to turn to a re-examination of *märr* as 'spiritual power', but first it will be necessary to distinguish it from another Yolngu word for power, *ganydjarr*.

## 'Spiritual Power' on the Crocodile Islands

There is another word, *ganydjarr*, that also translates as 'power'. Simply put, the feature that sets *ganydjarr* apart from *märr* is that *ganydjarr* power has no supernatural or spiritual associations.[24] *Ganydjarr* is a noun meaning 'power', 'strength', 'energy' and 'speed' (Zorc 1986: 148). It is the kind of power used to describe power in mobile phones, batteries or the force of an engine. As an adjective *ganydjarr* means 'hard', 'powerful' or 'with force'. Commonly, one will be entreated to 'hurry up' with the expression *ganydjarriyu!* (lit. 'power-emphasis'), and to be exhausted is to be *ganydjarr-miriw* (lit. 'power-without'), a condition endemic to mobile phones. Substitution with *märr* is very case-specific. It will not do, for example, to substitute *ganydjarr* with *märr* in most *märr* constructions; for example, *ganydjarr-mirriw* ('without power') with *märr-miriw*; this construction would be like a second-language gaffe. There are times in which the two are transferrable: for example, the constructions *märr dhumurr* (lit. '*märr*-large') and *ganydjarr dhumurr* (lit. 'power-large') can be used to mean the same thing, but the kind of power that is *ganydjarr* is understood to have no sacred connotation. It is, of course, possible to use *ganydjarr* to describe ancestral power if *ganydjarr* is linked with the ancestors, as in *wangarryu ganydjarr* ('ancestral power'), but the ancestral aspect of the power is not inherent in the word *ganydjarr*, as it is in the word *märr*.

Ethnographic anecdotes drawn from everyday practices of island life ranging from the mundane to the ritual will further explain *märr* as 'spiritual power'. The following anecdotes describe a number of aspects of *märr* as an ever-present spiritual power that resides in the bones of the land (*bäpurru*-based), a personal spiritual essence passed on after death and linked to the *bäpurru*, and passed on by spirit familiars to spirit healers and sorcerers (*marrnggit*), again indelibly joined to the *bäpurru*.

*Märr* has an everyday influence on social behaviour in part because of the widespread recognition of powerful ancestral essences known to dwell in the sites, in the rocks and stones, and in the waters of the estate. The potential of these powers to bestow benefit or impart sickness is well recorded in the literature (Biernoff 1978; Keen 1978, 1991; Reid 1983; Morphy 1991; Bagshaw 1998; Magowan 2001). There are many kinds of ancestral entities understood to be watching and listening: the *wangarr* creator ancestors; the *malagatj* or dangerous spirits; the *mokuy* ghosts of the dead. None but the very young

---

24   Warner also used the term *däl* in a way synonymous with power; *däl* is, however, more correctly translated as 'strong, hard, steady, firm' (Zorc 1986: 61).

or foolhardy would set out alone or contemplate any action on country or sea without first considering the implications of ancestral powers known to be present.

For example, I learned about a certain kind of ancestor or forerunner (*ngurunganggabu*) from a Yan-nhangu person (and Yan-nhangu-language speaker) of the Gamalangga *bäpurru* on their estate on Murrungga Island. While walking around checking the fish traps we passed a number of sites. As we walked my companion related the names and stories and sang snatches of song related to the ancestral journeys that linked these sites with others further afield. Such narrated walks produce a kaleidoscopic mental map of signification in the landscape linking every conceivable aspect of the environment. Upon rounding the point at Garlayamirringuli my guide held me by the arm and told me that I must not look landward, but to the seaward side for the next part of our journey. She then rubbed sweat over my eyes and made an incantation in old Yan-nhangu, that I could not follow. She then told me only that she had introduced me to the ancestor (*ngurunganggabu*) Gurrmirringu so that I would be safe from harm, and that I should refrain from asking any questions.[25] The Gurrmirringu, she explained later, is known to dwell at this site, telling how the spirits of place are always present and listening, but the Gurrmirringu is particularly dangerous:[26]

*Gurrmirringu nhani nininyngu märr barrngarrannhanin nhan'ku mananha mungubnuma wangalanganga.*

The Gurrmirringu 'spirit man's' power is in the ground and is listening forever.

In this example we get a glimpse of site-based ancestral power—the power of the Gurrmirringu is recognised as present, and dangerous to the uninitiated. The Gurrmirringu is understood to have both agency and power. His ability to act on the world comes from his *märr*; it is the power through which he may protect or destroy and by means of which he continues to shape the behaviours of the living.

People's social worlds are shaped by the recognition of essential links understood to exist between people, places and ancestors infused with *märr*. On the islands it is a common experience to 'hear' a bird call 'announcing' a death. For example, one day after a funeral I was talking to someone who had just got a fright. This person (Gupapuyngu Birrkili *bäpurru*, speaking the Gupapuyngu language)

---

25  Ian Keen has examined Yolngu doctrines and related practices to do with totemic ancestors and their traces, magic and sorcery, drawing on beliefs about intrinsic relations between part and whole, image and object, and the powers of bodily substance and spirits of the dead (Keen 2006).
26  An image of the Gurrmirringu painted by David Malangi Daymirringu appeared on the Australian $1 note in 1966.

explained how they had just seen the dead person's spirit, or essence, described as *märr*, inside a bird recognisable as one of the iconic species identified with the deceased's *bäpurru*:

> *Dharra ngarranha malng'thunminy, ngunhapuy märrpuy, nhakun ngayi dinggam, märrndja nhanngu ngunhidiyi birrkbirrkanga warrakanngur, djinagangur, nkakun, ga ngarranha dhakay nhakul marrararyun, marnggi ga wandinanhan.*

> I was standing and it appeared to me, that *märr*, when he/she died her (*märr*) entered a bird and I felt it [like the shiver you get when you feel somebody behind you], and you know it, and you take fright and run away.

It is not uncommon for people to interpret the appearance of a bird, bird song or apparition, as the incarnation of the spirit of the dead, the *mokuy* (ghost), however in this case it was not a ghost. In this example *märr* is used to denote the spirit of the deceased called *birrimbirr* (the *bäpurru* [totem] soul that returns to the sacred well), quite distinct from the *mokuy*.[27] This *märr* is distinctly that of the deceased, *märr-ndja nhanngu* (*ndja* = focus/emphasis, *nhanngu* = his or hers [the deceased's]), and as such this *märr* refers to the *birrimbirr* which returns to the *bäpurru*. That is, the *birrimbirr* (*bäpurru*-ancestral essence) as *märr* (*bäpurru*-ancestral essence), returns to the focal sites of the *bäpurru* in a way that reflects the return of the spirit to the 'totemic well' as described by Warner (1969: 380). This example provides an indication of the bond between the spiritual essence of the deceased person, bird ancestor (iconic species) and *bäpurru*—a relationship comprised of and expressed in terms of *märr*.

After a funeral the clothes of the departed are burned as they are thought to contain the *märr* of the deceased.[28] This is why images and speaking the name of the deceased are also proscribed. Ian Keen has discussed Yolngu notions of intrinsic connection between persons, parts of persons, hair, bone and sweat, spirits' ancestral icons, and sites (1978: 337; 2006: 522). It is recognised that such intrinsic connections can be harnessed for special purposes through ritual, such as those rituals performed by the *marrnggit*. The *marrnggit*, or healer, is said to be able to harness these intrinsic connections. The *marrnggit* harnesses the *märr* of spirit familiars in the form of birds, animals and 'spirit children' (*djamarrkuli*) (Webb 1938; Thomson 1961). For example, the following story was told to me in Djambarrpuyngu by a Djambarrpuyngu man (Wanybarrnga *bäpurru*, Dhuwal language) at Murrungga Island. This story tells how *märr* is given to healer witch doctors by familiars known as spirit children (*djamarrkuli*):

---

27 Nor is it *bamay* (distinct from *mokuy* and *birrimbirr*), which is now described as more like the soul Christians believe goes up to heaven. I was unable to discover a pre-mission translation for *bamay* from people of the oldest generation who remembered the coming of the mission.

28 People will often say *djikay bäpurru bulthana* (lit. 'bird-death-tell'). The *bäpurru* (group) and the *bäpurru* (death and funerary rite) are thus denoted by the same term.

> *Marrnggit ngayi dhu nhäma ngunhi baman bili djamarrkuli walal nguli djama märr gurrupan marrnggitjkurr ganaman nhanukal.*

> The witch doctor can see right through you because the (children) spirit familiars give him (insight/power/understanding-*märr*).

The *märr* of the spirit familiars is not a kind of generalised spiritual power. The *marrnggit* knows *exactly* which kind of *djamarrkuli* (*bäpurru*-specific iconic spirits), or what kind of named bird (*bäpurru*-specific iconic species), in such situations. Each kind of spirit familiar *djamarrkuli* is linked to a *bäpurru* and each kind of bird belongs to a specific *bäpurru*. The *märr* of each is a very particular kind of *märr*, each linked to a specific *wangarr* consubstantially identified with particular *bäpurru*.

The following is an excerpt of a story about how people lived together on the island of Murrungga in the old days, ending with a clear warning:

> *Djini dawal ngali gurrku nyena walipma ga bulthun mägaya, rulka ngali mana gurrku nhama bayngul djiningul mari mägaya yolngu rulka nyena mana gurrku. Rulka wanggalanga märr ngaraka ranu, bilamunu.*

> In the past we lived together, and met and told stories in peace, we never caused any trouble. Do not offend the bones of the land, so be it (amen).

The sentiment expressed in *rulka wanggalanga märr ngaraka ranu*, 'do not offend the bones (spirit) of the land, so be it (amen)', is customary. Always used by an older generation, it reveals the open recognition that the listening spirits of the land have the potential to wreak havoc if offended. What is tacit here, and thus well understood, is that the agent of retribution is the *wangarr* of the site; and the bones of the land upon which we stand, and their *märr*, are that of the *bäpurru*. These ancestral actors, the *ngurunganggabu*, *malagatj* or *wangarr*, possess the *märr* or power to destroy, as agents of the originating myths; they are part of the *bäpurru*. In the final analysis, the *märr* of the *bäpurru* is the 'spiritual power' that provides the social force behind the injunction. This *märr*, the *märr* that identifies the distinctive site-based laws of each *bäpurru*, which discerns each powerful spiritual entity, obligates its members to protect and care for kin and country—an inviolable moral duty to protect and to care, through ritual and practice, the re-invigoration of *märr*.

The familiarity of *märr* as a term in the everyday contrasts with its specificity as 'spiritual power', as the named ancestral essences of the *bäpurru*. This *märr* as the 'ancestral essence' is fundamental to the constitution of the *bäpurru*, and so a central focus of Yolngu society. It is this notion of *märr* as the inalienable ancestral links between ancestors, their descendants, their country, language and the law, that comprises a Yolngu site-based ontology. The esoteric knowledge of these connections and how to deploy them within and without the ritual context is the very coin of an economy of sacred knowledge.

## Conclusion

When W. Lloyd Warner came to the Crocodile Islands, he found the notion of 'spiritual power' to be a fundamental principle and used the Melanesian term *mana* to describe the concept known to the Yolngu as *märr*. I have sought to render a more nuanced reading of the Yolngu concept *märr* in a way that reveals a more complete meaning than that captured in the term *mana*.

In this chapter, I have argued that rendering *märr* simply as a generalised 'spiritual power' is misleading, not only because of its polysemy, but because of its complex nature. What at first appears to be a generality in the use of the term *märr*, on closer examination reveals very distinctive and highly distinguishable kinds of named inherited ancestral essence. These kinds of named ancestral essence constitute and identify the distinctive, multivalent, dynamic entities known as *bäpurru*, focused around common connections of shared ancestral essence. *Märr* comprises the inalienable connection between kinds of ancestors, people, stories, language, and place that make up the Yolngu site-based ontology. Ancestral essences, comprised of *märr*, are key distinguishing forms at the centre of the Yolngu world. This, in part, gives a clearer understanding of the meaning of *märr* in the language of 'spiritual power' on the Crocodile Islands.

Perhaps in the long run the fate of *märr* will resemble that described for *mana* by Blust. He described how, over time, notions of 'unseen supernatural agency' from such forces as thunder and lightning had detached from the meaning of *mana*, and so '*mana* assumed a life of its own' (Blust 2007: 404). But we know that *mana* is an even more important and potent concept in the lives of Melanesian people today. Perhaps the policies of 'normalisation' on the Crocodile Islands will diminish the role of site-based ontologies and blanch the meaning of *märr*. Or, what if these forces drive an increasing need for the revivification of this very special kind of site-based 'spiritual power', this *märr*?

# References

Bagshaw, G. 1998. *Gapu dhulway, gapu maramba*: conceptualisation and ownership of saltwater among Burarra and Yan-nhangu peoples of northeast Arnhemland. In N. Peterson and B. Rigsby (eds), *Customary Marine Tenure in Australia,* pp. 154–78. Oceania Monograph 48. Sydney: University of Sydney.

Biernoff, D. 1978. Safe and dangerous places. In L.R. Hiatt (ed.), *Australian Aboriginal Concepts*, pp. 93–105. Canberra: Australian Institute of Aboriginal Studies.

Berndt, R.M. 1951. *Gunapipi*. Melbourne: Cheshire.

Berndt, R.M. 1952. *The Djanggawul: An Aboriginal Religious Cult of Northeastern Arnhem Land*. London: Routledge and Kegan Paul.

Berndt, R.M. 1955. 'Murngin' (Wulamba) social organization. *American Anthropologist* 57: 84–106.

Blevins, J. 2008. Some comparative notes on proto-Oceanic *mana: inside and outside the Austronesian family. *Oceanic Linguistics* 47(2): 253–74.

Blust, R.A. 2007. Proto-Oceanic *mana revisited. *Oceanic Linguistics* 46(2): 404–23.

Capelli, C., J.F. Wilson, M. Richards, M. Stumpf, F. Gratrix, S. Oppenheimer, P. Underhill, V. Pascali, T.-M. Ko and D. Goldstein. 2001. A predominantly indigenous paternal heritage for the Austronesian-speaking peoples of insular Southeast Asia and Oceania. *American Journal of Human Genetics* 68(2): 432–43.

Christie, M. 1994. Grounded and ex-centric knowledges: exploring Aboriginal alternatives to Western thinking. In I. Edwards (ed.), *Thinking: International Interdisciplinary Perspectives*, pp. 24–34. London: Hawker Brownlow Educational Press.

Codrington, H. 1891. *The Melanesians: Studies in their Anthropology and Folk-lore*. Oxford: Clarendon.

Devlin, B.C. 1986. Language Maintenance in a North East Arnhem Land Settlement. EdD Thesis, Columbia University, New York.

Durkheim, E. 1912. *Les Formes Elementaries de la Vie Religieuse: Le System Totemique en Australie*. Paris: Alcan. Translated by J.W. Swain as *The Elementary Forms of the Religious Life*. New York: Free Press.

Firth, R. 1940. *The Work of the Gods in Tikopia*. Melbourne: Melbourne University Press.

Fox, C.E. 1924. *The Threshold of the Pacific: An Account of the Social Organization, Magic and Religion of the People of San Cristo-val in the Solomon Islands*. London: Kegan Paul.

Galpagalpa, J. et al. 1984. *Djambarrpuyngu Wordlist*. Yirrkala: Yirrkala Community School Literature Production Centre.

Garnggulkpuy, J. and M. Christie. 2002. *Yolngu Balandi-watangumirr: People with Connections*. Darwin: Northern Territory University.

Geertz, C. 1973. *The Interpretation of Cultures*. New York: Basic Books.

Hocart, A.M. 1914. Mana. *Man* 14: 97–101.

Hogbin, I. 1936. Mana. *Oceania* 6: 241–74.

Humphreys, C.B. 1926. *The Southern New Hebrides: An Ethnological Record*. Cambridge: Cambridge University Press.

James, B. 2009. Time and Tide in the Crocodile Islands: Change and Continuity in Yan-nhangu Marine Identity. PhD Thesis, The Australian National University, Canberra.

James, B. (forthcoming). Fish traps of the Crocodile Islands: windows on another world. In T. King and G. Robinson (eds), *At Home on the Waves: Human Habitation of the Sea from the Mesolithic to Today*. New York: Berghahn Books.

James, B. and L. Baymarrwanga 2014. *Yan-nhaŋu Atlas: Illustrated Dictionary of the Crocodile Islands*. Carlingford, NSW: Tien Wah Press.

Keen, I. 1978. One Ceremony, One Song: An Economy of Religious Knowledge among the Yolngu of Northeast Arnhem Land. PhD Thesis, The Australian National University, Canberra.

Keen, I. 1991. Images of reproduction in the Yolngu Madayin ceremony. *The Australian Journal of Anthropology* 1(2–3): 192–207.

Keen, I. 1994. *Knowledge and Secrecy in an Aboriginal Religion*. Oxford: Clarendon Press.

Keen, I. 1995. Metaphor and the metalanguage: 'groups' in northeast Arnhem Land. *American Ethnologist* 22(3): 502–27.

Keen, I. 2006. Ancestors, magic and exchange in Yolngu doctrines: extensions of the person in time and space. *Journal of the Royal Anthropological Institute* 12(3): 515–30.

Keesing, R.M. 1984. Rethinking *mana*. *Journal of Anthropological Research* 40(1): 137–56.

Keesing, R.M. 1987. Anthropology as interpretive quest. *Current Anthropology* 28(2): 161–76.

Lowe, B. M. 1957. Grammar Lessons in Gupapuyngu: A North East Arnhem Land Dialect. Mimeograph.

MacClancy, J. 1986. Mana: an anthropological metaphor for island Melanesia. *Oceania* 57(2): 143–53.

Magowan, F. 2001. Waves of knowing: polymorphism and co-substantive essences in Yolngu sea cosmology. *The Australian Journal of Indigenous Education* 29(1): 22–35.

Morphy, H. 1989. From dull to brilliant: the aesthetics of spiritual power among the Yolngu. *Man* (N.S.) 24(1): 21–40.

Morphy, H. 1991. *Ancestral Connections: Art and an Aboriginal System of Knowledge*. Chicago: The University of Chicago Press.

O'Grady, G.N., C.F. Voegelin and F.M. Voegelin. 1966. Languages of the world: Indo-Pacific fascicle 6 (with appendix by K.L. Hale). *Anthropological Linguistics* 8(2): 1–197.

Prytz-Johansen, J. 2012. *The Maori and His Religion in its Non-Ritualistic Aspects*. Hau Classics of Ethnographic Theory Series, Volume 1. Edinburgh: School of Social and Political Sciences, University of Edinburgh. (Original work published 1954)

Oliver, D.L. 1974. *Ancient Tahitian Society*. Honolulu: University of Hawai'i Press.

Reid, J. 1983. *Sorcerers and Healing Spirits*. Canberra: Australian National University Press.

Schebeck, B. 1968. Dialect and Social Groupings in North East Arnhem Land. MS held at the Australian Institute of Aboriginal and Torres Strait Islander Studies, MS 351, 352.

Schneider, D.M. 1965. Some muddles in the models or 'how the system really works'. In M. Banton (ed.), *The Relevance of Models for Social Anthropology*, pp. 25–86. London: Tavistock Publications; New York: Frederick A. Praeger.

Shapiro, W. 1981. *Miwuyt Marriage: The Cultural Anthropology of Affinity in Northeast Arnhem Land*. Philadelphia: Institute for the Study of Human Issues.

Speiser, F. 1990. *Ethnographische Materialien aus den Neuen Hebriden und den Banks-Inseln*. Berlin: C.W. Kreidel's Verlag. Translated by D.Q. Stephenson. Bathurst NSW: Crawford House Press. (Original work published 1923).

Thomson, D.F. (1975). The concept of 'marr' in Arnhem Land. *Mankind* 10(1): 1–10.

Thomson, D.F. 1961. Marrngitmirri and kalka: medicine man and sorcerer in Arnhem Land. *Man* 61: 97–102.

Toner, P.G. 2001. When the Echoes are Gone: A Yolngu Musical Anthropology. PhD Thesis, The Australian National University, Canberra.

Warner, W.L. 1937. *A Black Civilization: A Social Study of an Australian Tribe*. London: Harper and Brothers Publishers.

Revised edition 1969. Gloucester, MA: Peter Smith.

Waters, B.E. 1989. *Djinang and Djinba: A Grammatical Historical Perspective*. Pacific Linguistics, Series C, No. 114. Canberra: Department of Linguistics, Research School of Pacific Studies.

Webb, T.T. 1933. Tribal organisation in eastern Arnhem Land. *Oceania* 3: 406–11.

Webb, T.T. 1938. From spears to spades. *The Missionary Review* February. Melbourne, VIC: Methodist Overseas Missionary Society.

Wilkinson, M.P. 1991. Djambarrpuyngu: A Yolngu Variety of Northern Australia. PhD Thesis, University of Sydney, Sydney.

Williams, N. 1999. The nature of 'permission'. In J.C. Altman, F. Morphy, and T. Rowse (eds), *Land Rights at Risk? Evaluations of the Reeves Report*, pp. 53–64. CAEPR Research Monograph No. 14. Canberra: Centre for Aboriginal Economic Policy Research.

Zorc, R.D. 1986. *Yolngu Matha Dictionary*. Darwin: School of Australian Linguistics, Darwin Institute of Technology.

# 12 Reconstructing Aboriginal Economy and Society: The New South Wales South Coast at the Threshold of Colonisation

John M. White

Ian Keen's 2004 monograph, *Aboriginal Economy and Society: Australia at the Threshold of Colonisation,* represents the first anthropological study to draw together comparative pre- and postcolonial data sets and sources to explain the nature and variety of Aboriginal economy and society across the Australian continent. Keen's (2004: 5) rationalisation for comparing the economy and society of seven regions was 'mainly descriptive and analytical', in order to 'shed light on the character of each region, and to bring out their similarities and differences'. In doing so, as Veth (2006: 68) commented in his review of the book, 'It speaks to meticulous and exhaustive research from myriad sources including social anthropology, linguistics, history, ecology and, not the least, archaeology'. Following its publication, *Aboriginal Economy and Society: Australia at the Threshold of Colonisation* won Keen his second Stanner Award from the Council of the Australian Institute of Aboriginal and Torres Strait Islander Studies in 2005.

In this chapter, I draw upon Keen's comparative method to profile the ecology, institutions and economy of the Yuin people of (what is now) the Eurobodalla region of the New South Wales south coast at the time of European colonisation.[1]

---

1   Elsewhere I have documented the role of Aboriginal workers in the New South Wales south coast horticultural sector in the mid-twentieth century (White 2010a, 2010b, 2011) and have detailed the reactions of Yuin people to colonial incursions, which involved the development of intercultural relations that were mediated by exchange (White 2012).

The reasons for this are twofold. First, Keen's model breaks down the observable (or reconstructable) aspects of economy and society into relatively comparable categories to enable a profile to be built based on the available sources. Accordingly, I profile the Yuin under the interconnected themes of ecology, institutions and economy, drawing on a range of ethnographic, linguistic and archaeological material. Second, Keen refers to the Kŭnai of Gippsland, eastern Victoria, as occupying a broad resource zone in the southeast—a resource zone that is shared by the Yuin. In this chapter, I will draw some conclusions about whether the similar environments and resources utilised by both groups gave rise to similarities in the economy and society of the Kŭnai and Yuin. Evidence of substantial similarities between the two groups will support Keen's (2004: 3) assertion that ecology is integral to economy: 'Environments constitute arenas for human action and being, they yield resources to be exploited, and they impose constraints and provide enabling conditions for practices.'

## Why Compare?

Arguably, Keen's comparative approach developed as a product of his dissatisfaction with both the relative disinterest by anthropologists and historians in documenting Aboriginal economies and participation in the settler economy, and previous attempts to present a range of Aboriginal beliefs and practices in some kind of systematic way. On the former, Keen (2010: 1) noted that historians have been particularly guilty in rendering Indigenous Australians 'more or less invisible in many economic histories of Australia', while anthropologists were mainly concerned with Aboriginal beliefs and practices until Rowley (1970, 1971) 'brought about a sea change in the recognition of Indigenous involvement in the colonial economy' (Keen 2010: 2). On the latter, Keen's (1993) scathing review of Swain's (1993) *A Place for Strangers* signposts the comparative and systematic research on Aboriginal economies, beliefs and practices that Keen published a decade later. On Swain's argument that some aspects of all Aboriginal precolonial cultures were the same across the continent, Keen proposes that it serves a useful purpose—to 'help one to imagine the intellectual climate in which functionalism, an empiricist methodology and an emphasis on long-term fieldwork were engendered in reaction to "conjectural history" and especially to the excesses of extreme diffusionism' (Keen 1993: 107).

Several authors have attempted to provide reconstructions of Aboriginal economies (Butlin 1993; Dingle 1988; Lawrence 1968). One of the main problems in these studies is that their analytical frames are often too general and miss the highly localised and idiosyncratic nature of Aboriginal economies and societies. Several other studies have documented community economies in articulation with capitalist modes of production and the state (Altman 1987; Anderson

1984). These studies provide a more adequate comparative framework for reconstructions of Aboriginal economies, and contributed to the development of the categories used in by Keen in *Aboriginal Economy and Society: Australia at the Threshold of Colonisation*.

Keen sketches a 'possibilist' model of 'the relationship between environment and society, according to which the environment imposes limiting conditions or boundaries on human action and social relations rather than causing them' (Keen 2004: 21). Furthermore, relationships between human practices and environments and resources are viewed as 'mutual, interactive' ones (ibid.). Keen argues that ecological factors must be taken into account because 'the location and seasonality of resources greatly affected the organisation of production, for people had to move to the locations of food resources' (ibid.: 23). Technologies (defined as the material instruments Aboriginal people use and the knowledge of their appropriate use) were also tailored to locally specific needs that were shaped by ecological constraints. These ecological factors also placed constraining conditions or boundaries on 'the ways in which Aboriginal people moved around the country, the degree of mobility, the range of movement, the size and dynamics of residence groups' and population densities (ibid.: 103).

Keen takes the middle road between what Giddens refers to as institutions (the more 'enduring' aspects of social life which 'are deeply sedimented in space-time') and Bourdieu's (1977) notion of a 'social field' to provide a category for analysis he terms 'institutional fields' (Giddens 1979: 80; Keen 2004: 3). Keen acknowledges that 'the categories of institutional field' he uses (for example, 'cosmology') 'probably overlap only partially with Aboriginal ones' but that, 'nevertheless, similarities between ethnographic descriptions such as kin relations ... are sufficient to make the domains proposed here workable' (Keen 2004: 3–4). In examining the institutional fields across seven regions, Keen includes the categories of identities (including 'country groups', language varieties, marriage rules, totemic identities and naming systems), kinship and marriage, and cosmology, quasi-technology and ancestral law.

Keen's perspective on 'economy' borrows from Sahlins's (1974) substantivist approach and discussions of gift exchange by Mauss (1954), Gregory (1982), Weiner (1992) and Godelier (1999) to outline a range of categories for analysis under more general topics, including control of the means of production, organisation of production, distribution and consumption, and exchange and trade.

## Overview of Sources

Four main ethnographic sources provide key information for a reconstruction of Yuin economy and society when Europeans first reached southeastern Australian shores: George Augustus Robinson, Harry Warner, Alfred William Howitt and Robert Hamilton Mathews. Robinson was the Chief Protector of Aborigines for Port Phillip and travelled widely during his tenure. He travelled through the Monaro and parts of the south coast during 1844 and his field journals contain valuable information relating to customary journeys and intermarriage between Aboriginal people at Twofold Bay and far-east Gippsland. Robinson's journals illustrate that the majority of marriages occurred between people living within the broad south coast geographic region, although several marriages were with people from Gippsland and also the Monaro Plateau. Unfortunately Robinson never ventured north beyond the Bega River and therefore his journals provide little information relating to Yuin people living within what is now known as the Eurobodalla. By contrast, Harry Warner, the son of a wattle-bark buyer, travelled through the Eurobodalla region between 1916 and 1940 and recorded extensive information on the Brinja-Yuin. Although Warner's observations occurred long after European invasion and settlement, his undated notes provide useful information on the location of different countries and economic practices.

Both Howitt and Mathews conducted their research after more than five decades of European intrusion into the region. A.W. Howitt worked as a geologist, mining warden and magistrate during the 1870s, and as a result of his work (and interests in surveying and ethnography) also travelled broadly throughout eastern Victoria and southeastern NSW. Howitt's major work, *The Native Tribes of South-East Australia*, was published in 1904 and provides useful information relating to Yuin social organisation, identities, marriage networks and totemic classifications.

Mathews was also a surveyor who had served as a magistrate and coroner while pursuing his interests as an amateur linguist and ethnographer. However, Mathews and Howitt were two very different men with different preconceptions and predilections that produced very different insights.[2] Through observations collected while he was working as government surveyor, Mathews wrote a number of journal articles and a large body of unpublished papers relating to his research, yet never produced a major work in the style of Howitt.[3]

---

2  For an examination of Howitt's work, see Keen (2000). For an examination of Mathews's contributions to anthropology, see Elkin (1975a, 1975b, 1976) and Thomas (2004, 2006, 2011).

3  Arnold Van Gennep wrote to Mathews from Paris in 1909, despairing that Mathews had not synthesised his material into a magnum opus in the manner of Howitt (1904) and Baldwin Spencer (1899).

Sadly for the ethnographic record, Howitt and Mathews did not share information about the social organisation of the people whom they both studied.[4] Rather, as Thomas observed, Howitt and Baldwin Spencer 'formed a compact between themselves that Mathews' numerous publications should never be cited or even acknowledged' (Thomas 2004: 2). Thomas (2011: 8) gives a number of reasons for Mathews' treatment by his contemporaries, the most compelling being Mathews' dismissal of 'the great shibboleths of evolutionism' to which Spencer ('a leviathan of the discipline') subscribed. Thomas (2004: 2) further notes that 'the usual policy (apparently also shared by Roth) was to treat Mathews as a non-person'.

While Howitt might be credited as the key ethnographer in the south coast region because of his 1904 monograph, his account of social organisation is contradictory and frustrating because of its lack of complexity. Howitt believed that the Yuin 'had only traces of a class organisation', with two vaguely defined intermarrying classes and exogamous patrilineal totems (Howitt 1904: 261). Mathews' understanding of Yuin social organisation is as difficult to ascertain today as it was for his European correspondent Arnold Van Gennep in 1907; however, many clues remain that present a far more complex perspective than Howitt's model.[5]

The linguistic record is similarly patchy, with the main sources of linguistic evidence of Yuin dialects being collected by Mathews during his period of research on the south coast (c. 1890–1900), by Robinson (c. 1844), by Larmer (c. 1853) and by McKenzie (c. 1872). Drawing on Mathews' work, their own original research and a range of other sources, Tindale (1974) and Eades (1976) mapped the distribution of south coast languages. As Wesson notes, Eades' study differed from Tindale's in that she made a distinction between language groups and 'named groups' (Wesson 2000: 155).[6]

The New South Wales south coast region encompasses a rich array of sites of archaeological significance. Accordingly, a large body of archaeological research has been conducted that offers time-depth to the early ethnographies (see, for example, Bowdler 1976; Flood 1982; Lampert 1971 and Poiner 1976).[7] Attenbrow (1999) provides a detailed review of archaeological research in the

---

4   The only letters from Howitt in the R.H. Mathews collection were from Howitt to H.E. Hockey requesting information about Aboriginal people at Brewarrina (Howitt 1907a, 1907b). Presumably Hockey had handed the letters over to his good friend Mathews.
5   Elkin's (1975a, 1975b, 1976) examination of Mathews' legacy and extensive study of Mathews' papers provide a montage of observations and understandings about Aboriginal people in southeastern Australia.
6   Wesson has made a significant contribution to the understanding of Aboriginal history in southeastern Australia and both her historical atlas (2000) and thesis (2002) contain a wealth of information on the distribution of languages, named groups, place names, families and individuals in the nineteenth century.
7   Much of the body of archaeological research in the region relates to details of, and changes in, indigenous resource use and technologies.

study region and argues that significant knowledge has been gained about changes over time through numerous excavations of coastal middens, rock shelter deposits and open camp sites. The overall picture is that, at the time of colonisation, Aboriginal people in the Eurobodalla were mainly fisher people who roamed inland when resources were scarce on the coast. Furthermore, coastal groupings were generally associated with drainage basins that had relatively narrow 'beach frontages' and stretched inland to the top of the escarpments. The archaeological record makes it clear that Aboriginal people experienced a long and dynamic precolonial history, and that Aboriginal economy and society were by no means static.

## Ecology

Under the general heading of 'ecology', Keen surveys the environments, resources, technologies, population densities and patterns of settlement and mobility of each of the seven regions. For Keen (2004: 3), these 'ecological aspects' are 'integral to economy' because 'environments constitute arenas of human action and being, they yield resources to be exploited, and they impose constraints and provide enabling conditions for practices'. Following Keen, in this section I survey the ecological aspects of the Eurobodalla, which are broadly similar to those of the Kŭnai in Gippsland.

What is now referred to as the Eurobodalla Shire lies in southeastern NSW, to the east of the Great Dividing Range, between 35° 40´ and 36° 2´ south and 149° 5´ and 150° 2´ east. The region is bordered by the Pacific Ocean to the east and the escarpments rising to the Monaro Plateau to the west, and consists of three major drainage basins (from north to south) of the Clyde, Deua and Tuross River systems, and smaller drainages feeding the Wagonga Inlet and Wallaga Lake estuarine systems. The broad, shallow valleys are subject to flooding during times of heavy rainfall, and the worst flooding occurs when the river mouths have been closed by sand deposition. The escarpments rise gradually out of these drainage basins to the Monaro Plateau. The highest mountains in the escarpments are now known as Pidgeon House Mountain, Mount Dromedary/Gulaga (956 metres above sea level), Mumbulla Mountain and Mount Imlay (from north to south). These mountains have been described as providing important 'spiritual reference points to Aboriginal people' (Wesson 2000: 129).

Yuin people lived, and continue to live, in an environment with a temperate climate and high rainfall, characterised by long, warm (and occasionally hot) summers and cool winters. The average annual rainfall for Moruya Heads is 953.7 mm, with the heaviest rainfalls occurring in the summer months. While the Eurobodalla climate enjoys relatively high rainfall all year round, the winter months coincide with the lowest monthly averages. In comparison to nearby Braidwood (located on the Monaro Plateau at an elevation of 643 metres), the Eurobodalla coast is considerably wetter and the relative proximity to the ocean produces a far less variable range in seasonal temperatures. On the plateau, Braidwood's average annual rainfall is 718.2 mm, and its climate is characterised by colder nights and considerably colder winters, with severe frosts common from June to September.

The Eurobodalla environment consists of diverse terrestrial ecosystems ranging from various kinds of dry eucalypt forests and rainforests in the escarpments, to grasslands, wetlands, coastal sand scrub, dune complexes and rocky outcrops. These ecosystems were (and are) home to a diverse range of edible species, including plants, mammals, reptiles, birds, fresh and saltwater fish, crustaceans and molluscs. The main river systems are fed by numerous small streams and, combined with relatively high annual rainfall and occasional flooding, produce an abundance of potable water.

The ethnographic and archaeological accounts provide little information on the contribution of plant foods to Yuin people's diets. The oral history record identifies a range of edible fruits, and it is likely that various edible roots, rhizomes, tubers and other plant food sources provided year-round staples or were used for medicinal and other practical purposes (Chittick and Fox 1997; Dale Donaldson 2006, 2008). A variety of terrestrial mammals (found mainly in the grasslands and eucalypt forests), reptiles and birds contributed to the diet of the Yuin (Dale Donaldson 2006: 163–6). The remaining sources of protein available to Yuin people were derived from the various freshwater, estuarine and marine ecological zones.

According to Howitt, the functional name 'Katungal Yuin' referred to a people whose lifestyle was oriented towards gaining subsistence from the sea. Howitt's observations are supported by archaeological and ethnographic evidence. For example, Lampert argues that the archaeological evidence supports the theory that there was an 'almost complete dependence by coastal groups on seafoods for the protein portion of their diet. Only a few items, mainly vegetable foods, were derived from the bush' (Lampert 1971: 118). Similarly Harry Warner (n.d.: 2) observed that the Yuin relied mainly on the gathering of shellfish and hunting small land fauna, while the gathering of supporting plant foods was a seasonal activity of minor importance.

However, Poiner asserts that coastal groups did not live exclusively in camps close to the coast. Through an examination of the availability of potential dietary contributions of fish, shellfish and plant categories, Poiner argued that the cold winter months yielded the least in coastal and estuarine food resources. Poiner suggests that these months of relative scarcity reduced community size and resulted in smaller, 'more nomadic' coastal groups roaming inland as part of the food quest (Pointer 1976: 193; cf. Lampert 1971: 121). Based on the freezing conditions in the escarpments and on the plateau during winter, I suggest that this inland movement would have been limited and mobility was relatively aseasonal for coastal groups.

With an orientation towards coastal and estuarine environs, coastal Yuin people utilised a range of technologies to catch fish or to collect shellfish. The most significant material instruments of this type prior to colonisation were fishing lines, hooks and spears, flat water canoes, and flat water and ocean-going rafts. Aboriginal people also utilised a range of tools, weapons and facilities (including fish traps).[8] It is likely that Yuin people also used what Hotchin (1990) described as a general east-coast toolkit consisting of cloaks and rugs of possum skin, various types of fighting clubs, and hunting and fighting spears (Keen 2004: 96). Warner observed that, amongst the Brinja-Yuin of the northern Tuross Lakes area, certain movable technologies (spears, canoes and axes) were more or less 'owned' by the individuals who produced them, although they were shared (or 'loaned') for mutual economic benefit. Warner differentiated between 'movable' and 'real' property, and argued that the latter category (including wurleys, wurley bark slabs, windbreaks, freshwater storages, bark canoes, hearths and hearth-stones and support forks) were 'freely appropriated for use by other Aborigines' once the camp was vacated (Warner n.d.: 5).

The Eurobodalla region appears to have been an environment favourable to human habitation (in terms of high rainfall and a temperate climate) and of relative abundance in a wide variety of available food sources. It is therefore curious that contemporary estimates suggest a relatively small population of around a thousand people living between Twofold Bay and Narrawallee at the time of European settlement (1822–23) (Wesson 2000: 130). It is possible that Yuin people were affected by smallpox epidemics that spread southwards from the north of the continent prior to European colonisation (Butlin 1985; Campbell 2007). Regardless of the overall population size prior to colonisation (and the obvious problems associated with estimation), the evidence suggests that relatively large groups of people congregated when resources were plentiful along the coast during summer, and at larger gatherings including those associated with the beaching of whales and the Bogong moth feasts in the highlands (see Flood 1980; Mathews 1904: 252–3). During the months of relative scarcity (June–September), Keen's comparative material suggests that group size would have been lower, both on the coast and in the escarpments.

---

8   See Chittick (1992–93) and Mathews (1965, 1967).

A combination of the ethnographic, archaeological and oral history sources suggests that a number of smaller 'socio-territorial political ensembles' held areas of land and water in the Eurobodalla (Correy et al. 2008: 7–8). Yet the evidence also suggests that individuals within those groups had rights to use the country of several groups based on various kinds of connections. Rather than moving around in large numbers, these smaller socio-territorial political ensembles (or 'country groups') probably also consisted of smaller familial groups that moved from one residence group to another (Keen 2004: 107).[9] In this manner, Yuin mobility appears similar to that of the Kŭnai where 'individuals and families travelling to the country of other groups could visit relatives and gain access to particular resources in particular seasons' (Keen 2004: 108).

## Institutions

The categories of institutional fields that Keen uses for the seven regions include identities, kinship and marriage, cosmology and quasi-technology, and governance. This section examines the available sources according to these categories to argue that Yuin, as an identity, existed as an ensemble of smaller intermarrying 'country groups' that shared a similar orientation towards living in the coastal/escarpment environs, participated in shared ceremonial activities and spoke mutually intelligible languages.

Howitt observed that the Yuin 'tribes' claimed the country along the coast from the Shoalhaven River in the north to Cape Howe in the south, bounded by escarpments rising to the Monaro Plateau in the west.[10] According to Howitt, the Yuin were constituted by two subdivisions: the Kurial in the north, and the Guyangal in the south (Howitt 1904: 81).[11] Howitt described the local organisation in terms of these two 'sub-tribes', which were further divided into six smaller 'clans'. Besides the north/south differentiation of Yuin identities, Howitt thought that the Yuin were also divided by way of their proximity to the ocean, with Katungal used to describe people living on the coast, and Paiendra

---

9 It is important to make the distinction between landowning groups and residence groups. Following Keen, I use 'country groups' to refer to groups that '"held" or "owned" one or more defined countries and the associated myths, ceremonies, and sacred objects' (Keen 2004: 421). For a detailed examination of the development of, and debate around, anthropological models of Aboriginal rights and interests to land and resources, see Hiatt (2006: 13–35).
10 Wesson notes that 'the term *yuin/yoo-inj/uin/youeen* has been translated as man although it may have meant both person and man' (Wesson 2000: 129).
11 According to Howitt, the names originated from the words *guya*, meaning 'south', and *kuru*, meaning 'north'. The word *gal* was the possessive postfix (ibid.).

for people living further inland (Howitt 1904: 82).¹² Wesson (2000) describes these east/west differentiations as 'functional names' that were influenced by the distinctive ecological zones associated with the livelihoods of the respective groups (Wesson 2000: 151).

More recent work by Tindale (1974) similarly differentiated between Yuin people living on the coast as opposed to those living in the escarpments and on the plateau, and divided the north/south territory of the Katungal Yuin into smaller territorial units including (from Burrill Lake in the north to the Wallaga Lake region in the south) the Wandandian, Walbanga and Djiringanj. While conducting research on the south coast at roughly the same time, it is implicit that Warner thought that the territory of the Walbanga subgroup was further divided into different country groups including that of the Brinja-Yuin (see Warner n.d.: 73, 194).

Drawing on the work of Tindale, Flood argued that the archaeological evidence suggests that Katungal Yuin

> occupied a series of tribal territories along the coast. In general their country stretches up onto the top of the coastal escarpment, and has the shape of a rectangle or wedge, the shorter side being along the coast. It seems that in the past, as in the present, beach frontage was at a premium. (Flood 1982: 29)

If we return to Howitt's observations, Flood's association of these different subgroups with topographic features and drainage basins has some resonance. Howitt observed that 'when a child was born among the Yuin, its father pointed out some hills, lakes or rivers to the men and women there present as being the bounds of his child's country' (Howitt 1904: 83).

In terms of linguistic differences between Yuin country groups, Eades (1976) and Wesson (2000) have presented somewhat different maps of language distribution. Tindale (1974) also provided a map of tribal and linguistic diversity, though his work makes no distinction between language groups and groups with proper names. Eades' study included the languages Dharawal (Tharawal), Dhurga (Thoorga), Dyirringan (Jeringan) and Thawa (Thauaira) (Eades 1976: 6). Wesson's study differs in the geographical range of these languages and used a comparison of vocabulary lists to determine the relative commonality between the languages (Wesson 2000: 156). A combination of these studies suggests that in the Eurobodalla, the dialects of Jeringan and Thoorga comprised a common language for the Yuin ranging from Wallaga Lake to Batemans Bay, with the

---

12   The origin of these names were the words *katung* (meaning 'the sea'), and *paien* ('a tomahawk'). The groups were known to the colonists as 'fishermen' and 'waddymen', respectively. The word 'waddy' was an Aboriginal word for tree and was used in reference to Paiendra people's proclivity to climb trees as part of the food quest (Howitt 1904: 82).

Thurumba dialect being spoken north to Conjola Creek. Tharawal, a distinct language, appears to be common from Ulladulla to as far north as Sydney. To the west, the languages of the highlands and plateau were Ngarigo and Ngunawal.

Howitt provides details about Yuin marriage practices and observes that marriage was exogamous both through totemic classification and locality. One of Howitt's informants stated that the rules of marriage were that no one 'should marry so as to mix the same blood, but he must take a woman from a different name (*Mura*, totem) than his own; and besides this, he must go for a wife to a place as far as possible from his own place' (Howitt 1904: 262). Howitt also describes the arrangement of marriages by respective fathers at the conclusion of the male initiation ceremony, the style of punishment meted out for elopement, and mother-in-law avoidance. Howitt further observed that

> many of the old men among the Yuin, especially the principal *Gommeras*, had more than one wife, and there was one man who had ten, but not at the same time. He was in the habit of giving a wife to some poor fellow who had not any, and thus securing his adherence, and at the same time reducing the number he had to hunt for. (Howitt 1904: 266)

This level of polygyny amongst senior and powerful men reflects Keen's observation that 'since marriage was an exchange, highly polygynous men occupied a key place in exchange networks' (Keen 2004: 179). However, there is little to support Howitt's observations in the census lists, which leads me to believe that high levels of polygyny were anomalous in the nineteenth century and were restricted to the principal *Gommeras* and, perhaps, a handful of senior men.

The combination of observations and understandings that can be drawn from Mathews' scattered papers (and Elkin's analysis) offers far more complexity than Howitt's description of marriage rules, by describing betrothal based upon relationships. Mathews learnt that the first step was for elders to identify a possible wife's mother who would then give birth to the wife of the male child. As Elkin stated, 'The selection of mother-in-law, rather than of wife, was widespread in Australia, though possibly RHM was the first to say so in specific words' (Elkin 1976: 210).[13]

---

13  Both Mathews (see Elkin 1976: 211) and Howitt (1904: 266) described the practice of mother-in-law avoidance amongst the Yuin.

As Elkin noted, Mathews changed his views on Aboriginal social organisation in 1900.[14] Mathews had previously thought that

> all Australian tribes are divided into two exogamous inter-marrying classes, with subdivisions into smaller segments, each having a distinctive title. In cases where these divisions have been believed to be absent, it has probably been rather from their having escaped the notice of investigators than from their non-existence. These class divisions have been called organisations or systems. (Mathews 1894: 18)

Similarly, Howitt observed that 'the class system is in a decadent condition' for the 'Yuin tribes' because 'there are no class names or even traces of them, but very numerous totems scattered over the country, as in the case in the tribes with descent in the female line' (Howitt 1904: 133). According to Mathews' reasoning at the time, any absence of (or unclear delineations between) class divisions could be explained either by poor research or 'that they had formerly existed, but had dropped out of use, leaving traces which the diligent searcher might find' (Elkin 1976: 209).[15] Following extensive fieldwork at a number of locations during the late 1890s, Mathews found that there was no evidence on the south coast of discrete exogamous intermarrying classes.

Considering himself to be a diligent researcher, Mathews came to the conclusion that it was possible that these class divisions did not exist. Rather, 'marriages were regulated by a system of betrothals, based primarily on relationship' (Elkin 1976: 210). Mathews realised that appropriate marriages were between a man and the daughter of his father's cross-cousin—either the daughter of his father's father's sister's daughter or the daughter of his father's mother's brother's daughter. What Howitt thought was simply 'sister exchange' between two exogamous (but barely recognisable) 'classes' was, according to Mathews, the exchange of the man's sister to the wife's brother; that is, the marriage of the latter with the daughter of his mother's male cross-cousin.[16] This system of marriage (*not* organised between exogamous totemic categories, except for the avoidance of marriage between those with the same guardian totem) is congruent with Keen's (2004: 181) analysis of the Kŭnai.

---

14 Elkin notes that all the 'big names' of the era (Howitt, Fison and Spencer) were influenced by 'Lewis Morgan's theory of the development of marriage from primitive promiscuity, through a phase of group marriage and eventually to individual marriage' which associated class divisions 'with a form of group marriage' (Elkin 1976: 234). Mathews' diversion from this school of thought led to widespread criticism of his work. Elkin clearly believed that Mathews' theories were groundbreaking and that his own analysis of Mathews' material provided vindication.
15 I take this to be a thinly veiled criticism of Howitt.
16 Elkin argues that 'such marriages could not be correlated with exogamous classes and sub-classes (moieties and sections), and if they occurred after the introduction of such divisions, they would be regarded as irregular' (Elkin 1976: 211).

There is insufficient information in the sources to provide a model of Yuin kinship based on the classification of relatives. Mathews' and Howitt's observations are concordant that Yuin society was not organised around a moiety or section system. The available evidence also suggests that Yuin systems of kin classification do not fit with Kariera-like terminology, which Keen found to 'have been very adaptable, occurring in a range of environments' (Keen 2004: 396). Based on the evidence in hand, we can generalise that Yuin kinship involved extensive networks of relatedness within and between exogamous intermarrying country groups. These marriage rules are consistent with Howitt's observation that totemic classifications were exogamous.[17] Mathews also observed that 'each tribe is made up of a number of families or groups, each of which has a local position in some part of the tribal country ... In tribes with agnatic descent ... the totems are perpetuated through the man' (Mathews 1894: 21). Patrifilial *budjan* totems were associated with different places and different country groups or patri-clans that probably reflected some proliferation of the totemic species in that location. Therefore, in a similar manner to what Keen describes in the case of the Kŭnai, 'totemic affiliations both distinguished localities and created connections' (Keen 2004: 279).[18]

Totemic identities were (and are) also incorporated into Yuin cosmology or a general worldview including

> non-totemic male and female creator beings, and other non-ordinary beings ... The creator beings made the other beings and the totems ... The spirits of creators such as Tunku and Ngardi have been metamorphosed in the features of sacred sites in the area, just as Umbarra, the black duck, has become the form of the island in the middle of the Lake.
>
> Yuin people's cosmology of creation starts with Darumala (Daruma, or Darumalan), and his mother, Ngalalbal, along with two other creator beings, Tunku and Ngardi. (Rose et al. 2003: 40–1)

---

17  Through more recent ethnographic research, Deborah Rose is highly critical of Howitt's approach, and argues that 'his work generally does not take women's knowledge or practice into account' (Rose et al. 2003: 40). Rose found evidence that totemic classifications were (and are) bestowed upon children by both men and women (ibid.). While Rose is correct that there is a significant bias towards male knowledge and practice in Howitt's work, the presence of matrilineal totems in the nineteenth century is problematic for Mathews' schema of appropriate marriages. This can be explained in two ways: either matrilineal totems (which were observed neither by Howitt nor Mathews) might have been a separate category that did not affect marriage practices, or the significant disruptions to Yuin social worlds in the late nineteenth and twentieth centuries meant that it was necessary for the conferral of totems to become more flexible according to gender.
18  Mathews believed that this system of social organisation was characteristic of all the 'tribes' of the 'south-eastern coastal district' of NSW (see Mathews and Everitt 1900: 262–3).

The activities of these creator beings are mapped onto the landscape as Dreaming stories and tracks. As Rose notes, 'The term "Dreaming" covers a range of interconnected concepts including Dreaming ancestors and their creative journeys, religious laws, sacred designs and songs, and codes of social order' (ibid.: 21–2).

The nature of Yuin male initiation is the only reference Howitt gives to ceremonial practices in the study region. Yuin youths were given cicatrices after the initiation ceremonies and, as Howitt observed, 'scars are cut on both boys and girls' (Howitt 1904: 746). There is no evidence that Yuin people practised circumcision or subincision, however tooth avulsion was part of the male initiation ceremony. The ceremonies were coordinated by the principal *Gommera* of the officiating 'tribe'. According to Howitt, *Gommeras* were the headmen of the local divisions and 'must be a medicine-man, must be aged, able to speak several languages (dialects), be skilful as a fighting-man, and be, above all, able to perform those feats of magic which the *Gommeras* exhibit at the initiation ceremonies' (Howitt 1904: 314). While governance within these local divisions largely rested on the will of the powerful *Gommeras*, Howitt also observed what he called 'tribal councils' that included all the initiated men to discuss particular problems. Howitt was 'struck by the restrained manner of the younger men at these meetings' (Howitt 1904: 325). This 'restraint' reflected the norms of respect and ancestral laws that were impressed upon initiates during the ceremony.

## Economy

Under the broader heading of economy, Keen (2004: 275) examines 'resources, relations, and practices according to economic categories'. Accordingly, this section examines the way in which country groups accessed resources and controlled the means of production through use-rights, the organisation of production through gendered divisions of labour, the organisation of distribution and consumption, and exchange and trade.

Howitt observed that male children were given rights to their father's country and to the country of their birth. However, he also wrote (1904: 83) that the Yuin observed a range of use-rights to country, including man's place of birth, a man's father's place of birth, a father's sons' place of birth, a woman's place of birth, a woman's mother's place of birth, and a mother's daughters' place of birth. In addition to use-rights associated with the place of one's birth or parents' place of birth, use-rights were also governed by totemic classifications. Oral history documents 'the restrictive Aboriginal lores governing access to traditional ecological knowledge, including that relating to the location, distribution, collection and preparation method of flora used for food and medicines' (Dale Donaldson 2006: 13). Prior to colonisation, these restricted knowledges probably governed use-rights for particular resources.[19] Therefore, Aboriginal people in the Eurobodalla benefited from a mix of rights in a number of different countries.[20]

In terms of the division of labour, Bowdler argues that the procurement of food was 'according to technique. Men invariably used the four-pronged bone-barbed spear; women fished with a hook and line, using a shell hook and a vegetable fibre line' (Bowdler 1976: 254). Bowdler further remarks:

> Woman doubtless spent a good deal of their time gathering shellfish; and this was probably done in a thorough and systematic fashion, with due regard to the schedules imposed by the tides ... While spears were sacrosanct to men, the new implement, the shell hook which appeared some 600 years ago, had no such status adhering to it. (Bowdler 1976: 256)

Lampert's research supports this view and argues that Yuin people were organised around a 'strict sexual division of labour in using this equipment: women always fished with hook and line, men with spears' (Lampert 1971: 118).

Unfortunately, Howitt did not provide information on the composition of residence groups and patterns of distribution and consumption on the south coast. Warner's papers provide more helpful (if limited) details relating to the Brinja-Yuin, for whom the economic unit was observed to be a family group living at one wurley (Warner n.d.: 73). Warner thought that the Brinja-Yuin were organised around a 'semi-nomadic' lifestyle centred on 'semi-permanent' campsites that provided a base for food gathering expeditions (Warner n.d.: 94). Warner's papers suggest that during times of abundance, residence groups were considerably larger and gendered 'work teams' exploited coastal resources collectively. The ecological and archaeological evidence suggests that women and men generally worked and hunted separately, with women collecting shellfish and fishing with hooks and line during the day. It appears that much of the fishing men did was during the evening when fish could be startled using a torch and then speared, while during the day men sometimes hunted terrestrial game (including macropods).

Drawing on archaeological and ethnographic evidence and comparative material, Bowdler argues that 'fish—like other meat—was monopolised by men, despite the contribution of female effort in making the catch' (Bowdler 1976: 256). Bowdler postulates that Aboriginal men and women had different diets, with

---

19   Not only did totemic classifications denote use-rights for individuals and groups, but they also entailed responsibility for 'holding' that country by protecting and nurturing it.
20   This is consistent with Keen's (2004) comparison of seven different regions.

men consuming the lion's share of scale fish and any mammals that were caught, while women subsisted mainly on shellfish.[21] From a comparative perspective, this picture of distribution and consumption is overly simplistic. As Keen notes for Aboriginal economies in general, 'certain kinds of relationships required particular kinds of gifts' (Keen 2004: 337). While the evidence doesn't exist in the record, it is likely that the produce from both men's and women's labour were distributed according to particular kinds of kin obligations. Furthermore, distribution amongst Yuin people probably also followed patterns of what Peterson calls 'inertial generosity' in which people simply 'respond to demands as they are made' (Peterson 1993: 864).[22] However, as Keen further suggests, 'degrees of familiarity and constraint entailed by different kin relationships also affected the ability to make demands' (Keen 2004: 337).

Howitt's observations illustrate that a range of restrictions were placed on male initiates relating to consumption prohibitions during the seclusion phase of their initiation. Following the removal of the tooth, the *Gumbang-ira* ('raw-tooth novice') was prohibited from eating emu, any animal which burrows in the ground (e.g. wombat), creatures that have prominent teeth (e.g. kangaroo), any animal that climbs to the treetops (e.g. koala), any bird that swims, echidna, possum, lace-lizard, snakes, eels and perch, and the *budjan* (totem) of the novice. Howitt noted: 'Thus the young man during his probation is placed in an artificial state of scarcity as to food, although perhaps surrounded by plenty' (Howitt 1904: 560).[23] Most of these food prohibitions related to cosmology and processes undertaken during the ceremony.[24]

While various consumable items were distributed within Yuin residence groups, durable objects were exchanged with other groups based on regional specialisations. It appears that the *Kuringal* gathering also served as an opportunity for trade. Howitt writes, 'At the termination of the initiation ceremonies, at which the whole intermarrying community were present, a meeting was held near the camp at which things were bartered' (Howitt 1904: 263). Howitt (ibid.: 718–20) provides a valuable level of detail regarding these exchange practices, in which durable goods (alienable possessions) were

---

21  This argument hinges on evidence that shellfish remnants are broadly spread over a number of sites, leading Bowdler to believe that much of an Aboriginal woman's 'food is consumed while gathering away from the camp' (Bowdler 1976: 252).

22  Peterson's model of 'demand sharing' addresses the problem of negative reciprocity (or 'freeloading') (Peterson 1993: 860).

23  Howitt thought that these restrictions were removed when the *Gommeras* had deemed the novices fit to return to their groups. However, Mathews suggests that food prohibitions were incrementally lifted when men had attended a certain number of initiation ceremonies, although he doesn't state explicitly how many (Mathews 1896).

24  For example, the emu was prohibited because it was *Ngalalbal* (the mother of *Darumalan* the creation being), while kangaroos (and other animals with prominent teeth) were thought to remind the *Gumbang-ira* of the missing tooth.

exchanged and relationships were reaffirmed through gifts to important or powerful leaders (inalienable gifts). Similarly, ceremonial and auspicious items were exchanged along what appears to be a much broader trading network.

## Conclusion

This chapter has provided the first systematic profiling of Yuin economy and society within the Eurobodalla region of the New South Wales south coast at the threshold of colonisation. It has demonstrated the usefulness of Keen's approach of using the comparable and relatively reconstructable categories of ecology, institutional fields and economy to shed light on the character of this region, and has paid homage to Keen's invaluable contribution to economic anthropology, and to a comparative understanding of the variation in Aboriginal economies and societies across Australia.

In view of the ethnographic, archaeological and linguistic evidence, Yuin (as an identity) existed as a conglomerate of intermarrying country groups sharing a coastal/escarpment orientation, mutually intelligible language and who participated in common ceremonial activities. In the Eurobodalla, these country groups had their own range, and individual rights to country were determined by a variety of claims. The conclusions for this chapter are presented in Table 12.1, borrowing from Keen's comparable categories within Aboriginal economies and societies. Sadly, the available evidence for the Eurobodalla region is inadequate to comprehensibly profile the full extent of Yuin institutions and economy, particularly in relation to kinship terminology, cosmology and patterns of distribution.

The profile of the Yuin in this chapter is broadly consistent with Keen's profiling of the Kŭnai, with a great deal of similarity in the ecology, economy and institutions of each group, and a degree of intermarriage, and mutual involvement in shared ceremonial practices and trade, between the two groups.[25] Keen refers to the Kŭnai as occupying part of a broad resource zone in the southeast, rather than as exemplifying economic or social characteristics shared by people in that region (Keen 2004: 382–3). Both the Kŭnai and the Yuin populated an area with a vast array of similar lacustrine, estuarine and coastal resources and developed similar technologies to utilise those resources (including nets, fish hooks, spears

---

25  Both Mathews and Howitt observed the presence of Kŭnai people at Yuin ceremonies, which included exchange and trade. The genealogical records I was able to compile during my PhD research detail a number of marriages between Kŭnai and Yuin people in the 1800s—a pattern that may have predated European incursions into the region. While the information on Yuin marriage practices is incomplete, Howitt observed that the Yuin, like the Kŭnai, discouraged marriage between geographically close people, and close relatives—a practice that probably encouraged marriage between the two groups.

and canoes). The Kŭnai and Yuin had similar population densities and range of seasonal movements, as well as similarly comprised country groups holding a range of use-rights to various estates. In both these cases, totemic affiliations distinguished localities and created connections for Kŭnai and Yuin people. Further, Yuin creation stories have a similar celestial emphasis to those of the Kŭnai, telling of the creator-ancestors, Tunku and Ngardi, coming down from a star to inhabit the earth. Howitt also documented Yuin ancestral stories involving the Milky Way (Howitt 1904: 664), where the spirits of the dead inhabited the sky. This evidence is consistent with Keen's assertion of a celestial emphasis in the cosmology of the southeast region, as opposed to the strong terrestrial emphasis in the Western Desert (Keen 2004: 387).

Table 12.1 Key features of Yuin economy and society in the Eurobodalla in the late eighteenth century.

| Environment | Estuarine systems, intertidal zones, marine habitats, drainage basins, plains, temperate forests. |
|---|---|
| Resources | Mainly coastal and riverine resources, food plants (fruits, roots, rhizomes and tubers), birds, reptiles and mammals. |
| Population density | Keen's estimates for the Kŭnai seem to be a reasonable comparison based on similar environments and resources. Population densities may have been as high as one person per square kilometre around the estuaries. In the foothills population densities may have been medium to high (one person per 6–12 square kilometres) and considerably lower in the upper escarpment (see Keen 2004: 107). |
| Technologies | Canoes and rafts, fishing spears with variable tips, torches for startling fish at night, bone or shell fishing hooks, fishing lines, fish traps, possum cloaks/rugs, wurleys, an assortment of clubs, axes, spears and boomerangs. |
| Seasonal patterns | Generally aseasonal but some movement inland during winter. |
| Language and regional identities | Three dialects and possibly four regional identities within the Eurobodalla (Kurial/north, Guyangal/south, Katungal/east, Paiendra/west). |
| Local identities | Based on countries with totemic significance. Countries associated with geographical features and/or drainage basins. Coastal 'estates' with narrow beach frontages. |
| Totemic identities | Patrifilial *budjan* totems, country-groups identified by locality. Strong correlation between patrifilial totems and totemic significance of country. |
| Kinship terminology | Insufficient information in sources. Evidence suggests an extensive network of relatedness with no moiety system. |
| Level of polygyny | Possibly high. The evidence suggests that some senior or powerful men were highly polygamous (see Keen 2004: 178–9, 206–7). |
| Governance | *Gommeras* (headmen) acted as local bosses, magicians, ritual leaders and healers. |
| Cosmology | Strong celestial emphasis. |

| | |
|---|---|
| Use rights | Country of birth, father's country, mother's country, country of child's birth, country associated with totemic identity. |
| Organisation of production | Highly gendered by resource and technologies associated with those resources. |
| Distribution and consumption | Insufficient information in sources. Comparative material suggests generalised reciprocity, demand sharing and kin obligations shaped distribution. Totemic and ceremonial restrictions on consumption. |
| Exchange and trade | Exchange and trade of alienable possessions and inalienable gifts during ceremonial gatherings. |

Given the strong similarities between the Yuin material and Keen's profile of the Kŭnai, it is tempting to conclude that the Yuin and Kŭnai occupied a broad 'south-east zone' of shared economic and social characteristics, although more work on uncovering and understanding information about Yuin institutions (particularly kinship terminology) would be necessary. Further research of this type in the southeast of the Australian continent could establish whether such a zone was spread more broadly, further adding to the nuances of similarity and difference in Aboriginal ecology, economy and society that Keen has so compelling presented.

Keen concludes his 2004 monograph by suggesting that the character of Aboriginal economy and society in a particular region may have assisted in shaping the course of intercultural relations on the frontier and beyond, whereby 'certain forms of social organisation and leadership made stronger resistance possible in some areas, or made it possible for Europeans and others to become incorporated into Aboriginal exchange systems' (Keen 2004: 398). In doing so, Keen foreshadows a productive dialogue between the theoretical and methodological approaches of anthropology and history, an exchange of ideas that was developed by contributors to the two edited volumes of *Indigenous Participation in Australian Economies* (Keen 2010; Fijn et al. 2012), documenting the nature and variety of Aboriginal and Torres Strait Islander engagements with the settler economy from the colonial era to the present day. Further research of this type will assist in developing anthropological analyses of Aboriginal and Torres Strait Islander economic relations, and the articulation of Indigenous economies with market capitalism and the state.

# References

Altman, J. 1987. *Hunter-Gatherers Today: An Aboriginal Economy in North Australia*. Canberra: Australian Institute of Aboriginal Studies.

Anderson, C. 1984. The Political and Economic Basis of Kuku-Yalinji Social History. PhD Thesis, University of Queensland, Brisbane.

Attenbrow, V. 1999. Archaeological research in coastal southeastern Australia: a review. In J Hall and I. McNiven (eds), *Australian Coastal Archaeology*, pp. 195–210. Canberra: The Australian National University.

Bourdieu, P. 1977. *An Outline of a Theory of Practice*. Cambridge: Cambridge University Press.

Bowdler, S. 1976. Hook, line and dilly bag: an interpretation of an Australian coastal shell midden. *Mankind* 10(4): 248–58.

Butlin, N. 1985. Macassans and aboriginal smallpox: the '1789' and '1829' epidemics. *Australian Historical Studies* 21: 315–35.

Butlin, N. 1993. *Economics and the Dreamtime: A Hypothetical History*. Melbourne and Cambridge: Cambridge University Press.

Campbell, J. 2007. *Invisible Invaders: Smallpox and Other Diseases in Aboriginal Australia, 1780–1880*. Carlton, Vic.: Melbourne University Press.

Chittick, L. 1992–93. Interviews—Percy Mumbulla Project Canberra, Recorded Sound Archive, AIATSIS.

Chittick, L. and T. Fox. 1997. *Travelling with Percy: A South Coast Journey*. Canberra: Aboriginal Studies Press.

Correy, S., D. McCarthy and A. Redmond. 2008. The differences which resemble: the effects of the 'Narcissism of Minor Differences' in the constitution and maintenance of native title claimant groups in Australia. Australian Anthropological Society Annual Conference. Auckland, NZ.

Dale Donaldson, S. 2006. *Stories about the Eurobodalla by Aboriginal People*. Eurobodalla Aboriginal Cultural Heritage Study. Stage Two. Moruya, NSW: Susan Dale Donaldson Environmental and Cultural Services.

Dale Donaldson, S. 2008. *Aboriginal Men and Women's Heritage: Eurobodalla*. Moruya, NSW: Eurobodalla Shire Council.

Dingle, A.E. 1988. *Aboriginal Economy: Patterns of Experience*. Melbourne: McPhee Gribble.

Eades, D. 1976. *The Dharawal and Dhurga Languages of the New South Wales South Coast*. Canberra: Australian Institute of Aboriginal Studies.

Elkin, A.P. 1975a. R.H. Mathews: his contribution to Aboriginal studies. Part one. *Oceania* 46: 1–24.

Elkin, A.P. 1975b. R.H. Mathews: his contribution to Aboriginal studies. Part two. *Oceania* 46: 126–52.

Elkin, A.P. 1976. R.H. Mathews: his contribution to Aboriginal studies. Part three. *Oceania* 46: 206–34.

Fijn, N., I. Keen, C. Lloyd and M. Pickering (eds). 2012. *Indigenous Participation in Australian Economies II: Historical Engagements and Current Enterprises.* Canberra: ANU E Press.

Flood, J. 1980. *The Moth Hunters: Aboriginal Prehistory of the Australian Alps.* Canberra: Australian Institute of Aboriginal Studies.

Flood, J. 1982. Katungal, Paindra and Bemeringal. In S. Bowdler (ed.), *Coastal Archaeology in Eastern Australia: Proceedings of the 1980 Valla Conference on Australian Prehistory*, pp. 29–31. Canberra: Australian National University Press.

Giddens, A. 1979. *Central Problems in Social Theory: Action, Structure and Contradiction in Social Analysis.* London: Macmillan.

Godelier, M. 1999. *The Enigma of the Gift.* Chicago: University of Chicago Press.

Gregory, C. 1982. *Gifts and Commodities.* London: Academic Press.

Hiatt, L.R. 2006. *Arguments About Aborigines: Australia and the Evolution of Social Anthropology.* Cambridge: Cambridge University Press.

Hotchin, K. 1990. *Environmental and Cultural Change in the Gippsland Lakes Region, Victoria, Australia.* PhD Thesis, The Australian National University, Canberra.

Howitt, A.W. 1904. *The Native Tribes of South-East Australia.* London: Macmillan.

Howitt, A.W. 1907a. Howitt to Hockey. 13 December 1907. R.H. Mathews Papers. Canberra: National Library of Australia.

Howitt, A.W. 1907b. Howitt to Hockey. 16 September 1907. R.H. Mathews Papers. Canberra: National Library of Australia.

Howitt, A.W. n.d. Papers 1049/3b, 1050/2a, 1050/2c, 1050/4d, 1053/3a, 1053/3b, 1053/4a, 1053/5b, 1054/2a, 1054/2c. Melbourne: State Library of Victoria and Museum of Victoria.

Keen, I. 1993. Ubiquitous ubiety of dubious uniformity. *The Australian Journal of Anthropology* 4(2): 96–110.

Keen, I. 2000. The anthropologist as geologist: Howitt in colonial Gippsland. *The Australian Journal of Anthropology* 11: 78–98.

Keen, I. 2004. *Aboriginal Economy and Society: Australia at the Threshold of Colonisation*. South Melbourne, Vic.: Oxford University Press.

Keen, I. (ed.) 2010. *Indigenous Participation in Australian Economies: Historical and Anthropological Perspectives*. Canberra: ANU E Press.

Lampert, R. 1971. Coastal Aborigines of south east Australia. In D.J. Mulvaney (ed.), *Aboriginal Man and Environment in Australia*, pp. 114–32. Canberra: Australian National University Press.

Lawrence, R.J. 1968. Aboriginal Habitat and Economy. MA Thesis, The Australian National University, Canberra.

Mathews, R.H. 1894. The Kamilaroi class system of the Australian Aborigines. *Proceedings and Transactions of the Queensland Branch of the Royal Geographical Society of Australasia* 10: 18–34.

Mathews, R.H. 1896. The Bunan ceremony of New South Wales. *American Anthropologist* 9: 327–44.

Mathews, R.H. 1902. The Thoorga (and Yoolumbill) languages. *Queensland Geographical Journal* 17: 49–73.

Mathews, R.H. 1904. Ethnological notes on the Aboriginal tribes of New South Wales and Victoria. *Journal of the Royal Society of New South Wales* 38: 203–381.

Mathews, R.H. and M.M. Everitt. 1900. The organisation, language and initiation ceremonies of the Aborigines of the south-east coast of New South Wales. *Journal of the Royal Historical Society of New South Wales* 34: 262–80.

Matthews, J. 1965. Language elicitation, local and family histories, and material culture. Canberra: Recorded Sound Archive, AIATSIS.

Mathews, J. 1967. Vocabulary, songs and cultural discussions from south-east Australia. Canberra: Recorded Sound Archive, AIATSIS.

Mauss, M. 1954. *The Gift: Forms and Functions of Exchange in Archaic Societies*. Glencoe, IL: The Free Press.

Peterson, N. 1993. Demand sharing: reciprocity and the pressure for generosity among foragers. *American Anthropologist* 95(4): 860–74.

Poiner, G. 1976. The process of the year among Aborigines of the central and south coasts of New South Wales. *Archaeology and Physical Anthropology in Oceania* 11: 186–200.

Robinson, G.A. 1844a. Field journals, 13 April–11 May 1844. Unpublished transcription by I.D. Clark (1998). Sydney: Mitchell Library.

Rose, D.B., D. James and C. Watson. 2003. *Indigenous Kinship with the Natural World in New South Wales*. Hurstville, NSW: NSW National Parks and Wildlife Service.

Rowley, C.D. 1970. *The Destruction of Aboriginal Society*. Aborigines in Australian Society 4. Canberra: Australian National University Press.

Rowley, C.D. 1971. *Outcasts in White Australia*. Aborigines in Australian Society 6. Canberra: Australian National University Press.

Sahlins, M. 1974. *Stone Age Economics*. London: Tavistock.

Spencer, B. and F. Gillen. 1899. *The Native Tribes of Central Australia*. London: Macmillan and Co.

Swain, T. 1993. *A Place for Strangers: Towards a History of Australian Aboriginal Being*. Cambridge: Cambridge University Press.

Tindale, N.B. 1974. *Aboriginal Tribes of Australia*. Berkeley: University of California Press.

Thomas, M. 2004. R.H. Mathews and anthropological warfare: on writing the biography of a self-contained man. *Aboriginal History* 28: 1–32.

Thomas, M. 2006. A Very Human Survey. *Public History Review* 12: 12–26.

Thomas, M. 2011. *The Many Worlds of R.H. Mathews: In Search of an Australian Anthropologist*. Crows Nest, NSW: Allen and Unwin.

Van Gennep, A. 1909. Van Gennep to Mathews. 16 November 1909. R.H. Mathews Papers Canberra, National Library of Australia.

Veth, P. 2006. Review of *Aboriginal Economy and Society Economy and Society: Australia at the Threshold of Colonisation* by Ian Keen. *Australian Archaeology* 63: 68–9.

Warner, H. n.d. Ethnography summary of the late Brinja-Yuin tribe of Tuross, N.S.W. Closed Stack. Canberra, AIATSIS.

Weiner, A. 1992. *Inalienable Possessions: The Paradox of Keeping-While-Giving*. Berkeley: University of California Press.

Wesson, S. 2000. *An Historical Atlas of the Aborigines of Eastern Victoria and Far South-Eastern New South Wales*. Melbourne: School of Geography and Environmental Science, Monash University.

Wesson, S. 2002. The Aborigines of Eastern Victoria and Far South-eastern New South Wales, 1830 to 1910: An Historical Geography. PhD Thesis, Monash University, Melbourne.

White, J.M. 2010a. Peas, beans and river banks: seasonal picking and dependence in the Tuross Valley. In I. Keen (ed.), *Indigenous Participation in Australian Economies: Historical and Anthropological Perspectives*, pp. 109–26. Canberra: ANU E Press.

White, J.M. 2010b. On the Road to Nerrigundah: An Historical Anthropology of Indigenous-Settler Relations in the Eurobodalla Region of New South Wales. PhD Thesis, The Australian National University, Canberra.

White, J.M. 2011. Histories of indigenous-settler relations: reflections on internal colonialism and the hybrid economy. *Australian Aboriginal Studies* 1: 81–96.

White, J.M. 2012. Before the mission station: from first encounters to the incorporation of settlers into indigenous relations of obligation. In N. Fijn, I. Keen, C. Lloyd, and M. Pickering (eds), *Indigenous Participation in Australian Economies II: Historical Engagements and Current Enterprises*, pp. 37–56. Canberra: ANU E Press.

# 13  Long-Distance Diffusion of Affinal Kinship Terms as Evidence of Late Holocene Change in Marriage Systems in Aboriginal Australia

Patrick McConvell
The Australian National University

## Introduction

Ian Keen has made significant contributions to the comparison of Australian Aboriginal societies, and specifically to the relationship between types of marriage, kinship systems and other aspects of society and economy. He has maintained a commitment to the rigorous study of kinship systems and to comparative anthropology, or ethnology, when these orientations became unpopular in sociocultural anthropology. One of his major works (2004) systematically compared representative groups throughout Australia, emphasising how aspects of social organisation linked to economies. On a smaller scale was his brilliant study of how the scale of polygyny differed in two neighbouring areas of Arnhem Land, seeking the explanation in matrilateral cousin marriage and networks, age structures and economy (1982).

In recent times he has also joined forces with linguistics in investigating the prehistoric development of these relationships of kinship, marriage and other aspects of social organisation, in the AustKin project (Dousset et al. 2010). One study looked at how asymmetrical cross-cousin marriage developed, with crucial evidence supplied by the change in meaning of kinship terms. Notably the change in marriage type played a strong role in changing meanings of terms. The kinship terms in this case are inherited words within the Pama-Nyungan language family and its subgroups (McConvell and Keen 2011; Keen 2013b).

However, another striking phenomenon is the preponderance of affinal (in-law and spouse) terms among loanwords in kinship vocabulary. Consanguineal terms tend not to be borrowed widely unless they also function as affinal. Apart from affinal terms, kinship terms are rather rarely borrowed.[1] Affinal terms, however, include some of the most long-distance travelling loanwords (*Wanderwörter*). Why is this so? One might readily guess that words related to marriage are among those that tend to be shared in wide areas since exogamous marriage between language groups is a most salient and frequently discussed topic. Further than this, though, it may be that these new words for spouses and in-laws were first introduced because they were key elements in new marriage practices that were diffusing. This opens a window on changes in the nature of societal and intersocietal alliance in the last few thousand years in the late Holocene in Australia.

In this chapter, two examples of such long-distance affinal kin loans are examined:[2]

1. A term *ramparr*, originally associated with mother-in-law and avoidance in the northeast Kimberley region, which diffused into the west Kimberley with a change of meaning to father-in-law, then (affected by sound change) spread east as *lamparr(a)* through the southern Kimberley into the Northern Territory. These changes appear to be associated with an increase in power of the father-in-law in the arrangement of marriage.

---

1   There are also cases of borrowing of consanguineal terms but they are rarer. One circumstance which can trigger this type of borrowing is a shift to a different type of kinship system (for instance from Kariera to Aranda), which requires additional terms that are imported from neighbouring languages, as in the case of borrowed 'father's father' terms in Ngumpin-Yapa (McConvell 1997a: 217–20). Arguably, this change is related to new marriage patterns between an incoming and a resident population, and is thus not totally divorced from the question of affinal networks being discussed for the diffusion of affinal terms in this paper. Some language families appear to have borrowed a wide range of kinship terms over a long period, like Nyulnyulan from Pama-Nyungan subgroups and other neighbours, discussed below in the section 'Mother-in-Law > Father-in-Law'. The pattern of these spreads is different from that of the *Wanderwörter* considered in this paper (cf. Haynie et al. 2014).

2   Space does not permit consideration of other examples, such as (a) the term *ngumparna* ('husband'), found throughout the Ngumpin-Yapa subgroup, but also in neighbouring areas and some distance away in Arnhem Land; and (b) the term *nyupa* (also *ngupa, nyuwa,* etc.), found in a very wide area of Pama-Nyungan across Australia mainly with the meaning 'spouse'. These require detailed analysis to determine to what extent they are inherited in Pama-Nyungan subgroups (or for (b), within Pama-Nyungan as a whole). (b) may be inherited in Pama-Nyungan, or partly or mostly diffused at an early stage in the development of the Pama-Nyungan family. If the latter is the case, then this is one of the most widespread ancient *Wanderwörter* in Australia, with the most central meaning of 'spouse' from the start, or very soon after the start.

2. A term *tyamVny* (where V stands for an indeterminate vowel), which is quite widespread as an inherited term for 'mother's father' in Pama-Nyungan, that also diffused quite virulently into non-Pama-Nyungan languages in the north Kimberley and Arnhem Land. While the core meaning does not appear to be affinal, the mother's father term is frequently also used to mean 'cross-cousin' and then 'spouse' where cross-cousin marriage is practised.

(1) is clearly a *Wanderwort* from early on in its career, and spread across an area of northern Australia. (2) only became a *Wanderwort* as a late departure, when it acquired a new function and started to be borrowed into non-Pama-Nyungan families.

These studies point towards possible generalisations relevant not just to Indigenous Australia but to population dynamics, and its relation to kinship terminology systems and their distribution, more generally. They link to work on the study of exogamous marriage and in-law chains between language groups in Indigenous Australia, and beyond (Denham 2013), adding to the themes and discoveries in Ian Keen's work.

# Inheritance and Diffusion of Kinship Terms

It has been remarked for several language families that kinship terms are highly stable over long periods. This is generally because they are inherited from the proto-language without replacement. This is true for instance of Indo-European, where of a sample of 36 terms (six kintypes in six branches) reconstructed to proto-Indo-European some 6,000–7,000 years ago, 27 (75 per cent) are retained in the daughter subgroups and only nine (25 per cent) replaced (Clackson 2007: 207). These rates of retention are considerably higher than those predicted by the loss of 14 per cent of basic vocabulary items per millennium proposed in glottochronology.

There are differences in the stability of terms, which seem to have some correlations with the meanings of terms. The most stable appear to be the core consanguineal terms (such as 'mother', 'father', 'brother', etc.), whereas collateral terms ('uncle', 'aunt', 'cousin', etc.) and affinal terms (spouse and in-law) are less so, not only in Indo-European but also in other families (Matras 2009: 169–72).[3]

---

3   This does not mean that collateral and affinal terms are not stable, just that they tend to be less so. Marck et al. (2011) argue that terms for cross-cousin (collateral, and affinal because of cross-cousin marriage) are stable and inherited in East Bantu.

Those terms which are not inherited (and therefore not stable) can be either loanwords or coined from other resources in the language. For instance, regarding coinages, 'husband' can be the word for 'man' and 'wife' the word for 'woman' as in a number of Indo-European languages—and the spouse terms have this kind of origin in some Australian Aboriginal languages. I focus here not on this kind of process but on the diffusion of kinship loanwords.

The borrowing, often widespread borrowing as *Wanderwörter*, of affinal terms has been noted for instance by Dixon and Aikhenvald (1999: 8) for 'mother's brother'/ 'father-in-law' *kuku* or *koko* in Amazonia, and we will be seeing this kind of situation echoed in our Australian examples. Tuite and Schulze (1998) cite this as a parallel example to the borrowing of the Indo-European term for 'daughter-in-law' (*snus) into a large number of Caucasian languages (cf. Matasović 2012). In both cases, they claim, avoidance between in-laws motivated the replacement of original inherited terms by loans—the Amazonian case between a father-in-law and daughter-in-law, and in the Caucasus the ambivalent and often negative treatment of wives taken into the husband's lineage and community.[4] This importance given to avoidance seems to constitute a distinct general hypothesis about why some affinal terms diffuse so widely. While avoidance also comes into our stories of affinal term diffusion in Australia, it is doubtful if its role is primary: we return to this topic later in this chapter.

In Australia, kinship terms in general also seem to be quite stable, but some affinal terms are labile due to their propensity to be borrowed. In the very widespread Pama-Nyungan language family it has been possible to reconstruct a significant proportion of kin terms with some confidence (e.g. McConvell 2008, 2009). This contrasts with other semantic fields where the proportion of reconstructible roots is much lower. Narrowing to a smaller range, within the Ngumpin-Yapa subgroup of Pama-Nyungan, spoken in the Tanami Desert and Victoria River district of the Northern Territory and the South Kimberley of Western Australia, the majority of kinship term roots are retained and can be reconstructed. They are replaced in a number of cases by loanwords whose origin can be traced. The loanwords include several with affinal meanings, for instance in Gurindji *ngumparna* ('husband; husband's brother') and *lamparra* ('father-in-law, and reciprocally child-in-law'), the latter discussed in this chapter. The cognates of the proto-Pama-Nyungan term *$tya(m)(p)i$ 'mother's father' (*tyamirdi, tyawityi*, etc.) are primarily not affinal in this language subgroup, but in this chapter it is illustrated how their extended affinal functions (as spouse, sibling-in-law) elsewhere contribute to their diffusion. There are also consanguineal loanwords mentioned in note 2.

---

4   Dziebel (2012) claims that marriage exchange existed between speakers of Indo-European and North Caucasian languages and adduces genetic evidence.

In the following sections, the examples of the two affinal *Wanderwörter* to be discussed are introduced in turn. Maps are provided for each example showing their diffusion paths, and where relevant, changes in their meaning.

## *Ramparr* > *Lamparr*: 'Mother-in-Law > Father-in-Law'

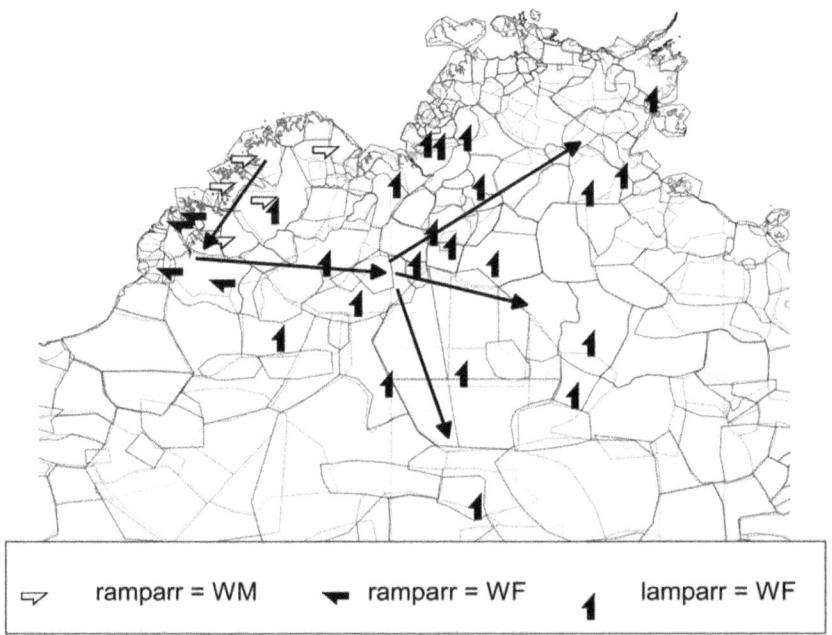

Figure 13.1 Spread of *ramparr/lamparr(a)*.[5]
Source: Patrick McConvell.

Here the stages of diffusion are dealt with in summary in reverse chronological order, starting with Stage 5 and going back to the origin, Stages 0–1. This labelling is also used in Figure 13.1. The following sections go into more detail about the loans, meaning changes and probable socio-historical contexts.

---

5   Thanks to Billy McConvell for work on this map and Figure 13.3.

Strings of Connectedness

## Stage 5: The Recent Eastward Diffusion in the Eastern Northern Territory

The term *lamparra* is widespread across a swathe of the Northern Territory from the Victoria River District east into the northern part of Central Australia and central Arnhem Land. It has the primary meaning of a man's wife's father, and reciprocally also of a man's daughter's husband, but also covering husband's father and reciprocal woman's son's wife in a number of groups. Throughout this region the term and associated practice (see below) are acknowledged by Aboriginal people to be a recent innovation arriving from the west within the last 100–150 years. For some languages the term is ascribed to Pidgin or Kriol, a lingua franca which spread in the same time period (e.g. Heath 1981: 109–10). In Figure 13.1 the stage of diffusion through the southern Kimberley is called Stage 4, and the mainly twentieth-century diffusion east of Mudburra Stage 5.

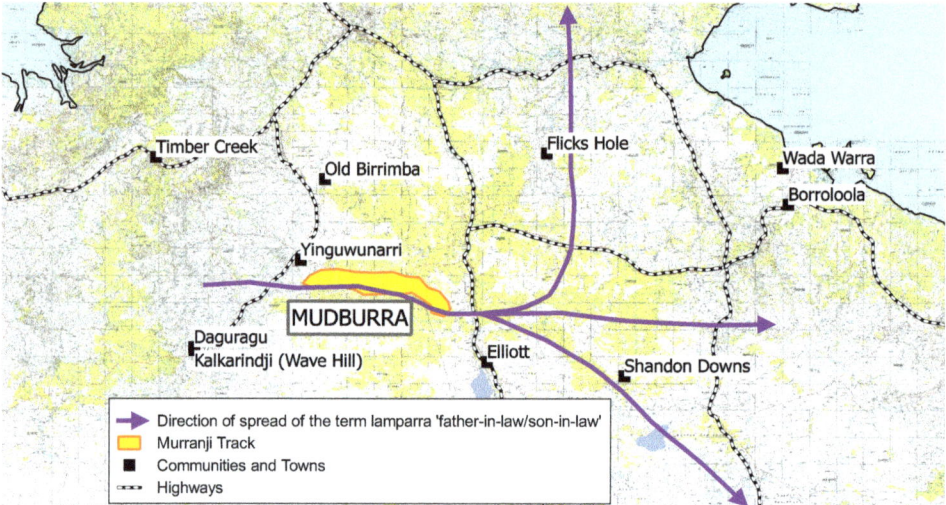

Figure 13.2 Recent eastward diffusion in the eastern Northern Territory.
Source: Patrick McConvell.

The form in the western Ngumpin language Walmajarri is *lamparr,* without the final vowel –*a*. The addition of a final –*a* on consonant-final nouns is a regular sound change only in the most easterly of the eastern Ngumpin languages, Mudburra (McConvell 2009: 800, 803). The fact that further diffusion (Stage 5) to the east (and also back into Gurindji (Meakins et al. 2013: 200), and partially Jaru) is of the form with a final –*a* indicates that the root passed through Mudburra on its journey. Mudburra was the language of the Murranji Track (Stock Route), heading east from Top Springs, along which drovers and their Aboriginal 'stockboys' took cattle in large numbers beginning in the 1880s

(Lewis 2007). This is, no doubt, the channel of communication through which the Mudburra term was carried to Aboriginal people being linked up by the new cattle industry.

## Stage 4: The Diffusion from Southern Nyulnyulan in the Western Kimberley into and through the Ngumpin Languages of the Kimberley and Victoria River District of the Northern Territory

Less well known is the earlier history of diffusion of the term. The immediate source of the term *lamparr* 'wife's father' in the Central Kimberleys Pama-Nyungan (Ngumpin-Yapa) languages is the adjacent Nyulnyulan (non-Pama-Nyungan) language family of the west Kimberley, where the term is *ramparr*. The meaning of the term is also 'wife's father' in some Nyulnyulan languages and, particularly significantly, in the easternmost language Nyikina which is in contact with the western Ngumpin-Yapa languages (for earlier meanings in northern Nyulnyulan and Worrorran, see below).

As with the addition of *–a* in Mudburra, here again the change in sound—from initial *r* to initial *l*—is highly significant for tracing the history of diffusion of the term. The regular sound change of lateralisation (r>rl, a retroflex l, written l at the beginning of the word) has been identified as one of the common innovations which serve to define the Ngumpin-Yapa subgroup, to which both Mudburra and Walmajarri and several languages in-between belong (McConvell and Laughren 2004). This change r>rl must then have happened roughly at the proto-Ngumpin-Yapa language stage, around the time before Ngumpin-Yapa differentiated into several distinct languages. Using archaeology to calibrate (McConvell and Smith 2003) this era can roughly be dated at around 3,000–2,500 years ago, in the first millennium BC. The word *ramparr* must have entered the proto-Ngumpin-Yapa language before this sound change stopped operating, approximately at the same period, so the change applied, yielding *lamparr*.

## Stages 3 and 2: From Worrorran to Western Nyulnyulan and Eastern Nyulnyulan

Going one stage further back into the history of *ramparr*, we find its source to the northwest of the Nyulnyulan languages, in the Worrorran language family in the north Kimberley. The diffusion from Worrorran into Nyulnyulan labelled Stage 3, does not involve any change in form of *ramparr* but does involve a major change in its *meaning*, from 'wife's mother' and 'wife's mother's brother' in some languages to 'wife's father'. This is discussed further below, in the section 'The Wider System Context of Change in Meaning of *Ramparr/Lamparr*'.⁶

The absence of a change in the sounds of the word makes it difficult to attempt any chronology for this diffusion in the same way as for Stages 4 and 5. Clearly, though, if Stage 4 is placed at 2,500–3,000 years ago, Stages 2–3 must have preceded that period.

In Stage 2, which preceded Stage 3, *ramparr* diffused west from western Worrorran to western Nyulnyulan. The form remained the same and its meaning remained focally the same, at least in Bardi, but the gender was restricted to the brother of wife's mother, not WM herself (Aklif 1999: 119). The shift to WF began to occur in Stage 3 as the term travelled southwest to western Nyulnyulan, and more completely as it went into eastern Nyulnyulan and reached the eastern boundary of the family, in Nyikina.

## Stages 1 and 0: Meaning Change between Eastern and Western Worrorran: Barrier > Avoidance Relations > Mother-in-Law

There is an evolution of meaning from an original more concrete meaning of 'screen' or 'barrier' to 'avoidance kin relations' in general in northeastern Worrorran. This is labelled Stage 0. Further west in Worrorran, closer to the zone of contact with Nyulnyulan, the meaning of *ramparr* becomes focused on the mother-in-law (wife's mother) specifically—Stage 1, and that is the meaning that is diffused farther west in Stage 2.

Avoidance of 'taboo' in-laws is symbolised and actualised by barriers, which include physical screening with some object or the hands over the face (referred to by Coate and Elkin (1974) as the '*rambar* wall'), as well as metaphorical usage, referring to the ban on looking at or talking to the avoidance in-law. Vocabularies of the eastern Worrorran languages in particular emphasise the physical barrier sense, including 'windbreak'; so, based on the general principle that concrete senses are earlier, the direction of change is likely to have been from 'barrier' of a general physical kind to the class of relations who are avoided. In Ngarinyin (Coate and Elkin 1974 (Volume 2): 448–9), a verb derived from this root has both senses, illustrating the stage of transitional polysemy:

---

6    Stokes and McGregor (2003: 66) reconstruct a term *\*rambarr* to proto-Nyulnyulan in the meaning 'male parent-in-law: HF'—but with a query beside WF. See below for further discussion. Bowern (2007) has proposed that the development of the western branch was driven by a movement of people from the coast to the Fitzroy River Valley in the inland, with changes of meaning of lexical items accompanying this.

*rambara bijorengka*
1. they screened themselves;
2. they became in-laws.

The second main sense of *ramparr* in northeastern Worrorran (Drysdale and Forrest Rivers) is the avoidance relationship itself and the relations who fall under this rule. Hernandez (1941: 227) states that 'it would be more correct to say that *rambar* is not a kinship term but only a taboo existing between certain relations'. *Ramparr* are primarily 'a man and his actual, future or possible mother-in-law, and her brothers'.

This origin gives some insight into the self-reciprocal nature of the suite of *ramparr/lamparr* terms in many of the languages, referring not just to the member who 'promises' a wife, but also the one who receives her, the son-in-law. In relation to the western Worrorran language, Worrorra, the dictionary (Clendon 2000: 56; Clendon 2014: 462) gives the following definition:

> **rambarr mana** (noun): the set of avoidance-category kin who are related to you as wife-givers; includes *kurruma, kurrumaanya, ngalinjaaya, jalinjaanya, walbaya* and *walbayinya* … DaHu-WiMo pairs are *walbaya* and *kurrumaanya* to each other respectively, and constitute the strongest form of the *rambarr* relationship category.

This definition encompassing a broad category of 'wife-givers' links back to the common feature of avoidance involved.

This notion of 'wife-giver' thus refers to a group of people. What becomes important as we look into the transformations of meaning of this term in its etymological history is *who exactly* has the main say over the bestowal of a woman in marriage. This is taken up in the next section, 'Mother-in-Law > Father-in-Law'.

In the whole region we have been speaking of, the most severe avoidance is practised with a man's mother-in-law. Of course, we should not assume that this was the case going back several thousand years, and elsewhere in Australia other affines such as siblings-in-law are equally or more subject to verbal and physical avoidance. There appear to have been two types of meaning of the term in Worrorran: a general term for avoidance relations, and primarily 'wife's mother'. These two meanings are distributed across the different languages in such a way that we cannot be sure if they represent two chronological stages. Unlike in the other later phases of the movement of this word which have been discussed, in this earliest phase, we do not know that these two meanings are linked by diffusion of the word: the term may be inherited from the proto-language with a complex meaning change in the western branch.[7]

As *ramparr* diffused into western Nyulnyulan (e.g. Nyulnyul and Bardi (Elkin 1932; Aklif 1999)) its meaning shifted from a group of people focused on wife's mother, to wife's mother's brother. In both cases the meaning included the reciprocal; man's sister's son's wife in Worrorran and sister's daughter's husband in western Nyulnyulan. In Worrorran, e.g. Ngarinyin (Elkin 1932: 317–9), it is reported that rights of bestowal in marriage rest with the wife's mother's brother, and the same is reported for Nyulnyul (Elkin 1928; Scheffler 1978: 179, 190). It seems likely that the actual wielder of the power of making the contractual decision with another group became the focus of the meaning in the new situation.

## Mother-in-Law > Father-in-Law

The shift of meaning of *ramparr* from the group and the mother of the bride to the actual bestower, the wife's mother's brother, in the above diffusion from Worrorran to Nyulnyulan, sets the stage for the more dramatic change of meaning to father-in-law, as greater power over bestowal was transferred to him in eastern Nyulnyulan, e.g. Nyikina and Yawuru.[8] It is probable that the eastern Nyulnyulan speakers expanded into the hinterland (Bowern 2007), and that the migrants were 'moving in on' groups of people already resident in the area.[9]

The most problematic part of the history of *ramparr* is the change of the term from mother-in-law and her brother in western Worrorran and eastern Nyulnyulan to father-in-law in eastern Nyulnyulan. While these meanings both refer to parents-in-law, the change from WM(B) to WF is unexpected. Significantly, a change from mother-in-law to father-in-law apparently represents a contravention of a principle of semantic change set forth by Evans and Wilkins (2000) that I further developed in relation to kinship terms

---

7   Worrorran is analysed as having three branches in McGregor and Rumsey (2009). As we have moved two steps backwards in time from stage 3,000–2,500 BP, it is possible that the origin of *ramparr* in the North Kimberley was 4,000–5,000 years ago or more. This could be compatible with it being in the proto-language as Worrorran has significant internal divergence, but at that time *ramparr* may not have had the connotations of affinal avoidance, and subsequently 'mother-in-law' until some time later, perhaps 4,000–3,500 years ago. These dates need confirmation, but there is a good chance of the linguistic stratigraphy and chronology improving in the coming years, and archaeology, rock-art and plant and human genetics being brought into the picture, to provide calibration (McConvell, Saunders and Spronck 2014; Rangan et al. 2015).

8   The 'wife's father' meaning is also recorded for Jawi which is centred around the islands of Northern Dampier Peninsula, and is a western Nyulnulan language closely related to Bardi.

9   This is the type of language expansion which I have called 'downstream spread' (McConvell 2010). This name can be confusing: in this case as the spread in this case is geographically upstream, so I suggest 'encroaching spread' as a better term. I have suggested that this form of expansion is related to particular types of kinship system, specifically Omaha skewing, which supports linguistic exogamy (McConvell 2012).

(McConvell 2013: 194–6). According to this hypothesis, a change from sense A to sense B passes through a stage of polysemy in which the term has both senses A and B, and that such a transitional polysemy should be evident in historical sequences, or contemporaneously elsewhere, and specifically in the region where the change is being proposed. While many changes in kinship term meanings do show these properties of transitional polysemy in Australia, there is doubt about where mother-in-law and father-in-law share the same term anywhere, even in any of the Kimberley languages under discussion.

However, in this case, as we have noted, in its early history the term *ramparr* has a wider meaning of an avoidance relationship which encompasses several types of in-laws who may also be designated by more specific kinship terms. This may be, then, a case of a term in which there is what we might call hypopolysemy—that is, one of two meanings involved is broader and includes the other, narrower, meaning. This is common as a synchronic pattern in fauna terms in Australia and also explains semantic shift from generic term for a life form to a species term or vice versa (McConvell 1997b).[10]

There is at least one more fairly clear case in Australian kinship where a similar change has happened. In Cape York Peninsula (Paman subgroup of Pama-Nyungan) the term *mukVr* means 'mother's brother',[11] but in the rest of the country where cognates of the term are found (mainly in Pama-Nyungan) it means 'father's sister and/or wife's mother'. Where the primary meanings of the terms seem to be consanguineal, they also both have affinal senses deriving from the rules of marriage: the equation FZ=WM is quite widely distributed in Australia, especially where there is or was a Kariera system and cross-cousin marriage. The common ground between MB (WF) and FZ (WM) could be their key role as decision-makers about their daughter's marriage.[12]

Ian Keen (2013b) has helped us on the road to solving this puzzle by pointing out the similarities and differences between the Yolngu and some eastern Cape York Peninsula groups, on the one hand, and the northern Kimberley groups, on the other. Both of these areas have a central area of asymmetrical matrilateral marriage and kinship, bracketed by areas of symmetrical (Kariera) marriage and kinship to the east and west. In the case of CYP-Yolngu, it can be proposed

---

10  The term 'hyperpolysemy' has already been claimed by Evans (1992) to mean something quite different.
11  In a number of Paman languages reflexes of *mukr* have the meaning 'mother's elder brother', with a distinct term for mother's younger brother. In eastern CYP what McConnel (1950) called 'junior marriage' is practised: a man should marry his MyBD, and a woman her MeBS. A *mukr* is therefore a woman's husband's father in this area.
12  The same is true of the change in the meaning of the term *ramparr* between WM in Worrorran and western Nyulnyulan and WF in western Nyulnyulan, where the direction of change is the opposite to that between Cape York Peninsula and the Yolngu of Arnhem Land. Note however that the term *mukr* is a proto-Pama-Nyungan term which is inherited, and the change of meaning occurs as part of this inheritance. *Ramparr/lamparr*, on the other hand, is a *Wanderwort*, a widespread loanword.

that the initial state was that found in the east, of a symmetrical Kariera system which gave way to an asymmetrical matrilateral system in the west. In the original system, the term *mukr* was 'mother's brother/wife's father', but in the changed western Yolngu system it became 'father's sister/wife's mother'.

In the case of the north Kimberley, the central area is dominated by an asymmetrical (matrilateral) system of marriage and kinship, with however more Kariera symmetrical features in the northeast Worrorran languages which, according to Keen (2013b: 144) may be a forerunner of the Ngarinyin (asymmetrical) type. In the central south among the Ngarinyin, 'the marriage system ... comes to resemble the Yolngu asymmetry of exchange between groups' (ibid.: 142). The asymmetrical system gives way to a symmetrical system in the south-west (ibid.: 141), that is, in the Nyulnyulan area.[13]

There is, then, a contrast between marriage arrangements in the Worrorran and Nyulnyulan groups which could affect how the affinal terms are interpreted. In western Worrorran *ramparr* designates 'wife-givers', associated with unilateral alliance of wife-giver clans and wife-taker clans, whereas the Nyulnyulan marriage system is primarily bilateral. This reciprocality of *ramparr/lamparr* referring to both parent-in-law and child-in-law is a feature of the Nyulnyulan, Ngumpin-Yapa and other groups to the east.

The broadest definitions of *ramparr* encompass a wide grouping of 'wife-givers', but even where this is narrowed down to specific affines there is ambiguity of the 'wife-giver', between the wife's mother who is subject to the most stringent avoidance and the wife's father who 'actually promises' the bride. This ambiguity provides the seeds of the split in *ramparr* between the meaning WM(B) and the meaning WF which becomes dominant in the eastward diffusion.

Elkin, writing of the Ungarinyin (Ngarinyin, a southern Worrorran group), addresses this ambiguity, although the term *ramparr* is not mentioned:

> The possible wife must be the daughter of a woman who is a 'proper' mother-in-law, that is, she must belong to a horde [clan] which is *wolmingi*, wife's mother, to him [the husband] while the actual promising of the bride is done by her [the mother-in-law's] husband, ego's *waiingi*. (Elkin 1932: 314)

---

13  Just southwest of the Nyulnyulan languages is another unrelated language, Karajarri of the Pama-Nyungan Marrngu subgroup, whose system has been interpreted as asymmetrical, and whose name ('Karadjeri') was chosen by Elkin to designate asymmetrical systems (Scheffler 1978: 208). Scheffler (ibid.: 219) disputes that this is a true 'asymmetrical' system.

## The Wider System Context of the Change in Meaning of *Ramparr/Lamparr*

The kinship systems of the Nyulnyulan family such as Nyulnyul have been described by Elkin as Aranda, because of a preference for MMBDD marriage and prohibition on cross-cousin marriage. Scheffler (1978: 173), however, believes that they are fundamentally Kariera. Certainly some features of the Nyulnyulan systems do look more 'Aranda'—having four distinct grandparent terms for instance, illustrated in Table 13.1 for Nyulnyul.

Table 13.1 Grandparental loanwords from Marrngu in Nyulnyulan.

| Kintype | Elkin | McGregor | Additional senses | Reconstruction | Related K – Karajarri; M – Mangarla |
|---|---|---|---|---|---|
| FF | kalod | kalud, kalurd | mSC | *kalurtu | kalurtu (K) |
| FM | kabil | kabirl | fSC | *kaparli | kaparli |
| MM | kamad | kamard | | *kamirta | kami |
| MF | djam | tyam | | *tyamu(ny) | jampartu, jamu (M) |

The presence of four distinct grandparent terms is often considered a criterion of the Aranda system (but see Keen 2013a for a reformulation of the typology of Australian Aboriginal kinship systems). However, the approach being taken in this paper is diachronic, so it is necessary to consider not just the patterns of the current configurations of kinship terms, but where they came from and when. A glance at the table is enough to raise suspicions that all these Nyulnyulan terms are loanwords from the nearby Marrngu subgroup of Pama-Nyungan.

The Nyulnyulan kinship terminologies constitute one of the rare exceptions to the principle enunciated at the beginning of this chapter, that kinship terms are mainly inherited, not borrowed. The grandparental terms in Table 13.1, and a number of other kinship terms, appear to have been borrowed wholesale from a neighbouring group in the Marrngu subgroup of Pama-Nyungan, which is only very distantly related linguo-genetically. The motivation for this mass borrowing clearly goes far beyond filling gaps in a system.[14]

---

14   While there are a few inherited Nyulnyulan kinship terms still present, the historical change here is close to a complete takeover of both kinship systems and terminology from Marrngu. A full investigation of this cannot be carried out in this chapter. For instance, the changes in the second vowel of the MM and FM terms are regular and constitute evidence that the loans belongs to an older stratum, which may be datable. The hypothesised movement of Nyulnyulan speakers south and east would not necessarily provide the answer, since while the eastern Nyulnyulan languages may be more affected, the whole family has this kind of profile, pointing perhaps to this transformation being early in the history of the family. There are a fair number of other apparent early loans from Pama-Nyungan into Nyulnyulan, apart from in the kinship domain, perhaps indicating early contact with Pama-Nyungan. The dominance of Pama-Nyungan in the kinship system may have resulted from heavy intermarriage between the two groups with concomitant adoption of the Pama-Nyungan terminology. Nyulnyulan languages also adopted the section system from the west and this may have been the occasion of some assimilation of the kinship terminology to that of the Pama-Nyungan. However, section systems have diffused in many parts of Australia without causing this kind of unusual radical diffusion of kinship terminology.

Beyond this there is a kinship loanword in the affinal (in-law) category, from the opposite direction, Worrorran in the northeast, which we have introduced: *ramparr*.

Table 13.2 shows the changes of meaning of *ramparr/lamparr* and several other affinal terms of the +1 and −1 generations as they diffuse from Worrorran, to Nyulnyulan, then to Ngumpin (Pama-Nyungan).

The term *ramparr* begins in northeast Worrorran with a focus on WM although it has a wider 'barrier' and 'avoidance relations' meaning too. In western Worrorran the term also has a wide 'avoidance' meaning but retains a focus on mother-in-law, WM. As the term moves into Nyulnyulan the situation becomes more complex. There is a shift of focal meaning from mother-in-law to her brother, WMB. In Jawi in the northern islands, however, the meaning changes to father-in-law (WF).

In Nyulnyulan other affinal terms come into play affecting the distribution of senses. *Rangin/rangan*, which appears to be an inherited Nyulnyulan term, rather than a loan, covers a range of affinal +1 and −1 kin types in western Nyulnyulan, but not including WM, or WMB. These latter are respectively *yalirr* in Nyulnyul and a cognate in Bardi, and probably inherited; and *ramparr*.

While WF is *ramparr* in Jawi and *rangin* can have WF as one of its meanings in other western Nyulnyulan languages, there is another expression which is also WF in all the Nyulnyulan languages. Its full form is *kaka tyami-nyarri*, literally 'mother's brother (*kaka*) associated with mother's father (*tyami/u*)', but commonly only the second word is used. There is commonly an equation (polysemy) between the MB term and WF especially in groups with Kariera systems, where the mother's brother gives his (classificatory) daughter to her cross-cousin in marriage. The father-in-law relationship is usually not an actual genealogical close relationship, so to distinguish clearly the affinal relationship from the consanguineal uncle the qualification is added. This is a little puzzling as the consanguineal 'mother's brother' also has a consanguineal relationship to 'mother's father', literally speaking. However the term for MF is often equated with cross-cousin by alternate generation equivalence and then the cross-cousin has a connotation of marriage—spouse or sibling-in-law. This will be explored further in the second case in this chapter about the history of the term *\*tyam(p) V*. So in fact this expression connotes 'MB associated with marriage partners', i.e. father-in-law.

Table 13.2 Diffusion and change of meaning of affinal terms from north to west to southeast Kimberley.

|  | E. WORR. | W. WORR. | W. NYNY. | E. NYNY. | W. NGUMPIN |
|---|---|---|---|---|---|
| ramparr | WM | Wife-givers (Worrorra) | WMB | WMB | >lamparr |
|  |  |  | WF (Jawi) | WF (Nyikina) |  |
|  | ZSW | WM (Ngarinyin, Unggumi) | ZDH | fDH |  |
| lamparr | X | X | X | HF | WF |
|  |  |  |  |  | HF |
|  |  |  |  |  | SW |
|  |  |  |  |  | DH |
| rangin/ rangan | X | X | SW | HM (Nyikina) | **MARRNGU** |
|  |  |  | WF | BSW (Yawuru) | Karajarri: WM |
|  |  |  | DH |  |  |
|  |  |  | HM |  |  |
|  |  |  | HF |  |  |
| yalirr |  |  | WM |  |  |
|  |  |  | fDH |  |  |
| (kaka) tyaminyirr/ tyaminyarri |  |  | WF | WF |  |
|  |  |  |  | fDH |  |
| tyikal |  |  |  | WM |  |
|  |  |  |  | fDH |  |

As we move to the next step in the changes in the system, in eastern Nyulnyulan, we see that, for *ramparr,* the focal meaning of WMB is retained in Yawuru near Broome, but shifts decisively to WF in Nyikina upstream in the Fitzroy basin, with overlap persisting with *kaka tyaminyarri*. The term *rangin* loses several of the senses it had in the western branch, including WF, and is narrowed to HM in Yawuru and its near reciprocal BSW in Nyikina. A new term comes in for WM, *tyikal*, an innovation in this branch of Nyulnyulan, perhaps a loan from Karajarri *tyikari* WM. The direction could be the opposite, like *rangin* 'WM' which was clearly loaned from Nyulnyulan into Karajarri, although WM is not among the senses recorded for Nyulnyulan.

The term *lamparru* is borrowed back as a doublet from a later form in Walmajarri *lamparr* into western Nyulnyulan in the meaning 'husband's father' with an added *–u* due to it passing through Bunuba, which has this addition as a regular sound change (see note 16). This is just one of the senses of the term in Walmajarri. Perhaps the meaning was narrowed in the process of borrowing, because the other main meaning 'wife's father' is already covered by *kaka tyaminyarri,* and *ramparr* in Nyikina (cf. McConvell and Ponsonnet 2013 on semantic narrowing in borrowing).

Nyikina was in contact with languages in the south-central Kimberley such as the most western language in the Ngumpin-Yapa subgroup, Walmajarri. Nyikina had probably been moving southeast for some time (Bowern 2007[15]) with increasing interaction with Ngumpin languages, particularly Walmajarri, that was also moving north from the desert.

When the term *ramparr* was borrowed into Walmajarri the sound change of lateralisation *r>rl was still in progress (McConvell and Laughren 2004), yielding *lamparr* (the initial l is retroflex but not written rl in this position). This provides a time frame for this stage in the diffusion of this word, using calibration from a word for 'muller' (top grindstone; McConvell and Smith 2003). While this chronological aspect is not fully argued here, I estimate this loan of the word into Ngumpin with the lateralisation sound change as having occurred 2,500–3,000 years ago (but see note 15).

This phase of diffusion was significant not just because of a sound change but also because of a meaning change. The form *ramparr* had either the meaning 'wife's father' or 'husband's father' and reciprocals in some previous stages of diffusion but only partially, with overlaps from other terms and only in some languages. In the diffusion of *lamparr* to Ngumpin, though, all the meanings of WF and HF and reciprocals are combined. This coherent package diffused to the east over the next period, culminating in a rapid and virulent diffusion in the twentieth century, combined with and strengthened by a suite of cultural practices.

At bottom, the innovation was the recognition of the father-in-law as the prime wife-giver rather than the mother-in-law or her brother. This was supported by a new kind of interaction between the wife-giver and wife-taker which was no longer based on avoidance but on its opposite, a joking relationship. The unity of this relationship was enhanced by the fact that the two parties to the

---

15  Bowern (2007: 51) writes 'we might draw the tentative conclusion that speakers of eastern Nyulnyulan languages spread into an area already inhabited by speakers of Pama-Nyungan languages, and when they moved inland they encountered a new environment and borrowed the names for many new species from the previous inhabitants … Although more evidence is required, the distribution of loans is suggestive of a migration East and inland from the Dampier peninsula, rather than the reverse'. Bowern describes the degree of divergence within Nyulnyulan as not great, perhaps about that of Romance—the group of languages descended from Latin, such as French, Italian, etc. One might conjecture based on this parallelism that the age of the family is around 2,000 years, and the spread of eastern Nyulnyulan inland between 2,000 and 1,000 years ago. This raises a problem for the chronology outlined for the lateralisation of r in proto-Ngumpin-Yapa based on archaeolinguistic stratigraphy of 3,000–2,500 BP, if the term *ramparr* was borrowed from eastern Nyulnyulan when it contacted western Ngumpin, as *lamparr*. However an alternative could be that lateralisation continued to operate for a longer time until, say, between 2,000 and 1,000 years ago.

marriage arrangement and the joking arrangement, the father-in-law and child-in-law, were called by the same term, unlike for instance in languages where the father-in-law is called 'uncle' (MB) and the junior reciprocal is the nephew/niece term ZC.

The hypothesis that wide diffusion of affinal terms is caused by avoidance has been noted (Tuite and Schulze 1998). In one view of this, words for avoided in-laws are replaced by euphemisms or foreign words. It is possible that use of a term for 'barrier' instead of 'mother-in-law' began as euphemistic in Worrorran but we have no reliable way of knowing this. The diffusion of this word to Nyulnyulan may also have been motivated by wanting to avoid a more blunt local word for 'mother-in-law' and her brothers and husband, but this is again speculative. In fact there are other words for 'mother-in-law' in Nyulnyulan (e.g. *yalirr*) which are not subject to taboo avoidance as far as is recorded.

Rather, it is the key role of such vocabulary in interaction of groups over marriage that may be what leads to the spread of words across languages and ethnic groups. Those involved in making those connections (including the avoided affines) need to be called by terms which are recognised across a broad sociocultural space extending across interethnic alliances. In this case, it may be that both avoidance and the prime role of an in-law in arranging marriage are in play. Level of strictness of avoidance practices around the wife's mother may be in a mutual feedback relationship with the ability to direct operations in marital arrangements. Scheffler (1978: 216) stresses the need among the Karajarri for mother-in-law's husband WF, called *kaka* 'MB', to be drawn into the central role in negotiations over marriage and as intermediary in gift exchange due to avoidance of the prospective WM.

The term we have followed, *ramparr,* began as an avoidance term; indeed, in the first phases of diffusion it can mean 'avoidance' itself, together with metaphorical expressions of avoidance. But as the focus of the term changes from mother-in-law to father-in-law, the avoidance character of the relationship also lessens. Nevertheless, the term continues to diffuse along with a different kind of marked relationship of control of marriage. So it is not avoidance itself which causes such widespread diffusion of terms, but the interaction of groups in contracting marriages and remoulding their social arrangements for this.

The origin of the term *ramparr* is clearly bound up with avoidance between in-laws, primarily a man and his wife's mother and her brother. By the latter part of the journey of this *Wanderwort*, it still relates to in-laws, but centrally the wife's father, not her mother, and the relationship is no longer one of avoidance. In the east the *lamparra* father-in-law/son-in-law relationship is a joking relationship including hurling of obscenities and horseplay, in some ways the very opposite of the restraint and avoidance behaviour between the *ramparr* in-laws in the north and west.

There is significantly, though, an area between these two extremes where the change of meaning to 'wife's father' has occurred but the avoidance behaviour also applies in some measure to this father-in-law/son-in-law bond. In Ngarinyin, a Worrorran language, the wife's father (*wayingi*) is spoken to in 'polite' *rambad* language known as *akaruru* (Coate and Elkin 1974).[16] In some Nyulnyulan languages also, Jawi and Nyikina, the focal meaning of *ramparr* has shifted to WF, prefiguring the later shift in Ngumpin-Yapa.

## Tyam(p)V(ny) 'Mother's Father' > 'Cross-Cousin' > 'Spouse/Sibling-in-Law'

Unlike the first example *ramparr>lamparr*, which is confined to a central and western area in northern Australia, the second term *tyam(p)V(ny)* to be considered here is very widespread in Pama-Nyungan, particularly in the western part of the family (McConvell 2013). Unlike *ramparr>lamparr,* which was diffused from non-Pama-Nyungan to Pama-Nyungan, *tyam(p)V(ny)* was diffused from Pama-Nyungan into non-Pama-Nyungan in the Kimberley and across into part of the Northern Territory. The primary meaning of *tyam(p)V(ny)* is 'mother's father' in most of its attestations, but it has secondary meanings of 'cross-cousin', ' spouse' and/or 'sibling-in-law' in many languages, with sometimes a shift to one or other of these secondary meanings, with loss of the original meaning.[17] There is no great surprise in these polysemies and semantic shifts. MF is often equated with cross-cousin (MBC, FZC) in many Australian Aboriginal kinship systems, following the principle of alternate generation equivalence between kin separated by a generation. Since cross-cousin is the preferred spouse in the Kariera system, which was found in many regions of Australia, this extension and semantic shift is to be expected, and occurs with other terms too.

---

16   *Rampat* is an alternative form of *ramparr* in Ngarinyin. Father-in-law is also called *lamparru* in Ngarinyin. This is a doublet caused by the diffusion of the term northeast from Pama-Nyungan (probably Walmajarri) after lateralisation in Ngumpin-Yapa. The *–u* is added because the word was borrowed via Bunuba, which adds *–u* to consonant final roots. *Lamparru* is also found in Nyikina (eastern Nyulnyulan) and is included in Table 13.2, and its specific meaning is discussed there. *Wayingi* is glossed 'wife's father' and 'wife's brother' in the dictionary: this is because of Omaha skewing in Ngarinyin and other Worrorran languages whereby the same kinterm can be used for relatives related by patrifiliation (McConvell 2012).

17   There are also apparent cognates in Paman and Mayi languages of North Queensland which have less easily explicable meanings like 'father's sister' and 'wife's father', in the +1 generation instead of the 0 or +/– 2 generations. For discussion of how this might have occurred, see McConvell (2013). The term for 'mother's father' in this region and more generally in the east of the continent is descended from a different root *ngatyV.

The spread of the term *tyam(p)V(ny)* by inheritance in the very large Pama-Nyungan family is not the central concern here, and is covered in McConvell (2013). Instead the focus is on the diffusion of the term into non-Pama-Nyungan. The aim here is to show that, in accordance with the hypothesis proposed, its affinal function is the main trigger for the diffusion.

This is not immediately obvious, since the primary gloss given for reflexes of the term in a number of non-Pama-Nyungan languages is 'mother's father', apparently consanguineal. It is also possible that the second type of explanation of kinterm diffusion discussed in the introduction—'filling a gap' in a kinship system when it needs to be augmented—could be an alternative hypothesis. This alternative is discussed and rejected below.[18]

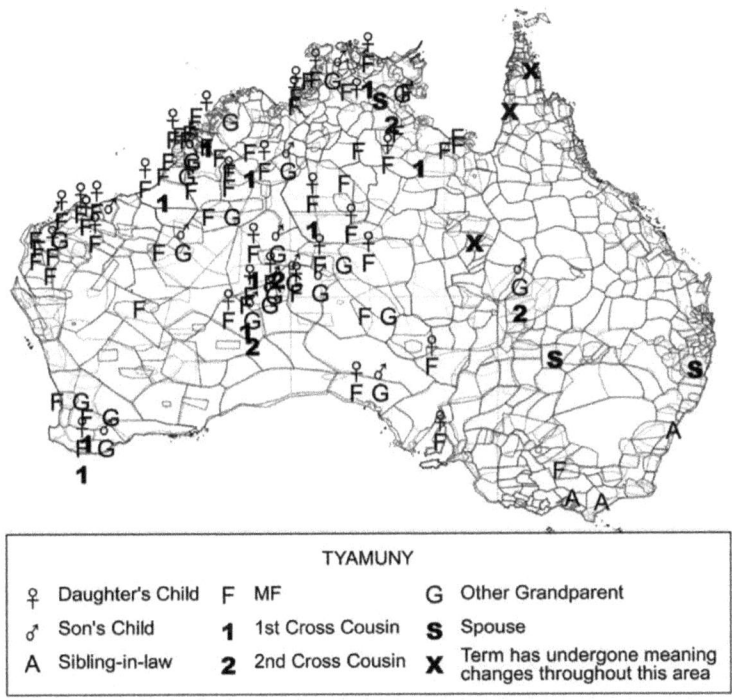

Figure 13.3 *TyamVny* in non-Pama-Nyungan.
Source: Patrick McConvell.

---

18   In an earlier attempt to describe and account for the distribution of the MF root *tyam(p)V(ny)* (McConvell 1997b) I remained agnostic about the origin of this root—whether it diffused into early Pama-Nyungan from non-Pama-Nyungan, or is a proto-Pama-Nyungan root which diffused into some non-Pama-Nyungan families. Additional data and analysis have come down heavily in favour of the second alternative (McConvell 2013). These include adding the term *tyampi* 'spouse, brother-in-law' found in southeastern Australia to this etymon. Harold Koch (personal communication) has disputed that the southeastern in-law term is connected because it has a different meaning from MF, and has the consonant cluster mp. As argued above the sequence of change MF>cross-cousin>spouse/sibling-in-law is highly credible. A number of the northern forms also have mp or p instead of m, and *mp could be plausibly reconstructed in this root. The sound change *mp>m is attested in various places in Pama-Nyungan (e.g. Yolngu Matha and the Sydney language), but aligning such a change to the set of languages where m is found in this root is not yet feasible.

The spread of the term in non-Pama-Nyungan languages is diffusional. It is found across at least eight adjacent language families in the Kimberley and part of the Northern Territory, going a considerable distance into Arnhem Land. The most northeastern occurrence in the diffusion through non-Pama-Nyungan found is in Burarra *tyamunya* ('MF and reciprocal') and the related *tyam-ttya* ('cross-cousin MBS/MBD; potential spouse') (Glasgow 1985: 95; Hiatt 1967; thanks to Gretel MacDonald for pointing this out to me). This may not be directly adjacent to other languages with related forms, but is not far away. The fact that there is another term for MF in Burarra, *mamam* (Glasgow 1985: 120) without the cross-cousin/spouse sense, may add to evidence that the *tyam* form is a loanword based on *affinal* relationship.

The northern non-Pama-Nyungan families through which *tyamV* forms are distributed are not thought to be related except in some very distant way to an unclear and very ancient entity usually named 'proto-Australian'. It is virtually impossible to suggest that the form is a joint inheritance from such a proto-language, because the forms are generally very similar, most of them being *tyamVny*. Much greater divergence would be expected from a joint inheritance from such a deep proto-language. If the ancestor were proto-Australian or something akin to it, then one would expect such forms to be much more widespread (and probably scattered). The restriction to a particular geographical zone and concentration in it, along what is plausibly a line of spread, point strongly to a diffusion in a relatively recent period.

The *tyamVny+* forms with the third consonant *ny* are the most frequent in non-Pama-Nyungan, stretching from western (and proto-) Nyulnyulan *tyamuny*, through *tyaminyi* (Bunuban—where augmentation of final consonants by *–i* is regular—and encroaching into Worrorran), *thamany* (Kija, southern Jarragan), to western Mirndi in the Barkly Tablelands (*tyaminy* with suffix *–tya* or *–tyila*). To the north *tyaminy* is also found in the meaning 'spouse' in Ngalakgan, *tyamunya* in Burarra 'MF/cross-cousin/spouse' (see above) and *thamuny* in the Daly languages as MF.

*tyapV+* forms are found in the central part of the distribution. The bare form *tyapi* is found in Walmajarri (together with forms with mp in an affinal meaning, e.g. *tyampi-rlangu* 'husband and wife' (Richards and Hudson 1990: 130)), and *tyapiy* in Bunuba, alternative to *tyaminyi;* and a form with the common Pama-Nyungan kinship suffix *–tyi* (McConvell 2008) in northern Jarragan (Gajirrabeng) and Jaru. The Miriwoong form *tyawityi,* produced by regular intervocalic lenition p>w, with the Miriwoong suffix *–ng* was borrowed into Jaminjungan (western Mirndi, non-Pama-Nyungan) and the eastern Ngumpin languages (Pama-Nyungan).

All the non-Pama-Nyungan forms are most likely to have spread from the west to the east, and there are forms in the area of Pama-Nyungan in contact with non-Pama-Nyungan which could have provided the initial loan source. *Tyamu* roots without *ny* are in Nyangumarta (Marrngu subgroup) and other Pama-Nyungan languages to the south and west in the meaning MF, and with a later broader 'grandfather' meaning throughout the Western Desert. *Tyami* roots without the *ny* and with the common Pama-Nyungan kinship suffix *-rti* are in Ngumpin-Yapa (as an alternative to *tyapi* in Walmajarri and in Warlpiri and Ngardi). These two could have provided the *tyamu* and *tyami* roots respectively as loans to Nyulnyulan, and Bunuban, and the *tyapi* variant to northern Jarragan in the east. In southern Jarragan (Kija) the form is *thamany*, meaning MF and cross-cousin, with *a* as second vowel, as also in *tyamaya*, MF and cross-cousin, found in Worrorra and a couple of other western Worrorran languages, but not in southern or eastern Worrorran.

One issue with the picture as presented so far is the preponderance of the *ny* final consonant in this root in the non-Pama-Nyungan languages but its absence in the putative loan sources, in recent times at least, in northwestern Pama-Nyungan. It is possible that the earlier forms in northwestern Pama-Nyungan had this final consonant and it was lost after it was borrowed into non-Pama-Nyungan; or alternatively it was a suffix added to the forms when they entered non-Pama-Nyungan. These questions have not yet been resolved.

\**tyaminy+tyV* MF is perhaps reconstructable for proto-eastern Mirndi (not in Harvey's 2008 list of proto-forms), but could also be an early loan into the family especially if the *-tya/-tyila* suffixes reflect the Pama-Nyungan \**tyV* (McConvell 2008). The western Mirndi form *tyawitying* is clearly a later loan from Jarragan, probably replacing an earlier *tyaminytya* or *tyaminytyi*. The ethnonym Jaminyjung, the major language group of western Mirndi, is part of an ethnonymic paradigm zone (McConvell 2006) with ethnonyms made up of a typical word of the language of the group concerned with a Jarragan suffix *-pung/-wung*. It is possibly to be analysed as containing the word *tyaminytyV*, the putative earlier pan-Mirndi form of the MF kinship term before it was replaced by *tyawityi*, thus meaning 'the people who say *tyaminytyV*'.[19] This is a speculation however, and it begs the interesting question in the context of this chapter, of why this kinship term should be salient enough to form an ethnonym.

This is related to the question of why this kinship term diffused so widely in this zone. Other examples of wide diffusion of kinship terms seem to involve terms with affinal senses and be motivated by changes in marriage systems (McConvell

---

19  Ethnonyms can contain archaic words pointing to early forms where the meanings have been replaced by other forms in everyday language; see McConvell (2006) for Australian examples.

2010). In this case for instance, as touched on in the section 'Mother-in-Law > Father-in-Law' above, in Nyulnyulan the term for father-in-law *tyamunyarri (Stokes and McGregor 2003: 62) can be analysed as 'associated with MF' and in Nyulnyul WF can be termed 'MB associated with MF' (Scheffler 1978: 183). *tyamunyarri is a contraction of such a phrase. Now as we have seen, MF is often extended to mean 'cross-cousin' and 'spouse' in a cross-cousin marriage regime, especially where there is a preference for matrilateral marriage of a man to his MBD, and this extension is common in the non-Pama-Nyungan languages of the Kimberley and east in the Northern Territory.

As for Ngalakgan in the northeast of the diffusion, the affinal meaning of *tyam(p)Vny has taken centre stage: tyaminy means 'spouse', not MF. It is a Gunwinyguan language but the root *tyami MF or similar is not reconstructed for this family (Harvey 2003), so it could well be a loanword in Ngalakgan. The form looks related to those far to the west, but the meaning is different. It can be linked via the polysemy chain of MF=cross-cousin>cross-cousin=spouse, as has been discussed previously, but the current marriage rule is not with a first cross-cousin but a MMBDC (an Aranda system) and the term tyaminy designates this kin type as well as spouse. This indicates the fact that once an affinal extension is consolidated, presumably in this case based on cross-cousin marriage, the actual consanguineal/classificatory kin designation can change to the new preferred marriageable kin type. Parallel arguments could be mounted for Burarra to the northwest of Ngalakgan, as already discussed.

This long-distance diffusion of the term for MF is indeed striking and calls for an explanation. While several indications exist of the role of affinal polysemies and connotations in this phenomenon, the explanation is not yet satisfying. Before concluding with a proposal about what might have driven it, let us examine an alternative.

As noted earlier, there are examples of diffusion of grandparent terms which are not directly related to marriage rules and patterns, but seem to be filling in gaps in the kinship terminology system to bring it into line with neighbours. This can be achieved by borrowing the missing terms from those neighbours, as occurred with the Ngumpin-Yapa subgroup as it 'upgraded' from a Kariera or Karadjeri terminology to an Aranda terminology.

Could the same type of situation have been the motivation for a large number of non-Pama-Nyungan language speakers to adopt the new *Wanderwort* term tyamVny in a chain diffusion? According to the kind of alternative hypothesis being assessed here, this would imply that the pre-existing kinship system among these groups lacked a distinctive term for MF and impelled them to borrow one. The most plausible type of system which would lack a distinctive term for MF in Australia is one in which there is a term which is polysemous between MF and FMB (and also perhaps FM)—a Kariera system.

Kariera systems are not known in recent history in the region with the exception of the Daly River.[20] However, there is evidence from the multiple borrowing of FF terms from different directions that the Ngumpin-Yapa subgroup had, at a previous stage, a Kariera system or a 'Karadjeri' system which did not distinguish between terms for paternal and maternal parallel grandparents FF and MM(B). A similar lacuna might have existed in those non-Pama-Nyungan languages to the north with no distinction between the cross grandparental terms FM(B) and MF, necessitating the importation of a new MF term. In this case, what occurred was not borrowing from all sides of different terms, but a surge of diffusion of a single MF term (*tyamVny*) from the south.

It is possible that this revolutionary change was driven by the spread of subsections and the second cousin (MMBDD) marriage associated with it, from its origin area around Katherine and the Lower Daly and Victoria Rivers (McConvell 1985, 1997a). However, part of the spread of the *tyamVny* terms was into areas which had no subsections, and either had sections (Nyulnyulan) or no such social categories (part of Worrorran). Most of the languages to which the terms spread in the 'Top End' and Arnhem Land of the Northern Territory have had subsections, at least in recent times, but it is likely that the more peripheral of them received subsections as late as the twentieth century. In some of these peripheral groups the classical type of marriage associated with subsections (MMBDD) did not fully take hold but typically Kariera marriage preferences (cross-cousins) were maintained, possibly in some areas earlier associated with a prior section system, for which we have little direct evidence. A link between the spread of these *tyamVny* terms and spread of sections or subsections is a possibility but must await further research (see also the previous discussion of the Burarra case where there seems to be evidence against a 'filling a gap' solution or subsection-driven diffusion of *tyam(Vny)*).

In any case, whether the diffusion was influenced by social categories or not, we cannot totally divorce the notion of 'filling a gap' to produce a more complex kinship terminology from the effect of the introduction of a new marriage system. In the case of the *tyamVny* diffusion the key move may have been the introduction of *tyamVny* with its cross-cousin/spouse sense to signal cross-cousin marriage, but part of the package would have been adding the other meaning of the word 'MF' to the terminology. Further research would be needed to establish whether this was 'filling a gap' in the grandparental terms

---

20  In the Daly languages the MF term in question was imported but in most cases extended to FMB to adapt to a Kariera system rather than to change it.

or replacing an earlier term for MF. Most likely the eastern diffusion of *tyamVny* in the north was related to the ascendancy of the matrilateral cross-cousin as marriage partner, referred to by a term for mother's father. As we have seen in Nyulnyulan in the previous section, the role of the mother's brother, son of MF, is pivotal in controlling marriage, and drives the key position of *tyamVny* in the affinal terminology.

## Conclusions

This brings us back to the insights of Keen in the book and papers mentioned above (and others). How do kinship terminologies and marriage systems relate to each other? Or are both related to more basic demographic factors? These are some of the fundamental questions of classical anthropology. Here the notion of 'coevolution' is critically evaluated and applied to the relationship of kinship and marriage in some actual cases as they develop through time. Diachronic analysis of the change in kinship systems in Aboriginal Australia over the short term is sometimes possible from historical documents, but over the longer term the work of comparative historical linguistics yields more evidence about the past state of kinship systems, and sometimes of at least ideal marriage patterns, for instance in the polysemies of affinal and consanguineal terms in a range of languages. The actual marriage patterns over time are not always readily available or analysed, but some genealogical databases do exist from which we can derive such diachronic data. Data on correlated change (or absence of correlation in change) can be much more valuable for theory in this area than correlations of synchronic snapshots.

With this perspective in mind, this chapter has been able to look at two diffusions of kin terms in northern Australia. The first, concerning *ramparr/lamparr*, was all about marriage and affinity from the start, bound up with concepts of in-law avoidance. As it moved through three language families first west, then east, it changed meaning from mother-in-law to father-in-law, and the dominant behaviours shifted from avoidance to joking. The borrowing of the term was intimately linked to its relationship to changes in authority structures in marriage, which put more control in the hands of the father-in-law. Such affinal terms and their implications are the elements which are most likely to be loanwords, as these are key concepts in a field of law and custom which crosses ethnic and language boundaries. In this interethnic field changes occur in marriage practice and these can spread concepts and terminology often quite rapidly.

The second example discussed is a set of terms descended from *tyam(p)i 'mother's father', reflexes of which are found across a wide area of Australia. This is a Pama-Nyungan proto-form and most of its occurrences are inheritances in Pama-Nyungan languages. However in northern Australia many related forms are found in a quite large area of several non-Pama-Nyungan languages adjacent to the northern boundary of Pama-Nyungan. These are clearly part of a pulse of loanwords from northern Pama-Nyungan. Unlike the in-law terms of the previous example, this looks at first blush like a consanguineal term, contradicting the hypothesis proposed that long-distance kinship loanwords are affinal. However there are very common equations (between MF and cross-cousin, and cross-cousin and spouse/sibling-in-law) which lead to this MF term having important secondary meanings. In this way, this example too supports the hypothesis that the motivations for kinship *Wanderwörter* to wander are primarily because of their role in marriage over wide areas of multiple ethnicity and language.

## References

Aklif, G. 1999. *Ardiyooloon Bardi Ngaanka: One Arm Point Bardi Dictionary*. Halls Creek: Kimberley Language Resource Centre.

Bowern, C. 2007. On eels, dolphins, and echidnas: Nyulnyulan prehistory through the reconstruction of flora and fauna. In A. Nussbaum (ed.), *Verba Docenti: Studies in Historical and Indo-European Linguistics Presented to J.H. Jasanoff by Students, Colleagues, and Friends*, pp. 39–52. Ann Arbor: Beech Stave Press.

Clackson, J. 2007. *Indo-European Linguistics: An Introduction*. Cambridge: Cambridge University Press.

Clendon, M. 2000. *A Provisional Worrorra Dictionary*. Halls Creek: Kimberley Language Resource Centre.

Clendon, M. 2014. *Worrorra: A Language of the North Kimberley Coast*. Adelaide: University of Adelaide Press.

Coate, H. and A.P. Elkin. 1974. *Ngarinjin–English Dictionary*. Sydney: Oceania Linguistic Monographs.

Denham, W. 2013. Beyond Fictions of Closure in Australian Aboriginal Kinship. *Mathematical Anthropology and Cultural Theory* 5(1): 1–90.

Dixon, R.M.W. and A. Aikhenvald. 1999. Introduction. In R. Dixon and A. Aikhenvald (eds), *The Amazonian Languages*, pp. 1–22. Cambridge: Cambridge University Press.

Dousset, L., R. Hendery, C. Bowern, H. Koch and P. McConvell. 2010. Developing a database for Australian Indigenous kinship terminology: the AustKin project. *Australian Aboriginal Studies* 1: 43–56.

Dziebel, G. 2012. Indo-European and North Caucasian: Linguistic Typology, Kinship Terms and Autosomal Genetics. kinshipstudies.org/2012/07/07/indo-european-and-north-caucasian-linguistic-typology-kinship-terms-and-autosomal-genetics/.

Elkin, A.P. 1928. Nyulnyul Social Organisation. MS.

Elkin, A.P. 1932. Social organization in the Kimberley Division, north-western Australia. *Oceania* 2(3): 296–333.

Evans, N. 1992. Multiple semiotic systems, hyperpolysemy, and the reconstruction of semantic change in Australian languages. In G. Kellermann and M. Morrissey (eds), *Diachrony Within Synchrony: Language, History and Cognition*, pp. 475–508. Bern: Peter Lang Publishing.

Evans, N. and D. Wilkins. 2000. In the mind's ear: the semantic extensions of perception verbs in Australian languages. *Language* 76(3): 546–92.

Glasgow, D. and K. Glasgow. 1985. *Burarra to English Bilingual Dictionary*. Darwin: SIL/AAB.

Harvey, M. 2003. An initial reconstruction of Proto-Gunwinyguan phonology. In N. Evans (ed.), *The Non-Pama-Nyungan Languages of Northern Australia: Comparative Studies of the Continent's Most Linguistically Complex Region*, pp. 205–68. Canberra: Pacific Linguistics.

Harvey, M. 2008. *Proto Mirndi: A Discontinuous Language Family in Northern Australia*. Canberra: Pacific Linguistics.

Haynie, H., C. Bowern, P. Epps, J. Hill and P. McConvell. 2014. Wanderwörter in languages of the Americas and Australia. *Ampersand* 1(1): 1–16.

Heath, J. 1981. *Basic Materials in Mara: Grammar, Tests, Dictionary*. Canberra: Pacific Linguistics.

Hernandez, T. 1941. Social organization of the Drysdale River tribes. *Oceania* 11(3): 211–32.

Hiatt, L. 1967. Unpublished field notes, held at AIATSIS.

Keen, I. 1982. How some Murngin men marry ten wives: the marital implications of matrilateral cross-cousin structures. *Man* 17(4): 620–42.

Keen, I. 2004. *Aboriginal Economy and Society: Australia at the Threshold of Colonisation.* South Melbourne: Oxford University Press.

Keen, I. 2013a. The legacy of Radcliffe-Brown's typology of Australian Aboriginal kinship systems. *Structure and Dynamics* 6(1): 1–31.

Keen, I. 2013b. The evolution of the Yolngu and Ngarinyin kinship terminologies: models of cumulative transformations. In P. McConvell, I. Keen and R. Hendery (eds), *Kinship Systems: Change and Reconstruction,* pp. 132–62. Salt Lake City: University of Utah Press.

Lewis, D. 2007. *The Murranji Track: Ghost Road of the Drovers.* Rockhampton: Central Queensland University Press.

Marck, J., P. Hage, K. Bostoen, and J.K. Muzenga. 2011. Kin terms in the East Bantu proto languages: initial findings. In B. Milicic and D. Jones (eds), *Kinship, Language, and Prehistory: Per Hage and the Renaissance in Kinship Studies.* Salt Lake City: University of Utah Press.

Matasović, R. 2012. Areal typology of proto-Indo-European: the case for Caucasian connections. *Transactions of the Philological Society* 110(2): 283–310.

Matras, Y. 2009. *Language Contact.* Cambridge: Cambridge University Press.

McConnel, U. 1950. Junior Marriage Systems: Comparative Survey. *Oceania* 21(2): 107–45.

McConvell, P. 1985. The origin of subsections in northern Australia. *Oceania.* 56: 1–33.

McConvell, P. 1997a. Long lost relations: Pama-Nyungan and northern kinship. In P. McConvell and N. Evans (eds), *Archaeology and Linguistics: Aboriginal Australia in Global Perspective,* pp. 207–36. Melbourne: Oxford University Press.

McConvell, P. 1997b. The semantic shift between 'fish' and 'meat' and the prehistory of Pama-Nyungan. In M. Walsh and D. Tryon (eds), *Boundary Rider: Essays in Honour of G.N. O'Grady,* pp. 303–25. Canberra: Pacific Linguistics.

McConvell, P. 2006. Shibbolethnonyms, ex-exonyms and eco-ethnonyms in Aboriginal Australia: the pragmatics of onymization and archaism. *Onoma* 41: 185–214.

McConvell, P. 2008. Grandaddy morphs: the importance of suffixes in reconstructing Pama-Nyungan kinship. In B. Evans and C. Bowern (eds), *Morphology and Language History: In Honour of Harold Koch*, pp. 313–28. Amsterdam: Benjamins.

McConvell, P. 2009. Loanwords in Gurindji, a Pama-Nyungan language of Australia. In M. Haspelmath and U. Tadmor (eds), *Loanwords in the World's Languages: A Comparative Handbook,* pp. 790–822. Berlin: de Gruyter.

McConvell, P. 2010. The archaeolinguistics of migration. In J. Lucassen, L. Lucassen and P. Manning (eds), *Migration History In World History*: *Multidisciplinary Approaches,* pp.155–88. Leiden: Brill.

McConvell, P. 2013 Proto-Pama-Nyungan kinship and the AustKin project: reconstructing terms for proto-mother's father and their transformations. In P. McConvell, I. Keen and R. Hendery (eds), *Kinship Systems: Change and Reconstruction,* pp. 192–216. Salt Lake City: University of Utah Press.

McConvell, P. 2012. Omaha skewing in Australia: overlays, dynamism, and change. In T.R. Trautmann and P.M. Whiteley (eds), *Crow-Omaha: New Light on a Classic Problem of Kinship Analysis*, pp. 243–60. Tucson: University of Arizona Press.

McConvell, P. and I. Keen. 2011. The transition from Kariera to an asymmetrical system: Cape York Peninsula to north-east Arnhem Land. In D. Jones and B. Milicic (eds), *Kinship, Language, and Prehistory: Per Hage and the Renaissance in Kinship Studies,* pp. 99–132. Salt Lake City: University of Utah Press.

McConvell, P. and M. Laughren. 2004. The Ngumpin-Yapa subgroup. In C. Bowern and H. Koch (eds), *Australian Languages: Classification and the Comparative Method*, pp. 151–77. Amsterdam: John Benjamins Publishing Company.

McConvell, P. and M. Ponsonnet. 2013. Results and prospects in the study of semantic change: a review of *From Polysemy to Semantic Change* (2008). *Journal of Language Contact* 6 (2013):180–96.

McConvell, P., T. Saunders and S. Spronck. 2014. Linguistic prehistory of the Australian boab. In L. Gawne and J. Vaughn (eds), *Selected Papers from the 44th Conference of the Australian Linguistic Society, 2013*. Melbourne: University of Melbourne.

McConvell, P. and M. Smith. 2003. Millers and mullers: the archaeolinguistic stratigraphy of seed-grinding in Central Australia. In H. Andersen (ed.), *Language Contacts in Prehistory: Studies in Stratigraphy,* pp. 177–200. Amsterdam: Benjamins.

McGregor, W. and A. Rumsey. 2009. *Worrorran Revisited: The Case for Genetic Relations among Languages of the Northern Kimberley Region Western Australia.* Canberra: Pacific Linguistics.

Meakins, F., P. McConvell, E. Charola, N. McNair, H. McNair, L. Campbell and G. Wightman (compilers). 2013. *Gurindji to English Dictionary.* Batchelor: Batchelor Press.

Rangan, H., K. Bell, D. Baum, R. Fowler, P. McConvell, T. Saunders, S. Spronck, C. Kull and D. Murphy. 2015. New genetic and linguistic analyses show ancient human influence on baobab evolution and distribution in Australia. *PLOS ONE* 10(4): e0119758. doi:10.1371/journal.pone.0119758.

Richards, E. and J. Hudson. 1990. *Walmajarri-English Dictionary.* Darwin: Summer Institute of Linguistics.

Scheffler, H. 1978. *Australian Kin Classification.* Cambridge: Cambridge University Press.

Stokes, B. and W. McGregor. 2003. Classification and sub-classification of the Nyulnyulan Languages. In N. Evans (ed.), *The Non-Pama-Nyungan Languages of Northern Australia: Comparative Studies of the Continent's Most Linguistically Complex Region,* pp. 29–74. Canberra: Pacific Linguistics.

Tuite, K. and W. Schulze. 1998. A case of taboo-motivated lexical replacement in the indigenous languages of the Caucasus. *Anthropological Linguistics* 40(3): 363–83.

# Afterword

Ad Borsboom
Radboud University

It goes without saying that I was happy to write this epilogue for this well-deserved festschrift. I was quite honoured by Peter Toner's request. After all, Ian Keen is not only one of the most prominent scholars of my generation in Australian anthropology—and I am sure for generations to come—but also has many other qualities, not the least being pleasant, humorous, and modest.

Also, his and Libby's hospitality is well known by his colleagues, students and friends. Staying at their lovely home is both intellectually stimulating and, as we like to say in Dutch, 'cosy'—the feeling of being comfortable at one's place because of the company present, a nice glass of wine at the fireplace and good conversation about almost any topic.

This was the easy part. Now that I have to provide my professional opinion I struggle to find the right words. Why so? Well, to prepare properly for this task I had to read the whole manuscript, and there exactly lies the problem. 'What value', I worried after I finished reading, 'could I possibly add to what already has been written?'

The book demonstrates how much of an inspiration Ian has been and still is for a great number of scholars. All 13 chapters reflect Ian's many intellectual skills and interests: Aboriginal religion, economics, linguistics, kinship, urban studies and, not least, applied anthropology as a number of pioneering land claims reveal. Inspired by Keen's work, my fellow authors present a great variety of rich ethnographic material—'thick description' as Clifford Geertz calls it—based on solid fieldwork coupled with stimulating theoretical discussions.

As Peter Toner explains in his introductory chapter, the present volume represents the full span of Ian's distinguished career and the diversity of his scholarly interests. There are chapters on language and meaning; the incommensurability of knowledge systems; problematic intercultural communication in court, based on fundamental insights contained in *Being Black*; and changes and succession in land claims with Ian's early emphasis on 'stories'. Others discuss the conceptual dynamism and dialogical features in Aboriginal religion, based on Ian's analyses of these phenomena; the relationship between Aboriginal people (women in particular) and Christianity; the central place of material culture in the engagement between Yolngu and Europeans at Milingimbi; the utility of Ian's framework developed in his *Aboriginal Economy and Society*; and the diffusion of kin terminology.

So again: what remains to be said without repeating what's already there? I decided to leave all that I had read behind me, and instead went for a jog for an hour or so. Physical exercise often helps one to make room in one's head for new thoughts and ideas. Fortunately, this time it had the desired effect. Towards the end of my favourite track, when the body starts protesting and begs for rest, one thought emerged. First it was vague, but slowly it became more persistent and clear. The bottom line, my brain kept suggesting, is this: Ian has the capacity to let you see phenomena from a different angle and, as a result, changes your perception of them.

Before moving on to more serious scientific business, let me first give you a somewhat simplified example of what I mean by this. When, many years ago, Ian was staying with me and my family in Nijmegen, we drove past the central station, and like almost any railway station, this one was full of graffiti. I didn't particularly like any of the drawings, but above all failed to understand why people would go through so much trouble to tag walls which in many cases were difficult to access. After a brief silence, Ian said something along the lines of 'Well, perhaps you should see them as modern-day variations on rock paintings'. This had never crossed my mind, but I have not been able to look at graffiti tags in any other way since then.

A rather trivial example, but perhaps illustrative of the point I made earlier about my assessment of Ian's scientific influence. His thorough re-examination of key concepts—property, rights, tribes, clans, cultural continuity, and knowledge and secrecy—has challenged orthodox positions on Aboriginal anthropology. It has changed current perceptions by looking at these phenomena from a different angle. As Craig Elliott writes in his contribution (Chapter 5), 'Keen has thoroughly critiqued the inadequacy of simplistic, taxonomical anthropological constructs such as "clan", "phratry", "dialect" and "tribe" to explain Arnhem Land local organisation'.

## Afterword

My emphasis on these aspects of Ian's work has much to do with my own experience in Arnhem Land. I did my initial fieldwork between 1972 and 1974 with Djinang people in the township of Maningrida. There was little reason to question the idea of bounded identities or of groups that could be named, counted and related to more or less fixed stretches of land. None of this was questioned by the literature I was taught as a student, nor by the administration or the hospital at the settlement. We all accepted and worked with fixed categories such as Djinang, Burarra, Gunabidji, and so on. And, not least, the Aboriginal people themselves used the same social and linguistic categories when identifying themselves. In retrospect, I suppose that they had become used to a colonial administrative system in which groups and group membership were fixed and bounded, and they accepted that this was the way the social world of the settlement was organised.

But soon things changed fast, very fast. There were winds of change from Canberra—Whitlam, under pressure from Aboriginal activists, replaced assimilation with self-determination. This led to an exodus from townships like Maningrida to newly established homeland centres on the clan estates of the various Aboriginal groups. When I returned in 1980 to continue my fieldwork, I spent a lot of time in the bush, commuting between the various Djinang outstations and the townships of Maningrida and Ramingining.

But where were the Djinang, that well-defined group of people from Maningrida that acted as a corporate entity? Some lived at Gattji, the most western outpost of Yolngu territory, with close ties to people from the Blyth River; others stayed in Raminigining or outstations nearby re-establishing relationships with people further east. Several appeared to have close links with families from Millingimbi in the northwest or with Rembarngga to the south.

Slowly I realised that the ever-so-solid name 'Djinang' had become ambiguous, contested and blurred. What's more, this conclusion not only applied to a language name but equally to other labels of social organisation. What is a *bapurru* (clan), *mala* (group), *mata* (language/dialect), lineage or phratry? What constitutes a group?

Long story short, I left the field in 1981 much more confused than in 1974 when I was convinced that I had proper understanding of the Djinang social world: a language group consisting of three well-defined Dhuwa-moiety clans and four Yirritja-moiety clans, each clan having bounded territories between Gattji lagoon, Ramingining and Nangalala.

Adding to my confusion were Dr Thomson's field notes, which I was able to study before I left for the Netherlands. Nicolas Peterson had encouraged me to visit Museum Victoria in Melbourne and read through Thomson's Arnhem Land field notes. Thomson had done extensive fieldwork in the Gattji-Ramingining area before World War II. But to my surprise he hardly mentioned the name 'Djinang' in his notes. Why? Well, he concluded that language (*mata*) did not constitute a very important basis for distinction between close groups. Instead, allegiances based on the same *rangga* (sacred objects) criss-crossed through language groups.

The main concept in Thomson's notes to understand these allegiances was *bapurru*. However, this Indigenous concept was not the solution to a better understanding of Indigenous group formations, but quite the opposite. It confused Donald Thomson more than it clarified. When asked what *bapurru* meant, one of his Aboriginal friends simply said that it could be a clan, an aggregation of clans or any group (*mala*). And he continued his explanation with a puzzling 'might be wangar time something he bin go and puttim something rangga and blackfella there, another place rangga and blackfella there'.

In short, Donald Thomson remained confused on the subject, as many entries in his field notes demonstrate. He constantly asked himself the same questions I struggled with some 50 years later: 'What is it that constitutes a *bapurru*, what factors join together or separate groups?', 'What makes this group one *bapurru*?' Elsewhere he concludes in some despair: 'I have spent days, even weeks, off and on, in investigations that lead, largely, nowhere'. In a strange way that last remark gave me some comfort when I left Australia for the second time.

Neither the heavy teaching load, nor the managerial functions at the University of Nijmegen in the years that followed made the problem go away. Here I was, stuck with a number of traditional conceptual tools that appeared inadequate to understand Indigenous social reality—tools that made it impossible to mould and fit the Indigenous perceptions in the anthropological (mainly structural-functionalist) theoretical framework of the day.

I expressed my own doubts in a chapter published in a Dutch festschrift; its title translated as 'The Djinang, Do They Exist?' My point of departure there was that although I knew *what* Djinang was, namely a language of the Pama-Nyungan family, I no longer knew with any certainty *who* the Djinang were. In that essay I was, in retrospect, on the right track when—also inspired by Thomson's field notes—I spoke of totemic affiliations, using phrases like 'loosely structured', 'flexible alliance' and 'totemic affiliations' as the main factors underlying various social formations. But I did not go far enough. The concept of the clan as a constant, fixed social reality remained, ultimately, unchallenged.

And then along came Ian's *Knowledge and Secrecy in an Aboriginal Religion*.

Family circumstances had prevented me from carrying out another year of fieldwork, so to get a better understanding of Indigenous social reality I relied mainly on the work of my distinguished colleagues. Ian Keen's work served that goal very well. As I write this, scanning through the pages of *Knowledge and Secrecy* I see again the many underlinings, exclamation marks and comments I made in the margins. In this landmark study Keen demonstrated that Yolngu social organisation is not a unified homogenous system; that sociality is based on open and flexible networks defined by discourse and action rather than clearly defined groups like 'clans'; and that rights over country are often contested instead of agreed upon.

Especially, Keen's original argument that Aboriginal society has long been depicted as a primitive form of English society makes sense to me. He convincingly argues that imposing these western concepts (e.g. clan, property, phratry) on Aboriginal societies is a far cry from Indigenous discourses. Although these concepts are rather fixed and well-defined in Western thought, quite the opposite—namely fluidity, ambiguity and flexibility—are at the heart of Indigenous perceptions about these phenomena. It was this approach that helped me to look at my own findings from a different perspective. As with all new ideas, they seem self-evident for the next generation, but were nowhere to be seen in the first two decades of my anthropological career.

Ian Keen did not work in an anthropological void of course. Flexibility and fluidity of group composition have been important subjects in the works of Nicolas Peterson and Peter Sutton. Howard Morphy's analysis of concepts like secrecy and *likan* ('elbow', 'fork', i.e. in an abstract sense the connection with a *wangarr* ancestor) also inspired Ian's landmark book *Knowledge and Secrecy*.

But as Peter Toner points out in his introduction and in Chapter 8, Ian developed a wide-ranging and systematic critique of the vestiges of anthropological orthodoxy and developed a coherent analysis of his own ethnographic data, extending important insights for work across the region—'Keen encourages us to shed the orthodoxies of established analytical frameworks … in favour of greater attention to heterogeneity and contingency'.

Well, having said what I wanted to say brings me to the end of this contribution. I am just looking for some famous last words to wrap up my appreciation for Ian's career. This time I do not have to go out running to find them because the words just come spontaneously:

'Good on ya, mate!'

# Appendix: Ian Keen's Publications, 1977–2015

## Books

- 1988. *Being Black: Aboriginal Cultures of 'Settled' Australia*. Canberra: Aboriginal Studies Press. (Reprinted 1992.)
- 1994. *Knowledge and Secrecy in an Aboriginal Religion: Yolngu of North-East Arnhem Land*. Oxford: Clarendon Press. (Reprinted in paperback, OUP Melbourne, 1997.)
- 2001. (ed. with Takako Yamada). *Identity and Gender in Hunting and Gathering Societies*. Osaka: National Museum of Ethnology.
- 2004. *Aboriginal Economy and Society: Australia at the Threshold of Colonisation*. Melbourne: Oxford University Press.
- 2010. *Indigenous Participation in Australian Economies: Historical and Anthropological Perspectives*. Canberra: ANU E Press.
- 2012. (ed. with N. Fijn, C. Lloyd and M. Pickering). *Indigenous Participation in Australian Economies II: Historical Engagements and Current Enterprises*. Canberra: ANU E Press.
- 2013. (ed. with P. McConvell and R. Hendery). *Kinship Systems: Change and Reconstruction*. Salt Lake City: University of Utah Press.

## Articles in Refereed Professional Journals

- 1977. Ambiguity in Yolngu religious language. *Canberra Anthropology* 1: 33–50.

- 1982. How some Murngin men marry ten wives: the marital implications of matrilateral cross-cousin structures. *Man* (N.S.) 17(4): 620–42.
- 1985. Definitions of kin. *Journal of Anthropological Research* 41: 62–90.
- 1985. On the notion of Aboriginality: a discussion (comment on S. Thiele's critique of the work of Tatz, with C. Anderson, Tim Rowse, J.R. von Sturmer, K. Maddock, C. Tatz, and S. Thiele.) *Mankind* 15(1): 43–5.
- 1985. Aboriginal tenure and use of the foreshore and seas: an anthropological evaluation of the Northern Territory legislation providing for the closure of seas adjacent to Aboriginal land. *Anthropological Forum* 5(3): 421–39.
- 1986. New perspectives on Yolngu affinity: a review article [review of W. Shapiro's *Miwuyt Marriage*]. *Oceania* 56(3): 218–30.
- 1987. Stanner on Aboriginal religion. *Canberra Anthropology* 9(2): 26–50.
- 1987. Gidjingali and Yolngu polygyny: a reply to Martin and Reddy. *Oceania* 58(1): 63–4.
- 1988. Report on the Fifth International Conference on Hunting and Gathering Societies, Darwin 1988. *Oceania* 59(2): 159–61.
- 1992. Undermining credibility: advocacy and objectivity in the Coronation Hill debate. *Anthropology Today* 8(2): 6–9.
- 1993. Aborigines and miners at Coronation Hill: the containing force of traditionalism. *Human Organization* 52(4): 344–55.
- 1994. Ubiquitous ubiety of dubious uniformity [review article of T. Swain's *A Place for Strangers*]. *The Australian Journal of Anthropology* 4(2): 96–110.
- 1995. Metaphor and the metalanguage: 'groups' in northeast Arnhem Land. *American Ethnologist* 22(3): 502–27.
- 1999. Cultural continuity and native title claims. *Land, Rights, Laws: Issues of Native Title; Issues Paper no. 28*. (Native Title Research Unit, Australian Institute of Aboriginal and Torres Strait Islander Studies.)
- 2000. The anthropologist as geologist: Howitt in colonial Gippsland. *The Australian Journal of Anthropology* 11(1): 78–97.
- 2000. A bundle of sticks: the debate over Yolngu clans. *Journal of the Royal Anthropological Institute* 6: 419–36.
- 2001. Introduction (Aboriginality in southeastern Australia). *Aboriginal History* 25: 173–5.
- 2002. Seven Aboriginal marriage systems and their correlates. *Anthropological Forum* 12(2): 145–57.
- 2003. Aboriginal economy and society at the threshold of colonisation: a comparative study. *Before Farming* 2003/3(2): 1–29.
- 2006. Constraints on the development of enduring inequalities in Late Holocene Australia. *Current Anthropology* 47(1): 7–38.

- 2006. Ancestors, magic and exchange in Yolngu doctrines: extensions of the person in time and space. *Journal of the Royal Anthropological Institute* 12(3): 515–30.
- 2013. The language of possession: three case studies. *Language in Society* 42(2): 187–214.
- 2013. The legacy of Radcliffe-Brown's typology of Australian Aboriginal kinship systems. *Structure and Dynamics* 6(1): 1–31.
- 2014. Does cognitive science need anthropology? *Topics in Cognitive Science* 6(1): 150–1.
- 2015. Language in the constitution of kinship. *Anthropological Linguistics* 56(1): 1–53.
- 2015. The language of morality. *The Australian Journal of Anthropology* (Special Issue on Language, Emotions and Morality, edited by Bree Blakeman and Ian Keen).

# Chapters in Edited Books

- 1977. Yolngu sand-sculptures in context. In P.J. Ucko (ed.), *Form in Indigenous Art*, pp. 165–83. Canberra: Australian Institute of Aboriginal Studies.
- 1980. The Alligator Rivers Aborigines—retrospect and prospect. In R. Jones (ed.), *Northern Australia: Options and Implications*, pp. 171–86. Canberra: Research School of Pacific Studies, The Australian National University.
- 1984. A question of interpretation: the definition of 'traditional Aboriginal owners' in the Aboriginal Land Rights (Northern Territory) Act 1976. In L.R. Hiatt (ed.), *Aboriginal Landowners: Contemporary Issues in the Determination of Traditional Aboriginal Ownership*, pp. 24–45. Sydney: Oceania Monographs.
- 1988. Aborigines and Islanders in Australian society. In J. Western and J. Najman (eds), *Sociology of Australia: A Reader*, pp. 182–212. Melbourne: MacMillan.
- 1988. Twenty-five years of Aboriginal kinship studies. In R.M. Berndt and R. Tonkinson (eds), *Social Anthropology and Australian Aboriginal Studies: A Contemporary Overview*, pp. 77–124. Canberra: Aboriginal Studies Press.
- 1988. Introduction. In I. Keen (ed.), *Being Black: Aboriginal Cultural Continuity in 'Settled' Australia*, pp. 1–26. Canberra: Aboriginal Studies Press.
- 1988. Aboriginal religions. In I. Gilmore (ed.), *Many Faiths, One Nation: A Guide to the Major Faiths and Denominations in Australia*, pp. 61–73. Sydney: Collins.

- 1988. Yolngu religious property. In T. Ingold, D. Riches and J. Woodburn (eds), *Property, Power and Ideology in Hunting and Gathering Societies*, pp. 272–91. London: Berg. (Paperback edition 1991.)
- 1989. Aboriginal governance. In J. Altman and F. Merlan (eds), *Emergent Inequalities Among Contemporary Australian Aborigines*, pp. 17–42. Sydney: Oceania Monographs.
- 1990. Ecology and species attributes in Yolngu religious symbolism. In R. Willis (ed.), *Signifying Animals*, pp. 85–102. London and Boston: Unwin Hyman.
- 1991. Images of reproduction in the Yolngu Madayin ceremony. In W. Shapiro (ed.), *Essays on the Generation and Maintenance of the Person in Honour of John Barnes*, pp. 192–207. (*Mankind* Special Issue).
- 1993. Aborigines and Islanders in Australian society. In J. Western and J. Najman (eds), *Sociology of Australia: A Reader* (extended and revised for the second edition). Melbourne: MacMillan.
- 1995. Some Yolngu songs about birds. In M. Duwell and R.M.W. Dixon (eds), *Little Eva at Moonlight Creek*, pp. 125–9. Brisbane: Queensland University Press.
- 1997. A continent of foragers: Aboriginal Australia as a 'regional system'. In P. McConvell and N. Evans (eds), *Understanding Ancient Australia: Perspectives from Archaeology and Linguistics*, pp. 261–73. Melbourne: Oxford University Press.
- 1997. The western desert vs the rest: rethinking the contrast. In F. Merlan, J. Morton and A. Rumsey (eds), *Scholar and Sceptic: Australian Aboriginal Studies in Honour of L.R. Hiatt*, pp. 65–93. Canberra: Aboriginal Studies Press.
- 1999. Applied anthropology, the academy, and the scientific attitude. In S. Toussaint and J. Taylor (eds), *Applied Anthropology in Australasia*, pp. 27–59. Nedlands: University of Western Australia Press.
- 1999. Norman Tindale and me: anthropology, genealogy, authenticity. In J.D. Finlayson, B. Rigsby and H.J. Bek (eds), *Connections in Native Title: Genealogies, Kinship and Groups*, pp. 13–57. Canberra: Centre for Aboriginal Economic Policy Research.
- 2000. The Djang'kawu story in art and performance. In S. Kleinert and M. Neale (eds), *The Oxford Companion to Aboriginal Art and Culture*, pp. 136–41. Melbourne: Oxford University Press.
- 2001. Introduction. In I. Keen and T. Yamada (eds), *Identity and Gender in Hunting and Gathering Societies*, pp. 5–11. Osaka: National Museum of Ethnology.

- 2001. Theories of cultural continuity and native title applications in Australia. In I. Keen and T. Yamada (eds), *Identity and Gender in Hunting and Gathering Societies*, pp. 163–79. Osaka: National Museum of Ethnology.
- 2001. The old airforce road: history, myth, and mining in northeast Arnhem Land. In A. Rumsey and J. Weiner (eds), *Mining and Indigenous Lifeworlds in Australia and Papua New Guinea*, pp. 157–81. Adelaide: Crawford House. (Republished by Wantage: Sean Kingston Publishing, 2004.)
- 2001. Agency, history and tradition in the construction of 'classical' music: the debate over 'authentic performance'. In C. Pinney and N. Thomas (eds), *Beyond Aesthetics: Art and the Technologies of Enchantment*, pp. 31–56. Oxford: Berg.
- 2003. Dreams, agency, and traditional authority in northeast Arnhem Land. In R.I. Lohmann (ed.), *Dream Travelers: Sleep Experiences and Culture in the Western Pacific*, pp. 127–49. New York: Palgrave Macmillan.
- 2004. Stanner on Aboriginal religion. In M. Charlesworth, F. Dussart and H. Morphy (eds), *Aboriginal Religions in Australia*, pp. 61–78. Aldershot: Ashgate.
- 2008. 'Religion', 'magic', 'sign' and 'symbol' in Stanner's approach to Aboriginal religions. In J. Beckett and M. Hinkson (eds), *An Appreciation of Difference: WEH Stanner and Aboriginal Australia*, pp. 126–36. Canberra: Aboriginal Studies Press.
- 2010. (with P. McConvell) The transition from Kariera to an asymmetrical system: Cape York Peninsula to north-east Arnhem Land. In D. Jones and B. Milicic (eds), *Kinship, Language, and Prehistory: Per Hage and the Renaissance in Kinship Studies,* pp. 99–132. Salt Lake City: University of Utah Press.
- 2010. The interpretation of Aboriginal 'property' on the Australian colonial frontier. In I. Keen (ed.), *Indigenous Participation in Australian Economies: Historical and Anthropological Perspectives,* pp. 41–61. Canberra: ANU E Press.
- 2010. Introduction. In I. Keen (ed.), *Indigenous Participation in Australian Economies: Historical and Anthropological Perspectives*, pp. 1–22. Canberra: ANU E Press.
- 2011. The language of property: analyses of Yolngu relations to country. In Y. Musharbash and M. Barber (eds), *Ethnography and the Production of Anthropological Knowledge: Essays in Honour of Nicolas Peterson*, pp. 101–19. Canberra: ANU E Press.
- 2011. (with P. McConvell). The transition from Kariera to an asymmetrical system: Cape York Peninsula to north-east Arnhem Land. In D. Jones and B. Milicic (eds), *Kinship, Language, and Prehistory: Per Hage and the Renaissance in Kinship Studies*, pp. 99–132. Salt Lake City: University of Utah Press.

- 2012. (with C. Lloyd) Introduction. In N. Fijn, I. Keen, C. Lloyd, and M. Pickering (eds), *Indigenous Participation in Australian Economies II: Historical Engagements and Current Enterprises*, pp. 1–15. Canberra: ANU E Press.
- 2013. The evolution of the Yolngu and Ngarinyin kinship terminologies: models of cumulative transformations. In P. McConvell, I. Keen and R. Hendery (eds), *Kinship Systems: Change and Reconstruction*. Salt Lake City: University of Utah Press.

## Encyclopedia Entries

- 1994. Aboriginal religion. In S. Bambrick (ed.), *The Cambridge Encyclopedia of Australia*. Cambridge University Press.
- 1994. Binyinyiwuy. In J. Turner (ed.), *The Dictionary of Art*. London: Macmillan.
- 1994. Sand sculptures. In J. Turner (ed.), *The Dictionary of Art*. London: Macmillan.
- 1994. Law. In D. Horton (ed.), *The Encyclopedia of Aboriginal Australia*. Canberra: Aboriginal Studies Press.
- 1999. Yolngu. In R.B. Lee and R. Daly (eds), *The Cambridge Encyclopedia of Hunters and Gatherers*, pp. 367–71. Cambridge: Cambridge University Press.
- 1998. Definitions of kin. In S.M. Channa (ed.), *International Encyclopaedia of Anthropology*. Columbia, MO: South Asia Books. (reprinted from Keen 1985).
- 2005. (with R.M. Berndt) Djan'kawu. In L. Jones, M. Eliade and C.J. Adams (eds), *Encyclopedia of Religion*. Detroit: Macmillan Reference USA.
- 2005. Aboriginal Mythology. In *Gods, Goddesses, and Mythology*. Brown Reference Group.
- 2005. Australian Aborigines. In J. Birx (ed.), *Encyclopedia of Anthropology*. Thousand Oaks, CA.: Sage.
- 2005. Clans. In J. Birx (ed.), *Encyclopedia of Anthropology*. Thousand Oaks, CA.: Sage.
- 2005. Polygyny. In J. Birx (ed.), *Encyclopedia of Anthropology*. Thousand Oaks, CA.: Sage.
- 2012. Dreams and the Dreaming in Aboriginal Australia. In D. Barrett and P. McNamara (eds), *Encyclopedia of Sleep and Dreams*. Santa Barbara, CA: Greenwood Publishers.
- 2013. Structural functionalism. In R.J. McGee and R.L. Warms (eds), *Theory in Social and Cultural Anthropology*, pp. 819–24. Sage Reference.

- 2014. Regional hunter-gatherer traditions: Australia. In *Oxford Handbook of the Archaeology and Anthropology of Hunter-Gatherers*, pp. 958–72. Oxford: Oxford University Press.

## Published Conference Papers

- 1980. Aborigines, anthropologists and Aboriginal studies. In C. Ferrier (ed.), *Australian Studies: Theory and Practice* (Australian Studies Centre Seminar Papers), pp. 35–40. Brisbane: University of Queensland.
- 1993. Indeterminacies in Yolngu religion and social order. In L. Ellana (ed.), *Hunters and Gatherers in the Modern Context: Book of Presented Papers Volume I*. (Seventh International Conference on Hunting and Gathering Societies, Moscow, 18–22 August 1993.), pp. 398–412. Fairbanks: University of Alaska.
- 1994. Conflict in Aboriginal land tenure. In J. Fingleton, M. Edmunds and P. McRandle (eds), *Proof and Management of Native Title*, pp. 26–31. Canberra: Aboriginal Studies Press.
- 2001. Variation in indigenous economy and society at the threshold of colonisation. *The Power of Knowledge and the Resonance of Tradition*, Australian Institute of Aboriginal and Torres Strait Islander Studies Conference, Canberra, 18–21 September 2001.
- 2001. (with T. Yamada) General introduction. In I. Keen and T. Yamada (eds), *Identity and Gender in Hunting and Gathering Societies* (Papers presented at the Eighth International Conference on Hunting and Gathering Societies, National Museum of Ethnology, October 1998), pp. 1–2. Osaka: National Museum of Ethnology.
- 2002. Similarities and differences in Aboriginal economy and society at the threshold of colonisation. *Ninth International Conference on Hunting and Gathering Societies*.

## Published Reports and Submissions

- 1977. Submission to the Parliamentary Select Committee on Aboriginal Land Rights. Canberra, Joint Select Committee on Aboriginal Land Rights in the Northern Territory. *Official Hansard Report*, Tuesday 3 May.
- 1977. (with N. Peterson and B. Sansom) Succession to land: primary and secondary rights to Aboriginal estates. In *Hansard of the Joint Select Committee on Aboriginal Land Rights in the Northern Territory*. Canberra: Government Printer, pp. 1002–14.

- 1980. *The Alligator Rivers Stage II Land Claim*. Darwin: Northern Land Council. (244 pp.)
- 1986. (with G. Koch, J. Stead and D. Alexander) *McLaren Creek Claim Book*. Alice Springs: Central Land Council. (164 pp.)
- 1990. (with F. Merlan) *The Significance of the Conservation Zone to Aboriginal People* (Resource Assessment Commission Kakadu Conservation Zone Inquiry Consultancy Series). Canberra: Commonwealth Government Printer. (124 pp.)

# Index

Aboriginal English, *see* English,
    Aboriginal use of
Aboriginality, deficit view of 16, 28,
    29–30, 46, 47
Aboriginal Land Commissioner 77
Aboriginal Land Rights Commission 76
*Aboriginal Land Rights (Northern
    Territory) Act* 7, 17, 62, 76, 80, 85, 88
Aboriginal Legal Services 33
Aboriginal people, East Kimberley, WA
    Gija and Jaru people 120, 129, 131,
        134, 136
    kin-based traditions 121, 131, 133–5,
        137
    traditional healers 129, 131–2, 135
Adelaide 226–8, 229
Adelaide River 87
affliction beliefs 102, 112
agency 16, 20, 167, 170–1, 210–1, 217–8,
    229–30, 238, 254, 257
Albert River 56–9
Alice Springs 221, 224–6
Ali Curung (place) 219, 223, 226–7
Alligator Rivers
    region 75–7, 79, 93–4
    Environmental Fact-Finding Study 87
    Stage I Land Claim xxii, 7, 17, 76, 88
    Stage II Land Claim, 7, 76–7, 88
ʕ*amal* 150, 153–5

ambiguity 16, 82, 248, 298, 321
    in Arnhem Land religion 6, 17–8,
        101–15, 161–2, 189
Anunga guidelines 37–8
Arabic grammatical tradition 19, 144–8,
    154, 156–8
Arnhem Land xx–xxi, 1–2, 4–5, 7, 17,
    54, 65, 75–6, 86, 101–15, 120, 161–84,
    187–211, 222, 235–57, 287, 288n.2,
    289, 292, 297n.12, 306, 309, 318–20
*Aubrey* case 37–9
AustKin 15, 21, 22, 287
Australian Institute of Aboriginal Studies
    xx, 75
Australian National Parks and Wildlife
    Service (ANPWS) 80–1
autonomy, personal 20, 217–8, 230
avoidance relations 21, 273n.13, 288, 290,
    294–5, 296, 297–8, 300, 302–3, 310

Badmardi (people) 86, 93, 94
Bakhtin, M. 19, 162–3, 165–74, 178,
    181–4
Balmbi (people) 104
*bäpurru* (*bapurru, baparru*) 9, 103–7, 171,
    182, 243–4, 245–6, 251–3, 255–6,
    319–20
Barramundie Creek 87
Bell, D. xxii, 20, 215–7, 219, 226, 229–30
Berndt, C.H. xx, 197

Berndt, R.M. xx, 104–5, 197
*birrimbirr* (spirit) 110, 113, 255
Birrinydji (Dreaming) 174
Borsboom, A. 5, 102, 106–9, 113
Bourdieu, P. 163, 169–70
Bream (*Wurdubal*) (Dreaming) 109–10
Breeden, S. and B. Wright 89
buffalo
    camps 77, 85, 94
    country 77, 79
    shooting 78, 87
Bumbaldjarri (place) 109, 111
Burarra (people and language) 105, 247, 306, 309, 319
Butler, J. 84–5, 86

Cabbage Palm (*Gul̠wirri*) (Dreaming) 109
ceremonies 107, 111, 164–8, 171–3, 183–4, 226
    mortuary ceremonies (*Bardurru*) 106–8, 110, 113–5
Chaloupka, G. xxii, 7, 76, 83–4, 86, 87–8, 89–91, 92, 93
Christianity
    East Kimberley, WA 18
        apocalyptic eschatology 119, 123–6, 129–30, 137
        Assemblies of God (AOG) 120, 130–6
        demonisation of Aboriginal spirit worlds 120, 124, 136
        dualisms 18, 126, 137
            Christian/sinner 132–3, 136
            God/Satan 125, 128, 130
            good/evil 119, 122–3, 128–31
            heaven/hell 119, 123, 125–6, 130, 134–5
            light/darkness 123, 126, 130
        half-Christians 133–4, 137
        United Aborigines Mission (UAM) 120, 130, 136
    influence on indigenous religious beliefs 18, 113–4
clan, critique of concept 8, 9–10, 103–4, 164–5, 166–8, 169, 171, 184
Clunies Ross, M. 108, 114
Codrington, H. 235, 236–7

cognition 144–6, 156, 158
Commonwealth government 55, 79–80
communication 29–30, 35–41, 42–7
comparative method 12, 21, 263–5, 287
conception beliefs 107, 110
*Condren* case 30–1
consultation 80–6, 94–5
cosmology, East Kimberley, WA 120, 128–9, 136
    ancestral spirits 120n.4, 129, 134
    *juwarri* 129, 131, 135
    *mamu* 129–31, 135
    *rayi* 135n.22
criminal justice system 28, 29–33
Crocodile Islands 20, 190, 235–6, 239, 244–6, 249, 257
Crow (*Wak Wak*) (Dreaming) 109

Darwin 77, 217, 220–4, 229
Deaf Adder Gorge 86–7, 91–2
demand sharing 224, 228, 230, 278n.22, 281
desinential inflection (*)i'rāb*) 145, 150, 153–5
Dhal̠wangu (people) 19, 162, 164–5, 171, 174, 177–8, 180–3
diglossia 146n.3
Djadiwitjibi (people) 104
*djalkiri* (anchor) (Dreaming) 177
Djambarrpuyngu (clan and dialect name) 105, 106, 191, 207, 246, 248n.22, 249, 255
Djambi (place) 109, 111
Djäwa xxi, 5, 20, 189, 194, 196–7, 199, 200–3, 205–8, 210–1
Djiliwirri (place) 202, 203–4
Djimbi Creek 102, 106, 111
Djinang (language and country) 17–8, 103–5, 319–20
Douglas, M. xx, 4

ecology 12, 21, 263–5, 268–71
economy 12, 13, 21, 67, 79, 124, 226, 231, 263–5, 268, 276–8, 279–81, 287
    'economy of knowledge' 6, 257
    fossicking economy 77, 85
    'hybrid economy model' 13

Elkin, A.P. 267n.5, 273–4, 294, 298
Ellemor, A. 195–6
English, Aboriginal use of 16–7, 30–1, 35–6, 38, 40, 41, 42–6
Eurobodalla region (NSW) 21, 263, 266, 268–72, 277, 279–80

Fernando case 33–4, 46
Fidock, A. 198
Fishtrap (*Mu̱litji*) (Dreaming) 108n.21, 110
Floodwater (*Wunggutj Gapi*) (Dreaming) 109–10
Forge, A. xx, xxi, xxii
Foucault, M. 84, 121, 136
Fox, J. xxi
Freeman, D. xix–xx
Friarbird (*Geggangie*) (Dreaming) 109

Galawdjapin (place) 103–4, 113–4
Ganalbingu (people) 103–4
Ganggalida (people) 17, 55–9, 61, 66–8
Ganingalkngalk (spirit being) 113
Gapuwiyak 8, 10, 105, 161, 162, 174, 207
Gattji (place) 102–4, 113–4, 319–20
Geertz, C. 240n.7, 317
Giddens, A. 163, 169–70, 218, 265
Gillespie, D. 82
Gorriba Island 110–1, 113
gratuitous concurrence 36, 43, 44
Groger-Wurm, H. 197
Gunabidji 319
Gupapuyngu (people and language) xxi, 113, 189, 191, 197, 199, 200–2, 204–7, 209–11, 246, 247, 249–52, 254
Guraknere (people) 106–7
Gurindji (language) 290, 292
Gurrumuru 174, 175n.6, 176n.7–8, n.10–1, 177, 180–1
  *Wängangur* song series 174–82

Halls Creek, WA 130–7
*Hart* case 44–6
Haynes, C. 82, 84, 92, 94
Hebrew 123, 124, 125, 127, 146–51, 153, 157
Hellenism 124–7, 135
heteroglossia 162, 165–6, 184

Hiatt, L. 3, 105, 108, 114
Howitt, A.W. 3, 12, 266–7, 269, 271–80
Hunter, J. 82

incommensurability 13, 19, 143–7, 155, 156, 158–9, 318
indeterminacy 9, 19, 161–2
initiation 59, 219, 245n.16, 273, 276, 278
Injilarija (people) 59, 61, 62, 63, 67
institutional field 12, 21, 265, 271–6
instruction 19, 144–50, 153–5, 157–9

Jabiluka 79, 81
*jilimi* (widows' camp) 216, 218, 224–6, 230
Jones, R. 88, 92
judge, *see* judicial officer
judicial officer/judiciary 28, 29, 32–3, 39, 41
jury directions 40, 42–4, 44–6

Kabirriki, N. 17, 79, 86–96
  knowledge 88–9
  life history 86–8
  research projects 87–9, 91–2
Kakadu National Park 17, 77, 78, 79, 81–3, 84, 88, 95
Kamminga, J. 87
Kariera (kinship system) 275, 297–300, 304, 308–9
Katherine 76, 87, 113, 217, 220, 223, 229, 309
Keen, Ian xx–xxiv, 1–22, 106n.16, 108n.18, 171, 204, 215, 239, 248, 251n.23, 254n.25, 255, 289, 310, 317–21
  analysis of Aboriginal Christianity 120, 136
  analysis of Aboriginal societies in southern Australia 11, 27–30, 47
  analysis of ambiguity in Arnhem Land cosmology 6, 101–2, 114–5, 161–2, 189
  critique of anthropological metalanguage 8–10, 103–5, 143–5, 158–9, 164, 166, 184, 236, 318
  research at Milingimbi 187, 202–3, 207, 211

research on Aboriginal economy and
   society 12–3, 263–5, 268, 270–1,
   273, 276–81
research on Kŭnai people (Gippsland)
   264, 274–5, 279–81
research on land claims 7–8, 53–4,
   65–6, 75–7, 83–4, 88, 92
research on kinship 6–7, 287, 297–8
research on property 13–5
Keen, Imogen, xx, xxii
Keen, John, xx
Keen, Libby, xx, xxii, xxiv, 5
Keesing, R. xx, xxii, 236, 238
*khabar* 149–51, 155–6
*Kina* case 36–7
kinship 2, 3, 6, 7, 11, 15, 16, 21, 54, 66,
   143, 148n.4, 206, 216, 220, 243, 265,
   271, 275, 287–8, 297–9, 304–5
   kinship terms 279–81, 288–90, 296–7,
      299, 307–10
      kinship terms, affinal 21, 288–90,
         297–8, 300, 303, 305–6, 307–8,
         310–1
      kinship terms, consanguineal 288,
         289–90, 300, 305, 308, 310–1
      kinship terms, diffusion of 21,
         290–1, 292–4, 296, 302–10
Kolondjorr (place) 87, 91
Koongarra 77, 79, 94
Kulumula (people) 105
Kŭnai (people) 11, 21, 264, 268, 271, 274,
   275, 279–81
Kunwinjku 113

Lajamanu 220–2
*lamparr(a)* 288, 290, 291–304, 310
*Lardil Peoples* case 55, 57
Layton, R. xx
leading questions 39–40, 42–4
Leichhardt River 56, 59, 61, 62
Lévi-Bruhl, L. 144
Liyagalawumirr (people) 5, 108n.18, 191
Liyagawumirr (people) 4–5
*Luma Luma* (spirit being) 110, 113

Macassans 113n.24, 174, 191
*maḏayin* (*mardayin*) 105–8, 189, 242–4
magistrate, *see* judicial officer
Makarrwala 200, 206
*mala* 103–7, 319–20
*mana* 20, 235–41, 257
*manikay* (song genre) 19, 106, 108–10,
   114–5, 162, 172–84, 204
   *dhamburru* (drum) song subject 176
   *garrurru* (flag) song subject 178–82
   *matha* (talking) song subject 175
   *ngarali* (tobacco) song subject 175, 177
   *nhina* (sitting) song subject 177
   *yakurr* (sleeping) song subject 175
   *yiki* (knife) song subject 176, 178
   *yuṯa manikay* (song version) 180
Maningrida 82, 103, 113, 319
Marrangu (people) 17–8, 102–15, 191
marriage 6–7, 60, 66, 103n.3, 105,
   106n.16, 219–20, 266, 271, 273–4,
   287–8, 297–8, 310
Marrngu (subgroup of Pama-Nyungan
   language family) 298n.13, 299, 301,
   307
Mason Alan 22, 161n.1
material culture 19–20, 174, 204, 211,
   318
   collections of 187–201
*matha* (*mata*) 103, 104n.4, 104n.8, 105,
   235n.1, 246, 305n.18, 319–20
Mathews, R.H. 61, 266–7, 273–5, 278–9
McCarthy, F. 197
melody 167, 182–3
Merlan, F. 11, 217n.2, 226
*Merri* (spirit being) 17–8, 102, 107–15
metalanguage 9, 14, 15, 20, 103, 235–6,
   240–1
metaphor 3, 9, 13, 15–6, 19, 103,
   107n.17, 143–4, 145, 158, 248, 250,
   294, 303
*Mewal* (spirit being) 17–8, 102, 105–15
Mildjingi (people) 103–4, 241n.8
Mildren, D. 39–40
Milingimbi xx–xxi, 2, 4–7, 8, 19–20,
   75–6, 103, 106, 111, 113, 187–211,
   239, 241, 246, 318
*mimi* (spirits) 91

334

Mingginda (people) 55–9, 61
Mirndi (language) 306–7
miscommunication 36–7, 43, 44–6
*mokuy* (spirits) 113, 253, 255
Monsoon (*Bara*) (Dreaming) 109–10
morphology 148, 152, 154
Morphy, H. 104–5, 111, 115, 162n.2, 168n.4, 242, 321
Morris, I. 82, 92
Mountford, C. 197
*mubtada*) 149–50, 154–8
Mudburra (language) 292–3
Mud Cod (*Morgal*) (Dreaming) 109–10
Mungurrpi (people) 106
Murayana (spirit) 207–9
Murrungga Island 191, 239, 241n.8, 245, 254, 255–6
Murrungun (people) 104–5
Myers, F. 162, 218–9

Nanggalala 4, 5
*narrpiya* (octopus) (Dreaming) 177
National Judicial College of Australia 32
native title xxii, 8, 10–2, 17, 27–8, 53–4, 55, 57–8, 65–8, 225,
Neidjie, B. 83
Ngalakgan (language) 306, 308
Ngarinyin (language) 294, 296, 298, 301, 304
Nguburindi (people) 59, 61, 62
Ngumpin-Yapa (subgroup of Pama-Nyungan language family) 288n.1, n.2, 290, 292–3, 298, 300–2, 304, 306–9
Nicholson River 57–9, 62
Nongere (people) 106–7
Northern Land Council (NLC), 7, 75, 76
Nowland, K. 198
Nyikina (language) 293–4, 296, 301–2, 304
Nyulnyulan (language family) 288n.1, 293–4, 296, 297, 298–304, 306–10

Oenpelli xxii, 76–7
ontology 21, 112, 143
    site-based 236, 240, 244, 257
Orientalist grammatical tradition 19, 144–7, 150, 152–3, 155, 157–8

Pama-Nyungan 288n.1, n.2, 289–90, 297–300, 302n.15, 304–7, 311, 320
Pelican (*Warbululu*) (Dreaming) 108n.21, 110
Pentecostalism 127, 216, 223–4, 231
Peterson, N. 241, 278, 319, 321
Pine Creek 77, 79, 87, 92
police interviews 30, 35–8
policy process 80, 91
politics of truth 84
polygyny 7, 273, 280, 287
Possum (*Narge Narge*) (Dreaming) 109
predicate 148–50, 151, 153–4, 156–7
promised marriage 295, 298
    escape from 216, 220–2, 227, 230

race 30–1
radical alterity 146, 150
Ramingining 106, 111, 113, 190, 319–20
*ramparr* 288, 291–304, 310
Ranger mine 79, 80, 93
Ranger Uranium Environmental Inquiry xxii, 17, 75–6, 79, 81, 93
Raymangirr (place) 105
religious property *see madayin*
Rembarrnga (people and language) 104, 113, 319
Robinson, G. 266
Roth, W. 60
Royal Commission into Aboriginal Deaths in Custody 31–2
Ruhe, E. 198–9, 202, 204, 207, 208

Saltwater Catfish (*Bullia*) (Dreaming) 108n.21, 110
sentencing 33–5
'settled Australia' 11, 16, 28
Setzler, F. 197
Shepherdson, E. 192
Shepherdson, H. 192–3, 196
sociality 2–3, 7–9, 13–4, 15–6, 17, 19, 102, 104, 161–9, 171, 178, 184, 321
song, *see manikay*
song texts 19, 174–81
southern Australia, *see* 'settled Australia'
speech genres 19, 171–4, 181–4
Spence, G. 198, 204, 207, 209

silence 36, 43, 44
skills 78–9, 83–6
*Stack* case 42–4
Stanner, W.E.H. 114
stories 82, 83–7, 91–5
Stringybark Tree (*Gundui*) (Dreaming) 102, 106–8, 110
subject 148–58
succession 17, 54–68
Sugarbag (*Djareware*) (Dreaming) 104–10, 113
syntax 148–9, 151–5, 158

Tawny Frogmouth (*Djudo Djudo*) (Dreaming) 109
Thomson, D. 103, 105, 113, 195, 202, 241–2, 247, 319–20
Tindale, N. 11, 56, 59, 267, 272
topicalisation 151–2, 155–7
translation 19, 20–1, 127, 130, 143, 145, 147–8, 150–3, 157–8, 235–6, 238
*tyamVny* 289, 290, 304–10, 311

Ucko, P. xx, 76
uranium 17, 75, 79, 81, 84, 87
utterance 19, 162, 164, 166, 168–9, 171–6, 178, 181–4

Vološinov, V. 162, 163–5

Waanyi (people) 17, 59–65, 66–8
Wagilak (people and language) 105
Walmajarri (language) 292–3, 302, 307
*Wanderwörter* (travelling loanwords) 288–91, 297, 303, 308
Warlpiri 20, 215–34
　Baptists 224–5
　diaspora, feminised 215–6
　in Adelaide 226–8
　in Darwin 222–4
　language 307
　Pentecostal 222–4, 231
　settlement conditions post-1980s 219
　women artists 227–8
Warnambi (people) 106
Warner, H. 266, 270, 272, 277

Warner, W.L. 105, 113, 194–5, 200, 235, 239–41, 253, 257
Water (*Gapi*) (Dreaming) 108–10
Watson, J. 191–2, 199
Webb, T.T. 191, 192–3, 241
Wells, E. 196–7, 200, 206
Wilkins, H. 191–2, 193
Worrorran (language) 293–4, 295–6, 298, 300, 303–4, 306–7
*Wuguli* (spirit) 110
Wurrkiganydjarr (people) 106

Yalungirr (people) 104
Yan-nhangu (people and language) 239n.6, 241, 244, 245–6, 247, 249, 251–2, 254
Yolngu (people and language) xxi–xii, 1–11, 17–22, 104, 109n.22, 114–5, 161–84, 235–6, 239–57, 297–8, 305n.18, 318, 319
　*manikay* (song) 171–84
　*märr* 20–1, 199, 235–6, 239–57
　material culture 187–211
　property, conceptions of 13–4
　religion 5–7, 18, 19, 101–2, 120, 136
　sociality 2–3, 8–10, 13, 15, 19, 143–4, 148n.4, 161–2, 163–9, 171, 321
Yuendumu 221, 226
Yuin (people) 21, 263–4, 266–81

Zoroastrianism 18, 119, 121–6, 130, 136

www.ingramcontent.com/pod-product-compliance
Lightning Source LLC
Chambersburg PA
CBHW040310240426
43666CB00022B/2921